SECURWARE 2018

The Twelfth International Conference on Emerging Security Information, Systems and Technologies

September 16 - 20, 2018

Venice, Italy

SECURWARE 2018 Editors

George Yee, Carleton University, Canada
Stefan Rass, Universitaet Klagenfurt, Austria
Stefan Schauer, Austrian Institute of Technology, Center of Digital Safety and Security, Vienna, Austria
Martin Latzenhofer, Austrian Institute of Technology, Center of Digital Safety and Security, Vienna, Austria

Printed from e-media with permission by:

Curran Associates, Inc.
57 Morehouse Lane
Red Hook, NY 12571

Some format issues inherent in the e-media version may also appear in this print version.

Printed by Curran Associates, Inc. (2018)

International Academy, Research, and Industry Association (IARIA)
412 Derby Way
Wilmington, DE 19810

Phone: (408) 893-6407
Fax: (408) 527-6351

petre@iaria.org

Additional copies of this publication are available from:

Curran Associates, Inc.
57 Morehouse Lane
Red Hook, NY 12571 USA
Phone: 845-758-0400
Fax: 845-758-2633
Email: curran@proceedings.com
Web: www.proceedings.com

Table of Contents

SECURWARE 2018

Forward

The Twelfth International Conference on Emerging Security Information, Systems and Technologies (SECURWARE 2018), held between September 16, 2018 and September 20, 2018 in Venice, Italy, continued a series of events covering related topics on theory and practice on security, cryptography, secure protocols, trust, privacy, confidentiality, vulnerability, intrusion detection and other areas related to low enforcement, security data mining, malware models, etc.

Security, defined for ensuring protected communication among terminals and user applications across public and private networks, is the core for guaranteeing confidentiality, privacy, and data protection. Security affects business and individuals, raises the business risk, and requires a corporate and individual culture. In the open business space offered by Internet, it is a need to improve defenses against hackers, disgruntled employees, and commercial rivals. There is a required balance between the effort and resources spent on security versus security achievements. Some vulnerability can be addressed using the rule of 80:20, meaning 80% of the vulnerabilities can be addressed for 20% of the costs. Other technical aspects are related to the communication speed versus complex and time consuming cryptography/security mechanisms and protocols.

Digital Ecosystem is defined as an open decentralized information infrastructure where different networked agents, such as enterprises (especially SMEs), intermediate actors, public bodies and end users, cooperate and compete enabling the creation of new complex structures. In digital ecosystems, the actors, their products and services can be seen as different organisms and species that are able to evolve and adapt dynamically to changing market conditions.

Digital Ecosystems lie at the intersection between different disciplines and fields: industry, business, social sciences, biology, and cutting edge ICT and its application driven research. They are supported by several underlying technologies such as semantic web and ontology-based knowledge sharing, self-organizing intelligent agents, peer-to-peer overlay networks, web services-based information platforms, and recommender systems.

To enable safe digital ecosystem functioning, security and trust mechanisms become essential components across all the technological layers. The aim is to bring together multidisciplinary research that ranges from technical aspects to socio-economic models

We take here the opportunity to warmly thank all the members of the SECURWARE 2018 technical program committee, as well as all the reviewers. The creation of such a high quality conference program would not have been possible without their involvement. We also kindly thank all the authors who dedicated their time and effort to contribute to SECURWARE 2018. We truly believe that, thanks to all these efforts, the final conference program consisted of top quality contributions.

We also gratefully thank the members of the SECURWARE 2018 organizing committee for their help in handling the logistics and for their work that made this professional meeting a success.

We hope that SECURWARE 2018 was a successful international forum for the exchange of ideas and results between academia and industry and to promote further progress in the field of security information, systems and technology. We also hope that Venice, Italy provided a pleasant environment during the conference and everyone saved some time to enjoy the unique charm of the city.

SECURWARE 2018 Chairs

SECURWARE Steering Committee
Yuichi Sei, The University of Electro-Communications, Japan
Carla Merkle Westphall, Federal University of Santa Catarina, Brazil
Hans-Joachim Hof, Technical University of Ingolstadt, Germany
Eric Renault, Institut Mines-Télécom - Télécom SudParis, France
Steffen Wendzel, Worms University of Applied Sciences, Germany
Aspen Olmsted, College of Charleston, USA
Calin Vladeanu, University Politehnica of Bucharest, Romania
Geir M. Køien, University of Agder, Norway
George Yee, Carleton University & Aptusinnova Inc., Ottawa, Canada
Sokratis K. Katsikas, Norwegian University of Science & Technology (NTNU), Norway
Hector Marco Gisbert, University of the West of Scotland, United Kingdom

SECURWARE Research/Industry Chairs
Rainer Falk, Siemens AG, Germany
Mariusz Jakubowski, Microsoft Research, USA
Malek ben Salem, Accenture Labs, USA
Jiqiang Lu, Institute for Infocomm Research, Singapore
Heiko Roßnagel, Fraunhofer IAO, Germany
Scott Trent, Tokyo Software Development Laboratory - IBM, Japan
Robert Forster, Edgemount Solutions S.à r.l., Luxembourg
Peter Kieseberg, SBA Research, Austria
Tzachy Reinman, Cisco, Israel

SECURWARE 2018
Committee

SECURWARE Steering Committee
Yuichi Sei, The University of Electro-Communications, Japan
Carla Merkle Westphall, Federal University of Santa Catarina, Brazil
Hans-Joachim Hof, Technical University of Ingolstadt, Germany
Eric Renault, Institut Mines-Télécom - Télécom SudParis, France
Steffen Wendzel, Worms University of Applied Sciences, Germany
Aspen Olmsted, College of Charleston, USA
Calin Vladeanu, University Politehnica of Bucharest, Romania
Geir M. Køien, University of Agder, Norway
George Yee, Carleton University & Aptusinnova Inc., Ottawa, Canada
Sokratis K. Katsikas, Norwegian University of Science & Technology (NTNU), Norway
Hector Marco Gisbert, University of the West of Scotland, United Kingdom

SECURWARE Research/Industry Chairs
Rainer Falk, Siemens AG, Germany
Mariusz Jakubowski, Microsoft Research, USA
Malek ben Salem, Accenture Labs, USA
Jiqiang Lu, Institute for Infocomm Research, Singapore
Heiko Roßnagel, Fraunhofer IAO, Germany
Scott Trent, Tokyo Software Development Laboratory - IBM, Japan
Robert Forster, Edgemount Solutions S.à r.l., Luxembourg
Peter Kieseberg, SBA Research, Austria
Tzachy Reinman, Cisco, Israel

SECURWARE 2018 Technical Program Committee
Nabil Abdoun, Université de Nantes, France
Habtamu Abie, Norwegian Computing Centre, Norway
Afrand Agah, West Chester University of Pennsylvania, USA
Yatharth Agarwal, Phillips Academy, Andover, USA
Rose-Mharie Åhlfeldt, University of Skövde, Sweden
Jose M. Alcaraz Calero, University of the West of Scotland, UK
Firkhan Ali Bin Hamid Ali, Universiti Tun Hussein Onn Malaysia, Malaysia
Basel Alomair, University of Washington-Seattle, USA / King Abdulaziz City for Science and Technology (KACST), Saudi Arabia
Eric Amankwa, Presbyterian University College, Ghana
Louise Axon, University of Oxford, UK
Ilija Basicevic, University of Novi Sad, Serbia
Carlos Becker Westphall, Federal University of Santa Catarina, Brazil
Francisco J. Bellido, University of Cordoba, Spain
Malek ben Salem, Accenture Labs, USA

Cătălin Bîrjoveanu, "Al.I.Cuza" University of Iasi, Romania
David Bissessar, Canada Border Services Agency, Canada
Wided Boubakri, ESSECT, Tunisia
Arslan Brömme, Vattenfall GmbH, Germany
Francesco Buccafurri, University Mediterranea of Reggio Calabria, Italy
Krzysztof Cabaj, Warsaw University of Technology, Poland
Cándido Caballero-Gil, University of La Laguna, Spain
Paolo Campegiani, Bit4id, Italy
Juan-Vicente Capella-Hernández, Universitat Politècnica de València, Spain
Aldar Chan, University of Hong Kong, Hong Kong
Tan Saw Chin, Multimedia University, Malaysia
Te-Shun Chou, East Carolina University, USA
Marijke Coetzee, Academy of Computer Science and Software Engineering | University of Johannesburg, South Africa
Gianpiero Costantino, Istituto di Informatica e Telematica | Consiglio Nazionale delle Ricerche, Pisa, Italy
Jun Dai, California State University, USA
Roberto Carbone, Security and Trust Research Unit - Fondazione Bruno Kessler, Italy
Jörg Daubert, Technische Universität Darmstadt, Germany
Ruairí de Fréin, Dublin Institute of Technology, Ireland
Fabrizio De Santis, Technische Universität München, Germany
P.P. Deepthi, National Institute of Technology Calicut, Kerala, India
Michele Di Lecce, iInformatica S.r.l.s., Matera, Italy
Changyu Dong, Newcastle University, UK
Safwan El Assad, University of Nantes/Polytech Nantes, France
Tewfiq El Maliki, University of Applied Sciences Geneva, Switzerland
Navid Emamdoost, University of Minnesota, USA
Rainer Falk, Siemens AG, Germany
Eduardo B. Fernandez, Florida Atlantic University, USA
Daniel Fischer, Technische Universität Ilmenau, Germany
Robert Forster, Edgemount Solutions S.à r.l., Luxembourg
Steven Furnell, University of Plymouth, UK
Amparo Fuster-Sabater, Institute of Physical and Information Technologies -CSIC, Madrid, Spain
François Gagnon, Cégep Sainte-Foy, Canada
Clemente Galdi, University of Napoli "Federico II", Italy
Michael Goldsmith, University of Oxford, UK
Stefanos Gritzalis, University of the Aegean, Greece
Bidyut Gupta, Southern Illinois University Carbondale, USA
Jinguang Han, Nanjing University of Finance and Economics, China
Petr Hanáček, Brno University of Technology, Czech Republic
Daniel Harkins, Hewlett-Packard Enterprise, USA
Ragib Hasan, University of Alabama at Birmingham, USA
Dominik Herrmann, University of Bamberg, Germany
Hans-Joachim Hof, Technical University of Ingolstadt, Germany

Fu-Hau Hsu, National Central University, Taiwan
Abdullah Abu Hussein, St. Cloud State University, USA
Sergio Ilarri, University of Zaragoza, Spain
Roberto Interdonato, Uppsala University, Sweden
Vincenzo Iovino, University of Luxembourg, Luxembourg
Mariusz Jakubowski, Microsoft Research, USA
P. Prasad M. Jayaweera, University of Sri Jayewardenepura, Sri Lanka
Thomas Jerabek, University of Applied Sciences Technikum Wien, Austria
Nan Jiang, East China Jiaotong University, China
Georgios Kambourakis, University of the Aegean, Greece
Erisa Karafili, Imperial College London, UK
Masaki Kasuya, Cylance Japan K.K., Japan
Toshihiko Kato, University of Electro-Communications Tokyo, Japan
Sokratis K. Katsikas, Norwegian University of Science and Technology, Norway
Peter Kieseberg, SBA Research, Austria
Hyunsung Kim, Kyungil University, Korea
Kwangjo Kim, Graduate School of Information Security (GSIS) | School of Computing (SOC) | KAIST, Korea
Ezzat Kirmani, St. Cloud State University, USA
Vitaly Klyuev, UniversityofAizu, Japan
Geir M. Køien, University of Agder, Norway
Sandra König, Austrian Institute of Technology, Austria
Hristo Koshutanski, Atos, Spain
Igor Kotenko, SPIIRAS, Russia
Lukas Kralik, Tomas Bata University in Zlin, Czech Republic
Lam-for Kwok, City University of Hong Kong, PRC
Ruggero Donida Labati, Università degli Studi di Milano, Italy
Romain Laborde, University Paul Sabatier (Toulouse III), France
Xabier Larrucea Uriarte, Tecnalia, Spain
Martin Latzenhofer, AIT Austrian Institute of Technology GmbH, Austria
Gyungho Lee, College of Informatics - Korea University, South Korea
Albert Levi, Sabanci University, Turkey
Wenjuan Li, City University of Hong Kong, Hong Kong
Giovanni Livraga, Università degli Studi di Milano, Italy
Patrick Longa, Microsoft Research, USA
Haibing Lu, Santa Clara University, USA
Jiqiang Lu, Institute for Infocomm Research, Singapore
Flaminia Luccio, Università Ca' Foscari Venezia, Italy
Feng Mao, WalmartLabs, USA
Hector Marco Gisbert, University of the West of Scotland, UK
Stefan Marksteiner, JOANNEUM RESEARCH, Austria
Isabella Mastroeni, University of Verona, Italy
Barbara Masucci, Università di Salerno, Italy
Ilaria Matteucci, Istituto di Informatica e Telematica | Consiglio Nazionale delle Ricerche, Pisa,

Stefan Schauer, AIT Austrian Institute of Technology GmbH - Vienna, Austria
Sebastian Schinzel, Münster University of Applied Sciences, Germany
Yuichi Sei, The University of Electro-Communications, Japan
Ana Serrano Mamolar, University of the West of Scotland, UK
Kun Sun, George Mason University, USA
Chamseddine Talhi, École de technologie supérieure, Montréal, Canada
Li Tan, Washington State University, USA
Enrico Thomae, Operational Services GmbH, Germany
Tony Thomas, Indian Institute of Information Technology and Management - Kerala, India
Scott Trent, Tokyo Software Development Laboratory - IBM, Japan
Alberto Tuzzi, iInformatica S.r.l.s., Trapani, Italy
Luis Unzueta, Vicomtech-IK4, Spain
Alastair Janse van Rensburg, University of Oxford, UK
Emmanouil Vasilomanolakis, Technische Universität Darmstadt, Germany
Eugene Vasserman, Kansas State University, USA
Andrea Visconti, Università degli Studi di Milano, Italy
Calin Vladeanu, University Politehnica of Bucharest, Romania
Steffen Wendzel, Worms University of Applied Sciences, Germany
Wojciech Wodo, Wroclaw University of Science and Technology, Poland
Wun-She Yap, Universiti Tunku Abdul Rahman, Malaysia
Qussai M. Yaseen, Jordan University of Science and Technology, Jordan
George Yee, Carleton University & Aptusinnova Inc., Ottawa, Canada
Petr Zacek, Tomas Bata University in Zlin, Czech Republic
Nicola Zannone, Eindhoven University of Technology, Netherlands
Tao Zhang, Chinese University of Hong Kong, Hong Kong

Copyright Information

For your reference, this is the text governing the copyright release for material published by IARIA.

The copyright release is a transfer of publication rights, which allows IARIA and its partners to drive the dissemination of the published material. This allows IARIA to give articles increased visibility via distribution, inclusion in libraries, and arrangements for submission to indexes.

I, the undersigned, declare that the article is original, and that I represent the authors of this article in the copyright release matters. If this work has been done as work-for-hire, I have obtained all necessary clearances to execute a copyright release. I hereby irrevocably transfer exclusive copyright for this material to IARIA. I give IARIA permission or reproduce the work in any media format such as, but not limited to, print, digital, or electronic. I give IARIA permission to distribute the materials without restriction to any institutions or individuals. I give IARIA permission to submit the work for inclusion in article repositories as IARIA sees fit.

I, the undersigned, declare that to the best of my knowledge, the article is does not contain libelous or otherwise unlawful contents or invading the right of privacy or infringing on a proprietary right.

Following the copyright release, any circulated version of the article must bear the copyright notice and any header and footer information that IARIA applies to the published article.

IARIA grants royalty-free permission to the authors to disseminate the work, under the above provisions, for any academic, commercial, or industrial use. IARIA grants royalty-free permission to any individuals or institutions to make the article available electronically, online, or in print.

IARIA acknowledges that rights to any algorithm, process, procedure, apparatus, or articles of manufacture remain with the authors and their employers.

I, the undersigned, understand that IARIA will not be liable, in contract, tort (including, without limitation, negligence), pre-contract or other representations (other than fraudulent misrepresentations) or otherwise in connection with the publication of my work.

Exception to the above is made for work-for-hire performed while employed by the government. In that case, copyright to the material remains with the said government. The rightful owners (authors and government entity) grant unlimited and unrestricted permission to IARIA, IARIA's contractors, and IARIA's partners to further distribute the work.

Analysing Trends and Success Factors of International Cybersecurity Capacity-Building Initiatives

Faisal Hameed, Ioannis Agrafiotis, Carolin Weisser, Michael Goldsmith, Sadie Creese

Department of Computer Science
University of Oxford, UK
email:{*firstname.lastname*}@*cs.ox.ac.uk*

Abstract—**The global community has been engaged extensively in assessing and addressing gaps in cybersecurity commitments and capabilities across nations and regions. As a result, a significant number of Cybersecurity Capacity Building (CCB) initiatives were launched to overcome cyber-risks and realise digital dividends. However, these efforts are facing various challenges such as lack of strategy, and duplication. Although extensive research has been carried out on CCB, no single study exists which focuses on analysing CCB initiatives. This gap presents an opportunity for investigating current trends in CCB efforts and identifying the principles for successful CCB initiatives. In this paper, we aim to bridge this gap by collecting and analysing 165 publicly available initiatives. We classify the initiatives based on Oxford's widely accepted Cybersecurity Capacity Maturity Model (CMM) and perform a descriptive statistical analysis. We further reflect on these initiatives, drawing on well-established success factors from the literature of capacity-building. Towards this end, we also conduct qualitative analysis based on CMM reports for two countries which have experienced socio-economic challenges, Mexico and Brazil, to understand which factors are essential in successful CCB initiatives. We conclude the paper with some interesting results on regional trends, key players, and ingredients of success factors.**

Keywords–Cybersecurity; Capacity Building Initiatives; Capacity Maturity Model.

I. INTRODUCTION

There has been an extensive engagement from the global community in combating cyber-risks, for numerous reasons. These efforts are in response to the increasing proliferation of cyber-threats and cyber-harm [1]–[4]. Such activities are adversely affecting the cyber-landscape that forms the foundation of today's interconnected societies. Thus, the desire to maintain cyber-hygiene and to protect against the proliferation of cyber-threats across nations is increasing rapidly [5]–[7]. Additionally, these efforts to protect investments in digitalising nations [8] [9] aim towards their economic and social development [10] [11]. Traditionally, CCB is also perceived as a pursuit of foreign-policy objectives such as advocating specific models of Internet governance, i.e., open and liberal vs closed and restrictive [5]. Moreover, foreign governments' involvements can promote their local companies to gain the competitive advantage of being influencers and decision-makers of these projects, which create opportunities and innovation [5]. Finally, donors are interested in capacity-building in order to promote and advance adoption of specific technical standards by recipient nations [5].

As such, there is a substantial investment being made by the international community aimed at helping nations to develop their capacity in cybersecurity [12]. However, various challenges emerged as nations and institutions rushed to implement instruments to combat cyber-risks. Key challenges includes duplication of initiatives [13], lack of strategy [8], and the widening of the 'cyber-capacity gap' between favored and neglected countries [12].

Thus, the research question to be addressed is *What are the lessons learnt from the current cybersecurity capacity-building activities and what aspects of these initiatives are crucial to their success?* This paper has a twofold objective: firstly, to analyse trends in regional and international capacity-building in cybersecurity, the nature of the work and the partnerships that exist to support it. That analysis of the initiatives will be guided by the University of Oxford Global Cyber Security Capacity Centre (GCSCC) CMM [14]. There are no efforts so far in linking initiatives with benchmarking models, and thus this effort from the GCSCC is presented. There is also no clear consensus on which capacity measures or initiatives work well [8]. Thus, the second objective is to provide the principles for successful cybersecurity initiatives based on a rigorous analysis of a small number of them reflected on Brazil and Mexico within the Latin America and the Caribbean (LAC) region to bring practical context. The LAC region was selected as it was available in both the International Telecommunication Union (ITU) Global Cybersecurity Index (GCI) and the CMM review by the Organization of American States (OAS). Within that region, Brazil and Mexico have been selected explicitly as both experienced significant regression and progression changes in cybersecurity maturity respectively, as identified by their GCI scores between the GCI 2014 and 2017 reports.

We define the term *initiative* in a capacity-building context to be any effort, activity, project, control, programme or instrument geared toward progressing capacity-building through assessing, implementing, supporting or developing the aims and objectives of that initiative. We adopt the definition of *Cybersecurity Capacity Building* (CCB) as "A way to empower individuals, communities and governments to achieve their developmental goals by reducing digital security risks stemming from access and use of Information and Communication Technologies" [8]. This definition incorporates consideration of the element of risk, which is an essential component of CCB.

The paper adopts mixed qualitative and quantitative approaches. We identify successful and unsuccessful factors of CCB initiatives, and we conduct a systematic review of current CCB initiatives. We accumulate 165 CCB initiatives and collect data related to critical success factors. We map these initiatives to the dimensions of Oxford's CMM and perform descriptive statistical analysis aiming at understanding trends in initiatives and areas which are neglected by the international community. We then engage in qualitative research to understand which factors are key in successful initiatives. To this end, we conduct a comparative analysis of CMM assessment and cybersecurity capacity-building initiatives to bring context and the overall understanding of trends in Brazil and Mexico. Our overall results present current trends among CCB initiatives, their distribution across regions, and key success factors to CCB.

In what follows, Section II provides a review of the literature underpinning the critical ingredients of unsuccessful and successful CCB. Section III investigates the assessments and indices relevant to the study and selects CMM and GCI as the guiding benchmarking instruments. It also provides preliminary insights into global trends in the field and analyses trends in capacity-building initiatives. Section IV compares and contrasts Brazil and Mexico cybersecurity capacity commitments, CMM comparison, relevant initiatives and the effects of externalities. Section V covers conclusion, limitations and future work.

II. Background and Related Work

To frame the research question, data collection and analysis, we conducted a literature survey answering the following questions: what are the known challenges in delivering effective CCB? What are the key ingredients of a successful CCB programme?

A. *Overview of challenges identified with current CCB efforts (factors of unsuccessful initiatives)*

One prominent challenge is that there is a lack of explicit linkage between developmental work in Information and Communications Technology (ICT) and cybersecurity. This lack of linkage is due to the lack of convincing empirically based evidence to demonstrate that improving cybersecurity in ICT projects would directly benefit development capacity initiatives [15]. Additionally, the development community does not perceive cybersecurity to be as mission-critical as terrorism or the migration crisis are [12]. Conversely, many cybersecurity strategies lack development-linked goals and activities [12]. Lack of such linkages discourages the community from integrating cybersecurity as a core element of their ICT development, and de-incentivises contributing efficiently to much-needed initiatives. Despite these challenges, there are initial steps in defining a CCB model that can be linked to the development agenda. This model is still struggling to operationalise a development-specific capacity-building approach that is both value-based [16], context-specific and brought in as a broader governance issue rather than tied to the technical silo [12]. There are other efforts that aim to bridge the gap by linking between ICT development and cybersecurity. Dutton et al. [17] examined various datasets related to national cybersecurity capacity for over 120 countries, and identified a strong positive correlation between increased ICT development, more mature cybersecurity posture and safer online environments for end-users [17]. The analysis is an initial step in the right direction regarding grounded evidence-based empirical proof, while admittedly lacking strong statistical proofs of their results [17]. Finally, the GCI 2017 report correlates ICT development and cybersecurity as it compares the GCI index with the ITU ICT for Development Index (IDI), without however providing strong statistical proofs of their results [18]. There is a general sense that improving cybersecurity would contribute to improving ICT yet there are a few outliers in which a country invests heavily in cybersecurity but does not invest in ICT, as in the case of Rwanda. Conversely, countries might invest heavily in ICT while neglecting cybersecurity. In summary, meaningful direct correlation between ICT development and cybersecurity would be a challenge, since multiple factors impact countries' cybersecurity readiness and commitment, such as geopolitical and socio-economical issues, as we highlight in the comparison of Mexico and Brazil below.

Another challenge is the double paradox of CCB maturity in which the development community requires rich empirical and conceptual foundations while also perceives CCB to have a mismatch with the core mission of the development community. However, when the development community decides to get involved with CCB, they often lack security expertise [12]. In contrast, the security experts in law enforcement and cybersecurity lack methodological toolkits and know-how to engage appropriately with the development community [12].

There is also the 'dual-use challenge' of cybersecurity, as cybersecurity capabilities and technologies can potentially be used adversely to increase surveillance and social control and to empower repressive governments as well as cyber-warfare, espionage and cybercrime [8]. Hence, CCB can also be considered a double-edged sword. As such, it is paramount to take a risk-aware approach when providing CCB capabilities to nations and regions [8]. Reflection on authoritarian regimes which have dubious human-rights records highlights the risk of abuse of capacity-building for repressive purposes. For that reason, some international partners such as the Global Forum on Cyber Expertise (GFCE) require their members to adhere to UN charters and laws which respect human rights such as freedom of expression and right to privacy [12].

Another critical challenge is discrimination between countries, a concept coined as 'cyber security gap'. Certain countries, known as 'darling countries', receive more attention in developmental benefits than marginalised or 'orphan' countries. Such discrepancies are observed in CCB according to the Official Development Assistance (ODA) distribution [12]. Typically, countries which are ready to cooperate, which explicitly express interest in joining efforts, which have an established rule of law, and which possess like-minded policy orientation are more likely to be considered for capacity-building assistance [12].

A further challenge is the absence of any widely accepted cybersecurity taxonomy, which results in a lack of mutual understanding of cybersecurity terminology. This confusion in the community is evident in the existence of more than 400 cyber and information-security related definitions within the Global Cyber Definitions Database [19] [20]. There are discrepancies in understanding the meaning of cybersecurity and capacity-building from various policy communities which result in fragmentation, leading to short-sighted and ad-hoc initiatives which are unsustainable [12]. It is essential to have a common level of understanding of the meaning of cybersecurity capacity-building, especially between crucial actors supporting any initiative. Established and accepted definitions serve to maintain a consistent approach to analysing and comparing initiatives, as well as to benchmarking these initiatives with assessments and indices.

Pawlak et al. [13] highlight specific factors shaping the politics of CCB due to the increased involvement of the international and regional communities: siloed mentality, the fragmentation of the CCB community and the duplication of work motivated by either institutional interests or potential business opportunities. Another factor shaping the politics of CCB is the persistence of mission-specific perspectives on capacity building within a policy area. These factors have resulted in adverse effects on donors, such as duplication of work, and inefficiencies amongst beneficiaries, confusion on objectives and conditions and motivations [13]. Another specific CCB challenge is the lack of policy coordination arising from lack of formal intergovernmental negotiations in their approval process. CCB initiatives that are not based on methods of assessment may cause harm as decisions by donors about engagement are not based strictly on the calculation of where the recipient country's most significant needs are or whether the intervention is appropriate to their level of maturity. Placing CCB within developmental traditions of increasing good governance, the rule of law and a human-rights-based approach would be a way forward.

Incomparable or clashing ideologies is yet another specific challenge that CCB encounters. This challenge is evident from lack of involvement in cybersecurity capacity-building from countries such as China and Russia due to their political and policy approaches. The absence of these countries demonstrates that it is not only the technical dimension that raises challenges, but also the political and socio-economical aspects of cybersecurity [12]. However, the formation of the Shanghai Cooperation Organisation (SCO) is an example of how countries within that region are perceiving CCB and conforming to the rapid advancements of technology, while retaining their views and understanding of CCB within that region and internationally [21].

Pawlak et al. [12] summarise signs of unsuccessful developmental initiatives as lack of coordination, budgetary constraints, overly ambitious targets, unrealistic timescales, and political self-interest [12]. Additionally, Hohmann et al. [8] summarise traits of unsuccessful CCB initiatives as lack of integration between key CCB players, few lessons-learned and best-practices available, a piecemeal approach to CCB by donor countries, competing agencies on the same initiatives, unclear mandates from donors, and lack of experts; also, a lack of clear consensus on which capacity measures work well and of adequate metrics to monitor and evaluate CCB projects are two further traits of unsuccessful CCB [8]. Finally, Muller highlights that there is often a lack of valid information due to the security context, as countries are unwilling to share valid information or follow up assessments to demonstrate progress [22].

B. *Key ingredients of successful CCB programmes*

A majority of the successful ingredients come as a negation of the challenges given in Section II.A above. An initiative is deemed successful if it achieves its aims and objectives and displays the characteristics summarised in the following: donors are major CCB influencers and thus what they deem successful is considered crucial. The UK Foreign and Commonwealth Office (FCO) CCB Programme summarises its requirements for supporting and funding any CCB program as follows: "When projects are part of the country's strategy; have strong host-government support; take a holistic approach that considers host government digital and cyber policies, national strategies, regulation, private sector interests, civil society, technical capability, development context and human rights; take account of what other donors are doing or planning; have co-funding from another country or organisation; and build on previous capacity building projects or partnerships [23]."

A more generic viewpoint at the CCB ecosystem as apposed to individual initiatives is proposed by Pawlak [12]:

- Cyber knowledge brokers at all levels of cross filtration and breaking silos to increase education and awareness.
- Principles-based CCB models and principle-based approach solutions.
- Closing the 'cyber capacity gap' Darling vs orphaned countries.
- Continuous mapping of CCB activities to identify substantial overlaps or gaps.
- Regional champions who are mature and willing to engage.
- Imminent needs to security translated into Computer Security Incident Response Teams (CSIRTs), forensics capabilities and strategies.
- Avoiding securitisation of development initiatives in fears of adverse effects on civil liberties.

Although these proposed solutions are critical components of successful CCB, they are intangible at an initiative level. It is a challenge to quantify and analyse the initiatives gathered against closing the 'cyber capacity gap' or identifying cyber-knowledge brokers at an individual initiative level, for example.

As an alternative view to Pawlak, Hohmann et al. [8] provides an initiative-specific viewpoint with five principles for advancing CCB initiatives. These are:

- National and international *coordination* (in activities) and *cooperation* (in measurements.) At national level coordination translates into an explicit national CCB approach with set strategy prioritisation, streamline institutional setup and stakeholders (academic, civil society, government, public and private) *coordination.* At an international level, *cooperation* would be in the form of sharing and leveraging the results of maturity models and indices to guide CCB efforts. *Coordination* can be enabled by strengthening multilateral and international coordination such as the efforts of the GFCE.
- The second principle would be *integration* of cybersecurity and development expertise as they work together and out of silos. Establishing common language and increased joint projects is also part of integration.
- Recipient countries need to take *ownership* and leadership from setting their own strategies to providing and backing capable institutions. The CCB programmes must be tailored to the country's specific requirements.
- *Sustainability*, in the sense of experts exchanging and benefiting from traditional capacity-building activities

that support sustainable long-term success and continuation of the projects with defined vision, goals and strategy-level components included.

- *Continued and mutual learning* by evaluating and learning how effective the initiatives are, and by developing clear capacity-measure frameworks for measurements and assessments, with useful metrics; also by encouraging openness over the results of assessments and conducting regular (annual) re-assessments, to follow up assessments in order to demonstrate progress and determine best practices available.

Moving forward, the focus in our analysis will be on success factors that are measurable at the initiative level. This will help guide the descriptive statistical analysis of the initiatives in Section IV to produce meaningful insights. As such, we are adopting the Hohmann et al. [8] five principles for advancing CCB, which incorporates the FCO mandates. We also adopt adequate *funding* and sufficient *duration* as the sixth and seventh success factors. These were taken from the budgetary-constraints and unrealistic-timescales points highlighted by Pawlak et al. [12] in the summarised signs of unsuccessful developmental initiatives and the FCO requirements [23] above. The following are therefore the selected key success factors of CCB initiatives:

1) Coordination & Cooperation.
2) Integration.
3) Ownership
4) Sustainability
5) Learning
6) Funding
7) Duration

III. Analysing trends in Cybersecurity Capacity-Building initiatives

A. Methodology

The paper adopts mixed qualitative and quantitative approaches. An initial literature review of existing research has been performed to underpin the key successful and unsuccessful factors of CCB initiatives and thus to identify critical metrics on initiatives, as a basis for the comparative analysis. To identify trends and gaps in CCB, we have collected information related to publicly available CCB initiatives. We have performed web searches to elicit current regional and international initiatives. To conduct the systematic review, a search for initiatives using phrases that focus on cyber-harm, cybersecurity and cyber-risk was performed, as these are crucial themes in combination with capacity-building initiatives, instruments, activities and efforts. Initiatives that exclusively focus on e-governance or privacy, as opposed to cybersecurity, as their core objective were excluded. The scope was limited to publicly available information in English. We accumulated 165 CCB initiatives in total and collected data related to the key success factors. The results were published on the Global Cybersecurity Capacity Portal [24]. Established in 2015, the portal is an output of the GCSCC in cooperation with the GFCE. The portal is a central point of reference of current regional and international capacity-building efforts globally in the critical areas of cybersecurity.

We then investigated various available regional and international CCB benchmarks, assessments and indices. The process was guided by the ITU 2017 Index of Cybersecurity Indices to determine which assessment and index to use to judge progression in cybersecurity. As a result, we have selected the CMM and GCI. A direct mapping between the initiatives and their respective dimensions and factors was performed to determine the linkage between the initiatives and their impacts on regions and nations. After the mapping, we then performed descriptive statistical analysis aimed at understanding trends in initiatives and areas which are neglected by the international community. We then engaged in qualitative research to understand which factors are key in successful initiatives.

A comparative analysis of the selected indexes for all countries within the Latin America and the Caribbean (LAC) region between 2014 and 2017 was performed to select countries that have progressed, remained static or regressed most regarding their cybersecurity capacity commitment.

To this end, we conduct a comparative analysis of CMM assessment and CCB initiatives to bring context and the overall understanding of the trends in Brazil and Mexico.

B. Selection criteria for cybersecurity maturity models and indexes

Various cybersecurity indices and maturity models have sprung up within the international community, academia and the private sector to capture the cyber-readiness and maturity progression. The ITU has developed the Index of Cybersecurity Indices [25] to form a reference that evaluates and presents various prominent organisational, regional and global efforts at producing maturity models and Indices. The 2017 Index of Cybersecurity Indices was instrumental in guiding our investigation of the effectiveness of CCB initiatives and the relevance of various cybersecurity Indices and assessments. The Index evaluates 14 prominent indices for assessing countries and organisations, as well as other scopes of assessment. See Figure 1. Our focus is on regions and nations, thus indices that focus on organisations (e.g. IBM X-Force [3] were excluded. As we are interested in answering the research question "What are the lessons learnt from current cybercapacity-building

	Metrics			Content										Presentation Format				
	Score	Ranking	Information Society Development Score (ISD) score)	Cyber Maturity	Cyber Threats	Cyber Vulnerabilities	Organizational	Technical	Economical	Legal Framework	Cooperation	Capacity Buiding	Recommandations	Profiles	Website	PDF	Visualization	No. of Iterations
Cyber Maturity in the Asia-Pacific Region	x			x					x	x	x			x	x	x		2
National Cyber Security Index	x	x	x	x	x		x	x		x	x	x			x	x	x	1
Global Cybersecurity Index	x	x					x	x		x	x	x		x	x	x	x	2
Kaspersky Cybersecurity Index	x				x				x					x	x	x	x	1
Asia-Pacific Cybersecurity Dashboard		x		x			x			x	x	x		x	x	x		2
Cyber Readiness Index 2.0	x	x		x		x	x		x	x	x			x	x	x		2
Cybersecurity Poverty Index	x			x			x	x							x		x	1
CyberGreen Index	x	x			x			x							x		x	1
The Accenture Security Index	x	x			x		x	x	x		x		x		x	x	x	1
Global Cybersecurity Assurance Report Cards	x				x	x		x							x		x	1
Index of Cybersecurity					x			x							x	x	x	73
Cybersecurity Capability Maturity Model				x			x	x		x	x	x			x	x		2
Cyber Power Index	x	x		x			x	x		x		x			x	x	x	1
IBM X-force Threat Intelligence Index					x			x							x			3

Figure 1. Overview of Cybersecurity Indices [25]

activities and what aspects of these initiatives are crucial to their success?" it is essential for our comparison to identify the countries or regions with the highest levels of progression (or regression) in their cybersecurity maturity and readiness journey. This assumes that initiatives would be most visible in terms of lessons learnt and key success factors when the progress of the country is demonstrable by the indices within the period. As such, we would be looking only at indices that provide metrics, whether scores or ranking, and also indices used for multiple iterations of evaluating countries. This further focuses the scope down to six indices and maturity models. Our preliminary research at this stage was across all nations and states before zooming in on a particular region. That eliminates sub-regional indices such as the Asia-Pacific Cybersecurity Dashboard [26] and the Cyber Maturity in the Asia Pacific Region model [27]. Since we are evaluating initiatives from various viewoints, our criteria include indices and models that incorporate at least four aspects of the five areas: Technical, Economical, Legal, Cooperation, and Capacity-Building. Based on the given criteria, the remaining applicable instruments for measurements were the GCI index [18] and the CMM assessment model [14].

The LAC region was selected as it was represented in both the GCI and the CMM review and it had a reasonably significant number of initiatives as well. Within that region, Brazil and Mexico have been selected, since both experienced significant changes (progression or regression) in their GCI scores between the GCI 2014 and 2017 reports. The Cyber Readiness Index 2.0 [28] would not be used in our analysis as it did not produce a report covering LAC region at the time of this research.

C. The Cybersecurity Capacity Maturity Model for Nations (CMM)

The GCSCC Cybersecurity Capacity Maturity Model for Nations supports comprehensive analysis of detailed appraisal of a country or region [14]. The analysis is based on self-assessments through partners or interviews and workshops with key stakeholders and representatives from donors, recipient countries and relevant organisations [14]. The CMM benchmarks a country's cybersecurity capacity across five distinct dimensions of cybersecurity capacity. The CMM has been developed and used to benchmark countries since 2015, with over 60 nations reviewed so far. The resulting CMM review report is in the form of an overview of the maturity level for the country in each dimension as well comprehensive detailed assessments with specific recommendations advising the state on ways to elevate its capacity to a higher maturity stage [14].

There are five dimensions of cybersecurity identified in the model:

1) Cybersecurity Policy and Strategy.
2) Cyber Culture and Society.
3) Cybersecurity Education, Training and Skills.
4) Legal and Regulatory Frameworks.
5) Standards, Organisations, and Technologies.

Each dimension is divided further into factors. Maturity levels are divided into five stages: start-up, formative, established, strategic, and dynamic.

D. The ITU Global Cybersecurity Index (GCI)

The index spans different mechanisms for evaluating cyber-maturity to derive rankings and scores that enable comparisons between nations and regions. It is being led by the ITU as part of its Global Cybersecurity Agenda (GCA) [29]. The GCI examines levels of commitment on five distinct pillars [18]: 1. Legal. 2. Technical. 3. Organizational. 4. Capacity building, and 5. Cooperation.

In addition to the overall ranking, the index includes regional rankings and an individual score for each country. This focus enables us to compare the country or region in question. The index is primarily based on surveying ITU's members and publicly available information. The identified weakness, however, is that the index is more policy and organisationally oriented more technical, and that distilling a single number to capture maturity necessarily equates incomparable considerations. The index assesses countries' commitments with regards to cybersecurity as opposed to actual readiness.

While there are in some cases a direct one-to-one mapping between the CMM Dimensions and the GCI Pillars, such as in the areas of strategy, legal and technical, there are GCI pillars such as Capacity Building and Cooperation that cut across all CMM Dimensions. See Table I.

TABLE I. MAPPING CMM DIMENSIONS WITH GCI PILLARS

GCSCC CMM Dimensions	*ITU GCI Pillars*	
Cybersecurity Policy and Strategy	Organizational	Cooperation
Cyber Culture and Society	–	
Cybersecurity Education, Training and Skills	Capacity building	
Legal and Regulatory Frameworks	Legal	
Standards, Organizations, and Technologies	Technical	

E. An overview of the Global Cybersecurity Capacity Portal.

Initiatives were collected and hosted on the Portal which contains a dedicated informational web-page per initiative. To bring more understanding and context to the initiatives, as well as to form the basis of the comparative analysis, an off-line dataset (spreadsheet) of the initiatives was created manually to help gain insights from these efforts, such as an analysis of stakeholders and linkage between the initiatives and the CMM model. The dataset includes the *Title* of the initiative; the name of the sponsoring or initiating *Organisation*; the *Target Region*; *Target Country*; the *GFCE Theme*; *Key Topic*; *Dimension* and *Factors*; and *Others Topics*; vital *Partners*; affected or *Target Groups*, planned *Budget*, main *Aims* and *objectives*, *Outputs*, underlying *Activities*, *Period* or duration of the effort, and finally *Contact* details. Mapping initiatives to dimensions and factors of the CMM can be demonstrated by the Dimension and Factors columns identified in the following colour scheme. See Figure 2:

- Red: Cybersecurity Policy and Strategy
- Blue: Cyber-Culture and Society
- Green: Cybersecurity Education, Training and Skills
- Yellow: Legal and Regulatory Frameworks
- Purple: Standards, Organisations, and Technologies

The purple is not illustrated in the following example as this particular initiative did not have mapping with the *Standards,*

Organisations, and Technologies CMM dimension. The unique numbers within the Dimensions and Factors columns are mapped directly to the CMM (e.g., 4.3 refers to Dimension 4 Factor number 3). A complete mapping between the initiatives in scope and the CMM has been performed.

Title	Organisation	Target region	Target country	GFCE Theme	Key Topic	Dimension / factors				Factor	Others topics
Privacy, Internet Governance, and "Children and Mobile Technology" Courses	GSMA	global	NA	Cybersecurity; Data Protection	Cybersecurity Strategy Development; Information Sharing; Cybersecurity Legislation; Legal Frameworks; Privacy Legislation	1.1	2	3	4.1	Media and Social Media; Cybersecurity Mindset; Reporting Mechanisms; Legal Frameworks; National Cybersecurity Strategy	Privacy, Internet Governance; Children and Mobile Technology;

Figure 2. Initiatives example

IV. Descriptive Statistical Analysis of the Initiatives

A. Regional analysis

As of July 2018, we had gathered 165 distinguished initiatives. Initiatives are either global in nature or within one of seven geographical regions. We are adopting the World Bank geographical regions [30]. Figure 3 displays the target regions, respective counts, and percentages of initiatives per region. An initiative that spans countries in multiple regions is counted in all those regions.

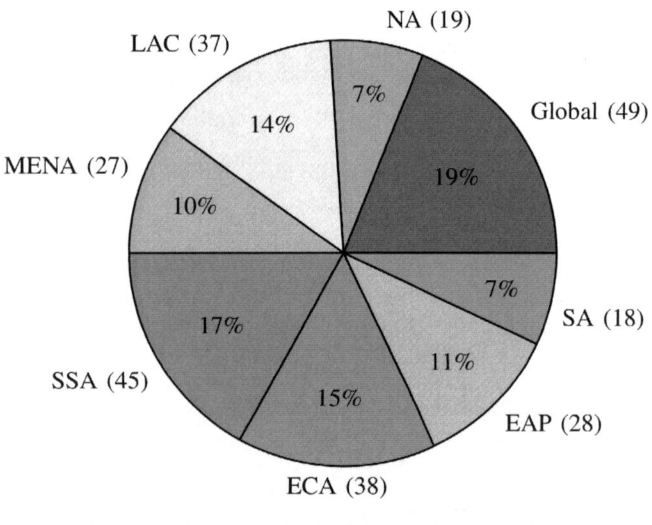

Figure 3. Global initiatives, and those for North America (NA), Latin America and the Caribbean (LAC), The Middle East and North Africa (MENA), Sub-Saharan Africa (SSA), Europe and Central Asia (ECA), East Asia and Pacific (EAP) and South Asia (SA)

B. Organisational analysis

105 organisations, countries or entities are initiating or leading initiatives across all regions and globally. Table II represents the Top 10 most active Organisations that are either initiating or leading initiatives. It is important to highlight that the top 10 active organisations account for 75% of initiatives. This is followed by a demonstration of the top Partners in supporting CCB across all initiatives within the portal. See Table III.

TABLE II. Organisational analysis

Organisation	*# of initiatives*
UK Foreign & Commonwealth Office	27
International Telecommunications Union (ITU)	15
e-Governance Academy (eGA)	12
Global Forum on Cyber Expertise (GFCE)	9
United Nations Development Programme	6
Council of Europe (CoE)	5
United Nations Economic Commission for Africa (UNECA)	5
United Nations Conference on Trade and Development (UNCTAD)	4
Association of Southeast Asian Nations (ASEAN)	3
DiploFoundation (Diplo)	3

TABLE III. Partner analysis

Partners	*# of initiatives*
ITU Oman Regional Cybersecurity Centre	8
European Union (EU)	6
Organization of American States (OAS)	5
Economic Community of West African States (ECOWAS)	4
European Cybercrime Centre – EC3 (Europol)	4
FIRST	4
Global Cyber Security Capacity Centre (GCSCC) – University of Oxford	4
INTERPOL (INT)	4
National Crime Agency	4
Netherlands	4
Norway	4
UK Foreign and Commonwealth Office	4
United States of America	4

C. Initiatives mapped to the CMM and GCI

When surveying the current trends over the gathered CCB initiatives, it visibly demonstrates that about half of the initiatives 47% are geared towards the first dimension of the CMM model, *Cybersecurity Policy and Strategy*; followed by the fourth dimension: *Legal and Regulatory Frameworks* 33%. The third dimension: *Cybersecurity Education, Training and Skills* concerns 14% of the initiatives, followed by the fifth dimension: *Standards, Organisations, and Technologies* with 7%, and finally the lowest number of initiatives are focused on the second dimension *Cyber Culture and Society* 7%. See Figure 4 which summarises the analysis.

Our results are in close alignment with the observations in ITU GCI 2017 report. The mapping between the initiatives and the CMM indicates that the current trends are focusing on building the foundational aspects of CCB, such as devising or enhancing national Cybersecurity strategies, establishing effective CSIRT programmes, or creating robust regulatory frameworks. Since only 38% of the surveyed countries have a published cybersecurity strategy, in which only 11% of it has a dedicated standalone tailored strategy [18], implementing or enhancing cybersecurity strategy is of paramount importance at this stage of global CCB. Similarly, efforts focusing on the development of legal and regulatory frameworks (33% of initiatives) endeavour to bridge the gap identified in ITU GCI report, where it was identified that 57% of legal actors lack specialist cybersecurity training [18].

Furthermore, there is also a close alignment between the initiatives that relate to incident management and gaps in CSIRTs that the 2017 GCI report has acknowledged. CSIRT enhancement is part of the Cybersecurity Policy, and Strategy CMM dimension with one third of the initiatives of that dimension focused on Incident Response, and 16 initiatives focused on Crisis Management. This is in line with the GCI finding that 79% of existing CSIRTs require metrics or measurements criteria to be used for effective management of incidents. There are, however, apparent gaps and imbalances since initiatives are oblivious to other dimensions such as Standards, Organisations, and Technologies and Cyber Culture and Society, which are vital in ensuring a balanced, capable, resilient, and dynamic cyberspace.

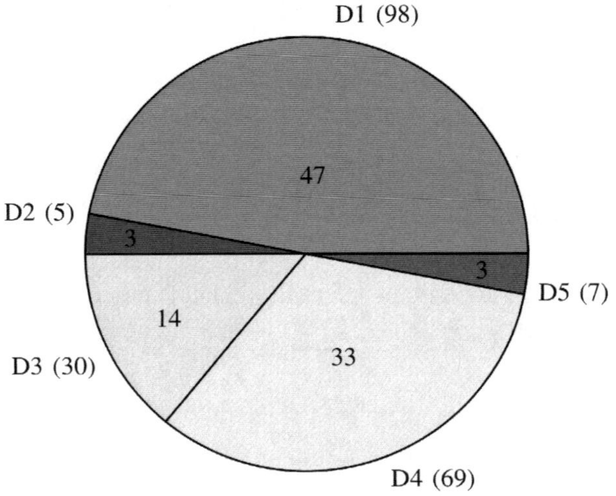

Figure 4. Percentage of initiatives per CMM Dimension: D1 *Cybersecurity Policy and Strategy*, D2 *Cyber Culture and Society*, D3 *Cybersecurity Education, Training and Skills*, D4 *Legal and Regulatory Frameworks*, D5 *Standards, Organisations, and Technologies*

D. Analysing initiatives based on key success factors

A direct mapping between key success factors identified in Section II.B and the initiatives gathered is a challenge, as such a mapping is subject to interpretation and subjective judgments. However, the following is an effort at translating what it is observed in the CCB initiatives against key success factors.

The first success factor is national and international *coordination* (in activities) and *cooperation* (in measurements). When applied properly, this factor should tackle challenges such as duplication of effort, lack of policy coordination, cyber-capacity gap and lack of strategy, as well as agencies competing on the same initiatives.

Coordination can be perceived by determining whether the initiating or sponsoring actor of an initiative is engaged with a partner or a set of partners. An actor could in itself be a consortium of multilateral entities, such as the ITU or the OAS. Thus, it has been observed that 84% of the initiatives have one or more partners supporting the effort. Although the remaining 16% do not have an explicit partnership, they are based on bilateral or multilateral entities, such as the Association of Southeast Asian Nations (ASEAN). These observations imply that the overwhelming majority of initiatives conform with the coordination factor of successful initiatives.

Cooperation is achieved when nations collaborate in cybersecurity assessments. It has been determined that there are twelve initiatives in which the aims and objectives contain some form of assessment. There are a further twenty-two initiatives where assessment or self-assessment is part of either their essential or other topics covered. All these are indications of high-level activity in cooperation between entities concerning measurement. This remains a challenge to quantify, however, as there are potential overlaps between the objectives of the initiatives.

The second identified factor is *intended Integration* of cybersecurity and development expertise. This is interpreted by the involvement and engagement of key stakeholders from across various levels of the targeted society. There were 10% of initiatives that included members of academic institutions, civil society, defence, non-profits, the private sector and governmental institutions. Further detailed analysis of each initiative is required to gain a deeper level of understanding of the true state of integration (or lack thereof) between the development sector and cybersecurity efforts.

Ownership by the recipient country or entity is the third success factor. Leveraging assessments, whether against the CMM or other models, represents an initial step in refining capacity-building to eliminate existing discrepancies between donors' objectives and beneficiaries' priorities. From the perspective of the initiatives gathered, investigating whether the target country or region is also part of the organisation leading the initiative or the partners supporting it was determines effective ownership. Many initiatives are global, however, and involve many countries and regions. Unfortunately, it was not possible to extract sufficient information to determine whether this factor is appropriately incorporated into the design of a given initiative.

The fourth factor of a successful initiative is *sustainability* of efforts, as evidenced by experts exchanging and benefiting from traditional capacity-building activities that support sustainable long-term success and continuation of the projects, as opposed to short-term one-off training activities. Successful initiatives tend to be based on an increase in the pool of experts in the recipient countries and in building on proven successful methodologies. Also, utilising cross-sectoral approaches to engage and involve the public and private sectors and academia, and getting them to work together, is another key ingredient. There were 10% of cross-sectoral initiatives identified based on this analysis.

The fifth factor is *continued and mutual learning* by developing clear capacity measurements while encouraging openness. This factor addresses the lessons learnt from designing and implementing CCB initiatives. Continued and mutual learning should also address the cybersecurity-context challenge, in which resistance by countries to information-sharing exists. There are only four initiatives which contain educational aspects, but there are a further twelve initiatives where education or learning elements are part of the aims and objectives. Finally, only two partners in all initiatives were associated with education. However, analysing continued learning within initiatives requires more in-depth data from each initiative, which is lacking.

Adequate *funding* is the sixth factor. It is challenging to obtain data on the funding aspects of initiatives. Currently, there are only three initiatives that indicate the initial budget of that initiative. As such, currently, the funding element is not being evaluated.

The seventh and final factor of successful initiatives is their *duration*. As capacity-building initiatives take time to develop and produce real impact, it can possibly be assumed that the longer the initiative remains, the more precise its measurement can be. Hence this factor is not necessarily a direct factor of a successful initiative. Caveatting that there are initiatives that are naturally limited in time, such as targeted workshops. 70% of the initiatives have their project duration identified among which 14% have a very short term.

V. Reflections on the Latin America and the Caribbean (LAC) region

To provide further insights on the key factors that render an initiative successful, we engage in qualitative research and analyse reports detailing the cybersecurity capacity maturity of countries in the LAC region. The LAC region was selected as it was represented in both the GCI and the OAS reviews. The Inter-American Development Bank (IDB) and the OAS have partnered together and carried out a CMM review of the thirty-two countries in LAC, based on the GCSCC CMM [24], [31]. The report reflects a dim view on the security posture and readiness of the region as only five countries have strategies, eight are planning or developing capabilities for Critical Infrastructure Protection, and 30% of citizens are not aware of cybersecurity risk [31]. Within that region, Brazil and Mexico have been specifically selected as they experienced significant regression and progression respectively in their GCI scores between 2014 and 2017.

The LAC region is a heterogeneous pool of countries with different economic developments, historical backgrounds, languages and different challenges. According to the World Bank 2017 annual report and regional perspective, the LAC region experienced an economic slowdown during the last six years including two recessions [30]. This slowdown has adversely reversed the gains realised due to hard earned social reforms at the beginning of the 21st century. As a result, GDP growth for LAC was 2.3% in 2000, 4.7% in 2010 and currently down -1.8%. However, the region is slowly gaining growth and recovering economically [30].

Cybercrime is proliferating within the Latin America and the Caribbean region due to multiple factors including the rapid digitisation of economies without considerations of appropriate cybersecurity controls; the foundational establishment of criminal networks; and the socio-economic and geopolitical situations affecting the region [32]. The cost of Cybercrime in Mexico was estimated to be $3 billion, while Brazil $8 billion in 2013 [33].

A. *Descriptive statistical analysis of the initiatives in LAC*

The distribution of the CCB initiatives within the LAC region reflects similar distributions among the global regions. See Table IV.

TABLE IV. CMM Dimensions and the corresponding number of initiatives for LAC.

D#	*GCSCC Dimensions*	*# of initiatives*
D1	Cybersecurity Policy and Strategy	31
D2	Cyber Culture and Society	1
D3	Cybersecurity Education, Training and Skills	3
D4	Legal and Regulatory Frameworks	11
D5	Standards, Organisations, and Technologies	1

Each country was measured and assessed by the GCI between 2014 and 2017 on various GCI pillars with a subsequent total score presented. Tables V and VI display the top 3 countries of the LAC region based on the GCI scores in 2014 and 2017, respectively. Mexico's 2014 results are also presented to highlight the progress achieved. According to the results, Brazil has descended from the highest rank of the LAC region regarding cybersecurity commitment in the year 2014 down to the third rank in 2017. Conversely, Mexico has ascended from the 7th rank to the first rank.

TABLE V. Top 3 LAC and Mexico GCI Index 2014 Results.

Regional Rank	*Country*	*GCI Score*	*Global Rank*
1	Brazil	0.7059	5
2	Uruguay	0.6176	8
3	Colombia	0.5882	9
7	Mexico	0.3235	18

TABLE VI. Top 3 LAC GCI Index 2017 Results

Regional Rank	*Country*	*GCI Score*	*Global Rank*
1	Mexico	0.6600	28
2	Uruguay	0.6470	29
3	Brazil	0.5930	38

The differences between countries' scores from 2014 and 2017 were computed to demonstrate progression, staticness or apparent regression concerning their commitments to cybersecurity. The differences demonstrate dramatic changes in the GCI scores, with Mexico being the highest positive change of 0.337, in stark contrast to Brazil (-0.113) as illustrated in Figure 5.

Country	Delta
Mexico	0.337
Uruguay	0.029
Colombia	-0.019
Brazil	-0.113

Figure 5. LAC Delta results between 2014 and 2017 GCI reports

According to the GCI 2017 report "The GCI 2014 and GCI 2017 are not directly comparable due to a change in methodology. While the 2014 index used a simple average methodology, the 2017 index employed a weighting factor for each pillar." [18]. However, both reports are based on the 5 pillars mentioned in Section III.D. The difference is that the 2017 index is finer grained with 157 scale points while the 2014 one has 34. The pillars are further broken down into 17 indicators in the 2014 GCI report. Each indicator is weighted against three levels of none (0), partial (1) and full compliance (2) with a full mark of 17 x 2 = 34. The ranking is calculated based on the following notations [34]:

χ_{qc} Value of the individual indicator q for country c, with q=1,..., Q and c=1,..., M.
I_{qc} Normalized value of individual indicator q for country c.
CI_c Value of the composite indicator for country c.

$$GCI2014 : CI_c = \frac{I_{qc}}{34}$$

$$I_{qc} = Rank(\chi_{qc})$$

The 2017 GCI is finer grained having 25 indicators with 157 binary none (0) or full compliance (1) questions distributed among the indicators and therefore the pillars based on weighting factor from experts [18].

$$GCI2017 : CI_c = \frac{I_{qc}}{157}$$

Brazil, for example, scored CI_c: 24 out of 34 in 2014 with GCI2014 score of 0.7059 out of 1 as in Table V. In contrast, Brazil in GCI 2017 scored CI_c: 93 out of 157 which is 0.5930 GCI out of 1 as shown in Table VI. Although GCI 2017 is finer grained as each mark is weighted (0.6%) in contrast to the (2.9%) of 2014, both GCIs benchmark countries between 0 and 1 or at a percentage scale. This deviation in granularity has been considered when performing the analysis and the averages of the GCI 2014 and 2017 scores between the two indices as we compute each country's delta with itself before comparing with others. As we use the delta as indicators that guides us in selecting Mexico and Brazil as countries of interest. The country's rank would be another indicator that we consider which is aligned with the delta comparison as well.

B. Comparative analysis between Mexico and Brazil

Figure 6 depicts security risks on (human, physical, and financial) areas including crime, riots, terrorism, military conflicts, and other threats. It also shows political risks which indicate the probability of political instability in a given country. In 2018, Mexico is Low in political risk and mixed between High, Medium and Low in security risks depending on the area of the country, whereas Brazil is Medium in both security and political risk according to the company Control Risks [35].

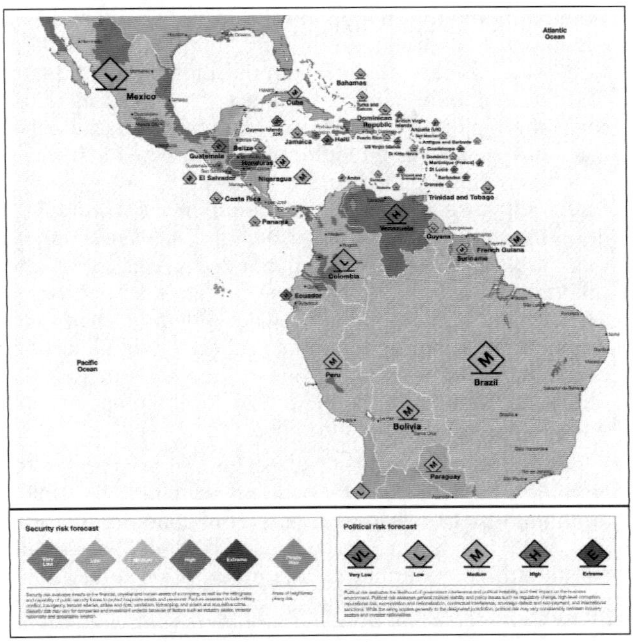

Figure 6. Americas Geopolitical socio-economical Risk Map 2018. [35].

According to the OAS reviews, both Brazil and Mexico have similar maturity levels across many dimensions; Brazil is further advanced in cyberdefence consideration, cybersecurity mindset, cybersecurity training, procedural laws, incident response and cybersecurity marketplace. In contrast, Mexico is more advanced in on-line privacy, responsible reporting and disclosure, identification of incidents, and critical infrastructure response planning. Both countries are rated in the OAS report between Formative (2) and Established (3) levels of maturity, with Brazil averaging at 2.55 and Mexico at 2.40.

Mexico has been demonstrating strength in the legal pillar of the GCI index as it invests substantial efforts in cyber legislation covering criminality, data protection, data privacy and electronic transactions [18]. As it aims to join the Budapest treaty on Cybercrime [36], Mexico has undergone tremendous amendments to substantive and procedural laws [31]. It also has hosted the 2016 Meridian Process [37] which produced The GFCE-MERIDIAN Good Practice Guide on Critical Information Infrastructure Protection for Governmental Policy Makers [38].

We have analysed the eight distinctive initiatives targeting Mexico and mapped the initiatives with the applicable key success factors. Table VII demonstrates that most of the initiatives have multiple success factors.

TABLE VII. INITIATIVES IN MEXICO WITH KEY SUCCESS FACTORS

Initiatives in Mexico	*Success factors*
Cybersecurity in the OAS Member States.	Coordination & Cooperation, Integration, Ownership, Sustainability, Learning, Funding, Duration
Japan International Cooperation Agency (JICA). Countermeasures Against CyberCrime.	Coordination & Cooperation, Integration, Funding
Mexican Financial Sector, FCO, Control Risks: Cybersecurity Health check.	Coordination & Cooperation, Ownership, Learning
Cybercrime Workshops, OAS, Federal Police: Mexican National Cybersecurity Week.	Coordination & Cooperation, Integration, Ownership
Cybercrime@Octopus, Council of Europe (CoE).	Coordination & Cooperation, Learning, Funding, Duration
Data Privacy Pathfinder APEC	Coordination & Cooperation, Integration
Latin American e-Commerce Legislation Harmonisation UN, Finland, ACS	Coordination & Cooperation, Ownership
Strengthening Cyber Skills in the Federal Police, FCO, BSI	Coordination & Cooperation, Integration, Ownership

In addition to these eight initiatives, Mexico is also part of the regional LAC initiatives, of which 24% cover Legal and Regulatory Frameworks.

In stark contrast to Mexico, Brazil had only five initiatives tailored to the needs of the country. These initiatives have commenced across a number of dimensions, focusing on the leadership role of the armed forces, or the establishment of the Cybersecurity strategy of the Federal Public Administration, or the coordination between the various CSIRTs, or the investments in education and awareness programs as well as establishing higher education centres of excellence [31]. However, Brazil was ranked the most dangerous country for Financial attacks in 2014 and has been the source and victim of cybercrime [39].

We have analysed the five distinctive initiatives targeting Brazil and mapped the initiatives with the applicable key success factors. Table VIII demonstrates fewer success factors linked to the initiatives at hand.

Brazil is one of the leading economies in LAC and has been investing heavily in ICT development. According to the World Bank national accounts data and the OECD national

TABLE VIII. INITIATIVES IN BRAZIL WITH KEY SUCCESS FACTORS

Initiatives in Brazil	*Success factors*
Fostering Cybersecurity Through Training the Judiciary on Digital and Cyber Issues. CFO, ITS	Coordination & Cooperation, Ownership
Introducing Estonian ICT Solutions for Delegations from Developing Countries. eGA	Coordination & Cooperation, Ownership, Learning, Funding, Duration
Tackling Cyber-Enabled Crime: Brazilian National Counter-Corruption and Anti-Money Laundering. FCO, NCA	Coordination & Cooperation, Learning
Cybersecurity and Cybercrime Workshop.	Learning
RNP-NSF for Research and Development Projects in Cybersecurity	Coordination & Cooperation, Ownership, Funding, Duration

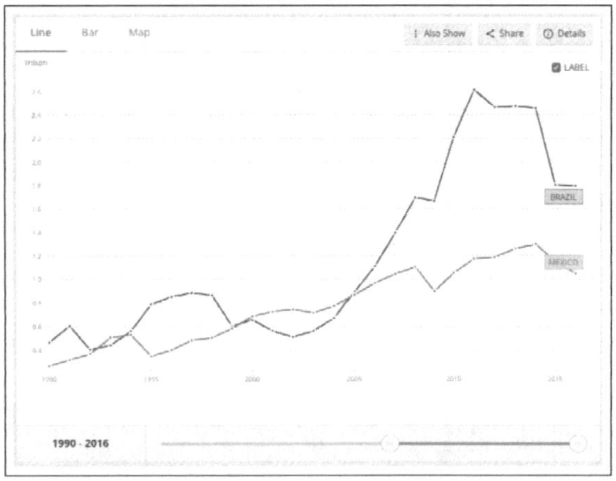

Figure 7. Economic (GDP) progress of Brazil and Mexico (1990-2016)) [40]

accounts data files, Brazil GDP in the year 2011 was 2.616 Trillion (USD) this has significantly fallen to a low 1.796 Trillion (USD) in the year 2016 losing 31% of GDP in this five-year period. See Figure 7. This slow economic progress might have contributed to the lack of progress in Brazil's cybersecurity maturity. Likewise, Mexico has also experienced economic slowdown but not as drastic as Brazil, and the number of targeted initiatives has facilitated the country's maturity growth.

VI. CONCLUSIONS, LIMITATIONS AND FUTURE WORK

The global community has been engaged extensively in assessing and addressing gaps in the cybersecurity commitments and capabilities of nations and regions. As a result, a significant number of Cybersecurity Capacity-Building (CCB) initiatives have been launched to overcome cyber-risks. These efforts face various challenges, however, such as lack of strategy and duplication of initiatives. To our knowledge, no study has explored the areas where cybersecurity initiatives focus and the possible gaps. In this paper, we have tried to close this gap by collecting and analysing all publicly available initiatives. We have further reflected on these initiatives with respect to well-established success factors in the literature on capacity-building. Towards this end, we have also engaged in qualitative research and analysed reports for two countries, Mexico and Brazil, trying to understand which of these factors may have been influential in designing and implementing successful cybersecurity initiatives.

Our results suggest that the distribution of CCB initiatives across the regions has been divided evenly, except that North America has received the least, only 7% of initiatives. This is because the gathered initiatives are focused on developing countries. The current focus, as observed from analysing the trends, is on building the foundational aspects of capacity such as devising or enhancing national Cybersecurity strategies, establishing effective CSIRT programmes, or creating reliable regulatory frameworks. These findings are in line with the observations of the ITU 2017 Global Cybersecurity Index. There are, however, evident gaps and imbalances with other CMM dimensions such as *Standards, Organisations, and Technologies* and *Cyber Culture and Society* which are vital in ensuring a balanced, capable, resilient, and dynamic cyberspace. As the top 10 active organisations account for (75%) of initiatives it demonstrates that few critical organisations are leading initiatives.

The comparison of Brazil and Mexico using the GCI scores demonstrates that Mexico was more committed to cybersecurity than Brazil during the 2014 and 2017 period, while it received a bigger number of initiatives. Our analysis suggests that the socio-economic and geopolitical challenges Brazil experienced over the recent years could be a key factor in why Brazil has apparently regressed or at least not progressed enough concerning cybersecurity maturity in contrast to the key success factors associated with the initiatives conducted by Mexico as highlighted in Section V.B.

The scope of this paper was limited to publicly available information in English. Moreover initiatives are primarily focused on developing and middle-income countries, since data was gathered mainly from sponsors and publicly available initiatives. Additionally, due to the security context dilemma, understandably various nations and entities would be hesitant to provide insights on their current and effective initiatives. As such the information is limited in scope and does not cover the majority of initiatives available. We may conclude that transparency in providing CCB information is essential in demonstrating effectiveness. Finally, lack of key attribute data such as the amount and commitment of funding for most initiatives adversely affected the analysis. Our scope was focused on the gathered initiatives, which limited our analysis to success factors at the initiative level as opposed the general CCB programmes and ecosystems. Generic success factors such as closing the 'cyber capacity gap' or identifying cyber-knowledge brokers requires alternative methodologies which would include interviews and focus groups of relevant stakeholders to gain deep insights.

In the future, we intend to perform a comparison of the existing efforts in capacity-building with the economic and technology metrics that exist for a set of countries or a specific region. There is a niche space in exploring what data should be collected from governments and organisation to better reflect capacity-maturity development. We aim to identify gaps in the funding of capacity-building and misallocation of these funds to less critical factors. Once the appropriate datasets are identified, relationships that exist between capacity-building activities may be revealed, hopefully leading to optimisation of the development of countries towards a more secure cybersecurity posture. A deeper analysis over the generic success factors, based on interviews and focus groups of relevant stakeholders, will provide us with more thorough and encompassing insights.

ACKNOWLEDGMENT

Special words of appreciations to Dr. Maria Bada for her valuable feedback and insights during the review phase of the project. Numerous words of appreciations to the Global Cyber Security Capacity Centre (GCSCC) for their invaluable guidance and feedback as well as providing materials from the GFCE portal. This work is supported by the UK Engineering and Physical Sciences Research Council (EPSRC) and the Saudi Ministry of Education.

REFERENCES

[1] J. Lewis, "Economic Impact of Cybercrime. No Slowing Down Report," McAfee, Center for Strategic and International Studies (CSIS), Tech. Rep., 2018. [Online]. Available: https://www.mcafee.com/us/resources/reports/restricted/economic-impact-cybercrime.pdf

[2] I. Agrafiotis et al., "Cyber Harm: Concepts, Taxonomy and Measurement," SSRN Electronic Journal, 8 2016, p. 23. [Online]. Available: http://www.ssrn.com/abstract=2828646

[3] M. Alvarez et al., "IBM X-Force Threat Intelligence Index 2017," IBM X-Forcec Threat Research, NY, Tech. Rep., 2017. [Online]. Available: https://assets.documentcloud.org/documents/3527813/IBM-XForce-Index-2017-FINAL.pdf

[4] ISACA Information Systems Audit and Control Association, "State of Cyber Security 2017 Resources and Threats," ISACA, Tech. Rep., 2017. [Online]. Available: https://cybersecurity.isaca.org/static-assets/documents/State-of-Cybersecurity-part-2-infographic_res_eng_0517.pdf

[5] P. Pawlak, "Capacity Building in Cyberspace as an Instrument of Foreign Policy," Global Policy, vol. 7, no. 1, 2 2016, pp. 83–92. [Online]. Available: http://doi.wiley.com/10.1111/1758-5899.12298

[6] World Economic Forum, "Risk and Responsibility in a Hyperconnected World: Pathways to Global Cyber Resilience," 2012. [Online]. Available: https://www.weforum.org/reports/risk-and-responsibility-/hyperconnected-world-/pathways-global-cyber-resilience

[7] H. Tiirmaa-Klaar, "Building national cyber resilience and protecting critical information infrastructure," Journal of Cyber Policy, vol. 1, no. 1, 1 2016, pp. 94–106. [Online]. Available: http://www.tandfonline.com/doi/full/10.1080/23738871.2016.1165716

[8] M. Hohmann, A. Pirang, and T. Benner, "Advancing Cybersecurity Capacity Building," Global Public Policy Institute (GPPI), 2017. [Online]. Available: http://www.gppi.net/fileadmin/user_upload/media/pub/2017/Hohmann__Pirang__Benner__2017__Advancing_Cybersecurity_Capacity_Building.pdf

[9] The World Bank Group, "World Development Report 2016: Digital Dividends." The World Bank Group, Washington DC, Tech. Rep., 2016. [Online]. Available: http://documents.worldbank.org/curated/en/896971468194972881/pdf/102725-PUB-Replacement-PUBLIC.pdf

[10] R. Heeks, "New Priorities for ICT4D Policy, Practice and WSIS in a Post-2015 World," Centre for Development Informatics, 2014, pp. 1–59. [Online]. Available: http://www.cdi.manchester.ac.uk

[11] Organisation for Economic Cooperation and Development (OECD), Digital Security Risk Management for Economic and Social Prosperity, 1st ed., Organisation for Economic Cooperation and Development (OECD), Ed. OECD Publishing, 10 2015. [Online]. Available: http://www.oecd-ilibrary.org/science-and-technology/digital-security-risk-management-for-economic-and-social-prosperity_9789264245471-en

[12] P. Pawlak and P.-N. Barmpaliou, "Politics of cybersecurity capacity building: conundrum and opportunity," Journal of Cyber Policy, vol. 2, no. 1, 2017, pp. 123–144. [Online]. Available: https://www.tandfonline.com/doi/full/10.1080/23738871.2017.1294610

[13] P. Pawlak, N. Robinson, M. G. Porcedda, E. Kvochko, and E. Calandro, "Riding the digital wave The impact of cyber capacity building on human development," EU Institute for Security Studies, Paris, Tech. Rep. December, 2014. [Online]. Available: http://www.iss.europa.eu/publications/detail/article/riding-the-digital-wave-the-impact-of-cyber-capacity-building/-on-human-development/

[14] Global Cyber Security Capacity Centre, "Cybersecurity Capacity Maturity Model for Nations (CMM). Revised Edition," University of Oxford, Oxford, Tech. Rep. CMM, 2017. [Online]. Available: https://www.sbs.ox.ac.uk/cybersecurity-capacity/content/cybersecurity-capacity-maturity-model-nations-cmm-revised-edition

[15] P. Pawlak, "Cyber Capacity Building in Ten Points Ten major take-away points," European Union Institute for Security Studies, vol. 7, no. 1, 2014, p. 8392. [Online]. Available: https://www.iss.europa.eu/sites/default/files/EUISSFiles/EUISS_Conference-Capacity_building_in_ten_points-0414.pdf

[16] M. Schaake and M. Vermeulen, "Towards a values-based European foreign policy to cybersecurity," Journal of Cyber Policy, vol. 1, no. 1, 1 2016, pp. 75–84. [Online]. Available: http://www.tandfonline.com/doi/full/10.1080/23738871.2016.1157617

[17] W. H. Dutton, S. Creese, R. Shillair, M. Bada, and T. Roberts, "Cyber Security Capacity: Does it Matter?" in Annual Meeting of the Telecommunication Policy Research Conference (TPRC), 2017, pp. 1–26. [Online]. Available: https://www.researchgate.net/profile/Ruth_Shillair/publication/319645577_Cyber_Security_Capacity_Does_it_Matter/links/59b7cdf4458515c212b505a3/Cyber-Security-Capacity-Does-it-Matter.pdf

[18] International Telecommunication Union, "Global Cybersecurity Index," International Telecommunication Union (ITU), Geneva, Switzerland, Tech. Rep., 2017. [Online]. Available: http://www.itu.int/en/ITU-D/Cybersecurity/Pages/GCI.aspx

[19] T. Maurer and R. Morgus, "Compilation of Existing Cybersecurity and Information Security Related Definitions," 2014. [Online]. Available: https://www.newamerica.org/cybersecurity-initiative/policy-papers/compilation-of-existing-cybersecurity-and/-information-security-related-definitions/

[20] V. Radunovic, "Towards A Secure Cyberspace Via Regional Co-operation," Geneva, Switzerland, Tech. Rep., 2017. [Online]. Available: https://www.diplomacy.edu/sites/default/files/Diplo-Towards_a_secure_cyberspace-GGE.pdf

[21] The Shanghai Cooperation Organisation, "About The Shanghai Cooperation Organisation SCO." [Online]. Available: http://eng.sectsco.org/about_sco/

[22] L. P. Muller, "Cyber Security Capacity Building in Developing Countries: Challenges and Opportunities," Norwegian Institute of International Affairs, Oslo, Norway, Tech. Rep., 2015. [Online]. Available: https://brage.bibsys.no/xmlui/bitstream/id/331398/NUPI+Report+03-15-Muller.pdf

[23] UK Foreign & Commonwealth Office (FCO), "Cyber Security Capacity Building Programme 2018 to 2021," 2018. [Online]. Available: https://www.gov.uk/government/publications/fco-cyber-security-capacity-building-programme-2018-to-2021

[24] The Global Cyber Security Capacity Centre (GCSCC), "Cybersecurity Capacity Portal," 2018. [Online]. Available: https://www.sbs.ox.ac.uk/cybersecurity-capacity/explore/gfce

[25] International Telecommunication Union (ITU), "Index Of Cybersecurity Indices." International Telecommunication Union (ITU), Geneva, Switzerland, Tech. Rep., 2017. [Online]. Available: https://www.itu.int/en/ITU-D/Cybersecurity/Documents/2017_Index_of_Indices.pdf

[26] BSA and The Software Alliance, "Asia-Pacific Cybersecurity Dashboard," Tech. Rep., 2015. [Online]. Available: http://cybersecurity.bsa.org/2015/apac/

[27] Fergus et al. Hanson, "Cyber Maturity in the Asia Pacific Region," Australian Strategic Policy Institute (ASPI), Tech. Rep., 2017. [Online]. Available: https://www.aspi.org.au/report/cyber-maturity-asia-pacific-region-2017

[28] M. Hathaway, C. Demchak, J. Kerben, J. Mcardle, and F. Spidalieri, "Cyber Readiness Index 2.0," Potomac Institute for Policy Studies, Virginia USA, Tech. Rep. November, 2015. [Online]. Available: http://www.potomacinstitute.org/images/CRIndex2.0.pdf

[29] International Telecommunication Union, "Global Cybersecurity Agenda (GCA)," 2017. [Online]. Available: https://www.itu.int/en/action/cybersecurity/Pages/gca.aspx

[30] The World Bank Group, "The World Bank Group Annual Report Regional Perspective. LAC region. 2017," 2017. [Online]. Available: http://www.worldbank.org/en/about/annual-report/region-perspectives#a

[31] The Inter-American Development Bank (IDB) and the Organization of American States (OAS), "Observatory Of Cybersecurity In Latin America And The Caribbean," 2016. [Online]. Available: http://observatoriociberseguridad.com/graph/countries//selected//0/dimensions/1-2-3-4-5

[32] N. Kshetri, Cybercrime and Cybersecurity in the Global South. London: Palgrave Macmillan, 2013, vol. 53, no. 9. [Online]. Available: https://doi.org/10.1057/9781137021946_7

[33] Symantec and Organisation of American States (OAS), "Cyber Security Trends In LAC," Symantec, Organisation of American States (OAS), Tech. Rep., 2014. [Online]. Available: https://www.thegfce.com/initiatives/c/cyber-security-initiative-in-oas-member-states/documents/publications/2014/06/01/latin-america-and-caribbean-cyber-security-trends

[34] International Telecommunication Union and ABI Research, "Global Cybersecurity Index 2014 & Cyberwellness Profiles," International Telecommunication Union ABI Research, Geneva, Switzerland, Tech. Rep., 2015. [Online]. Available: www.itu.int

[35] Control Risks, "RiskMap Americas Region," Control Risks, Tech. Rep., 2018. [Online]. Available: https://www.controlrisks.com/riskmap-2018/maps

[36] Council of Europe (CoE), "Convention on Cybercrime," pp. 1–22, 2001. [Online]. Available: https://rm.coe.int/CoERMPublicCommonSearchServices/DisplayDCTMContent?documentId=0900001680081561

[37] "The Meridian Process," 2016. [Online]. Available: https://www.meridianprocess.org/

[38] GFCE and Meridian, "Good Practice Guide on Critical Information Infrastructure Protection for governmental policy-makers," 2016. [Online]. Available: https://www.meridianprocess.org/siteassets/meridian/gfce-meridian-gpg-to-ciip.pdf

[39] F. Assolini, "Beaches, carnivals and cybercrime: a look inside the Brazilian underground," Kaspersky Lab, Tech. Rep., 2015.

[40] The World Bank Group WBG, "WBG World Bank national accounts data and the OECD national accounts data files." 2018. [Online]. Available: https://data.worldbank.org/indicator/NY.GDP.MKTP.CD?end=2016&locations=BR-MX&start=1990&view=chart

Towards a Quantitative Approach for Security Assurance Metrics

Goitom K. Weldehawaryat and Basel Katt

Department of Information Security and Communication Technology
Norwegian University of Science and Technology
Gjøvik, Norway
Email: {goitom.weldehawaryat,basel.katt}@ntnu.no

***Abstract*—The need for effective and efficient evaluation schemes of *security assurance* is growing in many organizations, especially Small and Medium Enterprises (SMEs). Although there are several approaches and standards for evaluating application security assurance, they are *qualitative* in nature and depend to a great extent on manually processing. This paper presents a *quantitative evaluation approach* for defining security assurance metrics using two perspectives, *vulnerabilities* and *security requirements*. While vulnerability represents the negative aspect that leads to a reduction of the assurance level, security requirement improves the assurance posture. The approach employs both *Goal Question Metric* (GQM) and *Common Vulnerability Scoring System* (CVSS) methods. GQM is used to construct measurement items for different types of assurance metrics and assess the fulfillment of security requirements or the absence of vulnerabilities, and CVSS is utilized to quantify the severity of vulnerabilities according to various attributes. Furthermore, a case study is provided in this work, which measures and evaluates the security assurance of a *discussion forum* application using our approach. This can assist SMEs to evaluate the overall security assurance of their systems, and result in a measure of confidence that indicates how well a system meets its security requirements.**

Keywords*–Quantitative security assurance metrics; Security testing; Goal question metric (GQM); Common vulnerability scoring system (CVSS); Security metrics.

I. INTRODUCTION

Our society has become increasingly dependent on the reliability and proper functioning of a number of interconnected infrastructure systems [1]. The security of most systems and networks depends on the security of the software running on them. This holds also for web applications that are usually accessible in public networks. However, most of the attacks on these systems occur due to the exploitation of vulnerabilities found in their software applications. The number of vulnerabilities also increase as the systems become more complex and connected [2].

Many organizations are implementing different security processes and procedures to secure their systems; however, some organizations need some evidence that show the security mechanisms are effectively put in place and carry out their intended functions to prevent, detect or divert a risk or to reduce its impact on assets [3][4]. Thus, it is important for organizations to know, on one hand, if their systems are vulnerable to threats, and on the other hand if the protection security mechanisms are effective to fulfill the security requirement and mitigate the threats [5].

Security assurance is the confidence that a system meets its security requirements [6]. The confidence is based on specific metrics and evidences gathered and evaluated with given assurance techniques, e.g., formal methods, penetration testing, or third-party reviews. The main activities in security assurance include threat and vulnerability analysis, definition of security requirements based on risk, testing, and architectural information of the environment where Target of Evaluation (ToE) resides. Although the research focus has been mainly on developing *qualitative* metrics that usually lead to security assurance levels that are either not accurate or not repeatable, recent efforts within the field have been directed towards utilizing *quantitative* indicators to capture the security state of a particular system [7]. However, the research efforts that applied quantitative methods have been mainly focused on vulnerabilities and to a lesser extent on the understanding of *vulnerability-security requirement interactions* [2][8].

This paper presents a quantitative evaluation approach for defining security assurance metrics that provides a high level security assurance evaluation and distinguishes two perspectives: *security requirement metrics* and *vulnerability metrics*. While vulnerability represents the negative aspect that leads to a reduction of the assurance level, security requirement improves the assurance posture. Specifically, the approach utilizes the GQM to construct measurement items for different types of assurance metrics and assess the fulfillment of security requirements or the absence of vulnerabilities, and the CVSS to quantify the severity of vulnerabilities according to various attributes. Furthermore, this work illustrates a case study on conducting security testing and assurance functions on an example application, *discussion forum*. The main contribution is the development of a quantitative evaluation approach for defining security assurance metrics that enables quantifying and estimating the level of security requirement and the degree of vulnerability severity. The metrics reflect the strengths of the protection mechanisms and the severity of vulnerabilities that impact a target of evaluation.

The rest of the paper is organized as follows. Section II presents a related work. Section III describes the quantitative assurance metrics, while Section IV discusses the security assurance process. Section V presents the case study, and Section VI provides a discussion of the quantitative assurance metrics approach. Finally, Section VII concludes the paper and presents future work.

II. Related Work

Research efforts have been made to address systems security assurance from the software development life cycle down to the operational systems level [6]. The reason for this is that without a rigorous and effective way of dealing with security throughout the system development process, the end product cannot be secure. However, the emphasis on design and process evidence versus actual implementation largely overshadows practical security concerns involving the implementation and deployment of operational systems [9].

A number of frameworks and standards exist for evaluating security assurance [10][11]. Examples include the Systems Security Engineering Capability Maturity Model (SSE-CMM) [10], OWASP's Software Assurance Maturity Model (OpenSAMM) [12], and the Common Criteria (CC) also known as ISO/IEC 15408 [13]. The CC describes a framework in which developers can specify security and assurance requirements that need to be valuated to determine whether a system meets the claimed security. Although evaluation methods are based on guidelines and best practices, they are done manually to a large extend and result in the creation of large amount of documentation. One major criticism against the CC, for example, is that it evaluates the process more than evaluating the implementation. They are also limited to a few application domains, like smart card security [14]. Furthermore, the assurance levels they define, especially those of Open Web Application Security Project (OWASP), CC and OpenSAMM are abstractly defined and have no quantifiable basis to be measured, which makes it harder for the vendors and third-party assessors to measure the actual security impact and confidence.

Recently, some initiatives have been taken towards developing operational methodologies for the evaluation of IT infrastructure security assurance. Pham *et al.* [15] introduce an attack graph based security assurance assessment system based on multi-agents. In their approach, the authors use attack graph to compute an "attackability" metric value (the likelihood that an entity will be successfully attacked) for static evaluation and define other metrics for anomaly detection at run time. Attack surface estimation [8] is another approach aiming at detecting vulnerabilities within a system. It does not evaluate the security directly, but rather estimates the number of access points to the subject system by counting available interfaces, supported protocols, open ports, open sockets, installed software, etc. The Building Security Assurance in Open Infrastructures (BUGYO) project [16][17] can be cited as the first project that proposed a methodology and tool for continuous security assurance evaluation; security assurance evaluation in the context of BUGYO was aimed at probing the security of runtime systems rather than products. This work investigates a quantitative approach for defining security assurance metrics that provides an overall security assurance evaluation of a target of evaluation.

III. Quantitative Assurance Metrics

Security assurance defines the confidence that a system meets its security requirements based on specific evidence provided by the application of assurance techniques (formal methods, penetration testing, etc) [6]. The need to provide organizations with confidence that deployed security measures meet their requirements at runtime has been acknowledged as a crucial issue [16][18][19]. This is because security mechanisms, even properly identified during the risk assessment stage, may still suffer from an inappropriate deployment that may render them less effective. Although the current evaluation methods rely to a great extent on security experts knowledge and are not adapted to real dynamic operational systems [17], recent research efforts have been directed towards utilizing *quantitative* indicators to capture the security state of a particular system [7]. The gathering of measurable evidence is facilitated by the specification of metrics that are necessary for the normalization of the security assurance levels. We consider three key concepts in our metrics specifications: *vulnerability metrics*, *security requirement metrics* and *assurance metrics*. These metrics will be described in the following subsections.

A. Security Requirement Metrics

Security requirements are associated to the protection of valuable assets in a system. Many authors implicitly assume that security requirements are identical to high-level security goals. Tettero [20] defined security requirements as the confidentiality, integrity, and availability of the entity for which protection is needed. Devanbu and Stubblebine [21] defined a security requirement as "a manifestation of a high-level organizational policy into the detailed requirements of a specific system". Thus, the aim of defining security requirements for a system is to map the results of risk and threat analyses to practical security requirement statements that manage (mitigate or maintain) the security risks of the target of evaluation.

Security requirement metrics reflect the vendor's confidence in a particular security control employed in the target of evaluation to fulfill one or more *security requirements*. Evaluating the confidence level of a security requirement is twofold. First, we need to check whether the current deployed security protection controls *fulfill* the security requirement. This can be manifested as a set of test cases associated with each security requirement. Second, it can be argued that not all security requirements of one application are equally important [22]. Thus, there is a need to consider the importance, or the *weight*, of each of the security requirements. The *weight* for a requirement represent the level of importance of the this requirement to the application in question.

In order to quantify the *fulfillment* factor of the security requirement metrics, we need to connect each requirement to a set of measurable metrics. This can be done using the Goal Question Metric (GQM) approach [23]. GQM provides a clear derivation from security goals to metrics by developing questions that relate to the goals and are answered by metrics [24]. A GQM approach is a hierarchical structure that defines a top-down measurement model based on three levels [23]:

- *Conceptual level* (Goal)
  A goal is defined for an object for various reasons, with respect to various models of quality, from various points of view and relative to a particular environment. Object of Measurement can be: Products, Processes or Resources. In our context, the main goal is to assess the assurance of the target of evaluation. This goal can be split into sub-goals that represent the identified security requirements.
- *Operational level* (Question)
  A set of questions is used to characterize the way the assessment or the achievement of a specific goal is

going to be performed based on some characterizing model. Test cases defined for each security requirement represent questions in our context.
- *Quantitative level* (Metric)
  A set of metrics is associated with every question in order to answer it in a measurable way. In our context, every question can be assigned to a value (for example, Full=1, Average=0.5, Weak=0), and metrics can be given based on *fulfillment* value to the test case.

As an example of applying the GQM for the *authentication* security requirement for web applications, Table I shows questions and metrics for this case. Based on the previous discussion, we define a security requirement metric (Rm_i) for a given security requirement at a specific time instance as:

$$Rm_i = (w_i \times \sum_{j=1}^{m} f_{ij}) \tag{1}$$

where m represent the number of test cases defined for this security requirement, w is the weight of the requirement and f is the fulfillment factor of the requirement. i is the index of the security requirement, and j is the index of the test cases for the security requirement. GQM is used to measure the fulfillment of the security requirements.

As a result, we define the accumulate security requirement metrics of an application at a specific time instance as:

$$RM = \sum_{i=1}^{n} (Rm_i) \tag{2}$$

where n represents the total number of security requirement defined for the ToE.

B. Vulnerability Metrics

A *vulnerability* is defined as a bug, flaw, behaviour, output, outcome or event within an application, system, device, or service that could lead to an implicit or explicit failure of confidentiality, integrity or availability [25]. Thus, vulnerability is a weakness which allows attacker to reduce a system's security assurance. Since organizations usually operate within limited budgets, they have to prioritize their vulnerability responses based on risk value of each vulnerability.

Vulnerability metrics allows to measure the existence and the severity level of system vulnerabilities. Thus assessing vulnerability metrics is twofold. First, there is a need to check the existence of the different types of vulnerabilities that pose a threat to the application. This can be assessed using the GQM method, in which (1) the goal will be to assess the existence of different vulnerabilities in the ToE, (2) the sub goals represent the vulnerability types that pose threat to the ToE, (3) questions represent the test cases that will check the existence of a given vulnerability type, and finally, (4) the quantified answer to the questions represent the metrics. Second, it is essential to quantify the severity level of vulnerabilities in the context of the ToE, which can be represented by the risk value of the vulnerability. For example, the *Common Vulnerability Scoring System* (CVSS) [25][26] cab be used for this purpose. A CVSS score is a decimal number in the range $[0.0, 10.0]$, where the value 0.0 has no rating (there is no possibility to exploit vulnerability) and the value 10.0 has full score (vulnerability easy to exploit). This score is computed using three categories of metrics, which assess the intrinsic characteristics of the vulnerabilities (*base metrics*), its evolution over time (*temporal metrics*), and the user environment in which the vulnerability is detected (*environmental metrics*). These three metric groups can be used to compute the vulnerability severity level of a target of evaluation.

We define a vulnerability metric (Vm_k) for a given security vulnerability at a specific time instance as:

$$Vm_k = (r_k \times \sum_{l=1}^{p} e_{kl}) \tag{3}$$

where, p represent the number of test cases defined for this vulnerability type, r_k is the risk of the kth vulnerability and e_{kl} is the existence factor for l^{th} test case defined for the kth vulnerability. The existence factor can have three values, 0 means that the test case indicates no vulnerability, 1 indicates the existence of the vulnerability for the test case, and 0.5 indicates the partial existence of the vulnerability for the test case.

Thus, the vulnerability metrics of a system at a specific time instance can be calculated using the risk of vulnerabilities and their existence factor as follows:

$$VM = \sum_{k=1}^{d} (Vm_k) \tag{4}$$

where d represents the total number of vulnerabilities defined for the ToE.

C. Assurance Metrics

Assurance Metrics (AM) determine the actual confidence that deployed countermeasures protect assets from threats (vulnerabilities) and fulfill security requirements. We define assurance metrics as the difference between security *Requirement Metrics* (RM) and *Vulnerability Metrics* (VM). Thus, the assurance metrics can be calculated as follows:

$$AM = RM - VM = \sum_{i=1}^{n} (Rm_i) - \sum_{k=1}^{d} (Vm_k) \tag{5}$$

where, AM is the security assurance metrics at a given time instance, RM is the security requirement metrics at a given time instance, and VM is the vulnerability metrics at a time given instance.

From (5), it can be noticed that AM is *minimum* when the following two conditions are met:

- All security requirements are not fulfilled (RM becomes zero), which causes the value of the first term to be minimum (zero), and
- All possible vulnerabilities exist and all have a maximum risk value. This makes the second term to be maximum (VM).

AM, on the other hand, can be *maximum* if (1) VM is minimum for all vulnerabilities, and (2) the protection mechanisms have been found to be effective to fulfill the defined security requirements (RM is maximum) for all requirements.

TABLE I. EXAMPLE OF GQM IN ASSESSING THE AUTHENTICATION VERIFICATION REQUIREMENTS

Goal		Question	Metrics
Purpose	assessing authentication	Are credentials and all pages/functions that require a user to enter credentials transported using a suitable encrypted link ?	Full, average or weak
Issue or Component	authentication	Do all pages and resources by default require authentication except those specifically intended to be public?	Full, average or weak
Object or Process	web application authentication	Do password entry fields allow, or encourage, the use of long passphrases or highly complex passwords being entered?	Full, average or weak
viewpoint	stakeholder, user, organization	Do all authentication controls fail securely to ensure attackers cannot log in?	Full, average or weak
		Does the changing password functionality include the old password, the new password, and a password confirmation?	Full, average or weak
		Is information enumeration possible via login, password reset, or forgot account functionality?	Full, average or weak

Rating Score: Full=1, Average=0.5, Weak=0

IV. SECURITY ASSURANCE PROCESS

An assurance process defines the different activities that need to be performed in order to assess the level of confidence a system meets its security requirements. Our assurance process deals with three types of metrics: *vulnerability metrics*, *security requirement metrics* and *assurance metrics*. Similar to the methodology defined in [17], the assurance process consists of five main activities: *application modelling, metric selection and test case definition, test case execution and measurement collection, assurance metrics and level calculation, evaluation and monitoring*. The input is an operational system running a target of application to be evaluated.

1) **Application modelling:** The application modelling allows decomposing the application in order to identify critical assets. An efficient way of identifying those critical components is an a priori use of a threat modelling and risk assessment methodology. Security functions and threats related to the basic security concepts of the application and its environment can be analysed. This results the security requirements expected to be present and running correctly in the system to fulfill security goals and protect assets from threats.
2) **Metric selection and test case definition:** A metric is based on the measurement of various parts or parameters of security functions implemented on the system with its service and operational environment. Depending on the measurements being performed, metrics can be classified as follows:
   - *Security requirement metrics* relate to a measurement that evaluates whether security protection mechanisms exist and fulfill defined security requirements using the GQM method.
   - *Vulnerability metrics* relate to a measurement that evaluates the weaknesses/severity and vulnerabilities existence in the systems using the CVSS and GQM methods.

   Test cases for both metrics can be defined to test the vulnerabilities and verify the security requirements on the target of evaluation.
3) **Test case execution and measurement collection:** Test case execution and measurement collection consist in deploying specific probes to implement the test cases on a target of evaluation and its operational environment. These probes can help to collect raw data from the system. This step will result in a measurement that will be normalized to produce an assurance level in step 4.
4) **Assurance metrics and level calculation:** Once the security requirement and vulnerability metrics are determined in step 3, the overall security assurance of the target of evaluation can be calculated using (5) presented in Section III.
5) **Evaluation and monitoring:** This step involves comparing the current value of the assurance level to the previous measure, or to a certain threshold and issuing an appropriate message. It can also provide a real time display of security assurance of the service to help the evaluator identify causes of security assurance deviation and assist him/her in making decisions.

V. CASE STUDY

This section presents the proposed assurance approach and processes applied for the web discussion forum developed for this purpose.

A. Application and Threat Modelling

Figure 1 shows a screenshot of the discussion forum. The forum has users who create topics in various categories, and other users who can post replies. Messages can be posted as either replies to existing messages or posted as new messages. The forum organizes visitors and logged in members into user groups. Privileges and rights are given based on these groups.

The tools used to develop the forum includes *PHP, MySQL,* and *Apache. WAMP* was used to do an all-in-one installation of Apache, MySQL, and PHP on a Windows 7 virtual instance. A Kali Linux [27] virtual instance was used as a security testing machine. The discussion application forum was tested using a number of tools such as *OWASP Zed Attack Proxy (ZAP), WebScarab, OpenVAS* and *Sqlmap*, and manual testing since some vulnerability types can only be found through testers observations. The infrastructure required to create a realistic environment for conducting the testing and assurance functions of the ToE was built using OpenStack cloud computing platform [28].

Threat modelling is a systematic process of identifying, analysing, documenting, and mitigating security threats to a software system [29]. Analysing and modelling the potential threats that an application faces is an important step in the process of designing a secure application. Some of these threats are very specific to the application, but other threats

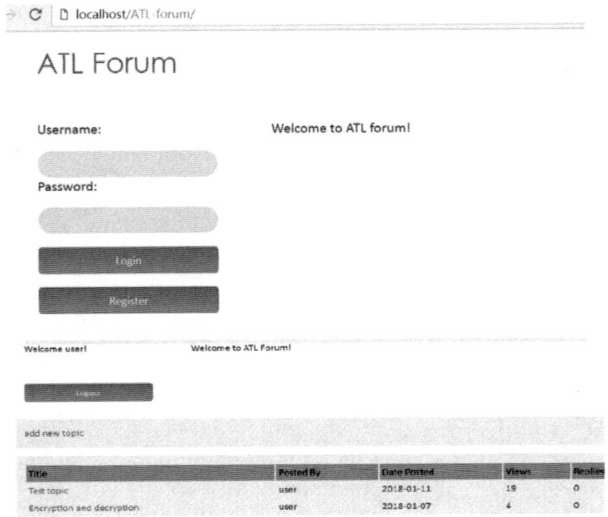

Figure 1. Discussion forum.

are directly or indirectly related to the underlying platforms, technologies or programming languages. The main steps of threat modelling process consists of the following three high-level steps: *characterizing the system, identifying assets* and *access points, and identifying threats* [30].

a) Characterizing the system: Characterizing the system involves understanding the system components and their interconnections, and creating a system model emphasizing its main characteristics. *Data Flow Diagram (DFD)* is used to model the application which dissects the application into its functional components and indicates the flow of data into and out of the various parts of system components. Figure 2 shows a flow diagram of the discussion forum, which was modelled with Microsoft threat modelling tool 2016.

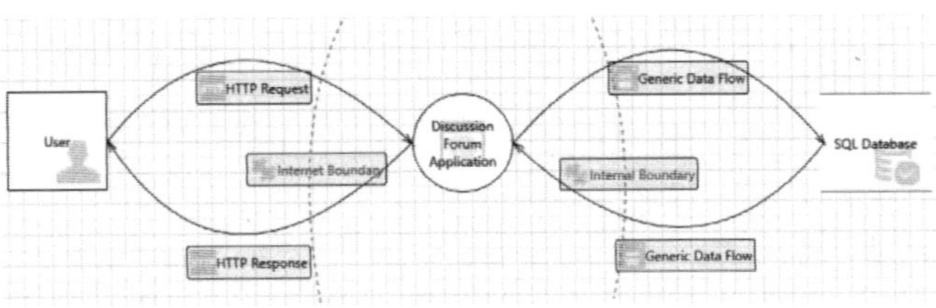

Figure 2. Data flow diagram for the discussion forum.

b) Identifying assets and access points: An asset is an abstract or concrete resource that a system must protect from misuse by an adversary. Identifying assets is the most critical step in threat modelling because assets are threat targets. Examples of identified list of assets of the application that may be targeted by attackers include:

- Forum users and assets relating to forum users
- User login details and the login credentials that a user will use to log into the discussion forum
- The discussion forum website and assets relating to the website

Access (entry) points are interfaces through which potential attackers can interact with the system to gain access to assets. Examples of access points include user login interfaces, HTTP Port, configuration files, file systems and hardware ports. It is also important to determine the *trust boundaries* in the system. A trust boundary is a boundary across which there are varied levels of trust. For example, administrators are trusted to do more than normal users.

c) Identifying threats: A threat is what an adversary might try to do to a system [31]. Threats can be identified by going through each of the identified critical assets and creating threat hypotheses that violate confidentiality, integrity, or availability of the assets. The output of threat identification process is a threat profile for a system, describing all the potential attacks, each of which needs to be mitigated or accepted.

A threat categorization is useful in the identification of threats by classifying attacker goals such as: *Spoofing, Tampering, Repudiation, Information Disclosure, Denial of Service, Elevation of Privilege* (STRIDE). An incomplete identified list of threats for the application are given in Table III .

Security requirements: Security requirements are driven by security threats. Although security requirements can also be extracted from standards, it is still important to conduct a thorough risk management to discover which threats are realistic, and analyse the suitability of security requirements to the system. However, these security requirements need to be validated and measured to achieve the security goals of the application. In this work, *Application Security Verification Standard (ASVS)* [11] verification requirements are considered as a source of security requirements, and GQM approach is used to measure/verify the fulfillment of these security requirements for the application. Security requirements used for the application are given in Table II.

B. Metric Selection and Test Case Definition

The metrics are categorized as (i) security requirement metrics, (ii) vulnerability metrics, and (iii) security assurance metrics. The first two are discussed in the first two subsections, and the third one is presented in subsequent subsection concentrating on security assurance metrics. OWASP ASVS is used to define the test cases for the security requirements, and OWASP Testing Guide and OWASP Cheat Sheets [32] were used as a reference while choosing the testing techniques and developing the vulnerability test cases.

a) Security requirement test cases: As the discussion forum is not a critical application, Level 1 is used to verify the security requirements. Level 1 consists of 68 security requirements to be verified. All of the requirements were analysed to find out how many of these requirements are applicable to the discussion forum, and the security requirements that are applicable to the application were assessed to measure the their fulfillment. Example test cases for the authentication requirement verification are given as follows:

- Verify that the weak lock out mechanism to mitigate brute force password guessing attacks
  - attempt an invalid log in by using the incorrect password a number of times, before using the correct password to verify that the account was locked out. An example test may be as follows:
    1) Attempt to log in with an incorrect password 3 times.

2) Successfully log in with the correct password, thereby showing that the lockout mechanism doesn't trigger after 3 incorrect authentication attempts.

- Verify that the forgotten password function and other recovery paths do not reveal the current password and that the new password is not sent in clear text to the user
- Verify that information enumeration is not possible via login, password reset, or forgot account functionality

b) Vulnerabilities test cases: This subsection specifies vulnerabilities test cases that can prevent the achievement of the security requirements. The severity impact of each vulnerability is measured based on the CVSS base score. Example vulnerability test cases for the application that transmits clear-text and uses default credentials are given as follows:

- Test for credentials transported over an unencrypted channel
  - Sending data with POST method through HTTP and trying to intercept the username and password by simply sniffing the network with a tool like Wireshark
- Test for default credentials of the application
  - Test for default credentials of common applications (as an example try the following usernames - "admin", "root", "system", "guest", "operator", or "super"), and an empty password or one of the following "password", "pass123", "admin", or "guest"

C. Test Case Execution and Measurement Collection

The discussion forum application was tested based on the the test cases developed to verify the security requirement and vulnerabilities in subsection V-B. After the test cases execution, security requirement measurement is collected from the application for all the security requirements. Due to space limitation, the measurement details for all test cases in each security requirement and each vulnerability type are not included; however the total measurement collected for each security requirements and vulnerabilities are summarized in Table II and Table III, respectively.

D. Assurance Metrics and Level Calculation

The *Assurance metrics* is calculated as the difference of *security requirement metrics* and *vulnerability metrics* using (5).

$$AM = RM - VM \quad \text{that is,}$$

$$AM = \left(\sum_{i=1}^{n} (w_i \times \sum_{j=1}^{m} f_{ij}) \right) - \left(\sum_{k=1}^{d} (r_k \times \sum_{l=1}^{p} e_{kl}) \right)$$

Thus, the assurance metrics for the discussion forum application can be calculated using the security requirement measurement in Table II and the vulnerability measurement in Table III as follows:

$$AM = \left(\sum_{i=1}^{11} (w_i \times \sum_{j=1}^{m} f_{ij}) \right) - \left(\sum_{k=1}^{10} (r_k \times \sum_{l=1}^{p} e_{kl}) \right) = 73 - 108.1 = -35.1$$

TABLE II. MEASUREMENT COLLECTED FOR ALL SEC. REQUIREMENTS

No.	Security Requirements	Weight	Fulfillment	RM = 73
1	Architecture, design and threat modelling	10	1	10
2	Authentication	8	3	24
3	Session management	5	4	20
4	Access control	7	1	7
5	Malicious input handling	5	1	5
6	Cryptography at rest	4	0	0
7	Error handling and logging	7	1	7
8	Data protection	4	0	0
9	HTTP security configuration	4	0	0
10	File and resources	4	0	0
11	Configuration	4	0	0

AM can be *minimum* if RM is minimum (zero) and VM is maximum. AM, on the other hand, can be *maximum* if VM is minimum and RM is maximum. Thus, the *minimum value* of the assurance metrics (AM_{min}) for the case study can be calculated as follows:

$$AM_{min} = RM_{min} - VM_{max} = 0 - 142.5 = -142.5 \quad (6)$$

The *maximum value* of the assurance metrics (AM_{max}) for this case study can also be calculated as follows:

$$AM_{max} = RM_{max} - VM_{min} = 255 - 0 = 255 \quad (7)$$

The normalized assurance metrics (AM_{norm}) can be calculated in the range of 0 to 10 using the *min-max normalization* formula as follows :

$$\text{AM}_{norm} = \left(\frac{AM - AM_{min}}{AM_{max} - AM_{min}}(AM_{newmax} - AM_{newmin}) + AM_{newmin}\right) = \left(\frac{-35.1 - (-142.5)}{255 - (-142.5)}(10 - 0) + 0\right) = \frac{1074}{397.5} = 2.7$$

Security assurance levels: For some purposes, it is useful to have a textual representation of the security assurance metric value of an application. Five subjective categories of assurance metrics and their corresponding values can be represented as follows:

1) Very low (0-0.9)
2) Low (1 - 3.9)
3) Medium (4 - 6.9)
4) High (7 - 8.9)
5) Very high (9 - 10)

As an example, the security assurance metric of the discussion forum application (2.7) has an associated security assurance level of *Low*.

TABLE III. MEASUREMENT COLLECTED FOR ALL VULNERABILITIES

No.	Threats/vulnerabilities	Av	Ac	Pr	UI	S	C	I	A	CVSS Base Score	Existence	VM=108.1
1	Web server generic XSS	N	L	N	R	C	L	L	N	6.1	2	12.2
2	Web server transmits cleartext credentials	N	L	N	N	U	L	L	L	7.3	1	7.3
3	Application error disclosure	N	H	N	N	U	L	N	N	3.7	2	7.4
4	Directory browsing	N	L	L	N	U	H	N	N	6.5	2	13
5	Cookie no HttpOnly flag	N	L	N	N	U	H	N	N	7.5	1	7.5
6	SQL injection vulnerability for the SQL-Database	N	L	L	N	C	L	L	N	6.4	1	6.4
7	Lack of input validation	N	L	N	R	C	L	L	N	6.1	5	30.5
8	Data tampering	N	H	N	N	U	H	H	N	7.4	1	7.4
9	Elevation of privilege using remote code execution	L	L	L	N	U	H	H	H	7.8	1	7.8
10	Network eavesdropping/Sniffing	N	L	N	N	U	H	L	L	8.6	1	8.6

VI. DISCUSSION

In this study, we have investigated the quantitative security assurance metrics using two dimensions of metrics to represent an overall security assurance: *vulnerability* and *security requirement*. In particular, vulnerability represents the negative aspect that leads to a reduction of the assurance level, and security requirement improves the assurance posture. Our approach employed both GQM and CVSS methods for metric definition and calculation. While the GQM is used to construct measurement items for security requirement metrics and assess the fulfillment of security requirements, CVSS is used to quantify the severity of vulnerabilities according to various attributes.

A case study is provided in this work, which measures the overall security assurance of the discussion forum application using our approach. The security assurance process was followed to measure and evaluate the degree of trustworthiness of the application. Specifically, we conducted a systematic threat modelling processes of the discussion forum application, test case definition, measurement collection, and security assurance metrics calculation. However, this work did not consider the security of the underlining infrastructure, non-technical attack vectors, new attacks, etc.

VII. CONCLUSION AND FUTURE WORK

This paper has presented a *quantitative approach* for defining security assurance metrics that provides a high level security assurance evaluation and distinguishes two perspectives: *security requirement metrics* and *vulnerability metrics*. The metrics reflect the strengths of the protection mechanisms and the severity of vulnerabilities that impact a target of evaluation. Specifically, we adopted the GQM method to estimate and quantify the level of protection, and the CVSS to quantify the vulnerability severity. The methodology described a process for security assurance evaluation emphasizing the role of security requirement metrics to probe the correctness of deployed security measures, vulnerability metrics to measure a severity level of a system vulnerability, and security assurance metrics. The computation of the assurance metric is focused on the current security state of a target of evaluation in order to consider the system dynamics in a particular time, e.g., the level of protection mechanisms and vulnerabilities.

This work has also conducted a case study on the discussion forum using the approach, and the results show that it is important to utilize a variety of tools, as well as conduct manual testing in order to find and test the most number of vulnerabilities and verify security requirements in a web application. This can assist organizations to evaluate the overall security assurance of a system and result in a measure of confidence that indicates how well a given system at a particular time meets particular security goal.

Our future work aims at automating the security assurance process and developing a platform that creates a network of systems based on testing scenarios, records the test execution and analyses its results, and scores the assurance level.

ACKNOWLEDGMENT

This work was partially supported by the the *Regional Research Fund* (RFF) Innlandet and *Playtecher* of Norway. The authors would like to thank the anonymous referees for their review comments that helped to improve the presentation of the paper.

REFERENCES

[1] G. K. Weldehawaryat and S. D. Wolthusen, "Modelling interdependencies over incomplete join structures of power law networks," in 2015 11th International Conference on the Design of Reliable Communication Networks (DRCN), March 2015, pp. 173–178.

[2] R. M. Savola, H. P. äinen, and M. Ouedraogo, "Towards security effectiveness measurement utilizing risk-based security assurance," in 2010 Information Security for South Africa, August 2010, pp. 1–8.
[3] S. M. Furnell, "The irreversible march of technology," Inf. Secur. Tech. Rep., vol. 14, no. 4, November 2009, pp. 176–180.
[4] G. Stoneburner, "Underlying technical models for information technology security," Special Publication (NIST SP)-800-33, 2001, pp. 1–28.
[5] M. Ouedraogo, R. M. Savola, H. Mouratidis, D. Preston, D. Khadraoui, and E. Duboi, "Taxonomy of quality metrics for assessing assurance of security correctness," Software Quality Journal, vol. 21, no. 1, March 2013, pp. 67–97.
[6] "Common criteria for information technology security evaluation part 3: Security assurance components, version 3.1 rev1," pp. 1–86, 2006.
[7] M. Ouedraogo, H. Mouratidis, D. Khadraoui, E. Dubois, and D. Palmer-Brown, "Current trends and advances in it service infrastructures security assurance evaluation," 2009, pp. 132–141.
[8] M. Pendleton, R. Garcia-Lebron, J.-H. Cho, and S. Xu, "A survey on systems security metrics," ACM Comput. Surv., vol. 49, no. 4, December 2016, pp. 62:1–62:35.
[9] W. Jansen, "Directions in security metrics research - NISTIR 7564," 2009, pp. 1–21.
[10] G. B. Regulwar, V. S. Gulhane, and P. M. Jawandhiya, "A security engineering capability maturity model," in 2010 International Conference on Educational and Information Technology, vol. 1, Sept 2010, pp. 306–311.
[11] OWASP, "Application security verification standard (ASVS)," 2015, pp. 1–70.
[12] C. Kubicki, "The system administration maturity model - SAMM," in Proceedings of the 7th USENIX Conference on System Administration, ser. LISA '93. Berkeley, CA, USA: USENIX Association, 1993, pp. 213–225.
[13] "Common criteria for information technology security evaluation," pp. 1–93, 2012.
[14] M. Vetterling, G. Wimmel, and A. Wisspeintner, "Secure systems development based on the common criteria: The palme project," in Proceedings of the 10th ACM SIGSOFT Symposium on Foundations of Software Engineering, ser. SIGSOFT '02/FSE-10. New York, NY, USA: ACM, 2002, pp. 129–138.
[15] N. Pham, L. Baud, P. Bellot, and M. Riguidel, "A near real-time system for security assurance assessment," in 2008 The Third International Conference on Internet Monitoring and Protection, June 2008, pp. 152–160.
[16] E. Bulut, D. Khadraoui, and B. Marquet, "Multi-agent based security assurance monitoring system for telecommunication infrastructures," in Proceedings of the Fourth IASTED International Conference on Communication, Network and Information Security. ACTA Press, 2007, pp. 90–95.
[17] S. Haddad, S. Dubus, A. Hecker, T. Kanstren, B. Marquet, and R. Savola, "Operational security assurance evaluation in open infrastructures," in Proceedings of the 2011 6th International Conference on Risks and Security of Internet and Systems (CRiSIS), ser. CRISIS '11. Washington, DC, USA: IEEE Computer Society, 2011, pp. 1–6.
[18] C. Criteria, "Common criteria for information technology security evaluation, v3.1, part 1-3," 2017, pp. 1–106.
[19] A. M. B. N. I. L. Nabil Seddigh, Peter Pieda and A. Hatfield, "Current trends and advances in information assurance metrics," 2004, pp. 197–205.
[20] O. Tettero, D. Out, H. Franken, and J. Schot, "Information security embedded in the design of telematics systems," Computers & Security, vol. 16, no. 2, 1997, pp. 145 - 164.
[21] P. T. Devanbu and S. Stubblebine, "Software engineering for security: A roadmap," in Proceedings of the Conference on The Future of Software Engineering, ser. ICSE '00. New York, NY, USA: ACM, 2000, pp. 227–239.
[22] K.-Y. Park, S.-G. Yoo, and J. Kim, "Security requirements prioritization based on threat modeling and valuation graph," in Convergence and Hybrid Information Technology, G. Lee, D. Howard, and D. Ślezak, Eds. Berlin, Heidelberg: Springer Berlin Heidelberg, 2011, pp. 142–152.
[23] V. R. Basili, G. Caldiera, and H. D. Rombach, "The goal question metric approach," Encyclopedia of software engineering, vol. 2, no. 1994, 1994, pp. 528–532.
[24] S. Islam and P. Falcarin, "Measuring security requirements for software security," in 2011 IEEE 10th International Conference on Cybernetic Intelligent Systems (CIS), September 2011, pp. 70–75.
[25] P. Mell, K. Scarfone, and S. Romanosky, "A complete guide to the common vulnerability scoring system version 2.0," 2007, pp. 1–24, [Accessed: 20/07/2018].
[26] FIRST, "Common vulnerability scoring system v3.0: Specification document," pp. 1–21, 2015, [Accessed: 20/07/2018].
[27] "Offensive security ltd. kali linux," https://www.kali.org/, 2018, [Accessed: 19/07/2018].
[28] "Openstack open source cloud computing software," https://www.openstack.org/, 2018, [Accessed: 18/07/2018].
[29] A. Marback, H. Do, K. He, S. Kondamarri, and D. Xu, "A threat model-based approach to security testing," Softw. Pract. Exper., vol. 43, no. 2, Feb. 2013, pp. 241–258.
[30] S. Myagmar, A. J. Lee, and W. Yurcik, "Threat modeling as a basis for security requirements," in in Proceedings of the IEEE Symposium on Requirements Engineering for Information Security, 2005, pp. 1–8.
[31] F. Swiderski and W. Snyder, Threat Modeling (Microsoft Professional), 2004.
[32] OWASP, "OWASP testing guide v4," pp. 1–224, 2014, [Accessed: 20/07/2018].

Sensitive Data Anonymization Using Genetic Algorithms for SOM-based Clustering

Fatemeh Amiri[1,2], Gerald Quirchmayr[1,2], Peter Kieseberg [3]
[1]University of Vienna, Vienna, Department of Computer Science, Austria
[2]SBA Research Institute, Vienna, Austria
[3]St. Poelten University of Applied Sciences, St. Poelten, Austria
Email: amirif86@univie.ac.at, gerald.quirchmayr@univie.ac.at, pkieseberg@sba-research.org

Abstract—**Improving privacy protection by using smart methods has become a major focus in current research. However, despite all the technological compensations through analyzing privacy concerns, the literature does not yet provide evidence of frameworks and methods that enable privacy protection from multiple perspectives and take into account the privacy of sensitive data with regard to accuracy and efficiency of the general processes in the system. In our work, we focus on sensitive data protection based on the idea of a Self-Organizing Map (SOM) and try to anonymize sensitive data with Genetic Algorithms (GAs) techniques in order to improve privacy without significantly deteriorating the accuracy and efficiency of the overall process. We organize the dataset in subspaces according to their information theoretical distance to each other in distributed local servers and then generalize attribute values to the minimum extent required so that both the data disclosure probability and the information loss are kept to a negligible minimum. Our analysis shows that our protocol offers clustering without greatly exposing individual privacy and causes only negligible superfluous costs and information loss because of privacy requirements.**

Keywords-Privacy-preserving; Big Data; Clustering; Kohonen's map; SOM; Genetic Algorithms.

I. Introduction

Owing to communal advantages, privacy-preserving data mining in e-business applications is very attractive [3][26]. The huge volume of data in e-business holds by big data and data mining methodologies. Data mining tasks can lead to the identification of data subjects as well as the disclosure of personal data. To address this problem, at first sight, contradicting requirements, privacy-preserving data mining techniques have been proposed [1][11][21]. Presenting privacy measures within data mining tasks enable them to become more popular and widespread; however, such measures may bring considerable costs and some difficulties concerning the topic of privacy-preserving systems. First, privacy measures require extra computational and storage costs that contribute to the scalability issues. Also, due to the privacy-preserving measures, it becomes an issue to run protected operations with reasonable accuracy [4].

Among the most popular algorithms in the data mining research community address, soft computing methods seem to be more capable to bring optimal solutions [2]. They apply generalization and suppression methods to the original datasets in order to preserve the anonymity of individuals data refer to. Privacy-Preserving on distributed data is important for both online companies and users due to mutual rewards. However, companies do not want to give up competitive knowledge advantages or violate anti-trust law [5].

Among data mining tasks, SOM as an unsupervised competitive learning works well on dividing an input data into closest clusters. SOM cluster approach improves the online computational complexity and expands the scalability of the recommendation process [24]. To implement SOM safely, we design our method based on the Genetic Algorithm. GAs [15] have recently become increasingly important for researchers in solving difficult problems. GAs could provide reasonable solutions in a limited amount of time. They are adaptive heuristic search algorithms derived from the evolutionary ideas of natural selection and genetics [6]. In this study, we propose a method for hiding sensitive data on Horizontally Distributed Data (HDD) among multiple parties without greatly jeopardizing their uniqueness. We assume that n users' preferences for m items are horizontally partitioned among L parties. Users are grouped into various clusters using SOM clustering off-line. After determining n's cluster, those users in that cluster are considered the best similar k users to each other. As off-line costs are not critical to the success of overall actions, our scheme performs GA reducing computations off-line. We analyze the scheme in terms of privacy and performance and perform real-data-based experiments for accurate analysis. Using our method, the local servers can overcome coverage and accuracy problems through partnership. Additionally, as they do not reveal their private data (by running our GA method) to each other, they do not face privacy issues. Let T be the whole data which is partitioned between K companies. Each local unit L holds TL, where TL is a nL×m matrix, k = 1, 2, ..., L; and nL shows the number of users whose data held by the unit L. Thus, each local unit L holds the ratings of nL users for the same m items. Figure 1 shows the first glance of the proposed model in this paper.

The contributions of the paper can be listed, as follows: (i) we propose a novel SOM method utilizing hiding sensitive items of information to alleviate privacy-preserving problems. (ii) We employ privacy-preserving measures to provide a sufficient level of privacy to individuals. (iii) We show the applicability of soft clustering techniques to the distributed framework to overcome scalability issues. (iv) We also show a comparison among utilized Traditional SOM technique with the proposed method. To the best of our knowledge, our paper presents the first analyses and evaluation on hiding sensitive information in SOM-based clustering on a distributed framework using GAs.

The remainder of this paper is organized as follows: Related work on privacy-preservation in SOM computing is reviewed in Section II. Section III discusses some technical preliminaries employed in the sequence of this paper. The presented protocol to protect transaction data against sensitive item disclosure based on Genetic Algorithms is described in Section IV. In Section V, we evaluate the data utility of the proposed protocol with real datasets. Finally, in Section VI, we summarize the conclusions of our study and outline future research directions.

II. RELATED WORK

To preserve privacy for partitioned data some methods have already proposed. Such studies help data owners cooperate when they own inadequate data and need to combine their fragmented data for improved facilities. A privacy-preserving ID3 algorithm based on cryptographic techniques for horizontally partitioned data is proposed by Lindell and Pikans [22] and followed by Clifton [5]. Vaidya and Clifton [27] presented privacy-preserving association rule mining for vertically partitioned data based on the secure scalar product protocol involving two parties. Privacy-preserving Naïve Bayes classier is also another common method to solve privacy issue in partitioned data [8][19][30].

SOM suffer from its considerable amount of communications in training steps that account for some security and privacy gaps. The number of studies on privacy-preserving in SOM is limited. The first study on solving this issue on SOM has been done by Han [13] that proposed a protocol for two parties each holding a private, vertical data partition to jointly and securely perform SOM. Kaleli and Polat[18] proposed a Homomorphic encryption privacy-preserving scheme to produce SOM clustering-based recommendations on vertically distributed data among multiple parties. They use this encryption, which is employed to privately encrypt and decrypt user vectors to avoid exposing of individual data. Bilge and his partners [4] focus on privacy-preserving schemes applied on clustering-based recommendations to produce referrals without greatly jeopardizing users' privacy. They investigate the accuracy and performance consequences of applying RPTs to some clustering-based CF schemes. Kaleli in [17] proposes offline SOM clustering with least jeopardizing the secrecy. He used the offline local server to run SOM independently in order to decrease the number of communications.

Soft computing methods in recent years brought novel results in privacy-preserving issue in different scenarios. One of the novel soft techniques is GAs. GAs are the search techniques, which are designed and developed to find a set of feasible solutions in a limited amount of time [29]. Fewer studies have adopted GAs to find optimal solutions to hide sensitive information. Han and Ng [12] presented a privacy-preserving genetic algorithm for rule discovery for arbitrarily partitioned data. To achieve data privacy of the participant parties, secure scalar product protocols were applied to securely evaluate the fitness value. Dehkordi [6] introduced a new multi-objective method for hiding sensitive association rules using GAs. The objective of their method is to support the security of database and to keep the effectiveness and certainty of mined rules at the highest level. In the proposed framework, four sanitization strategies were proposed with a different criterion. Lin et al.

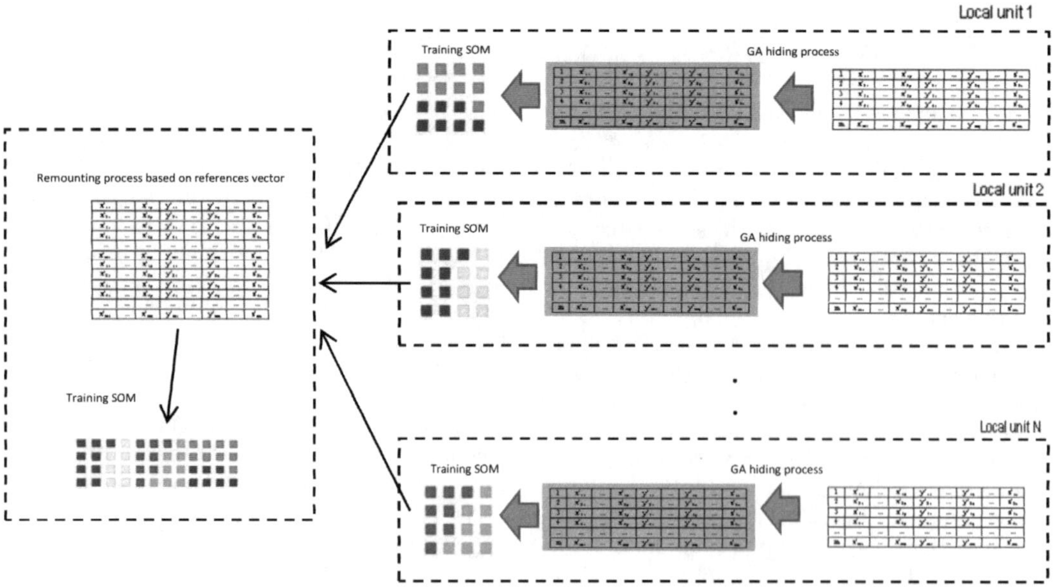

Figure 1. Overall scheme of GASOM protocol.

[20] compact pre-large GA-based algorithm to delete transactions for hiding sensitive items is thus proposed. Their method tries to refine the limitations of the evolutionary process by adopting the compact GA-based mechanism and also the pre-large concept.

To the best of our knowledge, there is no work to date on a privacy-preserving version of SOM using GAs in distributed servers. In this paper, we propose a protocol for multiple parties each holding a private, horizontal data partition to jointly and securely perform SOM. We prove that our protocol is correct and safe in front of some defined privacy attacks.

III. PRELIMINARY CONCEPTS

In this section, we review some technical preliminaries employed in our designed algorithms that are used in the sequence of this paper.

A. Problem definition

One of the most common techniques used to protect personal knowledge from disclosure in data mining is Hiding sensitive data [20]. In this paper, a hiding utility algorithm is proposed to hide sensitive items through optimal transaction deletion. To evaluate whether the transactions are required to be deleted for hiding the sensitive items, the hiding failure parameter is thus concerned. The transactions with any of the sensitive items are first evaluated by the GA algorithm designed to find the minimal hiding failure values among transactions. These transactions will be directly removed from the database. The procedure is thus repeated until all sensitive items are hidden. The reduced dataset is then sent for SOM training by local servers.

Definition 1. (SOM training) The SOM architecture entails of two fully connected layers: an input layer and a Kohonen's layer also called topology-preserving maps [31]. The steps of SOM clustering algorithm and the constants used in the algorithm are described in the following [9].

Based on the constants defined by Haykin [14], to find the Kohonen's layer neuron a random object x is selected from input data X and the winning Kohonen's Neuron (KNi) is determined by the computed minimum Euclidean distance between x and Wj using (1) as follows. Wj represents initial weights chosen randomly among objects in X for j = 1, 2, ..., T, where T shows a number of neurons in Kohonen's layer and s show an iteration:

$$KN_i^{(s)} = \min \left\| x^{(s)} - W_j^{(s)} \right\| \quad (1)$$

Update the weight vectors of all neurons by using (2), as follows:

$$w_j^{(s+1)} = w_j^{(s)} + \eta(s) h_{j.i}(s) \left(x - W_j^{(s)} \right) \quad (2)$$

where $\boldsymbol{h_{j.i}(s)}$ is the neighborhood function g(s) and $\boldsymbol{h_{j.i}(s)}$ are computed using (3) and (4), as follows:

$$\eta(S) = \eta_0 \exp(-s / \tau_2)). \quad s = 0.1.2. \dots \quad (3)$$

$$h_{j.i}(s) = \exp\left(-\frac{d_{i.j}^2}{2\sigma^2(s)} \right) \; and \; \sigma(s) = \sigma_0 \left(-\frac{s}{\tau_1} \right) \quad (4)$$

Repeat from all these steps until no noticeable change in the future map.

Definition 2. The input and output of the proposed protocol GA-based SOM (GASOM) including two algorithms are defined as:

Let *T* be the original database, a minimum support threshold ratio *MST*, and a set of sensitive items to be hidden $\boldsymbol{SX} = \{\boldsymbol{SX1}.\boldsymbol{SX2}.\cdots \boldsymbol{SXn}\}$. Let all of these parameters be input values, and $\boldsymbol{T^*}$ be reduced database with least and hided sensitive information as the output of genetic algorithm and the input dataset for SOM clustering algorithm.

Definition 3. (hiding failure value) To evaluate the hiding failures of each processed transaction in the sanitization process, the α parameter is used to evaluate the hiding failures of each processed transaction in the sanitization process. Figure 2 shows the relation of the main dataset and its intersection with reduced datasets.

When a processed transaction contains a sensitive item, the Sum of the α value for the processed transaction $\boldsymbol{T_j}$ is calculated as:

$$\alpha^j(S_x) = \frac{MAx_{sx} - freq(S_x) + 1}{MAx_{sx} - \lceil |T| \times MST \rceil + 1} \quad (5)$$

where $\boldsymbol{MST}$ is defined as the percentage of the minimum support threshold, sensitive items $\boldsymbol{S_x}$ is from the set of sensitive items SX, MAX is the maximal count of the sensitive items in the set of sensitive items $\boldsymbol{SX}$, $|\boldsymbol{T}|$ is the number of transactions in the original database, and $\boldsymbol{freq(S_x)}$ is the occurrence frequency of the sensitive items $\boldsymbol{S_x}$. The overall α value for transaction j is calculate as:

$$\alpha^j = \frac{1}{\sum_{i=1}^{n} \alpha^j(s_i) + 1} \quad (6)$$

Definition 4. (fitness function) to find the optimal transactions including sensitive items to be deleted, the genetic algorithm needs a novel fitness function. Base on the[16] the fitness function calculates as:

$$\text{Fitness function} = W1\alpha + W2\beta + W3\gamma \quad (7)$$

where w1, w2, w3 are weighting parameters, defined by users. α value calculate by formula 2. β is another factor as the number of missing items and γ is the number of artificial items. Based on the power of SOM clustering in safely training phase and keeping complexity simple in distributed execution, we define W1=1 and ignore the other factors.

B. Privacy attacks

User's data is considered to be protected effectively when an adversary could not identify a particular user's data through linkages between a record owner to sensitive feature in the published data [25]. Thus, these linkage attacks can be classified broadly into three types of attack models namely Record Linkage, Attribute Linkage and Table Linkage [28]. The proposed protocol in this paper aims to resist in front of Table Linkage sort of attacks.

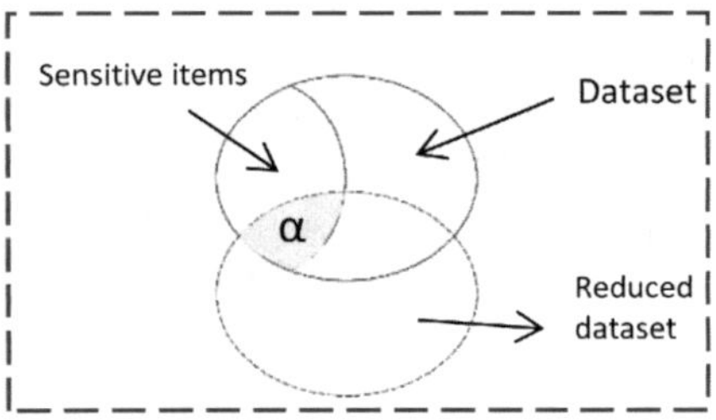

Figure 2. Hiding failure parameter.

Definition 5. (privacy attack) In all types of attacks, it is assumed that opponent knows the QIs (Quasi-identifiers) of the victim. If an opponent is talented to link a record holder to the published data table then such kind of privacy risk is known as Table linkage [28]. In this scenario, the attacker tries to govern the occurrence or nonappearance of the victim's record in the released table. To prevent table linkages privacy models such as δ-presence, ε-Differential privacy, (d, γ)-privacy and distributional privacy can be used. Our strategy in designing the method is trying to finding the optimal subsets to be deleted from the dataset, in order to preserve the data in front of such an attack.

C. Loss metric

Preventing sensitive item revelation may reduce the utility of data, as it involves data transformation [10]. One way is by measuring the difference between original data and transformed data, also called general purpose metrics, such as Generalization Cost, Normalized Average Equivalence Class Size, Normalized Certainty Penalty, and Information Loss Metric. For this paper, general purpose metrics apply to evaluate the information loss in this paper.

Definition 6. The information loss (IL) for a distributed GASOM partitioned and refined protocol is defined as $\sum_i len(T^*) - len(T)$ where T^* is the optimized and reduced dataset of T, and $len(T)$ denotes the number of transactions contained by T.

Definition 7. The information loss for a sensitive item i is defined as $SL(i) = len(i.T^*)$ where $len(i.T^*)$denotes the number of transactions that contain sensitive item i . Accordingly, the information loss for an anonymized integration dataset T is defined as:

$$IL(T) = \sum_{tran \epsilon T} IL(T) + \sum_{sen} IL(i) \qquad (8)$$

where sen is a set of items to be hide in the transactions defined by administrator. The IL measures the information loss of item hiding process through the number of sensitive items. The larger the IL is, the less certain the results are relating to the true information of trajectories and transactions.

IV. PROPOSED SOLUTION

In this section, we represent our distributed SOM-based protocol (GASOM) to protect transaction data against sensitive item disclosure based on Genetic Algorithms. It consists of two phases. First, eliminating sensitive items disclosure through our Genetic Algorithm designed for this purpose. Second, securely SOM training datasets by applying a horizontally distributed map in order to reduce the number of communication among local units. We assume that adversaries hold limited knowledge of the victim, such as the work-class that the victim has previously filled in tax forms and also know the corresponding public items that the victim purchased.

A. Eliminate sensitive items disclosure

In this paper, a sensitive data hiding approach GASOM based on the genetic algorithms is thus proposed to find the appropriate transactions to be deleted for hiding sensitive items. The sensitive items to be hidden can be defined as $SX = \{SX1. SX2. \cdots SXn\}$. In the proposed GASOM for hiding the sensitive items through transaction deletion, the support count of a sensitive item must be below the minimum support threshold (MST), in which each transaction to be deleted must contain any of the sensitive items in SX. Base on this concept, we assume each transaction from T as a chromosome. A chromosome with m genes is thus designed that is compatible with the m attribute in the real dataset to be solved. Each gene represents a positive integer of transaction ID (TID) value as a possible transaction to be deleted.

The general steps of this algorithm are as follows:

```
Algorithm 1. GA dataset reducing
INPUT:   T, SX, MST
OUTPUT:  a reduced dataset T*
1. Define the sensitive items as SX
2. for all the transaction Ti in T
     If Si ∈ Ti
          Project Ti from T to T '
     End if
End for
# initialize probability vector for each transaction Ti in T '
3. for all transaction Ti in T '
      Define p[i]=1
End for
4. Repeat
     # call GA function to compete for two transactions with
default crossover and mutation approach
       from T '
     1. randomly selecting TA and TB from T '
     2. compete for TA and TB by the fitness function
      For all transaction in T '
         Increase p[i] by 1/[ T '] for winner transactions
         decrease p[i] by 1/[ T '] for loser transactions
      End for
Until termination condition is not satisfied
#termination condition is reaching MST threshold
```

In competition process, each time two individuals are used for competition (in step 4). This approach can reduce the population size to speed up the evaluation process. As long as the termination condition is not satisfied, two other chromosomes are then generated again and compete on the probability of selected transactions in the winner chromosome. The final vector P as the output of this algorithm represents the probability of each transaction to delete from the main dataset.

B. Applying SOM clustering on a reduced dataset

The corporations, exclusively malicious ones, participating in distributed services attempt to derive information about each other's data. They can try to obtain useful information from interim results or final predictions. To protect data owners' confidentiality, our proposed scheme has to overcome privacy attacks. We use a two-step approach, where we cluster data off-line using SOM clustering (horizontally distributed) and utilize a genetic algorithm to hide sensitive items. We perform as many works as possible off-line to improve online efficiency. Also, with this technique, we reduce the number of communications in a network that known as on the most challenges in SOM. After determining local units online, clustering is estimated based on the users' data in local clusters.

The basic steps of our proposed protocol are as follows:

```
Algorithm 2. HDD SOM
INPUT:  main dataset T
OUTPUT:  - Index and reference vectors
(up to the request by central unit)
           - Local SOM clusters
1. Each local unit apply Algorithm 1 to get
 reduced safe database T*
2. Local unit i apply SOM algorithm on Ti*on the
 local data to obtain local clusters and also a reference
vector (to send to central unit)
3. In case of a request from the central unit, the local
index i
 send reference vector to the central server that will
represent the original data
4. The central unit remounts the dataset based on the
reference vector sent by local units and applies SOM
algorithm again to obtain a final output.
```

In step 1, algorithm 1 applies on each local dataset to get a reduced dataset T* which hide sensitive data. Applying genetic algorithm locally reduce the execution time which is a crucial factor especially in distributed networks. Then, in step 2, traditional clustering applies in each local dataset. These datasets are horizontally held same attributes. Thus, the algorithm applies to each subset, obtaining a reference vector and also locally trained clusters. This is the first time of applying SOM on the dataset and later in central unit another SOM training run to identifying the existing clusters. In case of a request from the central unit, in step 3, an index vector corresponding to the closest vector will be select and store in reference vector. This vector is very similar to the original object and in this way, data topology which is important will be kept. These vectors will be sent to the central unit and finally, in step 4, central unit combine these partial results and remount the dataset to obtain the main topology which is partially different with the original object but is very similar and more importantly protected. By applying another traditional SOM clustering method, the central unit could reach final output which all the clusters in all the unit exist and also sensitive data are hidden without losing accuracy.

V. EXPERIMENTS

In this part, we evaluated the data utility of the proposed protocol with real datasets. Also, privacy protection and information loss of the algorithm were tested. It should be noted that all the experiments accomplished on a local server and the idea of Algorithm 2 will be test in future works.

A. Experimental data

The test environment used for our initial Experiments was a VM/ Linux Ubuntu platform with 4 vCPU in Intel(R) Xeon (R) E5-2650 v4 processor and 4 GB memory. Two real database Adult [7], and Bank Marketing Dataset [23] is used to evaluate the performance of the proposed algorithms in terms of the privacy and also the execution time as well as the accuracy of clustering operations. The details of these databases are shown in Table 1.

TABLE 1. EXPERIMENTAL DATASETS

Database	Transactions	Attributes	Area	Missing value
Adult	48842	14	Social	Yes
Bank Marketing	45211	17	Business	N/A

At first level, we weighed the execution times of proposed GA method that is a discussing topic in privacy issues. Genetic Algorithms are time-consuming and this factor significantly influences toward the goodness of the protocol. We tried to apply an optimal fitness function to promote the complexity. The execution times obtained using the proposed genetic algorithm are then compared under different minimum utility thresholds with a fixed rate of sensitive percentage 5% for the database is shown in Figures 3 and 4.

With increasing factor of MST Runtime is reduced, which naturally means reducing the level of data safety. In this experiment, the number of transactions is relatively equal, but the features and conditions used to define sensitive data are more complex in the Bank Marketing dataset. So, results amount to a significant increase in runtime in Figure 3.

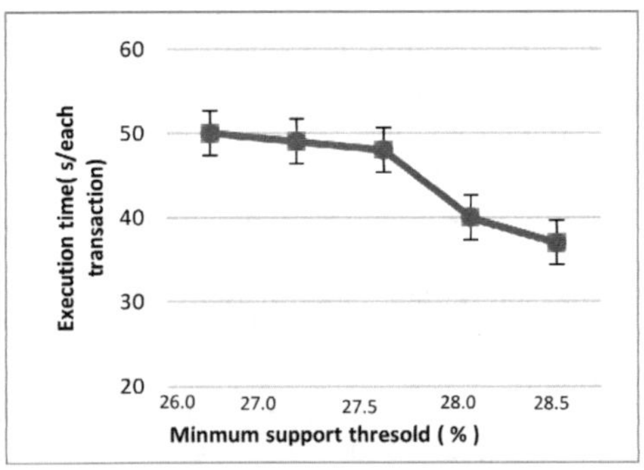

Figure 3. Execution time for adult data set with various minimum support thresholds.

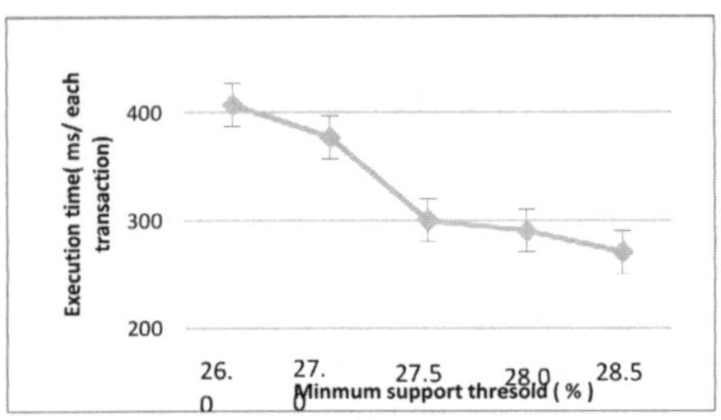

Figure 4. Execution time for adult data set with various minimum support thresholds.

Runtime is affected by the number of sensitive properties and validating conditions, but in general, the complexity of the algorithm is acceptable, especially as it runs locally on the server and does not add a bootloader to the system.

To evaluate the precision of the proposed algorithm, results are compared with those of traditional SOM clustering. Experiments were carried out using MATLAB 8.5 as well as SOM TOOLBOX. we set the radius of lattice to 3/2; and network topology to the hexagonal lattice, which is default topology in the MATLAB toolbox, and the optimum cluster number as three [17].

For the first experiments of our protocol, a test set of adult datasets has been used, which includes 1000 tuples with 14 attributes. Age and work-class are considered as sensitive attributes. A similar implementation of the Bank Marketing database was created with 3000 tuples and 17 properties. Sensitive features in this experiment were defined on three items of gender, age, and occupation, in order to verify the accuracy of the output of the genetic algorithm defined by the complexity of the sensitive items.

The neural network was implemented through MATLAB with the SOM toolbox and the attributes were represented in numeric format. The approach followed by firstly selecting the tuples matched with sensitive criteria, optimally hide those records with the genetic algorithm proposed. On our initial experiments, we cluster the data set only at the begging of the algorithm. In that case, the time needed for the hiding of the sensitive items in the dataset is depicted in Figures 3 and 4.

Afterward, the use of the neural network for training the partitioned dataset has been tested. Figures 5 and 6 show the U-Matrixes of clustering scheme of the two databases before and after data hiding task.

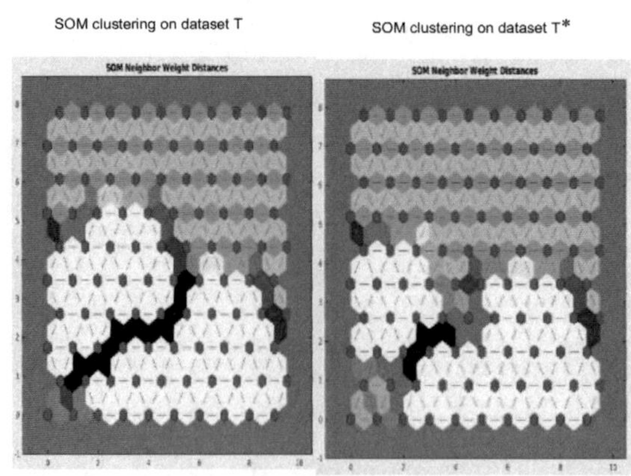

Figure 5. The U-Matrixes of traditional and proposed SOM clustering simulated on the Adult dataset.

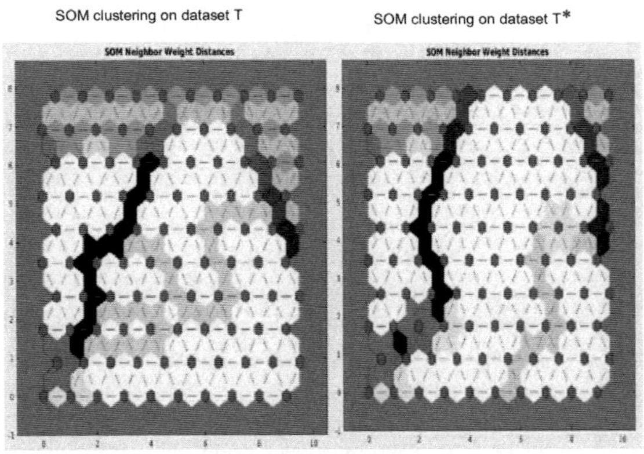

Figure 6. The U-Matrixes of traditional and proposed SOM clustering simulated on Bank Marketing dataset.

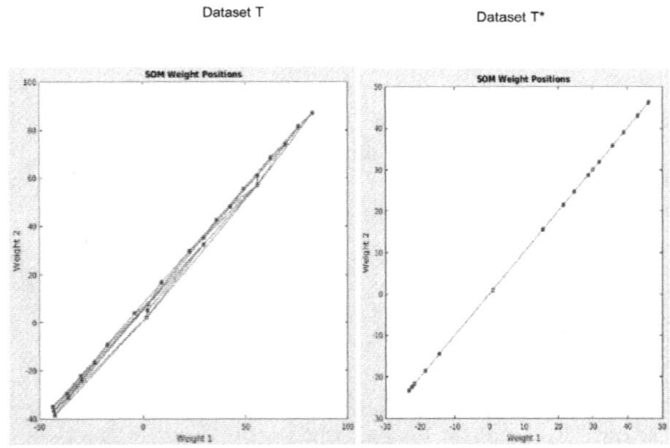

Figure 8. The Weight Position vectors of traditional and proposed SOM clustering simulated on Bank Marketing dataset.

It is clearly shown that the difference between weighting distance in found clusters is not too much, however, it is affected by the size of the database. Figures 7 and 8 demonstrate the certainty penalty of the weight positions which is significantly increased by parameter weight. A new well-promising algorithm which takes into account the above assumption with less penalty in similarity of results is being studied and it is expected to be even more efficient.

To validate the proposed algorithms, besides the visual comparison of the trained map and U-Matrix between classic SOM and proposed approach, some other comparative criteria were used including average quantization error between data vectors and BMUs on the map and topographic error counting of errors obtained in the application of the algorithm over the datasets. In the next section, these accuracy measure results are presented.

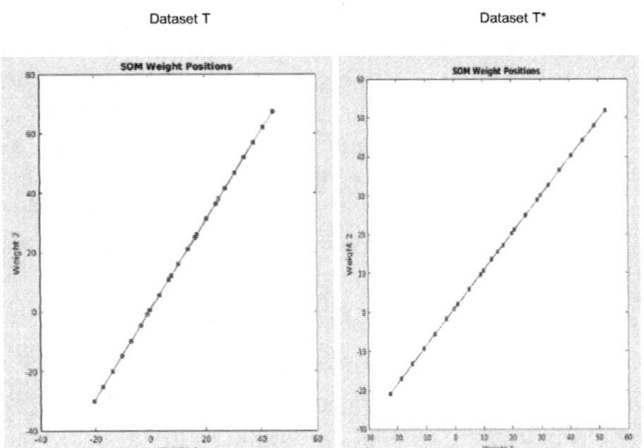

Figure 7. The Weight Position vectors of traditional and proposed SOM clustering simulated on Adult dataset.

B. Analysis of information loss and privacy

The well-known datasets Adult and Bank Marketing were used in a variety of privacy-preserving studies. Adult dataset It presents 48842 instances containing personal data with 14 attributes. We defined the sensitive items in this trial experiment as the age of the people under 30 with work-class 'Private'. Firstly, the dataset was analyzed initially using proposed GA method to extract a probability vector indicating the rate of failing in hiding sensitive items. The user then could decide about the rate of deletion from the dataset, which defined as MST in the proposed algorithm. Dataset was then horizontally partitioned, each containing all the attributes. In this phase, we implement experiment on a local server with 1000 tuples, both plan, and hexagonal lattice. For Bank Marketing dataset with 45211 instances and 17 attributes a similar criterion defined for age, job and marital attribute to test the influence of complexity of sensitive criteria on final results. 3000 tuples used for this experiment with the equal condition on the local server.

Maps size was defined by SOM Toolbox, based on data distribution in input space. In our experiments, maps were randomly initialized and batch SOM was used. We defined the constant fixed for both classic and proposed SOM as sigma initial=2 and sigma final=1 and trainlen defined to 1 epochs. Table 2 summarizes the clustering quality measures.

TABLE 2. COMPARING THE ACCURACY OF CLASSIC SOM AND GASOM

Dataset	Method	QE	TE
Adult	Classic SOM	0.0798	0.2290
	GASOM	0.0943	0.1435
Bank Marketing	Classic SOM	0.193	0.042
	GASOM	0.135	0.088

QE represents the average quantization error and TE represents the topological error. These results prove the usefulness of GASOM in keeping the clustering quality beside the improvement of protection. Also, to prove the protection level of the dataset, the difference between the number of sensitive items before and after hiding task in genetic algorithm calculated as follows:

$$\frac{Senfreq|T^*|}{Senfreq|T|} \quad (9)$$

where T* is the reduced dataset and T is the main dataset before hiding task. The result of (9) is always near to zero which proves the goodness of the proposed method of hiding the sensitive items. Although the results of experiments prove the usefulness of proposed protocol, try to refine the methods in order to keep the accuracy of clustering and the execution time sounds imperative. Figure 9 represents a comparison between the relation of hiding factor and Minimum Support Threshold (MST), which demonstrates privacy protection decrease with increasing the MST.

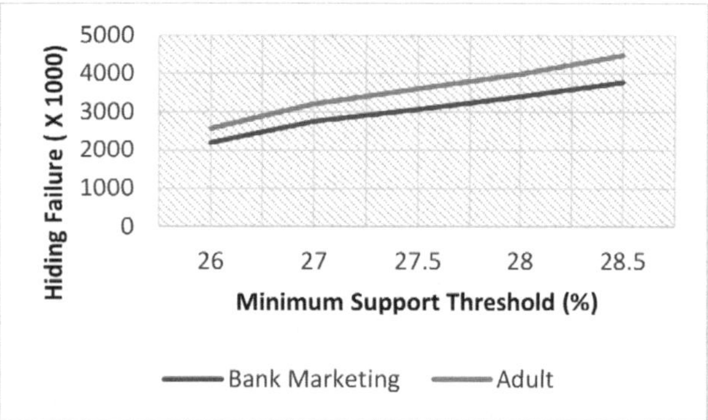

Figure 9. The relation between two factors of MST and Hiding Failure to check the information loss in front of privacy level.

Therefore, the boundary of information loss and privacy level are opposite and should be calculated and selected according to the requirements and conditions of the current database. Linkage attack by applying this protocol is completely deniable. The quasi-identifier for our method is defined as the whole subset of attributes that can uniquely identify a record. So, an attacker cannot find the complete quasi-identifier which we have already change with our GA method. However, this method is just a try to check the goodness of proposed GA methods in finding the sensitive items. Although the accuracy of GASOM is relatively acceptable, some other techniques like fuzzifying the optimal subset found by fitness function seem to be useful to implement to avoid of eliminating those transactions from the database.

VI. CONCLUSION AND FUTURE WORK

The crucial need for smarter approaches to analyze data distributed among several sites is obvious. This issue beside the increasing importance of privacy-preserving becomes much complicated. In this paper, a hiding sensitive technique for SOM clustering approach for partitioned data is thus proposed to hide the sensitive items using Genetic Algorithms. To determine the goodness of a transaction, a flexible fitness function with adjustable weights is also designed to consider the general side effect of hiding failure. Our offerings in this paper can be summarized as follows: First, a sanitization process to find the sensitive items from the main dataset will be done in order to shape a probability vector indicating the chance of each transaction to be deleted from dataset to hide the sensitive data. Second, the reduced dataset will be trained by local SOM to shape the topological map and finally the central unit merge the results of the local unit based on the reference vectors sent by local units to integrate the final clusters. Experiments are conducted to show that the proposed GASOM protocol beats better than classic algorithms considering the criteria of side effects but the execution time.

Final results demonstrate that the proposed protocol obtained similar results to those of classic clustering algorithms. The results of privacy protection prove the power of proposed GA methods. However, it is still necessary to find a more effective solution to keep the privacy with less information loss. Further research will include applying this protocol on distributed units and also trying a different soft based method like swarm intelligence to compare with the results of GA method form the privacy point of view. In this version of protocol, sensitive items defined by users which is context-based. In future works, we want to consider more details about these sensitive items regarding ownership, personal and semi-context sensitive data. Also, it makes a lot of sense to propose some way to change just a small portion of the database instead of deleting those records to reach all the goals defined in this paper at the same time. In this way, we want to integrate our protocol to some other machine learning techniques, such as fuzzy sets to refine the triple goals of privacy, accuracy, and speed. It should be noted that all the experiments accomplished on a local server and the idea of Algorithm 2 will be test in future works.

ACKNOWLEDGMENTS

This work was partially supported by SBA Research Institute, Vienna, Austria.

REFERENCES

[1] R.Agrawal and R.Srikant," Privacy-preserving data mining" ACM Sigmod Record, ACM, pp. 439-450, 2000.

[2] F. Amiri and G. Quirchmayr, "A comparative study on innovative approaches for privacy-preserving in knowledge discovery", ICIME, ACM, 2017.

[3] F. Belanger and R.E. Crossler,"Privacy in the digital age: a review of information privacy research in information systems", MIS quarterly vol. 35, no. 4, pp.1017-1042, 2011.

[4] A. Bilge and H. Polat, "A comparison of clustering-based privacy-preserving collaborative filtering schemes", Applied Soft Computing vol. 13, no. 5, pp. 2478-2489, 2013.

[5] C. Clifton, et al. , "Privacy-preserving data integration and sharing", Proceedings of the 9th ACM SIGMOD workshop on Research issues in data mining and knowledge discovery ACM, pp.19-26, 2004.

[6] M.N. Dehkordi, K. Badie, and A.K. Zadeh, "A novel method for privacy preserving in association rule mining based on genetic algorithms", Journal of software vol. 4, no. 6, pp. 555-562, 2009.

[7] D.K.T. Dheeru, "UCI Machine Learning Repository. University of California", Irvine, School of Information and Computer Sciences, 2017.

[8] W. Du, and M.J. Atallah, "Privacy-preserving cooperative statistical analysis", Computer Security Applications Conference, ACSAC , Proceedings 17th Annual IEEE, pp. 102-110, 2001.

[9] G. Gan , C. Ma, and J. Wu, "Data clustering: theory, algorithms, and applications", Siam , 2007.

[10] A. Gkoulalas-divanis, G. Loukides, and J. SUN, "Publishing data from electronic health records while preserving privacy: A survey of algorithms", Journal of biomedical informatics vol. 50, pp. 4-19, 2014.

[11] A. Gkoulalas-divanis and V.S Verykios, "An overview of privacy preserving data mining", Crossroads vol. 15, no. 4, p. 6, 2009.

[12] S. Han and W.K. Ng, "Privacy-preserving genetic algorithms for rule discovery", International conference on data warehousing and knowledge discovery Springer, pp. 407-417, 2007.

[13] S. Han and W.K. Ng, "Privacy-preserving self-organizing map", In DaWaK Springer, pp. 428-437, 2007.

[14] S. Haykin, "Neural Networks: A Comprehensive Foundation", Vol. 2. Segundo, Prentice Hall. España, 1999 .

[15] J.H. Holland, "Adaptation in natural and artificial systems. An introductory analysis with application to biology, control, and artificial intelligence", Ann Arbor, MI: University of Michigan Press, pp. 439-444, 1975.

[16] T.P. Hong, K.T. Yang, C.W. Lin and S.L. Wang, "Evolutionary privacy-preserving data mining", World Automation Congress (WAC), IEEE, pp. 1-7, 2010.

[17] C. Kaleli and H. Polat, "Privacy-preserving SOM-based recommendations on horizontally distributed data", Knowledge-Based Systems vol. 33, pp. 124-135, 2012.

[18] C. Kaleli and H. Polat, "SOM-based recommendations with privacy on multi-party vertically distributed data", Journal of the Operational Research Society vol. 63, no. 6, pp. 826-838, 2012.

[19] M. Kantarcoglu, J. Vaidya and C. Clifton, "Privacy preserving naive bayes classifier for horizontally partitioned data", IEEE ICDM workshop on privacy preserving data mining, pp. 3-9, 2003.

[20] C.W. Lin, B. Zhang, K.T. Yang, and T.P. Hong, "Efficiently hiding sensitive itemsets with transaction deletion based on genetic algorithms", The Scientific World Journal, 2014.

[21] Y. Lindell and B. Pinkas, "Privacy preserving data mining", Annual International Cryptology Conference Springer, pp. 36-54, 2000.

[22] Y. Lindell and B. Pinkas "Privacy preserving data mining. Journal of cryptology vol. 15, no. 3, 2002.

[23] S. Moro, P. Cortez, and P. Rita, "A Data-Driven Approach to Predict the Success of Bank Telemarketing", Decision Support Systems, Elsevier, vol. 62, pp. 22-31, 2014.

[24] T.H. Roh, K.J. Oh, and I. Han, "The collaborative filtering recommendation based on SOM cluster-indexing CBR", Expert systems with applications vol. 25, no. 3, pp. 413-423, 2003.

[25] P.N. Tan, M. Steinbach, and V. Kumar, "Association analysis: basic concepts and algorithms", Introduction to Data mining, pp. 327-414, 2005.

[26] E.C. Turner, and S. Dasgupta, " Privacy And Security In E-Business", Taylor & Francis, 2003.

[27] J. Vaidya and C. Clifton, "Privacy preserving association rule mining in vertically partitioned data", Proceedings of the eighth ACM SIGKDD international conference on Knowledge discovery and data mining ACM, pp. 639-644, 2002.

[28] K. Wang, R. Chen, B. Fung, and P. Yu, " Privacy-preserving data publishing: A survey on recent developments", ACM Computing Surveys, 2010.

[29] X.-Z. Wang, Q. He, D.-G. Chen, and D. Yeung, "A genetic algorithm for solving the inverse problem of support vector machines", Neurocomputing vol. 8, pp. 225-238, 2005.

[30] R. Wright and Z. Yang, "Privacy-preserving Bayesian network structure computation on distributed heterogeneous data",Proceedings of the tenth ACM SIGKDD international conference on Knowledge discovery and data mining ACM, pp. 713-718, 2004.

[31] Y. Yang, W. Tan, T. Li, and D. Ruan , "Consensus clustering based on constrained self-organizing map and improved Cop-Kmeans ensemble in intelligent decision support systems". Knowledge-Based Systems vol. 32, pp. 101-115, 2012.

New Covert Channels in Internet of Things

Aleksandra Mileva, Aleksandar Velinov, Done Stojanov
Faculty of Computer Science
University "Goce Delčev"
Štip, Republic of Macedonia
email: {aleksandra.mileva, aleksandar.velinov, done.stojanov}@ugd.edu.mk

***Abstract* — Network steganography is a relatively new discipline which studies different steganographic techniques that utilize network protocols for data hiding. Internet of Things (IoT) is a concept which integrates billions of embedded devices that communicate to each other. To the best of our knowledge, there are not many attempts that utilize existing network steganographic techniques in protocols specifically created for IoT. Therefore, in this paper, we present several new covert channels that utilize the Constrained Application Protocol (CoAP), which is a specialized Web transfer protocol used for constrained devices and networks. This protocol can be used regardless of its transport carrier (Datagram Transport Layer Security - DTLS or clear UDP – User Datagram Protocol). The suggested covert channels are categorized according to the pattern-based classification, and, for each covert channel, the total number of hidden data bits transmitted per CoAP message or its Packet Raw Bit Rate (PRBP) is given.**

Keywords-CoAP; network steganography; covert channels; data hiding.

I. INTRODUCTION

Network covert channels are used to hide data in legitimate transmissions in communication networks by deploying different network protocols as carriers and concealing the presence of hidden data from network devices. Covert channels (first introduced by Lampson [8]) can be divided in two basic groups: storage and timing channels. Storage covert channels are channels where one process writes (directly or indirectly) to a shared resource, while another process reads from it. In the context of network steganography, storage covert channels hide data by storing them in the protocol header and/or in the Protocol Data Unit (PDU). On the other hand, timing channels hide data by deploying some form of timing of events, such as retransmitting the same PDU several times, or changing the packet order.

Network-based covert channels may have black hat or white hat applications. Black hat applications include coordination of distributed denial of service attacks, spreading of malware (for example, by hiding command and control traffic of botnets), industrial espionage, secret communication between terrorists and criminals, etc. On the other hand, white hat applications include covert military communication in hostile environments, prevention of detection of illicit information transferred by journalists or whistle-blowers, circumvention of the limitation in using Internet in some countries (e.g., Infranet [3]), providing Quality of Service - QoS for Voice over Internet Protocol - VoIP traffic [10], secure network management communication [5], watermarking of network flows (e.g., RAINBOW [6]), tracing encrypted attack traffic or tracking anonymous peer-to-peer VoIP calls [16][17], etc.

Nowadays, there are a plenty of choices in the landscape of network protocols for carriers. There are several surveys about different covert channels in many TCP/IP (Transmission Control Protocol/Internet Protocol) protocols [12][19]. To the best of our knowledge, there are only a few papers about network steganographic research addressing protocols specialized for constrained devices in the IoT (sensors, vehicles, home appliances, wearable devices, and so on) [2] [7]. The Constrained Application Protocol (CoAP) [15] is a specialized Web transfer application layer protocol which can be used with constrained nodes and constrained networks in the IoT. The nodes are constrained because they have 8-bit microcontrollers, for example, with limited random-access memory (RAM) and read-only memory (ROM). Constrained networks often have high packet error rates and small data rate (such as IPv6 over Low-Power Wireless Personal Area Networks - 6LoWPANs). CoAP is designed for machine-to-machine (M2M) applications and its last stable version was published in June 2014 in the RFC 7252 [15]. In fact, it is a Representational State Transfer - RESTful protocol with multicast and observe support. In this paper, we try to apply existing network steganographic techniques for creating covert channels in CoAP.

Wendzel et al. [18] presented a new pattern-based categorization of network covert channel techniques into 11 different patterns or classes. They represented the patterns in a hierarchical catalog using the pattern language Pattern Language Markup Language (PLML) v. 1.1 [4]. In our paper, we use their classification to characterize our covert channels.

Covert channels are analyzed through the total number of hidden data bits transmitted per second (Raw Bit Rate - RBR), or through the total number of hidden data bits transmitted per PDU (for example, Packet Raw Bit Rate-PRBR) [11]. For each new CoAP channel, its PRBR value is given, where PDU is a CoAP message.

The rest of this article is structured as follows. The related work is presented in Section 2. Details about the

CoAP header, messages, functionalities and concepts are presented in Section 3. The main Section 4 describes eight groups of new covert storage and timing channels in CoAP, that can be used regardless its transport carrier (DTLS or clear UDP). Some possible applications of these covert channels are also briefly suggested in this section. In Section 5 we present the performance evaluation. We conclude the paper in Section 6.

II. Related Work

The research on network steganography for IoT has seen an increased interest recently.

One example for this is the work of Islam et al. [7], which uses Internet Control Message Protocol (ICMP) covert channels for authenticating Internet packet routers as an intermediate step towards proximal geolocation of IoT devices. This is useful as a defense from the knowledgeable adversary that might attempt to evade or forge the geolocation. Hidden data are stored in the data field of the ICMP Echo Request and ICMP Echo Reply messages.

Some applications of steganography in IoT are not connected with the protocols themselves, but with the applications on top of these protocols. For example, Denney et al. [2] present a novel storage covert channel on wearable devices that sends data to other applications, or even to other nearby devices, through the use of notifications that are normally displayed on the status bar of an Android device. For that purpose, a notification listening service on the wearables needs to be implemented. Data are hidden in the notification ID numbers (32 bits), and their exchange is done by using two functions notify and cancel. If the notifying function is immediately followed by the canceling function, the notification is never displayed to the user although it can be seen in the log files, so the communication is hidden from the user who wears the device.

There are several papers that deploy steganography in the physical and medium access control (MAC) layers of the IEEE 802.15.4 standard [9][13].

III. How CoAP Works

Similar to HTTP, CoAP uses client/server model with request/response messages. It supports built-in discovery of services and resources, Uniform resource identifiers (URIs) and Internet media types. The CoAP sends a request message requesting an action (using a Method Code) to the resource (identified by a URI) hosted on a server. The server responds to this request by using the response message that contains the Response Code, and possibly some resource representation. CoAP defines four types of messages: Confirmable (CON), Non-Confirmable (NON), Acknowledgment (ACK) and Reset (RST). These types of messages use method and response codes to transmit requests or answers. The requests can be transmitted as Confirmable and Non-Confirmable types of messages, while the responses can be transmitted through these and via piggybacked and Acknowledgment types of messages.

CoAP uses clear UDP or DTLS on transport layer to exchange messages asynchronously between endpoints. As shown in Figure 1, each message contains a Message ID used for optimal reliability and to detect duplicates. A message that requires reliable transmission is marked as CON, and if does not, it is marked as NON. The CON message is retransmitted using a default timeout and binary exponential back-off algorithm for increasing the timeout between retransmissions, until the recipient sends an ACK message with the same Message ID. When the recipient is

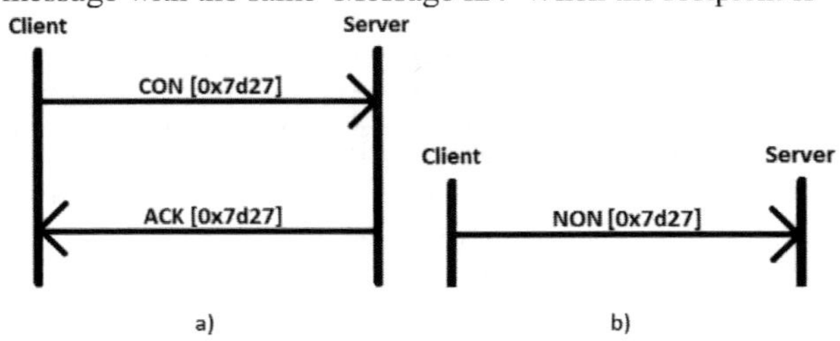

Figure 1. a) Reliable CoAP message transmission b) Unreliable CoAP message transmission.

not able at all to process CON or NON messages, it replies with a RST message.

CoAP messages are encoded into simple binary format (see Figure 2). Each message starts with a 4B fixed header, followed by a Token field, with size from 0 to 8B. Then comes the optional Options field and optional Payload field. If the Payload field is present it is preceded by one-byte Payload Marker (0xFF).

The fields that make up the message header are the following:

- Version (Ver) - 2-bit unsigned integer that identifies the CoAP version. Currently it must be set to 01.
- Type (T) – 2-bit unsigned integer that indicates the message type: Confirmable (0), Non-Confirmable(1), Acknowledgement (2), or Reset (3).
- Token Length (TKL) – 4-bit unsigned integer that stands for the length of the Token field (0-64 bits). Lengths 9-15 are reserved and must be processed as a message format error.
- Code – 8-bit unsigned integer. It is divided into two parts: 3-bit class (the most significant bits) and 5-bit details (the least significant bits). The format of the code is "c.dd", where "c" is a digit from 0 to 7 and represents the class while "dd" are two digits from 00 to 31. According to the class we can determine the type of the message, such as: request (0), a successful response (2), a client error response (4), or a server error response (5). CoAP has a separate code registry that provides a description for all codes [1].
- Message ID - 16-bit unsigned integer that is used to detect duplicate messages and to connect Acknowledgment/Reset messages with Confirmable/ Non-Confirmable messages.

The message header is followed by the Token field with variable size from 0 to 64 bits. This field is used to link requests and responses.

The optional Options field defines one or more options. CoAP defines a single set of options that are used both for requests and for responses. These are: Content-Format, Etag, Location-Path, Location-Query, Max-Age, Proxy-Uri, Proxy-Scheme, Uri-Host, Uri-Path, Uri-Port, Uri-Query, Accept, If-Match, If-None-Match, and Size1.

The payload of requests/responses that indicates success typically carries the resource representation or the result of the requested action.

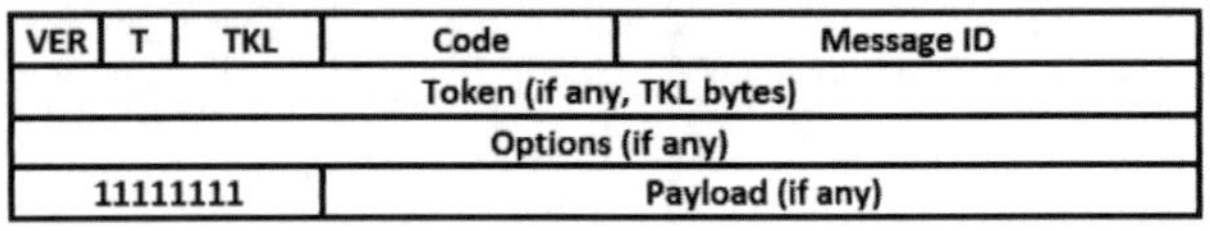

Figure 2. CoAP message format.

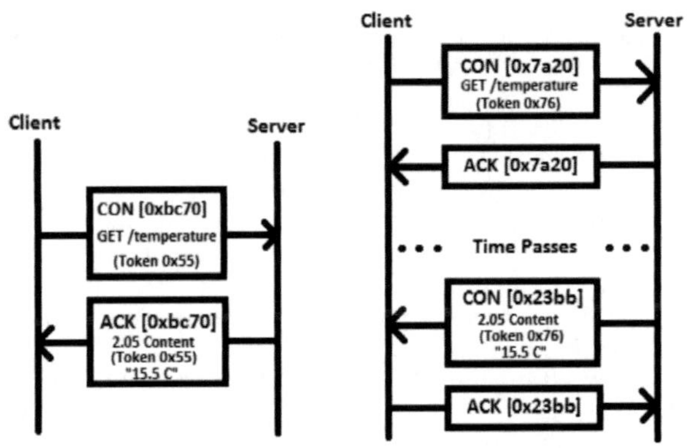

Figure 3. a) Piggybacked response b) Separate response.

There are two types of responses: piggybacked and separate (Figure 3). If the request is transmitted via CON or NON message, and if the response is available and transmitted via an ACK message, then it is piggybacked response. If the server is unable to respond immediately to the request, an Empty message (with code 0.00) is sent that tells the client to stop sending the request. If the server is able for later respond to the client, it sends a CON message that must then be confirmed by the client. This is called a separate response.

Similar to HTTP, CoAP uses GET (with code 0.01), POST (with code 0.02), PUT (with code 0.03), and DELETE (with code 0.04) methods.

IV. New Covert Channels in the CoAP

When someone creates a Covert Channel (CC) in network protocol, usually uses: a protocol feature that has a dual nature (i.e., the same feature can be obtained in more than one way), a feature that is not mandatory, a feature that can obtain random value, and so on. Therefore, if we use some of these features, we can create new covert channels in CoAP. From the beginning, CoAP offers some protection against network steganography. For example, by introducing a proper order in the appearance of different options in message, the steganographic techniques that deploy a different order of options can not be applied.

CoAP can be applied in different fields, such as: smart energy, smart grid, building control, intelligent lighting control, industrial control systems, asset tracking, environment monitoring, and so on. So, one useful scenario of application of the CoAP covert channels would be for support of the authentication of geolocation of IoT devices. Another possible scenario is clandestine communication between wearable devices in a hostile environment, for the needs of the soldiers, or, between nodes in a wireless sensor network.

As steganography offers security only through obscurity. A successful attack against any covert channel consists in detecting the existence of this communication. Next, the new CoAP covert channels are presented.

A. *Covert Channel Using Token and/or Message ID Fields*

The Message ID contains a random 16-bit value. In the case of piggybacked response for CON message, the Message ID should be the same as in the request, while in the case of separate response, the server generate different random Message ID (while the request Message ID is copied in the first sent Empty ACK message).

The same Message ID can not be reused (in the communication between same two endpoints) within the EXCHANGE_LIFETIME, which is around 247 seconds with the default transmission parameters.

The Token is another random generated field, with variable size up to 64 bits, used as a client-local identifier to make a difference between concurrent requests. If the request results in the response, the Token value should be echoed in that response. This also happens in the case when the server sends separate response. So, we can create an unidirectional or a bidirectional communication channel between two hosts, by sending 16 (from Message ID) plus/or 64 (from Token ID) bits per message (PRBR $\in$ {16, 64, 80}). According to the pattern-based classification [18], this channel belongs to the following class:

```
Network Covert Storage Channels
 --Modification of Non-Payload
  --Structure Preserving
   --Modification of an Attribute
    --Random Value Pattern
```

B. *Covert Channel Using Piggybacked and Separate Response*

Since the server has a choice for sending piggybacked or separate response, one can create an one-bit per message unidirectional or a bidirectional covert channel (PRBR=1), such as:

- piggybacked response to be binary 1, and
- separate response to be binary 0.

At heavy load, the server may not be able to respond (sending binary 1), so this covert channel is limited to the times when the server has the choice. According to the pattern-based classification [18], this channel belongs to the following class:

```
Network Covert Timing Channels
 --PDU Order Pattern
```

C. Covert Channel Using Payload of the Message

Both requests and responses may include a payload, depending of the Method or the Response Code, respectively. Its format is specified by the Internet media type and content coding providen by the Content-Format option. The payload of requests or of responses that indicates success is typically a representation of the resource or the result of the requested action.

If no Content-Format option is given, the payload of responses indicating client or server error is a Diagnostic Payload, with brief human-readable diagnostic message being encoded using UTF-8 (Unicode Transformation Format) in Net-Unicode form.

The CoAP specification provides only an upper bound to the message size - to fit within a single IP datagram (and into one UDP payload). The maximal size of the IPv4 datagram is 65,535B, but this can not be applied to constrained devices and networks. According to IPv4 specification in the RFC 791, all hosts have to be prepared to accept datagrams of up to 576B, while IPv6 requires the maximum transmission unit (MTU) to be at least 1280B. The absolute minimum value of the IP MTU for IPv4 is 68B, which would leave at most 35B for a CoAP payload (the smallest CoAP header size with Payload Marker before the payload is 5B, assuming 0B for Token and no options). On the other hand, constrained network presents another restriction. For example, the IEEE 802.15.4's standard packet size is 127B (with 25B of maximum frame overhead), which leaves (without any security features) 102B for upper layers. The sizes of the input/output buffers in the constrained devices are another restriction of the maximal payload. Thus, we can create a unidirectional or a bidirectional communication channel between two hosts, by sending a Diagnostic Payload with the smallest maximal size of 35B per message (PRBR=280). According to the pattern-based classification [18], this channel belongs to the following class:

```
Network Covert Storage Channels
 --Modification of Payload Pattern
```

Another similar channel can be created by encoding the data in some specific Internet media format (for example, "application/xml" media type) and sending this format as payload of a message with appropriate Content-Format option (41 for "application/xml").

D. Covert Channel Using Case-insensitive Parts of the URIs

CoAP uses "coap" and "coaps" URI (Uniform Resource Identifier) schemes for identification of CoAP resources and providing a means for locating the resource. The URI in the request are transported in several options: URI-host, URI-Path, URI-Port and URI-Query. They are used to specify the target resource of a request to CoAP origin server. The URI-host and the scheme are case insensitive, while all other components are case-sensitive. So, we can create a unidirectional covert channel between the client and the server using, for example:

- capital letter in the URI-host option to be binary 1, and
- lowercase letter in the URI-host option to be binary 0.

Taking into account that a valid Domain Name System (DNS) name has at most 255B, we can send at most 255B per message, or in other words, the PRBR of this channel is up to 255B. According to the pattern-based classification [18], this channel belongs to the following class:

```
Network Covert Storage Channels
 --Modification of Non-Payload
  --Structure Preserving
   --Modification of an Attribute
    --Value Modulation
     --Case Pattern
```

CoAP supports proxying, where proxy is a CoAP endpoint that can be tasked by CoAP clients to perform requests on their behalf. Proxies can be explicitly selected by clients, using Proxi-URI option, and this role is "forward-proxy". Proxies can also be inserted to stand in for origin servers, a role that is named as "reverse-proxy". So, we can create similar covert channel using schema and host part from the Proxi-URI option. A request containing the Proxy-URI Option must not include URI-host, URI-Path, URI-Port and URI-Query options.

E. Covert Channel Using PUT and DELETE Methods

The PUT method requires the resource identified by the URI in the request, to be updated or created with the enclosed representation. If the resource exists at the request URI, the enclosed representation should be considered as a modified version of that resource, and a 2.04 (Changed) Response Code should be returned. If no resource exists, then the server may create a new resource with the same URI that results in a 2.01 (Created) Response Code.

The DELETE method requires deletion of the resource, which is identified by the URI in the request. Regardless if the deletion is successful, or the resource did not exist before the request, a 2.02 (Deleted) Response Code should be send.

If somebody has a known representation of the existing resource R1 on the server and if he knows that specific resource R2 does not exist on the same server, a unidirectional covert channel to the server can be created, in this way:

- send request with PUT method to create the resource R1 with enclosed known representation as binary 1, and
- send request with DELETE method to delete non-existing resource R2 as binary 0.

In this way, one bit per message can be sent (PRBP=1). According to the pattern-based classification [18], this channel belongs to the following class:

```
Network Covert Storage Channels
 --Modification of Non-Payload
  --Structure Preserving
   --Modification of an Attribute
    --Value Modulation Pattern
```

F. Covert Channel Using Accept Option

The Accept option can be used to indicate which Content-Format is acceptable to the client. If no Accept option is given, the client does not express a preference. If the preferred Content-Format if available, the server returns in that format, otherwise, a 4.06 "Not Acceptable" must be sent as a response, unless another error code takes precedence for this response. We can create a unidirectional one-bit per message covert channel (PRBP=1), in this way:

- sending a given message without Accept option to be binary 1, and
- sending a given message with Accept option to be binary 0.

According to the pattern-based classification [18], this channel belongs to the following class:

```
Network Covert Storage Channels
 --Modification of Non-Payload
  --Structure Preserving
   --Modification of an Attribute
    --Value Modulation Pattern
```

G. Covert Channel Using Conditional Requests

Conditional request options If-Match and If-None-Match enable a client to ask the server to perform the request only if certain conditions specified by the option are fulfilled. In the case of multiple If-Match options the client can make a conditional request on the current existence or value of an ETag for one or more representations of the target resource. This is useful to update the request of the resource, as a means for protecting against accidental overwrites when multiple clients are acting in parallel on the same resource. The condition is not fulfilled if none of the options match. With If-None-Match option the client can make a conditional request on the current nonexistence of a given resource. If the target resource does exist, then the condition is not fulfilled.

If somebody knows for sure that given condition C1 is fulfilled (for example, the resource is created or deleted in previous message) and other C2 is not fulfilled, using either of If-Match and If-None-Match options, a unidirectional one-bit per message covert channel (PRBP=1) can be created in this way:

- sending a given message without fulfilled condition to be binary 1 (e.g., If-Match + C2), and
- sending a given message with fulfilled condition (e.g., If-Match + C1) to be binary 0.

According to the pattern-based classification [18], this channel belongs to the following class:

```
Network Covert Storage Channels
 --Modification of Non-Payload
  --Structure Preserving
   --Modification of an Attribute
    --Value Modulation Pattern
```

H. Covert Channel Using Re-Transmissions

If we are using CoAP in channels with small error-rate (to cope with the unreliable nature of UDP), we can create a unidirectional or a bidirectional covert channel using retransmissions with PRBP=1, in this way:

- sending a given message only once to be binary 1, and
- sending a given message two or more times to be binary 0.

In this way, one bit per message can be sent. According to the pattern-based classification [18], this channel belongs to the following class:

```
Network Covert Timing Channels
 --Re-Transmission Pattern
```

V. PERFORMANCE EVALUATION

Suppose that two IoT devices communicate with CoAP every *t* seconds.

TABLE I. PERFORMANCE EVALUATION OF THE NEW COVERT CHANNELS FOR SENDING THE MESSAGE "HELLO, WORLD!"

No.	Type of CC	PRBR	Time (*s*)		
			t=1*s*	*t*=5*s*	*t*=10*s*
1	CC using token and/or message ID Fields	16	6	30	60
		64	2	10	20
		80	2	10	20
2	CC using piggybacked and separate response	1	91	455	910
3	CC using payload of the message	280	1	1	1
4	CC using case-insensitive parts of the URIs	≤2040	1	1	1
5	CC using PUT and DELETE Methods	1	91	455	910
6	CC using Accept option	1	91	455	910
7	CC using conditional requests	1	91	455	910
8	CC using re-transmissions	1	91	455	910

Any covert channel with a given PRBR will need at least

$$\text{ceil}(l\ /\ \text{PRBR}) \cdot t\ (s)$$

for sending a message with length l bits.

We can evaluate the minimum time for sending the message "Hello, world!" using the newly suggested covert channels. The message has length of 13 7-bit ASCII characters or l=91 bits. Results are given in Table 1.

So, we can see that not all suggested covert channels in CoAP are able to send short messages in real time, especially the ones with PRBR=1. Still, the covert channels 3 and 4 can be used for sending a short message per one CoAP message, without raising any suspicions. If the time for sending the message is not so important, one can choose covert channels 1 or 2, without raising any suspicions.

Additionally, we can evaluate the minimum time for sending the 320x240 raw color image (with 24-bit pixels) using the newly suggested covert channels. The size of the image is 225KB or l=1843200 bits. Results are given in Table 2.

TABLE II. PERFORMANCE EVALUATION OF THE NEW COVERT CHANNELS WITH PRBR>1 FOR SENDING 320X240 RAW COLOR IMAGE (WITH 24-BIT PIXELS)

	Type of CC	**PRBR**	**Time(s)**	
			t*=1*s	***t*=5*s***
1	CC using token and/or message ID Fields	16	115200 (32h)	576000 (160h)
		64	28800 (8h)	144000 (40h)
		80	23040 (6,4h)	115200 (32h)
2	CC using payload of the message	280	6583 (>1,82h)	32915 (>9.1h)
3	CC using case-insensitive parts of the URIs	≤2040	904 (15 min)	4520 (76 min)

The results from Table 2 show that most of the new CoAP covert channels are not quite suitable for sending images, because of the large transmission time. The covert channel 3 is the most suitable for that purpose (it will send 225KB image in 15 minutes).

VI. CONCLUSION

New CoAP covert channels are suitable for sending short messages. CoAP is the first specialized IoT protocol for which network steganographic techniques are applied. Considering that IoT will consist of about 30 billion objects by 2020 [14], CoAP belongs to the group of most exploited protocols in the forthcoming years, and its traffic will not raise any suspicions. So, it is important to identify possible ways of hiding data in it and trying to mitigate them. This paper deals with the first part, leaving others to try to find a solution for mitigating presented covert channels. One solution is the deployment of active and passive wardens.

The next step is implementation and demonstration of some of these covert channels, to present their functionality and feasibility.

REFERENCES

[1] Constrained RESTful Environments (CoRE) Parameters, CoAP Codes [Online]. Available at: https://www.iana.org/assignments/core-parameters/core-parameters.xhtml [retrieved: July, 2018]

[2] K. Denney, A. S. Uluagac, K. Akkaya, and S. Bhansali, "A novel storage covert channel on wearable devices using status bar notifications," Proc. 13th IEEE Annual Consumer Communications & Networking Conference, *CCNC 2016*, Las Vegas, NV, USA, 2016, pp. 845-848, doi: 10.1109/CCNC.2016.7444898.

[3] N. Feamster, M. Balazinska, G. Harfst, H. Balakrishnan, and D. Karger, "Infranet: Circumventing Web Censorship and Surveillance," Proc. 11th USENIX Security Symposium, San Francisco, CA, 2002, pp. 247-262.

[4] S. Fincher et al., "Perspectives on HCI patterns: concepts and tools," Proc. Extended Abstracts on Human Factors in Computing Systems (CHI EA '03). ACM, New York, NY, USA, 2003, pp. 1044–1045, doi: 10.1145/765891.766140.

[5] D. V. Forte, "SecSyslog: An Approach to Secure Logging Based on Covert Channels," Proc. First International Workshop of Systematic Approaches to Digital Forensic Engineering (SADFE 2005), Taipei, Taiwan, 2005, pp. 248-263, doi: 10.1109/SADFE.2005.21.

[6] A. Houmansadr, N. Kiyavash, and N. Borisov., "RAINBOW: A Robust And Invisible Non-Blind Watermark forNetwork Flows," Proc. 16th Network and Distributed System Security Symposium (NDSS 2009), San Diego, USA, The Internet Society, 2009.

[7] M. N. Islam, V. C. Patil, and S. Kundu, "Determining proximal geolocation of IoT edge devices via covert channel," Proc. 18th International Symposium on Quality Electronic Design, ISQED 2017, Santa Clara, CA, USA, 2017, pp. 196-202, doi: 10.1109/ISQED.2017.7918316.

[8] B. W. Lampson, "Note on the Confinement Problem," Commun. ACM vol. 16, 10, Oct. 1973, pp. 613-615, doi: 10.1145/362375.362389.

[9] D. Martins and H. Guyennet, "Attacks with Steganography in PHY and MAC Layers of 802.15.4 Protocol," Proc. Fifth International Conference on Systems and Networks Communications (ICSCN), Nice, France, 2010, pp. 31-36, doi: 10.1109/ICSNC.2010.11.

[10] W. Mazurczyk and Z. Kotulski, "New Security and Control Protocol for VoIP Based on Steganography and Digital Watermarking," Annales UMCS Informatica AI 5, 2006, pp. 417-426, doi: 10.17951/ai.2006.5.1.417-426.

[11] W. Mazurczyk and K. Szczypiorski, "Steganography of VoIP Streams," in On the Move to Meaningful Internet Systems (OTM 2008) Robert Meersman, Zahir Tari (Eds.). LNCS, vol. 5332, 2008, pp. 1001-1018, doi: 10.1007/978-3-540-88873-4_6.

[12] A. Mileva and B. Panajotov, "Covert channels in TCP/IP protocol stack - extended version-," Central European Journal

of Computer Science vol. 4, 2, 2014, pp. 45-66, doi: 10.2478/s13537-014-0205-6.

[13] A. K. Nain and P. Rajalakshmi, "A Reliable Covert Channel over IEEE 802.15.4 using Steganography," Proc. IEEE 3rd World Forum on Internet of Things (WF-IoT), Reston, VA, USA, 2016, pp. 711-716, doi: 10.1109/WF-IoT.2016.7845486.

[14] A. Nordrum, "Popular Internet of Things Forecast of 50 Billion Devices by 2020 Is Outdated," IEEE Spectrum. 18 August, 2016.

[15] Z. Shelby, K. Hartke, and C. Bormann, "The Constrained Application Protocol (CoAP)," RFC 7252, 2014.

[16] X. Wang and D. S. Reeves, "Robust correlation of encrypted attack traffic through stepping stones by manipulation of inter packet delays," Proc. 10th ACM Conference on Computer and Communications Security (CCS'03), 2003, pp. 20-29, doi: 10.1145/948109.948115.

[17] X. Wang, S. Chen, and S. Jajodia, "Tracking anonymous peer-to-peer VoIP calls on the Internet," Proc. 12th ACM Conference on Computer and Communications Security (CCS'05), Alexandria, VA, USA, 2005, pp. 81-91, doi: 10.1145/1102120.1102133.

[18] S. Wendzel, S. Zander, B. Fechner, and C. Herdin, "Pattern-Based Survey and Categorization of Network Covert Channel Techniques," ACM Computing Surveys vol. 47, 3, Article 50, 2015, doi: 10.1145/2684195.

[19] S. Zander, G. Armitage, and P. Branch, "A survey of covert channels and countermeasures in computer network protocols," IEEE Communications Surveys and Tutorials vol. 9, 3, 2007, pp. 44-57, 10.1109/COMST.2007.4317620.

Towards a Protection Profile for User-Centric and Self-Determined Privacy Management in Biometrics

Salatiel Ezennaya-Gomez*, Claus Vielhauer*† and Jana Dittmann*
*Multimedia and Security Lab (AMSL)
Otto-von-Guericke-University Magdeburg
Email: {*salatiel.ezennaya / jana.dittmann*} *ovgu.de*
†Brandenburg University of Applied Sciences
Email: *claus.vielhauer@{ovgu.de / th-brandenburg.de}*

***Abstract*—While new concepts of data analysis bring new opportunities for technological and societal evolution, they also present challenges with respect to privacy. Misconduct on personal data usage, particularly of biometric data, may lead to expose it to identity thieves or unfair practices. It is necessary to define limits to the usage of personal data, involving the user actively in the process of defining and controlling their own data as it is gathered in the EU data regulation (GDPR). It includes the right for the user to be informed about the actual use of the data, as it is called notice and choice. In recent decades, security and privacy design aspects were analysed and incorporated as building blocks for IT systems, and now some aspects are mandatory in standardisation and certification procedures. As a first step towards a Protection Profile in biometrics meeting GDPR requirements, in this paper we propose new privacy enforcement concepts and essential privacy requirements to achieve the goal of designing user-centric and self-determined privacy management in mobile biometrics.**

Keywords–GDPR; privacy; biometric data; sensible data; informed consent; transparency.

I. INTRODUCTION

After data breach public scandals, such as Cambridge Analytica and Facebook, or the mainstream adoption of Home Voice Assistants [1], [2], [3], there is increasing social alarm concerning uncontrolled acquisition of personal data. Concerns about privacy rose some time ago, since social and individual liberties are attached to sensitive data, such as biometric data, as Lane, Stodden, Bender and Nissenbaum (2014) clearly expose about informational data and privacy [4].

The European General Data Protection Regulation (GDPR) [5] undermines practices carried out by organisations regarding the use of personal data and sets rules on informational privacy. This regulation defines the rights of the owner of the data, as well as the obligations for organisations responsible for the acquisition, processing and maintenance of the data. Regarding the treatment of sensitive data, the regulation is very strict and precise with the rights that the user has over them. For instance, processing personal data in categories, such as political opinions, religious beliefs, and ethnicity is prohibited. Moreover, GDPR includes the right to control the data, so individuals have the right to object to the processing of their data, unless the organisations demonstrate the contrary for legitimate reasons [6] and [7]. This implies that individuals must be informed about the use of their data and the organisations must provide the means for the identification of the data once they are in storage. This regulation presents concepts on data protection, e.g., purpose binding, data minimisation, transparency, information security and individual's rights by means of consent [7] and [5].

Some aforementioned principles are gathered in the Fair Information Practice Principles (FIPPs) introduced in the 70s by the U.S. government, as well as in several previous data protection laws of European countries. However, the terms are inefficient in providing users power over their personal data.

In the case of GDPR, one can claim that the term Consent will be a building block in the development of IT systems for years to come. The regulation obligates mandatory demonstrable consent for certain purposes, and it can be withdrawn at any time [5]. In short, the user has the right to access, delete, customise and choose which personal data are shared without the current tedious bureaucratic process, or simply having no option to carry out these actions after having given consent. Moreover, the regulation sets the user's right to obtain a copy of the data (Data Portability), to be informed, and to object if he/she does not agree with the use of his/her data. In summary, GDPR is crucial for personal data processing, thus having an economic impact on companies' procedures. It should be mentioned that there are guidelines and methodologies of data protection models embracing GDPR from a legal point of view, such as the Standard Data Protection Model published by the German data protection authorities (DPAs) [8].

With respect to the research agenda, on biometric data protection and for data holders, it can be summarised in the following domains: biometric devices, extraction and representation of biometric data, privacy, design of trusted systems [9]. However, for the sake of our scope, we focus our attention on the last two domains. The former refers to limiting risks of privacy and civil liberties, whilst offering policies to enable robust biometric systems. The latter refers to design of transparent and fair systems for user acceptance accomplishing social norms. Thereby, new technical mechanisms to limit personal data usage, and likewise, guidelines in technical implementation of informed consent are urgently to be developed to translate data accountability into an increasing volume of businesses.

Biometric data pose key privacy questions as are summarised by Bustard (2015) [6], e.g., what biometric data are being gathered and by whom? Are data being used solely for the purpose for which it was gathered? Misuse of biometric data is extremely dangerous to user privacy. Biometric systems can reveal health conditions of users, and uniquely identify users by means of de-anonymising or linking information, among other examples of hazards.

For this reason, research communities across different disciplines have discussed the privacy issue for several years. Proposals of Artificial Intelligence (AI) governance models for AI frameworks or standardisation of ethics in AI are under development [10] and [11]. Additionally, solutions to improve IT systems, privacy-enhancing technologies, and mechanisms to embed GDPR requirements, are all being studied in several European research projects. Technologies on Identity Management or Access Control are covered in European projects, e.g., PaaSword [12] or CREDENTIAL [13]. In the specific case of Biometrics, there is ReCRED which seeks to improve access control solutions relying on the uniqueness of biometrics [14] and AMBER (enhAnced Mobile BiomEtRics) [15], which addresses current issues facing biometric solutions on mobile devices. This includes new methods for user data privacy protection, to provide data anonymity and usage transparency with user-centric data management, and to implement informed consent by organisational and technical means.

In a large part of published documents in standardisation, security requirements are limited to evaluate risks in aspects, such as Confidentiality, Integrity, Authenticity, Availability and the latest added design aspect: Privacy-by-Design. For the aforementioned reasons on the relationship between privacy and biometric data, privacy-preserving design aspects besides those well-known (Anonymity, Unlinkability, Unobservability), namely Transparency and Intervenability [8], should be taken into account in system design that intends to process biometric data.

In this document, we briefly review some Protection Profiles (PP) existing in biometrics, and what privacy requirements should be considered, in addition to security aspects, which already meet some standards. Finally, we focus on the definition of protection profiles that are the guidelines for certification of security systems. A set of preliminary concepts of transparency requirements are proposed, which may be included in a forward protection profile on transparency for biometric systems environments. These must be centred on user privacy management to achieve the goal of implementation of Informed Consent. We analyse potential threats for privacy, and we propose informal functional requirements for a transparent biometric system. Note that the present work does not intend to define a protection profile to cover all types of systems, but to be a step to study the inclusion of terms and requirements defined in GDPR.

The paper is divided as follows: In Section II, background in protection profiles and standards related to biometric are briefly described, as well as work done in research and other disciplines as recommendations for evaluation of biometric systems. In Section III, we propose the essential privacy requirements that a biometric system should present for its performance according to GDPR requirements. In Sections IV and V, discussion and conclusions are presented along with future work.

II. Background in Protection Profiles and Standards

In order to have a secure privacy-preserving biometric system, it must comply with six basic security design aspects or protection goals, as they are required by any computer system: Confidentiality, Integrity of the data, Authenticity, Non-repudiation, Availability, and Privacy-by-Design. Regarding privacy, there are precise privacy aspects for privacy-preserving technology that are: Anonymity, Pseudonyms, Unlinkability and Unobservability [16].

With the upcoming future changes, new protection goals are essential to be included during the IT system design stage to achieve transparent secure privacy-preserving systems, they are *Transparency* and *Intervenability*. Transparency brings the right of notification, and information of data subjects or users. Intervenability is a term adopted in [8], which refers to the right of deletion, correction, and objection by data subjects, as they are gathered in GDPR, that is, to implement self-determination into systems. To achieve these two essential aspects, a possible and logical solution would be to seek *Informed Consent* of the user by technical means.

Once the protection goals are defined, there is a question to be asked: Are these protection goals collected in published technical standards or in any protection profile in biometrics?

The Common Criteria (CC) is an international standard (ISO/IEC 15408) that sets security requirements for the evaluation of IT products or systems [17]. Under the CC, PP documents are published for the certification of an IT security product. These define an implementation-independent set of security requirements, across different categories such as: access control devices, databases, and data protection (e.g., cryptographic modules) among others. According to the current requirements of the latest version of CC (version 3.1), biometric systems may perform either enrolment or verification under the authentication framework. So far, there are published PPs for biometrics on verification mechanisms and fingerprint spoof detection. However, PPs span different categories which enforce security aspects, such as confidentiality, integrity of data in IT products, thus suitable for biometric systems. Some of those PPs are for Access Control devices, Encryption Systems for data protection, Smart Cards (ePassport) or Trusted Computing. Current PPs, relevant for this paper, under the CC version 3.1 are:

- BSI-CC-PP-0043-2008 Biometric Verification Mechanisms Protection Profile: Describes the functionality of a biometric verification system, defining its functional and assurance requirements [18].
- BSI-CC-PP-0062-2009 Fingerprint Spoof Detection Protection Profile: The scope of this Protection Profile is to describe the functionality of a biometric spoof detection system in terms of CC [19].

Currently, a CC working group is developing the Essential Security Requirements (ESR) for biometric products in an upcoming PP, within which the security requirements do not depend on biometric characteristics [20].

Other technical standards on IT security techniques have been published by ISO or ANSI (American National Standards Institute). Concretely, the Joint Technical Committee SC37 of ISO is responsible for development of technical standards in biometrics. This is divided into working groups, each which works on a different topic, such as: harmonised vocabulary, biometric technical interfaces, data interchanges formats, and technical implementations among others.

An example of standards in biometrics that might be interesting to systems that process biometric data, is the ISO/IEC 24745. It provides guidance for protection of biometric information during transfer and storage, providing confidentiality, integrity and revocability as well as providing guidelines on the protection of user privacy while processing biometric data. Also, standards that cover data formats for interoperability which depend on the biometric modality, or for biometric presentation attack detection are defined in ISO/IEC 19794-1:2011 and ISO/IEC 30107-2, respectively [21].

We highlight the standard ISO/IEC 30136:2018 published recently which provides evaluation of accuracy, as well as the privacy of biometric templates, establishing definitions to evaluate the biometric template scheme performance [22].

In the literature, technical mechanisms and protocols to achieve user-centric management have been proposed in several works [23], [24], [25] for different frameworks (e.g., identity management in the cloud). The work is based on information exchange security isolating personal information. In the context of IoT and Smart cities, Martinez, Hernandez, Beltran, Skarmeta and Ruiz (2017) presented an IoT attribute-based access control platform which empowers the user to decide which energy data is shared with other entities defining XACML-based privacy policies [26]. In the context of biometrics, the efforts are focused on different areas of authentication, such as proposing more robust storage mechanisms, improving biometric authentication using cryptographic schemes, or biometric template protection systems. In the latter area, Gomez-Barrero, Rathgeb, Galbally, Busch, and Fierrez (2017) work on providing unlinkability and irreversibility in biometric templates [27]. Besides, the so-called biometric-system-on-cards (BSoC) or smartcards (considered in ISO/IEC 17839) are proposed for user-centric privacy in biometrics, [28]. In this case, the user has physically his/her biometric templates stored in a smartcard. The capture device, signal processing, feature extraction and comparison are embedded in a smartcard. In addition, in regulation and standardisation, proposals on PP for biometric systems under specific standards of the ISO, and protection profiles and evaluations of biometric system performance under the CC have been published [29].

Current standards and protection profiles in data protection neither include data subject preferences in relation to data sharing, nor consent to process his biometric data, both threats related to transparency or unfair use of personal data. Therefore, besides security design aspects, privacy-by-design requirements must be gathered in future PPs in biometrics.

III. Essential Privacy Requirements for Biometric Products

Data breaches or misuse of personal data, in the specific case of biometric data, can lead to the invasion of privacy of the individual, identity impersonation, or other hazards. These risk the disastrous consequence of the loss of user's trust to biometrics and its advantages. Therefore, a first step in the definition of the security problem is the risk analysis, wherein risks, to which a biometric system is exposed, are evaluated.

The following threats are applicable in many architectures, though we focus our attention on systems based on Cloud-as-a-Service (CaaS). These systems use biometric data to offer a service, such as voice-assistants including Alexa of Amazon [30], since voice templates are not solely used for authentication.

TABLE I. Threats: Unfair Use of Personal Data

Threat	*Description*
Profiling or discovering patterns	The application of machine learning techniques for profiling or predictive consumer scores, which also can lead to a re-identification of the subject. Data holders can learn from biometric data. Processing personal data, such as political opinions, religious beliefs, sexual orientation etc. to profile individuals into categories is now prohibited according to GDPR.
No-policy-transparency	No clear comprehensible communication regarding data management.
Violation of the principle of proportionality	Biometric data are not only used for what has been originally intended, but for other purposes [33].
Monetisation of information	Pricing data exchanges between agents which manages a user's personal data [34]
Processing children's biometric data	To process children's data, such as voice or faces, without parental authorisation or consent.
Second-hand data leakage	Private data are revealed (unintentionally) by a person who has any kind of relation with another person. Also named by Barocas, Solon and Nissembaum (2014) [35], the tyranny of minority
Cross-border data transfer	The effect of the transfer data to third countries which do not respect individuals privacy [8].

A. Risk Analysis for Privacy

Attacks or threats, regardless of biometric modality, can be identified based on where, what and how they are produced. In the literature, there are some taxonomies wherein threats of IT systems are identified, such as the CERT taxonomy or ENISA Taxonomy [31] and [32]. Protection profiles, as well as standards, collect complete lists of threats, such as eavesdropping/hijacking (communication channels), failures (physical or logical), outages, nefarious activity (malware, etc.), which affect different parts and elements of the architecture of a general IT system [32]. Specific threats related to biometric systems are high level threats as discussed in [33], and can be summarised as follow:

- Spoofing, coercion, mimicry or denial of service attacks can compromise the capture device.
- Pre-processing and feature extraction modules could be compromised by impostor data, or malware (in both enrolment and verification stages). This could happen in the matching and decision modules with attacks, such as reply, component replacement, or hill climbing.
- A reference database, i.e., where data are processed and stored, could be attacked by reading or modifying templates, or changing links between biometric templates and a user's ID.

Besides the aforementioned hazards, there are threats to privacy regarding the misuse of the biometric data. We evaluate the following threats in Table I as risks of *unfair* use of data, therefore, risks for privacy.

B. Informal Privacy Requirements for a Fair and Transparent System

Following with the exercise of the definition of the security problem, in this subsection, the informal privacy objectives are described. The goal of a user-centric and self-determined system is to provide a tool to inform, manage and make decisions concerning outsourced biometric data. In order to achieve the protection goals listed in [8], a transparent system must be designed to perform the specific functionalities for transparency and intervenability (in Table II), besides those that provide anonymity, unlinkability, pseudonym and unobservability. This is summarised as follows:

- Reduce collected attributes of the data subject (data minimisation principle): Attributes in the context of biometrics certainly include all kinds of features extracted for a specific classification task, such as language, race, gender and age determination, childhood, and health conditions, [36].
- Protect sensitive information-flow by means of security mechanisms already developed (e.g., access control, language-based techniques, among others), relying on existing PPs, and provide security and privacy to biometric data in order to address threats. Including the aforementioned threats to privacy (e.g., BSI-CC-PP-0043-2008 and Standard ISO24174).
- Provide biometric data stored in the system which is complete, legible, auditable, and understandable to the user. Moreover, the biometric data should be portable, which means, in case the user will copy the biometric data for any reason, it should be in a standardised data format (e.g., ISO/IEC 19785-1).
- Audit changes on biometric data and provide logs of any action performed on the data.

An practical example of a system that processes biometric data (user's utterances) with no biometric authentication purpose, is an intelligent voice assistant, (e.g., Amazon Alexa). Biometric data are processed in the cloud to perform the service. Note that these type of systems can be considered HbC (Honest-but-Curious), that is, it provides a service while it tries to retrieve information from the user's data.

A first step, before data disclosure, is the informed consent negotiation. The user must be notified about the points listed in Table II. According to his/her privacy preferences, the user must have control over those points. These preferences must be written in a profile (or a privacy certificate written in XML-based language, for instance) and shared with the system in the cloud. Note that the privacy profile should be updated periodically with user's preferences. The cloud must check the procedures that it will apply to the data, such as algorithms, outsourcing, purpose, retention time, etc. Later, it should inform the client which options it is able to fulfil. The client receives the server's options and checks the conditions. Sequentially, once the handshake is performed, the client is ready to share the biometric data, previously processed (i.e., applying anonymisation or marking algorithms, such as speech watermarking). Once these steps are performed, the data are sent to the cloud and stored following security requirements for sensitive data. In case that the negotiations ended in a deadlock, the user should able to decide to share the data with the best conditions that the server offers to preserve privacy, otherwise decline the use of his/her biometric data. In case of consent revocation, the system should look into the database, identify the user's data, and erase them.

TABLE II. SYSTEM DESIGN FUNCTIONALITIES

Privacy Design Aspects	*System Functionalities*
Transparency	Inform the user about: – Purpose of data collection. – Retention period of the data in data holder's servers. – Associated privacy risks. – Data collection periodicity. – Location of storage servers of data holder. – If decision making is done or not.
Intervenability	System must give options to: – Accept or decline the purpose of data collection. – Accept or decline data sharing with third-parties. – Revoke complete consent for processing. – Revoke partial consent, such as data sharing. – Erase data stored in data holder's servers. – Allow or deny decision making over user's data.

IV. DISCUSSION

GDPR pays attention to biometrics in Art. 9 Paragraph 1 which says: *"(...) the processing of genetic data, biometric data for the purpose of uniquely identifying a natural person, data concerning health or data concerning a natural person's sex life or sexual orientation shall be prohibited."* Following a list of exceptions is specified, where the first exception is described in Paragraph 2.a: *"the data subject has given explicit consent to the processing of those personal data for one or more specified purposes (...)"*. It may seem that the prohibition is in vague terms. Since once given the consent, it may give rise to continue with the misuse practices, with the difference that now the user is supposedly informed. This point is related to the user's behaviour at the time of reading the privacy policies. It has been observed that the user is aware of the importance of disclosure of sensitive data. In an experiment conducted by Naeini et al. in the context of the IoT, users appreciate being informed about the purpose and periodicity of data acquisition, [37]. Even so, when deciding about it, they tend to have a permissive behaviour. The causes can be diverse and are studied from a psychological point of view. Nonetheless, a reason has been proven to be linked to the prize obtained in exchange for granting the data, as preliminary results were shown by Bock (2018), who concludes that a solution for educating users is needed [38].

To the best of our knowledge, self-determination is impossible to implement with current technical mechanisms. The systems are not designed to allow such configuration. As we briefly reviewed, methods are being developed to incorporate intervenability into systems. A first intuition is to bring into mobile phones the same functional philosophy of smartcards, since they are more powerful computationally than a smartcard. In this case, as Sanchez-Reillo (2017) compels in [28], this option is not feasible, since the smartphones are multipurpose devices, respect for the security constraints of smartcards may be in conflict with other purposes. An example of this statement may be our case of use, voice assistants pre-installed in Android smartphones. They are able to perform more tasks beyond simply to search or send SMS. They can be launched remotely with no user privileges either by the manufacturer or by external attackers, as has been demonstrated by Alepis and Patsakis (2017), [39]. In such situations, current mechanisms of access control, encryption, or anonymisation are insufficient.

For these reasons, GDPR data subjects requirements regarding data management are currently not possible to guarantee. At present, we must rely on user data management platforms in the cloud provided by the data holder. In case of revocation of consent or account deletions, if this information has been disclosed to third parties previously, it is impossible to trace, and therefore to erase. For this reason, it is urgent to define protocols and common criteria security certificates with a thorough list of functional privacy and security requirements, as discussed in the paper.

V. Conclusion and Future Work

In order to create biometric systems respectful of user privacy while fulfilling GDPR requirements, new concepts in the design and implementation of privacy are needed. As stated earlier, along with the essential security requirements, privacy concepts and aspects (Unlinkability, Anonymity, Pseudonyms, Unobsevability) are defined in standards for IT systems. Nevertheless, two more aspects must be added to the list to accomplish users privacy expectations in sensible data processing: Transparency and Intervenability.

Since the use of biometrics in industry must provide accountability towards customers and data regulators, their systems should enforce the standards for biometrics. In this paper, we presented the outlook for biometric systems to embed the GDPR requirements, within which new privacy aspects are defined besides the well-known security aspects. We reviewed standards regarding biometric systems. With the idea to contribute to the analysis of further protection profiles for biometric systems, we presented the essential privacy requirements a biometric system should meet with focus on Transparency and Intervenability. For that purpose, potential threats of the unfair use of sensitive data were included in the list of threats related to biometric systems that are met in standard documentation. Some of those are profiling, no-policy-transparency, violation of the principle of proportionality, and cross-border data transfer. Regarding informal requirements, we consider it essential to reduce collected attributes of data subjects, apply user privacy preferences on data processing, and provide management permissions to the user allowing revocable consent.

For setting up PPs, basic aspects of transparency are necessary to be depicted in the CC. The current version 3.1 of CC lacks a family of the aforementioned essential privacy aspects, i.e., Transparency and Intervenability. Our contribution can be a first step to include in current version of the current CC. These two new families in the Functional Privacy Class (FPR) may be called (following the standard naming convention) FPR_TRP and FPR_INV, Transparency and Intervenability families, respectively.

Our future work continues with transparency, by means of the implementation of informed consent into protocols for user-centred systems.

Acknowledgment

The work presented has been supported in part by the European Commission through the MSCA-ITN-ETN - European Training Networks Programme under Project ID: 675087 ("AMBER - enhAnced Mobile BiomEtRics"). We would like to thank Nicholas Whiskerd for his formulations in developing this work. The information in this document is provided as is, and no guarantee or warranty is given or implied that the information is fit for any particular purpose. The user thereof uses the information at one's sole risk and liability.

References

[1] C. Cadwalladr and E. Graham-Harrison, "Revealed: 50 million facebook profiles harvested for cambridge analytica in major data breach," 2018, URL: https://www.theguardian.com/news/2018/mar/17/cambridge-analytica-facebook-influence-us-election, [accessed: 2018-07-16].

[2] H. Chung, M. Iorga, J. Voas, and S. Lee, "Alexa, can I trust you?" Computer, IEEE, vol. 50, no. 9, 2017, ISSN:0018-9162.

[3] J. Hubaux and A. Juels, "Privacy is dead, long live privacy," Communications of the ACM, vol. 59, no. 6, 2016, pp. 39–41, ISSN:0001-0782.

[4] J. Lane, V. Stodden, S. Bender, and H. Nissenbaum, Privacy, Big Data, and the Public Good: Frameworks for Engagement. Cambridge University Press, 2014, doi:10.1017/CBO9781107590205.

[5] "Regulation (EU) 2016/679 of the european parliament and of the council of 27 april 2016 on the protection of natural persons with regard to the processing of personal data and on the free movement of such data, and repealing directive 95/46/ec (general data protection regulation) (text with eea relevance)," 2016, URL: https://eur-lex.europa.eu/legal-content/EN/TXT/?uri=CELEX:32016R0679, [accessed: 2018-07-16].

[6] J. Bustard, "The impact of EU privacy legislation on biometric system deployment: Protecting citizens but constraining applications," Signal Processing Magazine, IEEE, vol. 32, no. 5, 2015, pp. 101–108, ISSN:1053-5888.

[7] G. Danezis, J. Domingo-Ferrer, M. Hansen, J. Hoepman, D. Metayer, R. Tirtea, and S. Schiffner, "Privacy and data protection by design-from policy to engineering," Tech. Rep., 2015, ISSN: 978-92-9204-108-3, URL:https://www.enisa.europa.eu/publications/privacy-and-data-protection-by-design, [accessed: 2018-07-16].

[8] K. Bock, W. Ernestus, M. Kamp, L. Konzelmann, T. Naumann, U. Robra, M. Rost, G. Schulz, J. Stoll, U. Vollmer, and M. Wilms, "The standard data protection model a concept for inspection and consultation on the basis of unified protection goals, version 1.1 (pdf)," 2018, URL: https://www.datenschutz-mv.de/static/DS/Dateien/Datenschutzmodell/SDM-Methode_V_1_1.pdf (in German), [accessed: 2018-07-16].

[9] N. R. Council, Biometric Recognition: Challenges and Opportunities. Washington, DC: The National Academies Press, 2010, ISBN= 978-0-309-14207-6. [Online]. Available: https://www.nap.edu/catalog/12720/biometric-recognition-challenges-and-opportunities

[10] U. Gasser and V. Almeida, "A layered model for AI governance," IEEE Internet Computing, vol. 21, no. 6, 2017, pp. 58–62.

[11] J. Havens, "Ethically aligned standards - a model for the future," 2017, URL: https://www.standardsuniversity.org/e-magazine/march-2017/ethically-aligned-standards-a-model-for-the-future/, [accessed: 2018-07-16].

[12] "European project: Paasword - a holistic data privacy and security by design platform-as-a-service framework introducing distributed encrypted persistence in cloud-based applications," 2015-2017, URL:https://cordis.europa.eu/project/rcn/194247/_en.html, [accessed: 2018-07-16].

[13] "European project: Credential - secure cloud identity wallet," 2018, URL: https://credential.eu/, [accessed: 2018-07-16].

[14] "European project: From real-world identities to privacy-preserving and attribute-based credentials for device-centric access control," 2015-2018, URL: https://cordis.europa.eu/project/rcn/194863/_en.html, [accessed: 2018-07-16].

[15] "European project: Amber - enhanced mobile biometrics," 2017, URL: https://www.amber-biometrics.eu/, [accessed: 2018-07-16].

[16] C. Vielhauer, J. Dittmann, and S. Katzenbeisser, "Design aspects of secure biometric systems and biometrics in the encrypted domain," in Security and Privacy in Biometrics. Springer, 2013, pp. 25–43.

[17] N. Mead, "The common criteria," 2013, URL: https://www.us-cert.gov/bsi/articles/best-practices/requirements-engineering/the-common-criteria, [accessed: 2018-07-16].

[18] T. Nils and L. Boris, "Biometric verification mechanisms protection profile bvmpp,v1.3," Bundesamt für Sicherheit in der Informationstechnik Common Criteria, Protection Profile, 2008, URL: https://www.commoncriteriaportal.org/files/ppfiles/pp0043b.pdf, [accessed: 2018-07-16].

[19] N. T. Boris Leidner, "Fingerprint spoof detection protection profile based on organisational security policies fsdpp_osp v1.7," Bundesamt für Sicherheit in der Informationstechnik Common Criteria, Protection Profile, 2010, URL: https://www.commoncriteriaportal.org/files/ppfiles/pp0062b_pdf.pdf, [accessed: 2018-07-16].

[20] C. W. G. for Biometric Product Security, "Biometric Product Essential Security Requirements," Common Criteria, Protection Profile, Nov. 2016, URL: https://www.commoncriteriaportal.org/communities/bio-esr.pdf, [accessed: 2018-07-16].

[21] C. Tilton and M. Young, Standards for Biometric Data Protection. Springer London, 2013, pp. 297–310, ISBN = 978-1-4471-5230-9.

[22] "ISO/IEC 30136:2018 Information technology – Performance testing of biometric template protection schemes," International Organization for Standardization, Standard, Mar. 2018.

[23] P. Dash, C. Rabensteiner, F. Hrandner, and S. Roth, "Towards privacy-preserving and user-centric identity management as a service," in Open Identity Summit 2017, L. Fritsch, H. Ronagel, and D. Hhnlein, Eds. Gesellschaft fr Informatik, Bonn, Oct. 2017, pp. 105–116.

[24] H. Gunasinghe and E. Bertino, "Privacy preserving biometrics-based and user centric authentication protocol," in Network and System Security. Springer International Publishing, 2014, pp. 389–408.

[25] S. Wohlgemuth, "Adaptive user-centered security," in Availability, Reliability, and Security in Information Systems. Springer International Publishing, 2014, pp. 94–109, ISBN = 978-3-319-10975-6.

[26] J. Martínez, J. Hernández-Ramos, V. Beltrán, A. Skarmeta, and P. Ruiz, "A user-centric internet of things platform to empower users for managing security and privacy concerns in the internet of energy," International Journal of Distributed Sensor Networks, vol. 13, no. 8, 2017, doi:10.1177/1550147717727974.

[27] M. Gomez-Barrero, J. Galbally, C. Rathgeb, and C. Busch, "General framework to evaluate unlinkability in biometric template protection systems," IEEE Transactions on Information Forensics and Security, vol. 13, no. 6, June 2018, pp. 1406–1420, ISSN: 1556-6013.

[28] R. Sanchez-Reillo, Biometric systems in unsupervised environments and smart cards: conceptual advances on privacy and security, ser. Security. Institution of Engineering and Technology, 2017, pp. 97–122, Chapter 5, URL: http://digital-library.theiet.org/content/books/10.1049/pbse004e_ch5.

[29] B. Fernandez-Saavedra, R. Sanchez-Reillo, J. Liu-Jimenez, and O. Miguel-Hurtado, "Evaluation of biometric system performance in the context of common criteria," Information Sciences, vol. 245, 2013, pp. 240 – 254, ISSN:0020-0255.

[30] A. D. S. LLC, "Alexa terms of use - amazon privacy notice," 2018, URL: https://www.amazon.com/gp/help/customer/display.html?nodeId=201909010, [accessed: 2018-07-16].

[31] C. James and Y. Lisa, "A taxonomy of operational cyber security risks," Software Engineering Institute, Carnegie Mellon University, Pittsburgh, PA, Tech. Rep. CMU/SEI-2010-TN-028, 2010, URL: http://resources.sei.cmu.edu/library/asset-view.cfm?AssetID=9395, [accessed: 2018-07-16].

[32] L. Marinos, "Enisa threat taxonomy: A tool for structuring threat information initial version, 1.0," ENISA, Heraklion, Tech. Rep., 2016, URL: https://www.enisa.europa.eu/topics/threat-risk-management/threats-and-trends/enisa-threat-landscape/etl2015/enisa-threat-taxonomy-a-tool-for-structuring-threat-information/view, [accessed: 2018-07-16].

[33] P. Campisi, Security and Privacy in Biometrics: Towards a Holistic Approach. London: Springer London, 2013, pp. 1–23, Chapter 1, ISBN= 978-1-4471-5230-9.

[34] L. Kugler, "The war over the value of personal data," Commun. ACM, vol. 61, no. 2, 2018, pp. 17–19, ISSN:0001-0782.

[35] S. Barocas and H. Nissenbaum, "Big data's end run around procedural privacy protections," Communications of the ACM, vol. 57, no. 11, 2014, pp. 31–33.

[36] N. Whiskerd, J. Dittmann, and C. Vielhauer, "A requirement analysis for privacy preserving biometrics in view of universal human rights and data protection regulation," 2018, to appear in Proc. EUSIPCO 2018.

[37] P. Naeini, S. Bhagavatula, H. Habib, M. Degeling, L. Bauer, L. Cranor, and N. Sadeh, "Privacy expectations and preferences in an iot world," in Proceedings of the 13th Symposium on Usable Privacy and Security (SOUPS), JUL 2017, pp. 399–412.

[38] S. Bock, "My data is mine - users' handling of personal data in everyday life," in Sicherheit 2018, Beiträge der 9. Jahrestagung des Fachbereichs Sicherheit der Gesellschaft für Informatik e.V. (GI), Konstanz., Apr. 2018, pp. 261–266, URL:https://dblp.org/rec/bib/conf/sicherheit/Bock18.

[39] E. Alepis and C. Patsakis, "Monkey says, monkey does: Security and privacy on voice assistants," IEEE Access, vol. 5, 2017, pp. 17 841–17 851, doi:10.1109/ACCESS.2017.2747626.

Exploiting User Privacy in IoT Devices Using Deep Learning and its Mitigation

Rana Al Ameedee, Wonjun Lee
Department of Electrical and Computer Engineering
The University of Texas at San Antonio, Texas, USA
Email: {rana.alameedee, wonjun.lee}@utsa.edu

Abstract — **Internet of Things (IoT) has seen a great growth in recent years; the number of devices is expected to be 80 billion by 2025. Although the IoT facilitates our life, however, it threatens our privacy if we do not take the necessary security measures. In this paper, we show how the user activities can be tracked using only network traffic packets sent from several commercial IoT devices with no need for deep inspection. The prediction about daily life activities of the user at home is made based on analysis of deep learning. In addition, we propose a practical idea to mitigate the privacy attack caused by the smart home devices, and introduce experimental results showing that our approach works very accurately.**

Keywords—Internet of Thing; Smart Home; Privacy; Deep Learning.

I. INTRODUCTION

Nowadays, IoT is being used in many places where installed devices are connected to the Internet providing smart and intelligent services such as smart home, smart cities, smart health, etc. In IoT, privacy is one of the most critical terms that need to be considered due to its close connection to the life of users at home, hospital, and work. For example, a sleep-monitor device is used to track sleeping patterns, heart rate, breathing, snoring, movements of users for improving sleep quality. Sensing devices that control home objects such as light, thermometer, electricity, windows, and doors are related to human life. The research in IoT privacy has focused on keeping data hidden during its transmission to the external Internet by encrypting these data in the strong security protocols [1]. However, even though the data is hidden, by combining and analyzing data transmitted from multiple devices, a malicious party can track user's life patterns revealing critical privacy issues. Especially, smart home devices should not reveal their presence at home, because exploiting these devices with their specific function could potentially disclose personal information. Thus, even though some IoT devices in the smart home do not produce personal information, it is still possible to find out the identity of devices [2]-[4] and then, indirectly track individual's personal life style through identified devices [5].

In this paper, we show how user privacy can be exploited in deep learning model, by implementing experiments on three commercial IoT devices. Identifying the devices through the devices' manufacturer name is the first step to exploit user privacy. Training dataset for this work is generated manualy simulating human's real life pattern while testing data is extracted from the network traffic sent by devices. Analyzing in deep learning method, it was possible to show how the vulnerabilities could lead to violate user privacy by making an accurate prediction about user activities at home.

In addition to attack method, we present the most recent defense approaches and an idea that mitigates the privacy violation as well as corresponding experiment results. These results bring a broad impact on nations, as well as IoT community in the sense that human life will be based on so many different types of smart home devices that are connected to the Internet in near future. From the simple technique to get device identity information and normal traffic data with the analysis on the deep learning methods, we show that user's personal life style can be revealed. This vulnerability becomes much bigger whenever a new device is added.

The paper is composed of following four sections. Section II describes how user privacy could be exploited with deep learning; Section III presents the suitable mitigation of the vulnerabilities that are found and have caused the privacy violation; Section IV describes related and similar works to our approach including the most recent attacks and mitigations concluding in Section V.

II. EXPLOITING USER PRIVACY WITH DEEP LEARNING

In the IoT system, Domain Name Server (DNS) queries reveal IoT devices' identities since DNS queries are mapped to a specific manufacturer, when exchanging data between the devices and manufacturer's servers. The revelation of device identities alone represents privacy violations regardless of consequent attacks. For instance, some people do not want anyone to know that they use a blood pressure device or device to measure diabetes [6]. Generally, IoT devices have individual purpose with one type of data for most of time [1]. Therefore, the traffic that comes from a particular device reveals its functionality. Under such characteristics of IoT devices, identifying the devices could predict user activities in terms of functioning of devices [7].

Some IoT devices may not provide sensitive information by themselves, but when it is joined with other devices' traffic, they give strong prediction. For instance, when traffics from vacuum device, sleep sensor, and smart TV [8] are jointly analyzed together, it's possible to predict when the user goes bed to sleep [9].

The following subsections describe how we exploit user privacy by analyzing data coming from devices.

A. *Smart home devices*

Tracking user's daily activities at home through network traffics sent by IoT devices can be performed using a deep learning method. In order to set up the IoT environment, three commercial devices are used as IoT devices; *Smart lock*, *Smart light*, *Smart alarm*. How these devices are installed in the experiment and what vulnerabilities are investigated in these devices can be found as follows:

Smart lock – Smart lock is installed on the deadbolt of the main door at home. The device sends an alarm to the user if the door is open. Device's App is installed on the phone, and the device is connected through a wireless network (i.e., Wi-Fi) to *raspberry pi3* (i.e., router in our IoT environment). From the domain name in the DNS queries which are in plain text while data transmitted between device and manufacturer's server are encrypted in Transport Layer Security (TLS), attackers can get the information about the lock and notice the identity of the device. The network traffic sent by the device denotes *open* or *close* of the door.

Smart light – Smart light is installed in the home lab and also connected to the raspberry pi router using Wi-Fi. Investigating the TLS packet header, manufacturer name (i.e., *tuyaus* in our experiment) appears clearly in the DNS queries, as shown in Figure 1. After filtering out packets other than TLS packets with the identified device name, it is found that the device sends traffics in encrypted data format whenever the device is used by the user. Thus, finding the packet here means turning *on* or *off* the light [10].

Smart alarm – Regarding device identification, DNS queries reveal device identity clearly through domain name which has a manufacturer name. Device identification through its DNS queries is a general problem for most of IoT devices including investigated six devices in [2], as well as three devices in this experiment. The smart alarm device sends encrypted data whenever it is used.

When the data coming from three devices are merged with time information and then analyzed, this analysis provides meaningful information which should not be revealed to the third persons other than users. For example, when the people have the pattern such that they wake up in the morning, turn off the light, lock the door in time order, and then no activities are sensed, it can be expected that they *left home* in the morning for a long time. If the malicious person gets a data such that the door is opened after a long time (i.e., after 16 hours), and then the light is on right after the door is open, he or she can confirm that these series of information reveal a life pattern such that the user comes back home at late night. Combining those two examples of scenario provides complete information about user's daily life such that the user wakes up in the morning, leaves home and then comes back home at late night. If the data that contains such pattern repeats multiple times, the adversary can confirm that the life pattern is really true. Based on the collected time of the same series of information, the analysis may reveal user's many different life patterns such as working at night and coming back home in the morning while sleeping at day.

	B	C	D	E	F	G	H
1	Time	Source	Destination	Length	Protocol	Encrypted Application Data	Info
2	8:52 AM	192.168.0.11	a1.tuyaus.com	694	TLSv1.2	bd717bcf50cf2338d3e3966c8cf6bc199bb714fc32755fdc...	Application
3	8:52 AM	a1.tuyaus.com	192.168.0.11	388	TLSv1.2	3aea8cd6615eb9fb93eed2755e6035a9b4bb9a3201f01783...	Application
4	8:52 AM	192.168.0.11	a1.tuyaus.com	770	TLSv1.2	26e90c55c9b66a39e32b8dfbb4877aa0dab52314b846c609...	Application
5	8:52 AM	a1.tuyaus.com	192.168.0.11	392	TLSv1.2	65c36a38ea4fad39d0302da6a6be786375e1795355562b91...	Application
6	8:52 AM	192.168.0.11	a1.tuyaus.com	774	TLSv1.2	bd717bcf50cf2339706d1690f4f5fc3c1bc04e1b8a9bfc80...	Application
7	8:52 AM	a1.tuyaus.com	192.168.0.11	417	TLSv1.2	3aea8cd6615eb9fccb30ab8127ea5655babc11dd8aad4791...	Application
8	8:52 AM	192.168.0.11	a1.tuyaus.com	765	TLSv1.2	bd717bcf50cf233a31d4225bd241f45d4a329a2c9b06d4be...	Application
9	8:52 AM	a1.tuyaus.com	192.168.0.11	1375	TLSv1.2	3aea8cd6615eb9fd51cdaa8e80ec8554260a2fabdc439c06...	Application

Figure 1. Sample raw data sent from smart light device

B. *Experiment*

For the experiment, we set up a home lab where raspberry pi3 is programmed as a Wi-Fi access point [11] and connected to Ethernet as an Internet provider. All IoT devices mentioned above (i.e., smart light, smart lock and smart alarm) were installed at home to be used in a real life and provided a real network packet to the simulated adversary. All the IoT devices as well as raspberry pi3 were connected to a smartphone where all IoT devices' Apps are installed to control the devices as depicted in Figure 2.

In order to get training data, network traffics are captured for a routinized 24 hours from home lab where three devices are used simulating real normal life during weekdays. If the more diverse patterns of life including weekend are collected and trained, it will give more accurate result. However, since it is good enough to show the privacy vulnerability in IoT devices even only with a weekday data, thus we used simple (e.g., 24 hours) data. The experiment consists of five steps; Capture network traffic from home lab; Filter the captured traffic; Extract features; Write training dataset; Build a deep learning model.

Capture network traffic – The entire network traffic packets coming from the router (i.e., raspberry pi) of the home lab are captured using *tcpdump* [12] and then saved as a *pcap* file.

Filter the captured traffic – First, the pcap file is opened in *Wireshark* and filtered based on DNS queries that show device identities (i.e., manufacturer name). After that, packets are separated for each device and then saved as a CSV file.

Extract features – Since the device sends encrypted data whenever it is used, sending itself gives information to the adversary about the time when users use the device. Based on the specific tasks of each device with respect to time, the adversary can predict user's living patterns by combining all

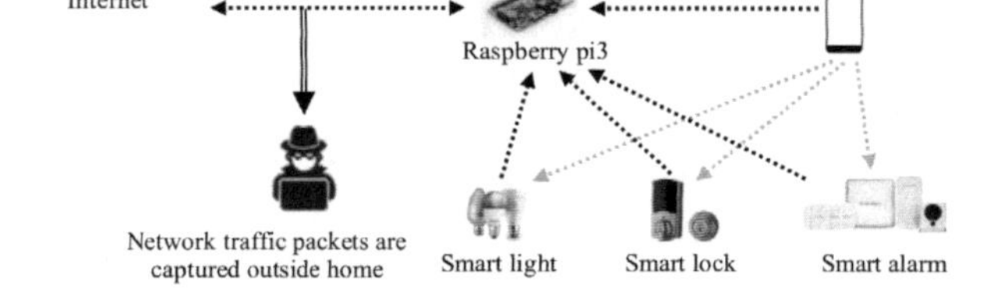

Figure 2. Experiment environment

user_activity	light	lock	smartalarm	Time	light_5h_ago	lock_5h_ago	smartalarm_5h_ago	light_5h_later	lock_5h_later	smartalarm_5h_later	lock_30 minute later	lock_1h_afte	lock_2h_afte	lock_3h_after
0	0	0	0	5:00	1	0	0	0	0	0	0	0	0	0
1	0	1	1	6:00	1	0	0	0	0	0	0	0	0	0
2	0	1	1	14:00	0	0	0	0	0	0	0	0	0	0
3	1	1	0	6:00	1	0	0	0	0	0	1	0	0	0
4	0	0	0	20:00	0	0	0	0	0	0	0	0	0	0

Figure 3. Samples of training data

data in CSV file to analyze. Using pandas library [13], a python code was written to extract features and merge CSV files. The features extracted for each device are as follows:

- *What time is the encrypted data sent?*
- *Which device sends this data at that time?*
- *Is this device used before five hours?*
- *Is this device used after five hours?*
- *Is the smart lock device used during the periods of 30 minutes, one hour, two hours, or three hours?*

The third feature helps the adversary to predict user activities, such as waking up or returning after a long time since users do not have any activities for five hours before waking up or returning home. The fourth feature helps the adversary to predict user activities, such as sleeping or leaving for a long time since users do not have any activities after they sleep or leave. The fifth feature helps to predict if the user left his home temporarily. All features are in binary format (i.e., *0* or *1*) except time feature which is also converted to numerical format using *sklearn* [14]. The value *1* represents that user used the device while *0* means the device was not used.

Write training dataset – The training dataset is manually written to reflect a real normal life at the same format as test dataset. This dataset considered all probabilities and times of using devices resulting in 135,668 records in CSV file. The training dataset is classified with five labels which we call, user_activity; *Wake-up*, *Leave-home-for-a-long-time*, *Return-to-home*, *Leave-home-temporarily*, and *Go-to-bed or Sleep*, which are represented as numeric values (i.e., 0, 1, 2, 3, and 4) as shown in Figure 3.

Build a deep learning – The model that we used is a Sequential *keras* [15] consisting of four layers including an input and output layer. All layers have 500 nodes except the last layer, which has five output nodes since we have five classes. We used a nonlinear function, *relu* as an activation function, stochastic gradient descent for optimizer, and *mean_squared_error* for loss function. After compiling the deep learning model inside a function, we used wrapper function to take *keras* model and pipe it to *scikit-learn*. In addition, *numpy* library from python was used to read and normalize data before entering it into the *keras* model.

C. Experiment result and evaluation

After training the model with 80% and validating with 20% of training data respectively, we obtained 98.81% of accuracy over the training dataset. Figure 4 shows that how the adversary predicted user's daily activities over 8 different scenarios in test data. The *X*-axis and *Y*-axis in Figure 4 denote predicted output and true output respectively. Our model correctly predicted user activities in that two predictions of *wake-up* for a test data were truly labeled as the same activities, and two predictions for the test data, labeled as *leaves-home-for-a-long-time* (i.e., *leave_home* in the Figure 4) were actually what they were as labeled in true outcomes. Even though there is one false result such that the model predicts *leave-home-temporarily* (i.e., *leave_temp* in the Figure 4 – up) as *leave-home-for-a-long-time*, it is still a good prediction because it does not go too far to a different class, such as *return-to-home* or *go-to-bed* predicting as a leave class. Therefore, as a result, the deep learning model provides high accuracy for the comprehensive prediction. If more IoT devices are added at home such as smart TV, smart refrigerator, smart vacuum, thermometer, camera, etc., more accurate and various personal living activities can be predicted from the accordingly added dataset. Furthermore, we can see that in the normalized confusion matrix (Figure 4 – down), the model predicted all the scenarios with accuracy of 100 %, except *leave-home-temporarily* scenario with 50%.

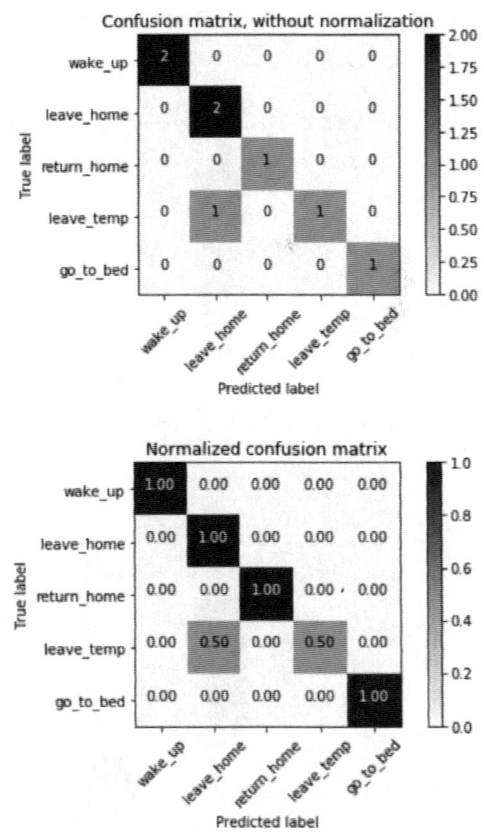

Figure 4. Up – Confusion matrix without normalization. Down – Confusion matrix with normalization.

III. MITIGATION

The time of sending data from IoT devices causes the privacy violation with accurate prediction of user activities when all device traffics are merged and analyzed in deep learning model. The critical problem here is that the adversary knows when these devices are activated or used through a time of sending encrypted data. Our idea to mitigate this attack is based on the simple technique in that by sending fake data from devices, the adversary is perturbed to precisely analyze user activities. Since the data has already been encrypted, the adversary cannot distinguish fake data from the real data. We implemented the proposed idea and applied the same deep learning method to prove its effectiveness.

It is found that the prediction accuracy has been decreased to the lowest level as shown in confusion matrix of Figure 5. This figure shows how the model incorrectly predicts user activities. For example, while the adversary predicted a test data as *go-to-bed*, the actual label of that data was *wake-up*. The two test data are predicted as user's *return-to-home* but the true labels were *leave-home-for-a-long-time* (i.e., leave_home) and *leave-home-temporarily* (i.e., leave_temp). Furthermore, Figure 6 shows the regression graph between predicted and expected output describing how those two outputs match closely. *X*-axis represents testing data representing 8 scenarios, of which each is predicted to 5 corresponding output labels in *Y*-axis.

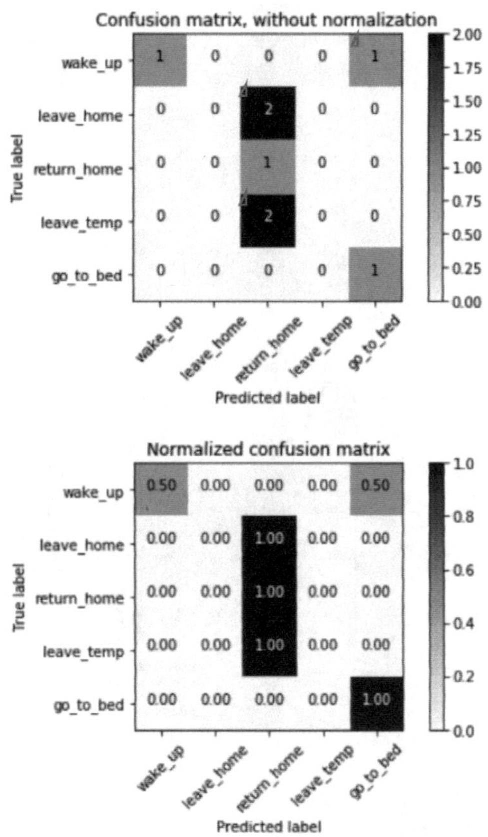

Figure 5. Confusion matrix after injecting fake data in testing data

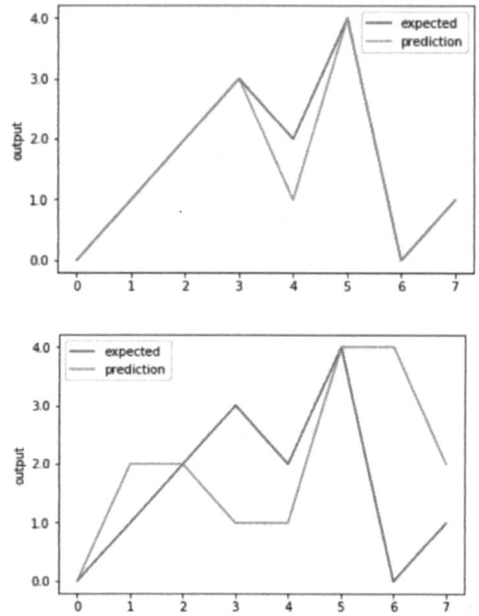

Figure 6. Regression graph without (Up) and with (Down) injecting fake data

Figure 6 – up shows that the prediction almost matches the true label meaning that the adversary successfully predicted the user activity at his home before sending fake data. Figure 6 – down shows how the prediction is far from the true labels showing that those outputs almost do not match. We can clearly see that the model predicts most of scenarios incorrectly except scenario 2 ad 5.

IV. RELATED WORKS

Apthorpe et.al. [2] analyzed four commercial IoT devices (i.e., Sense Sleep Monitor, Nest Security Camera, WeMo Switch, and Amazon Echo) to exploit user privacy. The analysis was conducted using DNS queries and metadata with no further deep inspection due to data encryption. Devices were identified through the domain name in DNS queries, which had the manufacturer name. They inferred user activities by mapping similar variations from live traffic after correlating variations of traffic rates with known user interactions. For instance, they recorded the traffic from light sensor for 12 hours at night and observed user's sleeping habits through the sent and received packet rate. After plotting this traffic, they found that traffic rate in high peak denotes user activities, such as going to bed, getting out of bed temporarily, getting out of bed in the morning. In our research, though the same approach has been used to record the traffic and identify devices using DNS queries, different IoT devices (smart lock, smart light, and smart alarm) were applied. In addition to applying to different devices, regarding network traffic packets, we only used a time of sending encrypted data and device identification information who sent it while there was no need to know the size of the sent packet, or the rate of sending these packets. In order to predict user's life style, we implemented deep learning methodologies which were only proposed by Apthorpe, et.al., [2] as their future work.

One of the proposed privacy attack mitigations is DNS concealing to prevent the adversary from recognizing the IoT device identity by Apthorpe, et.al., [4]. However, it is known that by applying a simple supervised machine learning technique, such as *k-nearest-neighbors classifier* on device traffic rates, it is possible to recognize identity of devices with accuracy 95%. Nevertheless, DNS concealing still motivates and makes device identification more complex.

A Virtual Private Network (VPN) could be used for mitigating device identification as introduced by Apthorpe, et. al. [4]. This approach includes tunneling of all traffics of a smart home to prevent the adversary from splitting the traffic into individual devices. VPN envelopes all traffic coming from the home and aggregated them into additional transport layer. Although VPN is considered a good solution to keep privacy and security for smart home, it is still possible to identify the device using supervised machine learning technique. If the home has only one IoT device, then VPN traffic rate will match the traffic from that device. In case of multiple devices, they send traffic at a different time in that the adversary still could identify the devices. For instance, a smart door lock and smart sleep monitor are less likely to be recording user activities simultaneously because it is impossible for the user to sleep and open the door at the same time.

One of the proposed approaches to mitigate attacks that use revelation of device usage patterns is to make IoT devices delay sending data to the server. For instance, sleep sensing device delays sending data for a couple of hours instead of sending right away to server. This mitigation could be successful for devices, such as sleep sensors that do not require direct outcome; however, devices that require a real-time response to triggers, such as smart alarm or personal assistant devices cannot be used for this type of mitigation because those devices cannot wait to answer user's question [4].

V. Conclusion

Smart home devices connected to Internet provide not only convenience in life to human but also private information of users to adversary. Even though many smart devices are prevalently being used in many places including house, many people are not aware of vulnerabilities that reveal their life pattern and its potential threats of misuse by malicious parties.

In this paper, we presented a deep learning based privacy attack method and its mitigation in IoT environment. From the experiment, we showed that data encryption is not enough to assure user privacy when using smart home devices and it requires additional technique to hide device usage patterns represented in time by adding noisy traffics.

As a future work, we will add additional mitigation methods such as sending fake traffics in random period, as well as its performance analysis.

References

[1] J. Singh, T. Pasquier, J. Bacon, H. Ko, and D. Eyers, "Twenty security considerations for cloud-supported Internet of Things", IEEE Internet of Things Journal, vol. 3, no. 3, pp. 269-284, 2016.

[2] N. Apthorpe, D. Reisman, and N. Feamster, "A smart home is no castle: Privacy vulnerabilities of encrypted IoT traffic", 2017, *arXiv preprint arXiv:1705.06805*.

[3] Y. Meidan, M. Bohadana, A. Shabtai, J. D. Guarnizo, M. Ochoa, N. O. Tippenhauer, and Y. Elovici, "ProfilIoT: a machine learning approach for IoT device identification based on network traffic analysis", In Proceedings of the Symposium on Applied Computing, pp. 506-509, ACM, April 2017.

[4] N. Apthorpe, D. Reisman, and N. Feamster, "Closing the Blinds: Four Strategies for Protecting Smart Home Privacy from Network Observers", 2017, arXiv preprint arXiv:1705.06809.

[5] D. Geneiatakis, I. Kounelis, R. Neisse, I. Nai-Fovino, G. Steri, and G. Baldini, "Security and privacy issues for an IoT based smart home. In Information and Communication Technology", The 40th International Convention on Electronics and Microelectronics (MIPRO), pp. 1292-1297, IEEE, May 2017.

[6] C. Debes et al., "Monitoring activities of daily living in smart homes: Understanding human be-havior", IEEE Signal Processing Magazine, vol. 33, no. 2, pp. 81-94, 2016.

[7] H. Lin and N. W. Bergmann, "IoT privacy and security challenges for smart home environments", Information, vol. 7, no. 3, 44, 2016;7:44 doi: 10.3390/info7030044.

[8] R. L. Rutledge, A. K. Massey, and A. I. Antón, "Privacy impacts of IoT devices: a SmartTV case study", IEEE International Conference in Requirements Engineering Conference Workshops, pp. 261-270, September 2016.

[9] C. Bettini and D. Riboni, "Privacy protection in pervasive systems: State of the art and technical challenges", Pervasive and Mobile Computing, 17, pp. 159-174, 2015.

[10] J. Huntley, "DoctorBeet's Blog: LG Smart TVs logging USB filenames and viewing info to LG servers": http://doctorbeet.blogspot.com/2013/11/lg-smart-tvs-logging-usb-filenames-and.html [retrieved: 07, 2018].

[11] L. Ada and T. Adafruit, "Setting up a Raspberry Pi as a WiFi access point", nd): n. pag. Adafruit. Adafruit, 5, 2016.

[12] N. Kumar, J. Madhuri, and M. ChanneGowda, "Review on security and privacy concerns in Internet of things", International Conference on IoT and Application (ICIoT), pp. 1-5, IEEE, May 2017.

[13] W. McKinney et al., "Pandas: Python Data Analysis Library": https://pandas.pydata.org/ [retrieved: 07, 2018].

[14] scikit-learn developers, "scikit-learn": http://scikit-learn.org/stable/index.html [retrieved: 07, 2018].

[15] Keras Google group, "Keras: The Python Deep Learning library": https://keras.io/ [retrieved: 07, 2018].

Secure Collaborative Development of Cloud Application Deployment Models

Vladimir Yussupov*, Michael Falkenthal*, Oliver Kopp†, Frank Leymann*, and Michael Zimmermann*
*Institute of Architecture of Application Systems
†Institute of Parallel and Distributed Systems
University of Stuttgart, Stuttgart, Germany
email: [lastname]@informatik.uni-stuttgart.de

Abstract—**Industrial processes can benefit considerably from utilizing cloud applications that combine cross-domain knowledge from multiple involved partners. Often, development of such applications is not centralized, e.g., due to outsourcing, and lacks trust among involved participants. In addition, manual deployment of resulting applications is inefficient and error-prone. While deployment can be automated using existing modeling approaches, the issues of data confidentiality and integrity in exchanged deployment models have to be addressed. In this paper, we tackle security challenges posed by collaborative cloud application development. We present a policy-based approach for modeling of security requirements in deployment models. Furthermore, we propose a method of peer-to-peer model exchange that allows enforcing modeled requirements. To validate our approach we apply it to Topology and Orchestration Specification for Cloud Applications (TOSCA), an existing cloud applications modeling standard, and describe the prototypical implementation of our concepts in OpenTOSCA, an open source toolchain supporting TOSCA. Usage of the resulting prototype in the context of a described model exchange process allows modeling and enforcement of security requirements in collaborative development of deployment models. We then conclude the paper with a discussion on limitations of the approach and future research directions.**

Keywords–Collaboration; Security Policy; Confidentiality; Integrity; Deployment Automation; TOSCA.

I. Introduction

Modern computing paradigms have great potential for accelerating the 4th industrial revolution, often referred to as Industry 4.0 [1]. One notable example is the rapidly evolving field of cloud computing [2], which allows on-demand access to potentially unbounded number of computing resources. Combined together with ubiquitous sensors usage in the context of the Internet of Things (IoT) [3], cloud computing facilitates the development of composite, cross-domain applications tailored specifically for automation and optimization of manufacturing. The overall complexity of the development process, however, might become a significant obstacle for industries willing to benefit from cloud applications.

A typical cloud application today has a composite structure consisting of numerous interconnected and heterogeneous components [4]. Deploying such complexly-structured applications in a manual fashion is error-prone and inefficient. Therefore, various deployment automation approaches exist. One well-established automation technique relies on the concept of *deployment models* that specify application structure along with the necessary deployment information. Automated processing of such models considerably reduces the deployment's complexity and minimizes required efforts. Another significant benefit, which improves the portability and reusability aspects of the application development process, is that standardized models can be exchanged instead of separate application components.

One common cloud application development scenario in the context of Industry 4.0 is a collaboration [5] among several multidisciplinary partners responsible for separate parts of the application [6]. The final goal of this collaboration is to combine all parts into a complete and deployable cloud application. Collaborative development can significantly benefit from the portability and reusability properties of deployment models. However, since not all parties are known in advance, e.g., due to task outsourcing or changes in organizational structure, the issues of intellectual property protection in decentralized settings arise. For instance, confidential information like sensor measurements and proprietary algorithms might be subject to various *security requirements*, including protection from unauthorized access and verification of its integrity. Therefore, modeling and enforcement of such requirements aimed at specific parts of deployment models, have to be supported.

In this work, we focus on the aspects of secure collaborative development of cloud applications' deployment models. The contribution of this paper is a method for modeling and enforcement of security requirements in deployment models which combines the ideas of sticky policies [7], policy-based cryptography [8], and Cryptographic Access Control (CAC) [9]. We describe how security requirements aimed at data protection in modeled cloud applications can be expressed using dedicated security policy types and analyze which parts of deployment models need to support the attachment of security policies. As a next step, we elaborate on how modeled security requirements can be enforced in a peer-to-peer exchange of deployment models. To validate our concepts, we apply them to an existing OASIS standard called Topology and Orchestration Specification for Cloud Applications (TOSCA) [10], [11], which specifies an extensible, provider-agnostic cloud modeling language [12]. As a proof of concept, we describe the prototypical implementation of the presented concepts in OpenTOSCA [13], an opensource ecosystem for modeling and execution of TOSCA-compliant deployment models. The resulting prototype used in the context of the proposed decentralized model exchange serves as a means to model the discussed security requirements and enforce them along the model's exchange path. Finally, we discuss the limitations of our approach and describe possible improvements.

The remainder of this paper is structured as follows. We describe the fundamentals underlying this work in Section II and discuss a motivational scenario in Section III. In Section IV, we present concepts for modeling and enforcement of security requirements in collaborative deployment models development. In Section V, we apply the concepts to a TOSCA-based deployment modeling process. The details about the prototypical implementation in OpenTOSCA are discussed in Section VI. In Section VII, we describe related work and Section VIII summarizes this paper and outlines future research directions.

II. FUNDAMENTALS

In this section, we provide an overview of several important concepts which serve as a basis for our work, namely: (i) deployment automation of cloud applications by means of deployment modeling approaches, (ii) usage of policies as means to specify non-functional system requirements, (iii) and a brief coverage of access control mechanisms.

A. Deployment Modeling

The compound application structure and increased integration complexity make it non-trivial to automate the deployment of modern cloud applications [4]. The concept of deployment modeling aims to tackle the automation problem, and there are several known approaches including imperative and declarative modeling [4], [14], [15]. Both paradigms are based on the idea of creating a description, or deployment model, sufficient enough for deploying a chosen application in an automated fashion. What makes these modeling approaches different is the way how corresponding deployment models are implemented.

In case of the declarative modeling [14], a deployment model is a structural model that conveys the desired state and structure of the application. Essential parts of the declarative deployment model include a specification of application's components with respective dependencies and necessary connectivity details. As a result, the model might contain binaries or scripts responsible for running some application's components, e.g., a specific version of Apache Tomcat, or a predefined Shell script for running a set of configuration commands. In addition, a description of non-functional system requirements in some form can be included into the model. Some examples supporting this type of modeling include Chef [16] and Juju [17] automation tools, as well as TOSCA. This type of models relies on the concept of deployment engines, which are able to interpret a provided description and infer a sequence of steps required for successful deployment of the modeled application.

Compared to declarative approach, the imperative modeling [14] focuses on a procedure which leads to automatic application deployment. More specifically, an imperative model describes (i) a set of activities corresponding to the required deployment tasks which need to be executed, (ii) the control and data flow between those activities. One robust technique for this modeling style is to use a process engine, e.g., supporting standards like Business Process Execution Language (BPEL) [18] or Business Process Model and Notation (BPMN) [19], that can execute provided imperative models in an automated fashion.

A combination of declarative and imperative approaches is also possible. In general, creating both types of models requires efforts from the modeler. However, the imperative modeling approach is generally more time-consuming and error-prone, since multiple heterogeneous components need to be properly orchestrated. Moreover, the structure of the application might change frequently which requires to modify imperative models. To minimize required modeling efforts, imperative models might be derived from the provided declarative models [4].

One important aspect of deployment models is that apart from valid descriptions they also need to include various files related to described software components and other parts of the application, e.g., scripts, binaries, documentation and license details. As a result, the term deployment model usually refers to a combination of all the corresponding metadata and application files required for automatically deploying a target application.

B. Policies

One well-known approach [20] for separation of non-functional requirements from the actual functionalities of a target system relies on the usage of policies. Essentially, a *policy* is a semi-structured representation of a certain management goal [21]. The term management here is rather broad, as it might refer to different aspects of management, e.g., high-level corporate goals or more low-level, technology-oriented management goals. For instance, from the system's perspective, performance, configuration, and security are among the classes of non-functional requirements that can be described using policies. Additionally, various policy specification languages exist in order to simplify the process of describing such requirements in a standardized manner [20]. From the high-level view, policies only declare the requirements which then have to be enforced using dedicated enforcement mechanisms [22].

The idea to specify security requirements in policies dates back to at least the 1970s [20]. Depending on the level of details security policies might specify, e.g., privacy requirements for the whole system or for particular data objects. In information exchange scenarios, security policies specified on the level of data objects have to be ensured during the whole exchange process [23]. For this reason, all receivers have to be aware of specified policies and enforcement must happen, e.g., by means of globally-available security mechanisms. Similarly, deployment models in collaborative application development are constantly exchanged and parts of them might be subjects to security policies. So-called *sticky policies* [23] is an approach to propagate policies with the data they target. This approach can be combined with cryptography in order to ensure that data is accessed only when requirements specified in policies are satisfied. Multiple approaches to combine sticky policies with different cryptographic techniques such as public key encryption or Attribute-Based Encryption (ABE) exist [24].

C. Access Control

A secure information system must prevent disclosure (confidentiality) or modification (integrity) of sensitive data to an unauthorized party and ensure that data are accessible (availability) [22]. These requirements can be enforced by assuring only authorized access to the system and its resources. Commonly, this process is referred to as *access control* and there exist multiple well-established access control mechanisms. For example, in Discretionary Access Control (DAC) mechanism, the access is defined based on the user's identity. This results in access rules that are specified specifically for this identity, e.g., in the form of an access control matrix [25]. Another well-known access control mechanism is called Role-Based Access Control (RBAC) where access is granted or denied based on the user roles and access rules defined for these roles.

One disadvantage of aforementioned access control mechanisms is that they commonly rely on some centralized trusted authority, making it difficult to implement them in large scale and open systems [9]. The idea of CAC is based on well-known cryptographic mechanisms and regulates access permissions based on the possession of encryption keys. In CAC, the stored data are encrypted and can only be accessed by those users who have the corresponding keys. One benefit of this approach is that the data owner can grant keys to receivers of his choice using established key distribution mechanisms, thus enforcing the access control without relying on the trusted third party.

III. Motivational Scenario

Developing distributed cloud applications and analytics applications in the context of Industry 4.0 typically requires combining numerous heterogeneous software components [26], [27]. Commonly, this process implies a collaboration among experts from various domains, such as data scientists, infrastructure integrators, and application providers. Furthermore, resulting applications are often required to be deployable on demand and, thus, are expected to be in the form of deployment models that allow automating application provisioning [6], [28].

An example of a collaborative cloud application development depicted in Figure 1 involves four participants responsible for distinct parts of the application. When joined together, all developed parts of the application, e.g., software components, datasets, and connectivity information, comprise a complete and provisioning-ready deployment model. In this scenario, the main beneficiary who orders the application from a set of partners and has exclusive rights on the resulting deployment model is called the *Application Owner*. The *Infrastructure Modeler* is responsible for integrating different components, such as analytics runtime environments, databases, or application servers. Moreover, two additional co-modelers are involved in the development process, namely a *Data Scientist* and a *Dataset Provider*. The former develops a certain proprietary algorithm, whereas the latter provides a private dataset, e.g., comprised of sensor measurements obtained from a combination of various cyber-physical systems used in production processes.

In contrast to the Application Owner who has full rights on the resulting deployment model, other participants might be subjects to security restrictions with respect to certain application parts. For example, access to the dataset provided by the Dataset Provider might need to be restricted to some of the involved parties. Similarly, the Data Scientist might want to impose a certain set of security requirements on the provided algorithm. Since the final infrastructure must include all corresponding sub-parts that were provided directly or indirectly by other participants, the Infrastructure Modeler is responsible for preparation and shipping of the finalized deployment model to the Application Owner who is then able to create new instances of the application on demand.

Generally, collaborative processes from various fields share some common characteristics. For instance, according to Wang et al. [29] such issues as (i) a *dynamically changing sets of participants*, (ii) the *lack of centralization*, (iii) *intellectual property and trust management issues*, and (iv) *heterogeneity of exchanged data* are important in collaborative development of computer-aided design models. Likewise, the lack of knowledge about all participants involved in collaborative cloud application development makes it difficult to establish a centralized interaction among them. Possible reasons include outsourcing of development tasks and introduction of additional participants due to rearrangements in organizational structures. Since no strict centralization is possible, communication with known participants happens in a peer-to-peer manner. Another important aspect of collaborative cloud application development is its iterative nature. Since exchanged deployment models might be impartial or require several rounds of refinement, a potentially complicated sequence of exchange steps is possible for obtaining a final result. Therefore, deployment models need to be exchanged in collaborations in a way that simplifies the overall process and enforces potential security requirements.

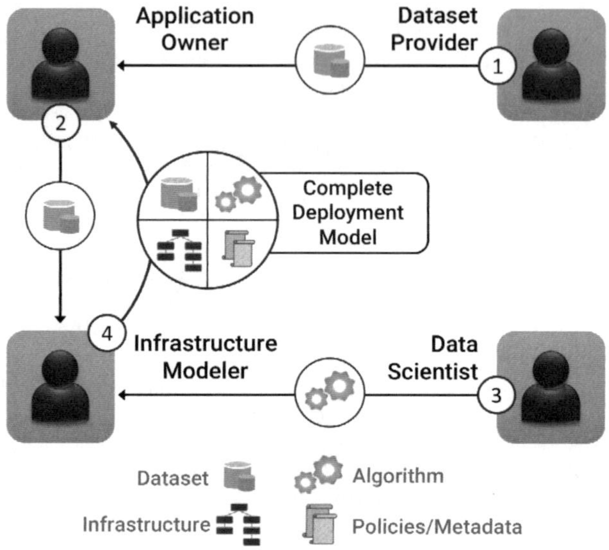

Figure 1. A collaborative application development scenario.

A deployment model, generally, can be exchanged either in a self-contained form or on a per-participant basis. In the former case, the deployment model is self-contained and its content is the same for all participants, whereas in the latter case its content is fragmented according to some rules separately for each participant. Sometimes, however, exchanging deployment models on a per-participant basis interferes with the actual goals of the collaboration. For example, in exchange sequence shown in Figure 1 the dataset is firstly passed directly to the Application Owner by the Dataset Provider. For integration of the dataset into the final model, the Infrastructure Modeler needs to model the required infrastructure, e.g., a Database Management System (DBMS) and related tooling. As only the Application Owner has full rights on all parts of the application, the provided dataset has to be protected from unauthorized access. Intellectual property issues become even more complex in highly-dynamic scenarios when multiple parties continuously exchange partially-completed deployment models. Unfortunately, encrypting an entire deployment model does not solve the problem since models might be intended to remain partially-accessible by parties with limited access rights. Apart from confidentiality problems, the authenticity and integrity of passed deployment models and their parts might be subjects to verification requirements. For instance, the Application Owner might need to check if an algorithm was actually provided by the Data Scientist and no changes were made by other parties. In such case, signing the hash value of an entire deployment model is not suitable as integrity of individual model's parts have to be verified. Hence, it should be possible to verify distinct parts of deployment models independently.

The aforementioned scenario highlights several important issues in collaborative development of deployment models which need to be solved, namely (i) confidentiality, authenticity, and integrity requirements of each involved participant have to be reflected in the model, (ii) various levels of granularity for these requirements need to be considered: from full models to its separate parts, and (iii) a method to enforce modeled requirements in a peer-to-peer model exchange is needed.

IV. Modeling and Enforcement of Security Requirements

Intellectual property in collaborations has to be protected from both, external and internal adversaries with respect to their relation to the process. The former describes any attacker from outside of the collaboration, i.e., who is not participating and is not reflected in any kind of agreements, e.g., Service Level Agreements (SLAs). Conversely, the latter refers to a dishonest party involved in the process. We focus on internal adversaries and data protection issues involving known parties.

This section presents an approach to ensure the fulfillment of security requirements in collaborative development of deployment models. Our approach relies on the well-established concept of representing non-functional requirements via policies [30], [31], [32], [33]. The semantics of security requirements is analyzed to derive a set of action and grouping policies. The former type represents cryptographic operations allowing to enforce confidentiality and integrity requirements, inspired by the idea of policy-based cryptography [8]. The latter type simplifies grouping parts of models which are subjects to action policies. Both policy types are data-centric and attachment happens with respect to a certain entity or a group of entities in the manner of sticky policies [23] to preserve the self-containment property of deployment models. The access control enforcement is inspired by the idea of CAC [9].

A. Assumptions

To focus on internal adversaries, we assume that participants establish bidirectional secure communication channels for data exchange and that the modeling environment of every involved participant is secure. We employ an "honest but curious" [34], [35], [36] adversary model in which adversaries are interested in reading the data, but avoid modifications to remain undetected. Despite the absence of modifications made by adversaries, authenticity and integrity requirements still need to be modeled and enforced. For instance, participants might want to track changes or verify the origin of some specific part in the model.

When describing how data encryption can be modeled, we assume that no double encryption is needed for distinct parts of deployment models. We do not distinguish between read and write rights when discussing access control based on cryptographic key possession. Therefore, a participant with the required key is assumed to have full access rights on the corresponding entity. For efficiency reasons, we adopt symmetric encryption for ensuring the confidentiality of data.

B. Security Policies in Collaborative Deployment Models

An assumption that data is exchanged in a secure manner among the participants does not guarantee that all involved parties can be trusted. Therefore, security requirements are important even under the secure communication channels assumption. Security requirements we focus on are: (i) protection of data confidentiality in deployment models, and (ii) verification of data integrity and authenticity of deployment models. On the conceptual level, two distinct types of policies, namely *encryption policy* and *signing policy*, can be distinguished. The former is aimed to solve the confidentiality problem, whereas the latter targets integrity-related requirements. However, having a completely encrypted deployment model does not solve the confidentiality problem, since a party with limited rights will not be able to access the parts of the application which were intended to remain accessible. Similar problem might arise for a signature of the complete packaged deployment model, e.g., in a form of an archive, since it will not be possible to check what exactly was changed unless all files are also signed separately as a part of the process. More specifically, if only the hash of an entire deployment model was signed, there will be no way to distinguish which specific part of the model is invalid. Therefore, we need to model security policies on the level of atomic entities in deployment models to support collaborations similar to the scenario described in Section III.

Naturally, if only parts of deployment models are subjects to confidentiality requirements, enforcement of encryption and signing policies must affect only respective entities. In our approach, an encryption policy attached to a certain entity of the deployment model signals that it has to be encrypted. In a similar manner, if a certain entity of the deployment model needs to be signed, the corresponding signing policy needs to be linked with it. In both cases, policies represent actual keys that are going to be used for encryption or signing. Since not all collaborations can rely on a centralized way to manage policies, the deployment model has to be transferred together with corresponding policies attached to its entities. The keys bound to policies, however, cannot be embedded, as deployment models will no longer remain suitable for sharing with all possible participants in a self-contained fashion. In such cases, either participants with proper access control rights can receive such models, or the models have to be split on a per-participant basis. Since not all scenarios favor participant-wise model splitting, a policy needs to be linked with a specific key in a decoupled manner to preserve self-containment of a deployment model. As a side effect of decoupling keys from policies, existing key distribution channels can be utilized independently from deployment model exchange channels.

For linking policies with particular keys, we need to maintain unique identifiers for every key involved in the collaboration. Since not all participants know each other, one simple solution is to compute a digest of the key and use it as an identifier or additionally combine it with several other parameters such as algorithm details, participant identifier, etc. Another option is to use identifiers which include some partner-specific parts so that policies can be easily identified. Several important points have to be mentioned here. Linking the policy only with the unique key identifier is not enough for decryption since the modeler needs to know the algorithm details to perform decryption. Such information can be provided either as properties of a policy itself or be a part of the key exchange. Additionally, specifically for encryption there is no obvious way to distinguish if the policy was already applied and the data is in encrypted state when a deployment model is received. Although the data format after encryption will not be identical to the original entity's format, checking this difference for every modeled entity is not efficient. For this reason, a policy needs to have an attribute stating that it was applied. Due to the usage of symmetric encryption, generating a respective *decryption policy* is unnecessary as it is identical to the encryption policy.

Conversely, the verification of signing policies differs from the encryption process since private keys are used for signing and certificate chains of one or more certificates containing the public key and identity information are used for verification. As a result, there are two options: to follow the encryption approach and decouple certificates from policies, or, to embed

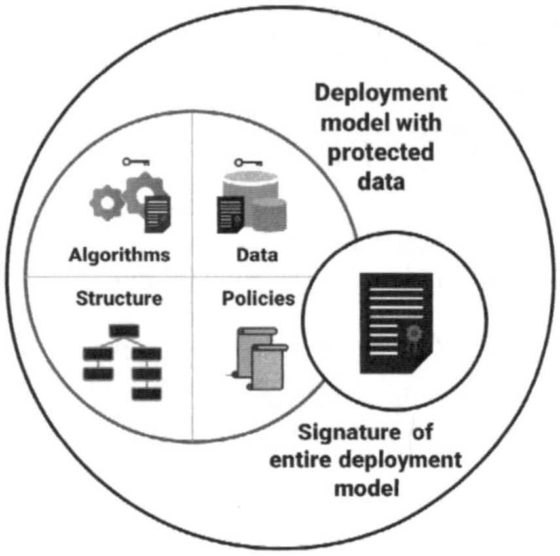

Figure 2. A conceptual model of the signed deployment model.

certificates into policies to simplify the verification process. While certificates are meant for distribution, there is one caveat in the embedding of certificates approach, however. Certificates commonly have a validity period and verification must be able to deal with the cases when certificates embedded into policies are no longer valid. Since such verification is more an issue of a proper tooling, the certificates are embedded into policies.

Unlike file artifacts, e.g., software components or datasets, which are referenced from models and supplied alongside with them, some sensitive information, e.g., model's properties, might be directly embedded into models. For instance, if user credentials for a third-party service have to be passed from one modeler to another and no other participant is allowed to see them, then these properties must be encrypted. Sometimes such properties also need to be verified, e.g., the Service Owner might want to check if the endpoint information for a third-party service was actually modeled by the Infrastructure Modeler. Therefore, an additional caveat one has to consider is that not only distinct artifacts, but also separate parts of artifacts might require encryption or signing. The corresponding artifact in this case has to store these properties with the modeled security requirements being enforced, e.g., encrypted or signed.

Hence, we need two more policy types: *encryption grouping policy* and *signing grouping policy* which contain lists of properties within an artifact that have to be encrypted or signed, respectively. From the conceptual point of view, the discussed policies can be classified as *action* and *grouping* policies. The former includes policies representing an action, i.e., encryption or signing, whereas the latter identifies groups of entities which require the action. As a result, the corresponding grouping policies are linked with the desired action policies, i.e. with actual keys which will be applied to selected properties.

C. Integrity and Self-Containment of Deployment Models

When security policies are modeled and enforced, the resulting deployment model contains a combination of encrypted and signed artifacts and properties. Integrity check at this point allows to verify the state of modifications and authenticity of entities modeled by other participants. However, verification of the entire deployment model's integrity including modeled security policies and other attached metadata requires an additional signature on the level of deployment model.

For this purpose we adopt the technique analogous to signing of Java archives (JARs) [37]. Essentially, a packaged deployment model is some sort of an archive containing grouped artifacts. It is then possible to assume the presence of a meta file similar to manifest in JARs, which provides the list of all contents plus some additional information. In situations when such manifest file does not exist, it can easily be generated by traversing the contents of a corresponding deployment model.

As both, integrity of the model's parts that are targeted by security requirements and integrity of the entire deployment model have to be considered, an enhanced packaging format is needed. The enhanced structure of a deployment model consists of its original content as well as the content's signature files. The latter is achieved via a combination of: (i) a manifest file with digests for every file, (ii) a signature file consisting of digests for every digest given in the manifest file plus the digest of the manifest file itself, and (iii) a signature block file consisting of a signature generated by the modeler and the certificate details. The resulting conceptual model is shown in Figure 2. To make a signed deployment model distinguishable from regular deployment models, the signature has to be generated in a standardized fashion, e.g., it can be stored in a predefined folder inside the package or entire deployment models can be archived along with the generated signature information.

One important issue is that, technically, there is no fixed concept of a deployment model in collaboration. Since parts of cloud applications might be exchanged separately or merged together, the definition of the exchanged deployment model is changing throughout the process. Thus, it is mandatory to preserve the self-containment of modeled security requirements on the level of atomic entities. Firstly, security policies are always included to the deployment model since they are tightly-coupled with target entities. With respect to actual entities, the problem is trivial in case of encryption since locations of files or properties remain unchanged and only their state changes. In other words, whether the encrypted entity is exported from or imported into the modeling environment, the information about encryption is always available. Conversely, signatures of modeled entities have to be created as separate files since embedding them might not always work. For instance, embedding a signature into the application's source code might result in an incorrect behavior at runtime. This leads to a requirement of generating and storing signatures in a self-contained manner when signing policies enforcement happens.

In contrast, the signature of an entire deployment model reflects a snapshot of its state at a particular point in time, e.g., when the deployment model was packaged by a certain participant. Semantically, this signature does not mean that all content of the deployment model belongs to a signing party, but only captures the state of the deployment model at export time. In our approach, we use this external signature only for integrity verification at import time, but do not explicitly store it if verification was successful. However, if stored in a centralized or decentralized manner, this type of signature might form an expressive log of all export states which can later be utilized for audit and compliance checking purposes.

D. Enforcement of Security Policies

As participants of collaboration might not know all involved parties, every side has to maintain a set of permissions for known participants, e.g., in a form similar to the access matrix

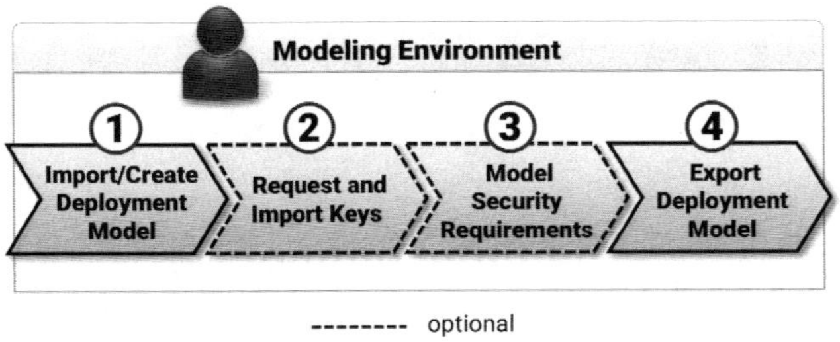

Figure 3. Actions of a collaborating participant.

model [22]. In our case, permissions have to reflect which policies are available to which participant and are therefore used for export and distribution of keys. One caveat is that in long sequences of steps there will be cases when a party does not know which rights with respect to the specific key have to be defined for some of the involved parties. The rules in such collaborations rely on various types of agreements, such as SLAs, which define the lists of trusted parties. Hence, we handle only explicitly mentioned access rights defined by participants and forbid transitive trust [38] propagation.

To enforce security policies in collaborations, participants have to follow a set of actions shown in Figure 3. A new or existing deployment model can be imported into the participant's modeling environment. Signatures are verified for an existing deployment model before import. An entire model's signature is verified first and if verification is successful, all signed entities are verified next. If certificate chains are embedded, all certificates must be valid. The import is aborted in case some signatures or certificates are invalid. Participant might request keys needed for encrypted entities and if access is granted by the key owner, keys can be imported into the modeling environment and used for decryption. The policy enforcement at export time happens transparently for participants as entities always get encrypted if the respective keys are present. Since decryption is only possible when the key is available, the encryption at export is ensured by the modeling environment.

Afterwards, participants can model additional security requirements and export a modified deployment model. One issue related to signatures and mutual modifications of the same entity is whether to keep the obsolete signature information. Since the original content of the entity has to be modified, we consider it being a new entity which can be modeled separately eliminating the problem of handling several signatures altogether. At export time, all modeled requirements are enforced with respect to the keys available in modeling environment. The decrypted data get encrypted again, in case the corresponding key is present and the entity was decrypted previously. Only signatures modeled by the participant who performs the export are generated. All entities that were signed by others remain in a self-contained state after import and thus exported in a regular fashion.

Generated signatures must be linked with corresponding modeling constructs. For instance, for every signed file the corresponding signature files must be added as additional linked references, e.g., following a predefined name format "filename#sigtype.sig". Signing properties requires a slightly different approach. Since properties are parts of artifacts and are subject to certain policies, their signatures have to be grouped with respect to the policy. This results in generation of the combined signature file and linking it with the artifact which holds the signed properties. Signature of this file is, again, generated similar to JAR files signing, but in this case the generated artifact contains the details about signed properties.

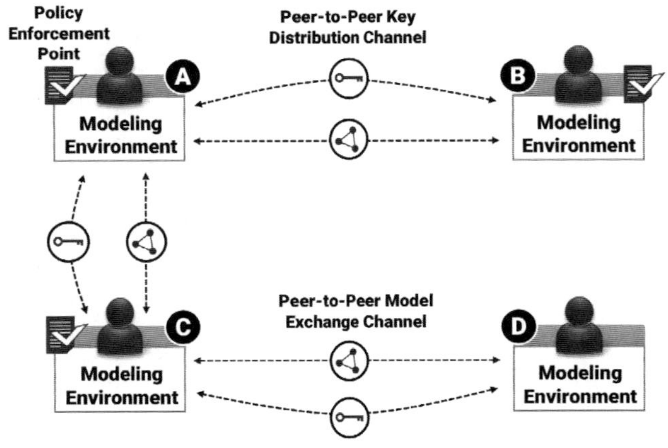

Figure 4. Model and key exchange in collaborations.

Figure 4 shows communication infrastructure for collaboration described in Section III. As key distribution is decoupled from the model exchange, two peer-to-peer channel types are distinguished. Generally, not all participants need to communicate with each other. For example, in outsourcing case, a contractor grants rights to the ordering party based on the contract rules and does not need to communicate with others. Therefore, access permissions of the ordering party have to also reflect access rules for the part of deployment model provided by the contractor. The access to encrypted data is inquired by requesting a key using the corresponding policy identifier. Without having a centralized Policy Enforcement Point (PEP) [39], [40], every participant's modeling environment acts as a separate PEP which regulates access control permissions based on inter-participant agreements. Participants are responsible for maintaining proper access control permissions including transitive cases.

V. Standards-Based Secure Collaborative Development of Deployment Models

In this section we discuss the specifics of collaborative development of deployment models using TOSCA. We analyze which TOSCA modeling constructs might require protection and describe how our concepts can be applied to this technology.

A. TOSCA Application Model

TOSCA [10] is a cloud application modeling standard which allows to automate the deployment and management of applications. The structure of a TOSCA application is characterized by descriptions of application's components with corresponding connectivity information, modeled as a directed, attributed graph which is not necessarily connected. In TOSCA terminology the entire application model is called a *Service Template*, whereas the connectivity information is a subpart of it and referred to as a *Topology Template*. The management information in TOSCA terms is called *Management Plans*. This information is necessary for execution and management of applications throughout their lifecycle and can be represented, e.g., in a form of BPEL [18] or BPMN [19] models.

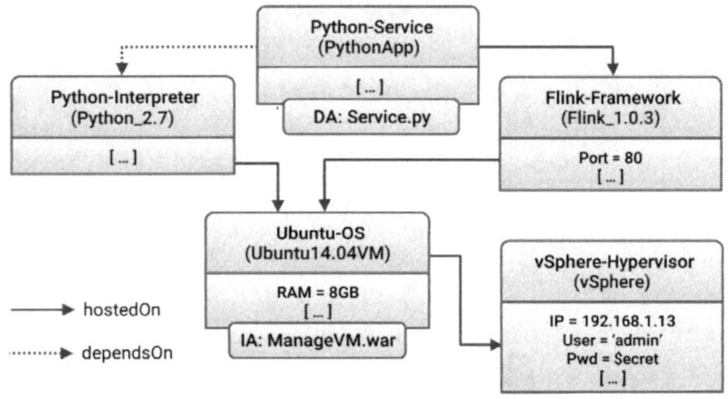

Figure 5. A simplified TOSCA model of a cloud application.

A simplified TOSCA topology of a Python cloud service [6] is shown in Figure 5. It consists of several *nodes* representing software components which are connected with directed edges describing the *relationships* among them. TOSCA differentiates between *entity types* and *entity templates*, where the term entity might refer to distinct TOSCA entities such as nodes, relationships, artifacts, or policies. Such separation eases reusing modeled TOSCA entities, since the semantics is always defined in the corresponding type. For instance, the "vSphere" in Figure 5 is called a *Node Type*. It describes a generic setup of a vSphere virtualization platform and defines all required configuration properties. Apart from defining common properties, any Node Type might provide definitions of interface operations required for managing its instances. For example, a virtual machine node might have two interface management operations, namely "start" and "stop" implemented using Java web services. Correspondingly, the "vSphere-Hypervisor" represents a particular instance of the "vSphere" *Node Type* and in TOSCA terms is referred to as a *Node Template*.

For deployment and management of the cloud service, all required artifacts have to be modeled, e.g., the application files and implementations of management interface operations. The artifact entity in TOSCA can be of two types, namely deployment artifacts (DA) and implementation artifacts (IA). The former defines an executable required for materialization of a node instance. The latter is a representation of an executable which implements a certain interface management operation.

One of the main goals of deployment models is to make cloud applications portable and reusable. For this reason TOSCA introduces a self-contained packaging format called Cloud Service Archive (CSAR). Essentially, it is an archive containing all application-related data necessary for automated deployment and management, including, e.g., the model definitions, artifact files, policies and other metadata. In addition, it contains a TOSCA.meta file which describes files in the archive similarly to a manifest file in JARs.

B. Security Requirements for TOSCA Entities

Several TOSCA modeling constructs can be associated with confidential information or be subjects to integrity checks. Modeled application files, i.e., artifacts in TOSCA terms, is one obvious example. All artifacts are always modeled as Artifact Templates of particular Artifact Type in TOSCA, e.g., a Java web application artifact is a template of Web application Archive (WAR) Artifact Type. While Artifact Type is a generic entity which does not store any sensitive data, the Artifact Templates include actual application files. However, in TOSCA specification there is no standard way to describe security requirements using policies for Artifact Templates. To provide such modeling capabilities, an extension to TOSCA is needed. Since properties are defined at the level of Types in TOSCA, e.g., Node Types, it is useful to have a mechanism allowing to enforce security requirements at this level. Semantically, this would mean that encryption or signing policies have to be applied to all Node Templates of a certain Node Type. TOSCA does not offer a standard way of attaching policies to specific properties, thus a proper way to enforce protection of properties at the level of Node Types is needed as well.

C. TOSCA Policy Extensions

To support the attachment of security policies to aforementioned TOSCA entities we introduce several extension points. All policies are defined in a dedicated extension element which belongs to a chosen entity. A simplified XML snippet in Figure 6 shows extension policies for Artifact Templates and Node Types from Figure 5. For Artifact Templates, a security policy is attached in a separate element directly to the Artifact Template. Essentially, an Artifact Template is a container grouping related files in a form of file references. We treat Artifact Templates as atomic entities meaning that policies are applied to all referenced files which makes the semantics of modeled security requirements clearer. If some referenced files need to be distributed without enforcement of policies, they can be modeled as separate Artifact Templates.

A combination of two policy types has to be defined in a dedicated extension element for encryption and signing of properties. A modeler has to specify a list of property names that must be encrypted or signed as well as to attach a corresponding action policy. These extensions allow participants to model desired security requirements for parts of the CSAR.

```
<ArtifactTemplate name="Python-Service" ...>
  <Policies>
    <Policy applied="false" name="encryption"
          policyType="csar:EncryptionPolicyType"
          policyRef="csar1:c0e9a0e7".../>
  </Policies>
  <ArtifactReferences>
    <ArtifactReference ref=".../Service.py"/>
  </ArtifactReferences>
</ArtifactTemplate>
...
<NodeType name="vSphere" ...>
  <PropertiesDefinition>...</PropertiesDefinition>
  <Policies>
    <Policy ... name="signing" .../>
    <Policy ... name="signedprops" .../>
  </Policies>
</NodeType>
```

Figure 6. Example of TOSCA extension policies specification in XML.

The introduced extensions, however, do not offer modeling capabilities for signing the entire CSAR. These two notions of integrity might contradict with each other, since a party having parts of the cloud service belonging to other parties is required to sign them as well. Hence, we separate the integrity check for a specific part of the model from an integrity check of the entire CSAR leaving the latter outside of TOSCA modeling.

The Policy Types and Templates representing action and grouping policies are lightweight. The Encryption Policy Type defines a key's hash value, an algorithm, and a key's size as its properties. In the corresponding Policy Template, these properties are populated using the respective key's data. Similarly, the Signing Policy Type has public key's hash and related certificate chain as its properties, filled in using the given key. Certificate chain can be embedded, e.g., in a form of a Privacy Enhanced Mail (PEM) encoded string in case of X509 [41] certificates. The only property defined in grouping policies is a space-separated list of property names. This Policy Type is abstract and is not directly bound to any specific entity. Therefore, the tooling is responsible for checking the consistency of specified property names in attached policies.

D. Self-Contained CSAR

Preservation of CSAR's self-containment property after enforcement of modeled policies requires embedding the signature information for artifacts and properties into the corresponding entities. More specifically, when a signature for an artifact is created, it has to be placed along with other files referenced in the artifact. For the signature of properties, one artifact containing all properties' signatures needs to be generated and attached to the corresponding Node Template. Following this approach, modeled entities remain self-contained even in case they are being reused in other Service Templates.

VI. PROTOTYPICAL IMPLEMENTATION

In this section we describe the prototypical implementation of the presented concepts. The prototype is based on the OpenTOSCA ecosystem, an open source toolchain for development and execution of TOSCA-compliant cloud applications. The OpenTOSCA ecosystem consists of such tools as Winery [42], [43], OpenTOSCA Container [13], and Vinothek [44].

Winery is the core part for implementation of the presented concepts, as most of them are coupled with the modeling process. Winery is a feature-rich modeling environment for TOSCA-compliant applications. It is written in Java programming language and uses Angular for the frontend. The prototype is open source and available via Github [45]. As discussed in Section IV, in our approach every modeler is required to use a local Winery instance due to the absence of a centralized environment. Since keys are used for enforcement of policies, Winery is extended to support key management functionalities. This includes storing, deletion, and generation of symmetric and asymmetric keys. For key storage we rely on usage of Java's Java Cryptography Extension KeyStore (JCEKS) keystore for storing all imported keys together. Assuming that Winery runs in a local and secure environment of a distinct party, publishing keys is not problematic since keys never leave the modeler's environment. This approach, however, has to be extended to support multiple-owner Winery instances. Corresponding policies are generated based on selected keys. For key distribution, a partner-wise specification of access control lists for security policies is added to Winery. Every participant needs to maintain the list of partner-specific rules negotiated by means of agreements in collaborations. Therefore, whenever a key is requested by some party, the key access rights are defined based on the local rules in Winery. All functionalities are accessible via the corresponding REST endpoints.

The prototype supports modeling of security requirements via Winery's built-in XML editors for respective TOSCA entities. Winery stores modeled TOSCA entities in a decoupled manner making a concept of CSAR important only at export or import time. At import time, CSARs are disassembled into distinct entities to prevent storing duplicates. In a similar manner, at export time CSARs are assembled from all the entities included in the chosen Service Template. This results in an issue that TOSCA meta files are not explicitly stored and are generated on-the-fly. Enforcement of modeled security policies at export time for selected TOSCA entities, e.g., Service Templates or Artifact Templates, happens in case specified keys are present in the system. Signatures for files in Artifact Templates are generated as additional files in the same Artifact Template. If the files of Artifact Templates are subjects to both, encryption and signing requirements, then the signatures of plain and encrypted files are attached. This allows verifying the integrity of target files to both, authorized and unauthorized parties. Signatures for properties are grouped as a separate Artifact Template of type "Signature" which is attached to the respective Node Template. This ensures the self-containment property of deployment models. If policies were applied, the corresponding attribute is set to signify this fact. After encryption and signing requirements are enforced, an external signature of a CSAR is generated using a so-called master key, which is specified by the modeler for the whole environment as discussed in Section IV. The corresponding certificate or chain of certificates for this external signature is embedded into the CSAR and is used for verification at import time. This signature is verified first at import time and is not stored if verification succeeds, since the CSAR is decomposed into distinct separately-stored entities. Import does not happen in case if integrity checks were not successful. In case keys requested by a modeler were provided, they can be imported and used for decryption of entities. Finally, only the modeler who has an entire set of keys is able to decrypt and deploy the final application. Deployment and execution in OpenTOSCA Container then happens in a regular manner, since the CSAR contains the original deployment model.

VII. RELATED WORK

The problem of data protection in outsourcing and collaboration scenarios appears in works related to different fields. Multiple works attempt to tackle security-related problems using centralized approaches. Wang et al. [29] present a method for protecting the models in collaborative computer-aided design (CAD), which extends RBAC mechanism by adding notions of scheduling and value-adding activity to roles. Authors propose to selectively share data to prevent reverse engineering. However, no clear description how to enforce the proposed model is given. Cera et al. [46] introduce another RBAC-based data protection approach in collaborative design of 3D CAD models. Models are split into separate parts based on specified role-based security requirements to provide personalized views using a centralized access control mechanism. Li et al. [30] propose a security policy meta-model and the framework for securing big data on the level of Infrastructure as a Service (IaaS) cloud delivery model using sticky policies concept. Policies are loosely-coupled with the data and the framework relies on a trusted party which combines policy and key management functionalities and enforces the access control. Huang et al. [47] introduce a set of measures allowing to protect patients data in portable electronic health records (EHRs). Authors propose a centralized system which combines de-identification, encryption, and digital signatures as means to achieve data privacy. Li et al. [34] describe an approach based on the Attribute-Based Encryption which helps to protect patient's personal health records in the cloud. In this approach, data is encrypted using keys that are generated based on the owner-selected set of attributes and then published to the cloud. Users can only access the data in case they possess corresponding attributes, e.g., profession or organization. More specifically, users are divided into several security domains and the attributes for these domains are managed by corresponding attribute authorities. Decryption keys, therefore, can be generated independently from data owners by the respective attribute authorities.

A number of approaches focus on the data encryption in outsourcing scenarios. Miklau and Suciu [48] introduce an encryption framework for protecting XML data published on the Internet. Contributions of the work include a policy specification language available in the form of queries and a model allowing to encrypt single XML documents. Access control is enforced based on key possession. Vimercati and Foresti [49] discuss fragmentation-based approaches for protecting outsourced relational data. The authors elaborate on several techniques allowing to split up the given data based on some constraints into one or more fragments and store them in a way to protect confidentiality and privacy. For instance, data can be split into two parts and stored on non-communicating servers. Whenever constraints cannot be satisfied for some attributes, the encryption is used. In the follow-up work, Vimercati et al. [50] present a way to enforce selective access control using the cryptography-based policies. Authors propose to use key derivation mechanisms to simplify the distribution of keys.

To the best of our knowledge, none of the discussed approaches successfully tackles our problem of deployment models protection in collaborative application development scenarios. Most of the discussed approaches rely on the idea of a trusted party which can regulate the access control. While it is desirable to have a central authority, in many cases it is unrealistic, leading to a need for peer-to-peer solutions. Moreover, having focus only on separate security requirements like encryption or strong assumptions about the underlying data make these approaches not suitable for the described problems.

VIII. Conclusion and Future Work

In this work, we showed how security requirements can be modeled and enforced in collaborative development of deployment models. We identified sensitive parts in deployment models and proposed a method which allows protecting them based on a combination of existing research work. For validation of the presented concepts, we applied them to TOSCA, an existing OASIS standard, which specifies a provider-agnostic cloud modeling language. The resulting prototypical implementation is based on the modeling environment called Winery, which is a part of the OpenTOSCA ecosystem, an open source collection of applications supporting TOSCA.

One issue in our approach that has to be optimized is the way keys are distributed. We rely on the fact, that not all participants need to exchange keys which, however, does not solve the scalability problem. If N keys were used for encryption, eventually all of them will be used in key distribution. For improving the efficiency, the key derivation techniques, e.g., described by Vimercati et al. [50], can be used to reduce the number of keys that need to be exchanged. Another problem for future work is the generalization of the adversary model. Since deployment models can be intentionally corrupted by an adversary, there is a strong need to store the provenance information which describes deployment model's states at every export with respect to certain collaboration. Having such provenance information stored in some accessible form makes it possible to track the entire collaboration history with all the deployment model states that were existing throughout the process. For this reason, one might employ a centralized system, which will also simplify the policy enforcement and key distribution processes, or store the provenance in a decentralized fashion, e.g., by utilizing the blockchain technology [51].

Finally, there is a pitfall for cases when files are modeled in a form of references, e.g., if they reside on a remote server. Encrypting and signing such files completely changes the verification semantics as only the references are checked. This is not safe since the actual content behind the reference can be changed multiple times by the data owner without changing the reference itself. Moreover, the usage of references invalidates the self-containment property of deployment models. In the future work, referenced files need to be materialized at export time which solves this problem and preserves deployment models in a self-contained state.

Acknowledgment

This work is funded by the BMWi projects *SePiA.Pro* (01MD16013F) and *SmartOrchestra* (01MD16001F).

References

[1] M. Hermann, T. Pentek, and B. Otto, "Design principles for industrie 4.0 scenarios," in 2016 49th Hawaii International Conference on System Sciences (HICSS). IEEE, 2016, pp. 3928–3937.

[2] P. M. Mell and T. Grance, "Sp 800-145. the NIST definition of cloud computing," Gaithersburg, MD, United States, Tech. Rep., 2011.

[3] L. Atzori, A. Iera, and G. Morabito, "The internet of things: A survey," Computer networks, vol. 54, no. 15, 2010, pp. 2787–2805.

[4] U. Breitenbücher et al., "Combining declarative and imperative cloud application provisioning based on tosca," in Proceedings of the IEEE International Conference on Cloud Engineering (IEEE IC2E 2014). IEEE Computer Society, March 2014, pp. 87–96.

[5] T. Kvan, "Collaborative design: what is it?" Automation in construction, vol. 9, no. 4, 2000, pp. 409–415.

[6] M. Zimmermann, U. Breitenbücher, M. Falkenthal, F. Leymann, and K. Saatkamp, "Standards-based function shipping – how to use tosca for shipping and executing data analytics software in remote manufacturing environments," in Proceedings of the 2017 IEEE 21st International Enterprise Distributed Object Computing Conference (EDOC 2017). IEEE Computer Society, 2017, pp. 50–60.

[7] G. Karjoth, M. Schunter, and M. Waidner, "Platform for enterprise privacy practices: Privacy-enabled management of customer data," in International Workshop on Privacy Enhancing Technologies. Springer, 2002, pp. 69–84.

[8] W. Bagga and R. Molva, "Policy-based cryptography and applications," in International Conference on Financial Cryptography and Data Security. Springer, 2005, pp. 72–87.

[9] A. Harrington and C. Jensen, "Cryptographic access control in a distributed file system," in Proceedings of the 8th ACM symposium on Access control models and technologies. ACM, 2003, pp. 158–165.

[10] OASIS, Topology and Orchestration Specification for Cloud Applications (TOSCA) Version 1.0, Organization for the Advancement of Structured Information Standards (OASIS), 2013.

[11] OASIS, Topology and Orchestration Specification for Cloud Applications (TOSCA) Primer Version 1.0, Organization for the Advancement of Structured Information Standards (OASIS), 2013.

[12] A. Bergmayr et al., "A systematic review of cloud modeling languages," ACM Comput. Surv., vol. 51, no. 1, Feb. 2018, pp. 22:1–22:38.

[13] T. Binz et al., "Opentosca – a runtime for tosca-based cloud applications," in Service-Oriented Computing. Berlin, Heidelberg: Springer, 2013, pp. 692–695.

[14] C. Endres et al., "Declarative vs. imperative: Two modeling patterns for the automated deployment of applications," in Proceedings of the 9th International Conference on Pervasive Patterns and Applications. Xpert Publishing Services (XPS), Feb. 2017, pp. 22–27.

[15] U. Breitenbücher, K. Képes, F. Leymann, and M. Wurster, "Declarative vs. imperative: How to model the automated deployment of iot applications?" in Proceedings of the 11th Advanced Summer School on Service Oriented Computing. IBM Research Division, Nov. 2017, pp. 18–27.

[16] Chef. [Online]. Available: https://www.chef.io/ [retrieved: July, 2018]

[17] Juju. [Online]. Available: https://jujucharms.com/ [retrieved: July, 2018]

[18] OASIS, Web Services Business Process Execution Language (WS-BPEL) Version 2.0, Organization for the Advancement of Structured Information Standards (OASIS), 2007.

[19] OMG, Business Process Model and Notation (BPMN) Version 2.0, Object Management Group (OMG), 2011.

[20] R. Boutaba and I. Aib, "Policy-based management: A historical perspective," Journal of Network and Systems Management, vol. 15, no. 4, Dec 2007, pp. 447–480.

[21] R. Wies, "Using a classification of management policies for policy specification and policy transformation," in Integrated Network Management IV. Springer, 1995, pp. 44–56.

[22] P. Samarati and S. C. di Vimercati, "Access control: Policies, models, and mechanisms," in International School on Foundations of Security Analysis and Design. Springer, 2000, pp. 137–196.

[23] S. Pearson and M. Casassa-Mont, "Sticky policies: An approach for managing privacy across multiple parties," Computer, vol. 44, no. 9, 2011, pp. 60–68.

[24] Q. Tang, On Using Encryption Techniques to Enhance Sticky Policies Enforcement, ser. CTIT Technical Report Series. Netherlands: Centre for Telematics and Information Technology (CTIT), 2008, no. WoTUG-31/TR-CTIT-08-64.

[25] B. W. Lampson, "Protection," ACM SIGOPS Operating Systems Review, vol. 8, no. 1, 1974, pp. 18–24.

[26] M. Falkenthal et al., "Opentosca for the 4th industrial revolution: Automating the provisioning of analytics tools based on apache flink," in Proceedings of the 6th International Conference on the Internet of Things, ser. IoT'16. New York, NY, USA: ACM, 2016, pp. 179–180.

[27] T. Binz, U. Breitenbücher, O. Kopp, and F. Leymann, TOSCA: Portable Automated Deployment and Management of Cloud Applications. New York, NY: Springer New York, 2014, pp. 527–549.

[28] M. Zimmermann, F. W. Baumann, M. Falkenthal, F. Leymann, and U. Odefey, "Automating the provisioning and integration of analytics tools with data resources in industrial environments using opentosca," in Proceedings of the 2017 IEEE 21st International Enterprise Distributed Object Computing Conference Workshops and Demonstrations (EDOCW 2017). IEEE Computer Society, Oct. 2017, pp. 3–7.

[29] Y. Wang, P. N. Ajoku, J. C. Brustoloni, and B. O. Nnaji, "Intellectual property protection in collaborative design through lean information modeling and sharing," Journal of computing and information science in engineering, vol. 6, no. 2, 2006, pp. 149–159.

[30] S. Li, T. Zhang, J. Gao, and Y. Park, "A sticky policy framework for big data security," in 2015 IEEE First International Conference on Big Data Computing Service and Applications (BigDataService). IEEE, 2015, pp. 130–137.

[31] T. Waizenegger et al., "Policy4TOSCA: A Policy-Aware Cloud Service Provisioning Approach to Enable Secure Cloud Computing," in On the Move to Meaningful Internet Systems: OTM 2013 Conferences. Springer, Sep. 2013, pp. 360–376.

[32] U. Breitenbücher, T. Binz, O. Kopp, F. Leymann, and M. Wieland, "Policy-aware provisioning of cloud applications," in Proceedings of the 7th International Conference on Emerging Security Information, Systems and Technologies (SECURWARE). Xpert Publishing Services (XPS), 2013, pp. 86–95.

[33] A. A. E. Kalam et al., "Organization based access control," in IEEE 4th International Workshop on Policies for Distributed Systems and Networks, 2003. Proceedings. POLICY 2003. IEEE, 2003, pp. 120–131.

[34] M. Li, S. Yu, K. Ren, and W. Lou, "Securing personal health records in cloud computing: Patient-centric and fine-grained data access control in multi-owner settings," in International conference on security and privacy in communication systems. Springer, 2010, pp. 89–106.

[35] F. Li, B. Luo, and P. Liu, "Secure information aggregation for smart grids using homomorphic encryption," in 2010 First IEEE International Conference on Smart Grid Communications (SmartGridComm). IEEE, 2010, pp. 327–332.

[36] S. Ruj and A. Nayak, "A decentralized security framework for data aggregation and access control in smart grids," IEEE transactions on smart grid, vol. 4, no. 1, 2013, pp. 196–205.

[37] Oracle. Understanding signing and verification. [Online]. Available: https://docs.oracle.com/javase/tutorial/deployment/jar/intro.html [retrieved: July, 2018]

[38] J. Huang and M. S. Fox, "An ontology of trust: formal semantics and transitivity," in Proceedings of the 8th international conference on electronic commerce: The new e-commerce: innovations for conquering current barriers, obstacles and limitations to conducting successful business on the internet. ACM, 2006, pp. 259–270.

[39] M. Falkenthal et al., "Requirements and Enforcement Points for Policies in Industrial Data Sharing Scenarios," in Proceedings of the 11th Advanced Summer School on Service Oriented Computing. IBM Research Division, 2017, pp. 28–40.

[40] F. W. Baumann, U. Breitenbücher, M. Falkenthal, G. Grünert, and S. Hudert, "Industrial data sharing with data access policy," in Cooperative Design, Visualization, and Engineering. Springer International Publishing, 2017, pp. 215–219.

[41] M. Cooper et al. Internet X.509 Public Key Infrastructure: Certification Path Building. [Online]. Available: https://tools.ietf.org/html/rfc4158 [retrieved: July, 2018]

[42] O. Kopp, T. Binz, U. Breitenbücher, and F. Leymann, "Winery – A Modeling Tool for TOSCA-based Cloud Applications," in Proceedings of the 11th International Conference on Service-Oriented Computing (ICSOC 2013). Springer, Dec. 2013, pp. 700–704.

[43] Winery. [Online]. Available: https://eclipse.github.io/winery/ [retrieved: July, 2018]

[44] U. Breitenbücher, T. Binz, O. Kopp, and F. Leymann, "Vinothek – a self-service portal for tosca," in Proceedings of the 6th Central-European Workshop on Services and their Composition (ZEUS 2014). CEUR-WS.org, Feb. 2014, Demonstration, pp. 69–72.

[45] Prototypical implementation of the secure csar concepts. [Online]. Available: https://github.com/OpenTOSCA/winery/releases/tag/paper%2Fvy-secure-csar [retrieved: July, 2018]

[46] C. D. Cera, T. Kim, J. Han, and W. C. Regli, "Role-based viewing envelopes for information protection in collaborative modeling," Computer-Aided Design, vol. 36, no. 9, 2004, pp. 873–886.

[47] L.-C. Huang, H.-C. Chu, C.-Y. Lien, C.-H. Hsiao, and T. Kao, "Privacy preservation and information security protection for patients' portable electronic health records," Computers in Biology and Medicine, vol. 39, no. 9, 2009, pp. 743–750.

[48] G. Miklau and D. Suciu, "Controlling access to published data using cryptography," in Proceedings of the 29th international conference on Very large data bases-Volume 29. VLDB Endowment, 2003, pp. 898–909.

[49] S. D. C. di Vimercati and S. Foresti, "Privacy of outsourced data," in IFIP PrimeLife International Summer School on Privacy and Identity Management for Life. Springer, 2009, pp. 174–187.

[50] S. D. C. di Vimercati, S. Foresti, S. Jajodia, S. Paraboschi, and P. Samarati, "Encryption policies for regulating access to outsourced data," ACM Transactions on Database Systems (TODS), vol. 35, no. 2, 2010, p. 12.

[51] S. Nakamoto. Bitcoin: A peer-to-peer electronic cash system. [Online]. Available: http://bitcoin.org/bitcoin.pdf [retrieved: July, 2018]

Pro-SRCC: Proxy-based Scalable Revocation for Constant Ciphertext Length

Zeya Umayya*, Divyashikha Sethia†
Department of Computer Science and Engineering, Delhi Technological University

New Delhi, India
Email: *zeyaumayya@gmail.com, †sethiadivya@gmail.com

Abstract—**Ciphertext-Policy Attribute-Based Encryption (CP-ABE) is a fine-grained encryption technique, which can provide selective access control. Although it is computationally expensive, it has been proved feasible on resource-constrained devices, such as mobile devices and Internet of Things (IoT) devices. We look into the use case of storing important information, such as health records or sensor information from such devices by the user locally or through direct selective access by various users based on their roles. It must protect the information from malicious users with the support of an efficient revocation scheme. It must provide uninterrupted access to the unrevoked users without re-encryption or redistribution of keys. In this paper, we review the Emura's constant ciphertext CP-ABE scheme, which offers the advantage of retaining constant-sized ciphertext on resource-constrained devices. We propose a novel scheme called Proxy-based Scalable Revocation for Constant Ciphertext Length (ProSRCC) to improve it for scalable revocation without re-encryption and re-distribution of keys. It uses a trusted proxy server for partial decryption and revocation of users. The paper presents ProSRCC's design and implementation on the Pairing-based cryptography (PBC) library and compares it with the Proxy based Immediate Revocation of ATTribute-based Encryption (PIRATTE) and Emura's constant length CP-ABE schemes. The results indicate that computation time for ProSRCC is least as compared to the other schemes. Hence, it is beneficial to encrypt information with ProSRCC and get constant-sized ciphertext, as well as support for scalable revocation especially on static and resource-constrained devices.**
Keywords:—**PIRATTE; CP-ABE; ProSRCC.**

I. Introduction

An Attribute-based Encryption (ABE) is an encryption scheme, where different users have specific attributes and can decrypt a given ciphertext, which is associated with an access policy of these attributes. Characteristics of a user, e.g., his name or date of birth can be used for access control of important resources and information. Schemes, such as [1] [2], are an example of the Identity-Based Encryption (IBE) scheme, which does not disclose the identity of the decryptor in any case. Canetti et al. [3] proposed the first ABE scheme inspired by IBE. In the IBE schemes, there is a one-to-one relationship between an encryptor and a decryptor and the schemes assign only one decryptor for an encryptor. Whereas the ABE schemes assign many decryptors to a single encryptor by assigning some common attributes to the decryptors, such as mail ID, gender, age and so on. The ABE schemes have two variants namely Key-Policy ABE (KP-ABE) and Ciphertext-Policy ABE (CP-ABE). The KP-ABE [1] [3] is a scheme such that it associates each user's private key with an access structure. However, in the CP-ABE schemes, an access-structure is defined for each ciphertext, which means that an encrypting party can decide who should be allowed to access the ciphertext. However, in the earlier ABE schemes [7] [8], the ciphertext length was dependent on the number of attributes present in the access structure. Also, the number of pairing computations increased with an increase in the number of attributes. Boneh et al. [4] and Katz et al. [5] presented the idea of the Predicate Encryption Scheme (PES) in which the predicates and attributes are associated with the users and ciphertexts respectively. According to Boneh et al. [4] and Katz et al. [5], PES is another variant of the CP-ABE scheme. However, both the schemes [4] [5] suffered from the problems of increase in the number of pairing computations and the length of the ciphertext with the increase in the number of attributes.

According to the survey of the existing techniques presented by Hwang et al. [6], an ideal ABE scheme must have the following capabilities:

- *Data confidentiality:* Any unauthorized participant cannot find out any information about the encrypted data.
- *Fine-grained access control:* For access control to be flexible, the access rights, even for the users of the same group, are different.
- *Scalability:* The overall performance of an ABE scheme will not go down with the total number of approved participants. Thus, we can say that an ABE scheme can deal with the case where the number of the authorized users increases dynamically.
- *Attribute or user-based revocation:* If any participant leaves the system, then his access rights will be revoked by the ABE scheme. Similarly, attribute revocation is inevitable.
- *Accountability:* In all previous the ABE schemes, the dishonest/illegal users were able to directly distribute some part of the transformed or original keys such that nobody will know the real distributor of these keys. Accountability should prevent the above problem, which is called key abuse.
- *Collusion resistance:* The unauthorized users cannot de-

crypt the secure data by combining their attributes to match the access policy.

The length of ciphertext plays an important role in any CP-ABE system. Cloud storage systems are capable of storing long ciphertexts, but for those devices where space is limited, an increase in the length of ciphertext can become a problem. Emura et al. [10] provided a solution of constant length CP-ABE scheme. The number of pairing computations also affects the time taken to either encrypt or decrypt. In the Emura et al.'s [10] scheme, the number of pairing computations is also constant for both encryption and decryption.

Revocation is an essential feature for CP-ABE schemes. According to Jiang et al. [16], revocation can be done using direct and indirect methods. The indirect methods require re-encryption of the ciphertext after revocation. Re-encryption involves the regeneration of ciphertext and secret keys. However, in the direct method, re-encryption is not necessary. There are different revocation techniques proposed to date. For resource constrained devices, re-encryption is costly and time-consuming and can interrupt the service for unrevoked users. Li et al. [18] have proposed a revocation scheme based on Emura et al.'s [10] CP-ABE scheme for both user and attributes. However, it requires re-encryption and key regeneration. Jahid et al. [19] proposed another such scheme for revocation, named Proxy based Immediate Revocation of ATTribute-based Encryption (PIRATTE). Their scheme uses a trusted proxy server and enhances the Bethencourt et al.'s [7] CP-ABE scheme. However, both the schemes suffer from the increasing ciphertext size problem. Proxy-based solutions have been proposed based on a proxy server, a third party which should be online all the time, to ensure malicious user revocation. Such schemes divide the user secret-key into two parts. The proxy server keeps a revocation list, and one part of the user secret-key to itself and the user keeps the other part. Whenever the Trusted Computing Authority (TCA) discovers a malicious user or some attributes to be revoked, it lists them in the revocation list held by the proxy server. Decryption involves two steps: First, the proxy does partial decryption using part of the key held by it. Then, the user receives this part and continues with the rest of the decryption process. The proxy causes the partial decryption to fail for revoked users and hence, they cannot decrypt the ciphertext successfully [20].

A. Contribution

- We propose a Proxy-based Scalable Revocation for Constant Ciphertext Length (ProSRCC) scheme for improving the Emura et al.'s [10] scheme for scalable revocation. A trusted proxy server calculates a partial decryption element and passes it to all users such that users in the revocation list get revoked, and the unrevoked users can decrypt without interruption. Based on this element, only the legitimate users can obtain access to the ciphertext. The ProSRCC does not require re-encryption of the ciphertext or re-distribution of the keys. The proxy server and the revocation list are enough to handle the access control.
- Experimental results and comparison of ProSRCC with the existing techniques indicate that it is an efficient and scalable revocation scheme.
- We present a Case Study using ProSRCC for resource-constrained devices with scalable revocation, such as accessing a food vending machine using the user's mobile device for allowing access to selective food items based on the user's role.

B. Organization

The rest of the paper is organized as follows. Section II discusses the related work for the previous CP-ABE schemes and revocation schemes. Section III presents the preliminary construction, some definitions and notations used in the paper. We also describe the CP-ABE scheme with constant ciphertext length in Section III. Section IV explains the proposed revocation scheme ProSRCC followed by its implementation in Section V. We present the experimental results in Section VI, which is followed by a case study on a smart food vending machine in Section VII. We finally conclude the paper in Section VIII.

II. Related Work

A. Basic CP-ABE

There are several CP-ABE schemes introduced to date. They require access policies using attributes within the encryption procedure. Sahai and Waters (SW) [7] first presented the idea of access policies over attributes. They suggest that there must be an association of both the secret keys and ciphertexts with some sets of attributes. Decryption is possible only if the secret key and ciphertext attribute set overlap each other.

Goyal et al. [1] suggested the possibility of a CP-ABE scheme, but they did not provide any constructions. In a CP-ABE scheme, every user's secret key is associated with an arbitrary number of attributes expressed as strings and the ciphertext is associated with an access structure. A user can decrypt a ciphertext, only if his attributes satisfy the access structure related to the ciphertext. Goyal et al. [11] and Liang et al. [12] use a bounded tree as access structure. Goyal et al. [11] presented a bounded CP-ABE scheme and gave an idea of generalizing the approach to show how to transform a KP-ABE scheme into an equivalent CP-ABE scheme. Ibraimi et al. [7] [13] have used the tree access structure to remove the boundary constraints presented in [11] [12] and proposed a new CP-ABE scheme without using Shamir's threshold secret sharing. Bethencourt et al. [7] provided an implementation of CP-ABE scheme and has an open source CP-ABE-toolkit.

B. CP-ABE Schemes Supporting AND Gate Access Policy

Cheung et al. [8] introduced a new CP-ABE scheme, which supports AND gate access policy with two types of attributes, positive and negative attributes. It terms the attributes, which participate in the access policy as positive terms. The scheme is secure under the standard model. For those attributes, which are not be a part of the access structure, it uses a wildcard (do not care) element. The scheme is Chosen Ciphertext Attack

(CPA) secure under the Decisional Bilinear Diffie-Hellman (DBDH) assumption. Moreover, it improves the security proof in Bethencourt et al. [7]. Unfortunately, Cheung et al.'s [8] scheme has two drawbacks. Firstly, it is not flexible enough since it supports only policies with the logical conjunction. Secondly, the size of the ciphertext and the secret key linearly increase as the number of attributes increase in this scheme. Hence, this scheme is less proficient as compared to Bethencourt et al.'s CP-ABE scheme [7].

Based on Cheung et al.'s [8] scheme, Nishide et al. [9] and Emura et al. [10] further improved the efficiency and provided hidden access policies. Nishide et al. [9] also proposed another scheme, which supported the AND gate access policy on multi-valued attributes. Emura et al. [10] have used the same access policy and further improved the scheme to achieve a constant number of bilinear pairing operations along with a constant length of ciphertext.

C. CP-ABE with Revocation

The revocation feature is essential for encryption systems to deal with the malicious behavior of users. However, addition of the revocation feature in ABE schemes is much more complicated than any public key cryptosystem or IBE schemes. The design of revocation mechanisms in previous CP-ABE schemes was difficult as users with same attributes might have been holding same user secret key.

There are two methods to realize revocation: indirect revocation method and direct revocation method. In an indirect revocation method, the owner delegates authority to execute the revocation function, which releases a key-update material after every delegation, in such a way that only non-revoked users will be able to update their keys. An advantage of the indirect revocation method is that the data owner does not need to know the revocation list. However, the disadvantage of the indirect revocation method is that all non-revoked users need communication from the respective authority at all time slots in the key-update phase. Some related attribute revocable ABE schemes, which used the indirect method, have been proposed. In the direct revocation method, the data owner performs direct revocation, which specifies the revocation list while encrypting the ciphertext. The benefit of the direct revocation method over the indirect revocation one is that there is no requirement for a key-update phase for all non-revoked users who are interacting with the authority.

Attrapadug et al. [21] first proposed a hybrid ABE (HR-ABE) scheme, which utilized the advantage of both indirect and direct methods. Jahid et al. [19] proposed a proxy-based solution for revocation scheme called Proxy-based Immediate Revocation of ATTribute-based Encryption (PIRATTE). In their scheme, the proxy is trusted minimally and also it is not able to decrypt ciphertexts on its own. The proxy has a part of the key, so each time before decryption proxy calculates a proxy data, which assists in decryption. The PIRATTE scheme provides both user and attribute-level revocation. It involves two additional costs before decryption: re-generation of the elements held by the proxy server and reconstruction of the ciphertext elements specific to the leaves in the tree access policy. The PIRATTE scheme uses the idea of re-encryption by the proxy server. However, it can revoke only a limited number of users.

In the PIRATTE scheme, the key authority generates a polynomial P of degree t over Z_p. Here, t is the maximum number of users, which can be revoked at a time. The user's secret keys are blinded with P(0). All users get a share of the polynomial P. For a revoked user, the proxy share takes its share and adds it into the proxy-key. Thus, any revoked user will not be able to get the plaintext from a ciphertext as it does not have enough points to unblind their secret key.

Sethia et al. [23] presented another novel scheme Scalable Proxy-based Immediate Revocation For CP-ABE Scheme (SPIRC) for user revocation. It improves the PIRATTE scheme for scalable user revocation. However, since it is based on Bethencourt's CP-ABE scheme [7], the length of the ciphertext is not constant.

Zhang et al. [22] have proposed a revocation technique using the subset difference scheme, which supports the attribute level revocation. In this scheme, the authors have changed the access structure completely. Instead of taking the attribute set, they have taken the set of users satisfying a subset of attributes. Their scheme ensures forward and backward secrecy. Li et al. [18] have proposed an efficient and attribute revocable scheme for cloud-based systems. They have used the same access policy as Emura et al.'s [10] scheme, which is AND-gates on multi-value attributes. Their scheme sends a key-update message to users for updating their keys. In case of user revocation, the non-revoked users must again update the authorization key, which interrupts the access.

In this paper, we propose a novel revocation scheme, which is based on Emura et al.'s [10] CP-ABE scheme. It improves it for scalable user revocation and allows uninterrupted access to non-revoked users. Hence, it can be used for direct selective access for information on resource-constrained static devices, such as a mobile-based health card or a static food vending machines.

III. PRELIMINARY CONSTRUCTION

A. Bilinear Group

Bilinear groups make the CP-ABE scheme secure against various attacks. The algebraic groups are called bilinear groups, which are groups with bilinear map.

Definition (Bilinear map). Assume $G1, G2$, and $G3$ are three multiplicative cyclic groups of prime order p. A bilinear mapping is done as follows

$e : G1 \times G2 \rightarrow G3$

e is a deterministic function; it takes one element from each group *G1* and *G2* as input, and then produces an element of group *G3*, which satisfies the following criteria:

1) *Bilinearity :* For all
$$x \in G1, y \in G2, a, b, \quad e(x^a, y^b) = e(x, y)^{ab}.$$
2) *Non degeneracy:* $e(g_1, g_2) \neq 1$ where g_1 and g_2 are generators of group G1 and G2 respectively.

TABLE I. LIST OF NOTATIONS

Notations	*Their Meaning*
PK, MK, SK_L	User's Public, Master and Secret Keys
M, C, RL	Message, Ciphertext, Revocation List
L/L_u	User attribute list associated with a user, also called user access structure
W/W_c	Access structure associated with ciphertext
$G1, G2, G3, GT$	Multiplicative cyclic groups of order p
e, g	Pairing, Generator of multiplicative cyclic group
C_{user_i}	An element computed by proxy server for the ith user to be used in decryption.
C_{attr_i}	An element computed by proxy server for the ith user to be used only in decryption.
K_{attr_i}	An element computed by key authority (KA) for the ith user to be used by proxy server.

3) *e* must be computed efficiently.

Table I defines the different notations used throughout the paper.

B. Emura et. al's Constant Ciphertext Length CP-ABE Scheme [10]

In this section we describe the basic algorithms for the different phases of the Emura et. al's [10] scheme.

- **Setup:** It takes the security parameter *K* as an input and produces two keys, a public key *PK*, and a master key *MK*.
- **KeyGen:** It takes the keys *PK*, *MK*, and a set of user attributes *L* as input and produces a user secret key SK_L associated with user's attribute list L_u.
- **Encrypt:** It takes the key *PK*, a message *M* and an access structure *W* as input. It produces a ciphertext *C* such that a user with secret key SK_L can decrypt the ciphertext *C* if $L_u \models W_c$, i.e the attribute list L_u satisfies the access structure W_c.
- **Decrypt:** It takes *PK*, ciphertext *C*, which is encrypted by W_c, and SK_L as inputs. It returns *M* if user attribute list L_u, which is associated with SK_L satisfies W_c.

1) Definition of Access Structures

Previous ABE schemes have used different variants of access structures, such as tree-based, threshold structure, linear, AND-gates with positive and negative attributes along with wild-cards and AND-gates on multi-valued attributes. This scheme uses the sum of master keys to achieve the constant ciphertext length. Hence, it uses AND-gates on multi-valued attributes. They are defined as follows:

Definition 1. Let $Univ = att_1, .., att_n$ be a set of all possible attributes. For $att_i \in Univ$, $Si = v_{i,1}, v_{i,2}, .., v_{i,n_i}$ is a set of all possible values, where n_i is the total number of possible values for att_i. Let $L_u = [L_{u1}, L_{u2}, .., L_{un}], L_{ui} \in S_i$ be an attribute list for a user, and $W_c = [W_{c1}, W_{c2}, .., W_{cn}], W_{ci} \in S_i$ be an access structure defined on a ciphertext. The notation $L_u \models W_u$ expresses that an attribute list L_u satisfies an access structure W_c , namely, $L_{ui} = W_{ci} (i = 1, 2, ..., n)$.

The number of access structures are $\prod_{i=1}^{n} ni$. For each att_i, an encryptor has to explicitly indicate a status $v_{i,*}$ from $Si = v_{i,1}, v_{i,2}, .., v_{i,n_i}$.

The access structure of our scheme ProSRCC is based on AND-gate access structure. It does not include wild-cards as it has been used in [7] [12]. In [12], an access structure W_c is defined as $W_c = [W_{c1}, W_{c2}, .., W_{cn}]$ for $W_{ci} \subseteq S_i$, and $L_u \models W_c$ is defined as $L_{ui} \in W_{ci} (i = 1, 2, ..., n)$. ProSRCC access structure is a subset of the access structures used in [7] [12]. However, even if previous CP-ABE schemes [7] [12] use AND-gate access structure with multivalued attributes, then the length of their ciphertext still depends on the number of attributes.

2) Details of the Algorithms

The details of the algorithms for the Emura et al.'s [10] scheme are:

- **Setup Algorithm**
  A Trusted Certified Authority (*TCA*) selects a prime number *p*, a bilinear group *(G1,GT)* with order *p*, a generator $g \in G1, h \in G1, y \in Z_p$ and $t_{i,j} \in_R Zp (i \in [1, n], j \in [1, n_i])$. *TCA* computes $Y = e(g, h)^y$, and $T_{i,j} = g^{t_{i,j}} (i \in [1, n], j \in [1, n_i])$. *TCA outputs* $PK = (e, g, h, Y, T_{i,j} i \in [1, n], j \in [1, n_i])$ *and* $MK = (y, t_{i,j} i \in [1, n], j \in [1, n_i])$.
  Note that we assume
  $\forall L_u, L'_u (L_u \neq L'_u), \sum_{v_{i,j} \in L_u} t_{i,j} \neq \sum_{v_{i,j} \in L'_u} t_{i,j}$.
- **Keygen Algorithm**
  KeyGen (PK, MK, L_u): The TA chooses $r \in_R Zp$, and outputs the secret key $SK_L = (h^y (g^{\sum_{v_{i,j} \in L_u} t_{i,j}})^r, g^r)$, and sends it to a user with access structure L_u.
- **Encrypt Algorithm**
  Encrypt (PK, M, W_c): An encryptor chooses $s \in_R Zp$ and computes $C1 = M.Y^s, C2 = g^s$ and $C3 = (\prod_{v_{i,j} \in W_c} T_{i,j})^s$. The encryptor outputs the ciphertext $C = (W_c, C1, C2, C3)$.
- **Decrypt Algorithm**
  Decrypt (PK, C, SK_L): Before decryption, it checks if the access structure of the user and access structure related to the ciphertext are equal or not. If they are not same, it means that particular user can not access the ciphertext. However, if they are the same then decryption is done as follows:

$$= \frac{C1.e(C3, g^r)}{e(C2, h^y.(g^{\sum_{v_{i,j} \in L_u} t_{i,j}})^r)}$$

$$= \frac{M.e(g, h)^{sy}.e(g, g)^{s.r.\sum_{v_{i,j} \in W_c} t_{i,j}}}{e(g, h)^{sy}.e(g, g)^{s.r.(\sum_{v_{i,j} \in L_u} t_{i,j})}}$$

$$= M$$

This way, the decryption of the ciphertext is successful.

IV. PROXY-BASED SCALABLE REVOCATION FOR CONSTANT CIPHERTEXT LENGTH (PROSRCC) SCHEME

In this paper, we propose a novel proxy-based scalable revocation scheme called Proxy-based Scalable Revocation for Constant Ciphertext Length (ProSRCC) scheme. It improves the Emura et al.'s [10] scheme with scalable revocation. It accomplishes revocation with the help of a trusted proxy server, which computes a proxy element to complete the decryption process. It modifies the proxy term only for a revoked unauthorized users. The ProSRCC scheme supports two types of revocation schemes attribute-based and user-based revocation.

Role of Proxy Server: In our scheme the proxy server assists in partial decryption by providing two proxy terms required to complete decryption process. The proxy server contains a list of revoked users, a list of revoked attributes and corresponding users from whom attributes have been revoked. This list is called the revocation list *RL*. The proxy server uses the list *RL* and the user's secret key to compute two components named as C_{user_i} and C_{attr_i}. It modifies the two components for revocation for a revoked user so that decryption fails. The non-revoked users can continue to access the ciphertext uninterruptedly without re-encryption or re-distribution of the keys.

The Key Authority (*KA*) handles all the attributes for a user. In case of attribute level revocation, the proxy server contacts *KA* to calculate K_{attr_i} value and uses it to compute C_{attr_i}. The proxy server does not need K_{attr_i} in case of user revocation or simple decryption for a non-revoked user. The proxy server calculates C_{user_i} and C_{attr_i} and uses it to complete the decryption process.

The setup(), keygen() and encrypt() phases are the same in all cases as similar to the Emura et al's [10] phases are discussed in the previous section.

The proxy and decrypt algorithms are different in all cases whether it is user-based revocation, attribute-based revocation or no revocation and are described in the following subsections.

A. CASE I: No Revocation

- **Proxy**
  Proxy(SK_L, RL): The proxy server computes the components C_{user_i} and C_{attr_i}.

$$C_{user_i} = (g^{\lambda}), \lambda \in RandomNumber$$
$$C_{attr_i} = h^y.(g^{\sum_{v_{i,j}\in L_u} t_{i,j}})^r.g^{\lambda}$$

  The proxy server forwards C_{user_i} and C_{attr_i} to the user for further decryption.
- **Decrypt Algorithm**
  Decrypt ($PK, C, SK_L, C_{user}, C_{attr}$): Decryption proceeds as follows:

$$= \frac{C1.e(C3, g^r)}{e(C2, C_{attr_i}/C_{user_i})}$$
$$= \frac{M.e(g,h)^{sy}.e(g,g)^{s.r.\sum_{v_{i,j}\in W_c} t_{i,j}}}{e(g^s, h^y.(g^{(r.\sum_{v_{i,j}\in L_u} t_{i,j})+\lambda}).g^{-\lambda})}$$
$$= \frac{M.e(g,h)^{sy}.e(g,g)^{s.r.\sum_{v_{i,j}\in W_c} t_{i,j}}}{e(g,h)^{sy}.e(g,g)^{s.r.(\sum_{v_{i,j}\in L_u} t_{i,j})+s(\lambda-\lambda)}}$$
$$= M$$

  Thus, the decryption of a non-revoked user is done successfully.

B. CASE II: Attribute-based Revocation

- **Proxy**
  Proxy(SK_L, RL): If attributes have been revoked for a user i then the proxy server calculates C_{user_i} and C_{attr_i} as follows: The proxy server will call the Key Authority (*KA*) to calculate the value K_{attr_i} and send it back to the proxy server. $K_{attr_i} = (g^{-r.\sum_{v_{i,j}\in RL} t_{i,j}})$
  After receiving K_{attr_i} from KA, the proxy server calculates C_{user_i} and C_{attr_i}.
  $C_{user_i} = (g^{\lambda}), \lambda \in RandomNumber$
$$C_{attr_i} = h^y.(g^{\sum_{v_{i,j}\in L_u} t_{i,j}})^r.K_{attr_i}.g^{\lambda}$$
$$= h^y.(g^{\sum_{v_{i,j}\in L_u} t_{i,j}-\sum_{v_{i,j}\in RL} t_{i,j}})^r.g^{\lambda}$$
  After calculating the components C_{user_i} and C_{attr_i}, the proxy server sends these values to the user for further decryption.
- **Decrypt Algorithm**
  Decrypt ($PK, C, SK_L, C_{user}, C_{attr}$): Decryption is performed as follows:

$$= \frac{C1.e(C3, g^r)}{e(C2, C_{attr_i}/C_{user_i})}$$
$$= \frac{M.e(g,h)^{sy}.e(g,g)^{s.r.\sum_{v_{i,j}\in W_c} t_{i,j}}}{e(g^s, h^y.(g^{(r.\sum_{v_{i,j}\in L_u} t_{i,j}-\sum_{v_{i,j}\in RL} t_{i,j})+\lambda}).g^{-\lambda})}$$
$$= \frac{M.e(g,h)^{sy}.e(g,g)^{s.r.\sum_{v_{i,j}\in W_c} t_{i,j}}}{e(g,h)^{sy}.e(g,g)^{s.r.(\sum_{v_{i,j}\in L_u} t_{i,j}-\sum_{v_{i,j}\in RL} t_{i,j})}}$$
$$\neq M$$

  It is clear from the above expression that in the denominator part, all the revoked attributes cancel out and thus numerator is not nullified by the denominator. In this way, decryption of the ciphertext fails.

C. CASE III: User-based Revocation

- **Proxy**
  Proxy(SK_L, RL): The proxy server computes the components C_{user_i} and C_{attr_i}. Suppose any user i is revoked completely then the proxy server computes the values of C_{user_i} and C_{attr_i} as follows:

$$C_{user_i} = (g^{\lambda_1}), \lambda_1 \in RandomNumber$$
$$C_{attr_i} = h^y.(g^{\sum_{v_{i,j}\in L_u} t_{i,j}})^r.g^{\lambda_2}, \lambda_2 \in RandomNumber$$

  The proxy server passes C_{user_i} and C_{attr_i} to the user i to complete the decryption process.

TABLE II. SYSTEM SETUP

Hardware Requirements	1.Disk space of 2 GB or more 2.RAM of 2048 MB or more 3.Intel Dual Core Processor of 1.7 GHz or faster
Software Requirements	1.32/64-bit Windows XP/2008/7/8 2..PBC Library [14] 3.GMP Library [25] 4.CP-ABE Toolkit

- **Decrypt Algorithm**
  Decrypt $(PK, C, SK_L, C_{user}, C_{attr})$: The decryption proceeds as follows:

$$= \frac{C1.e(C3, g^r)}{e(C2, C_{attr_i}/C_{user_i})}$$

$$= \frac{M.e(g,h)^{sy}.e(g,g)^{s.r.\sum_{v_{i,j}\in W_c} t_{i,j}}}{e(g^s, h^y.(g^{(r.\sum_{v_{i,j}\in L_u} t_{i,j})+\lambda_1}).g^{-\lambda_2})}$$

$$= \frac{M.e(g,h)^{sy}.e(g,g)^{s.r.\sum_{v_{i,j}\in W_c} t_{i,j}}}{e(g,h)^{sy}.e(g,g)^{s.r.(\sum_{v_{i,j}\in L_u} t_{i,j})+s(\lambda_1-\lambda_2)}}$$

$$\neq M$$

A revoked user cannot access the ciphertext since λ_1 and λ_2 do not cancel each other and this causes the decryption to fail.

V. IMPLEMENTATION

We have implemented the ProSRCC algorithm with the setup given in Table II.

We have first implemented the CP-ABE scheme with AND-gate access policy and revocation scheme using the CP-ABE toolkit. All pairing based operations have been implemented using the PBC library [14] and the GMP library [25]. The PBC library is the backbone of all pairing based crypto-systems. The PBC library uses the GMP library internally for performing on signed integers and floating-point numbers. We have implemented both the Emura et. al's scheme [10] and our proposed scheme ProSRCC using the PBC library. Secion VI discusses the evaluation of their performance.

VI. EXPERIMENTAL RESULTS AND ANALYSIS

We compare our scheme with Jahid et al.'s [19] PIRATTE scheme and Li et al.'s [18] schemes. We compare our proposed revocation scheme with the other revocation schemes for the access policy used, the time taken in encryption and decryption, scalability and security features. The scheme given by Jahid et al. [19] is a proxy-based scheme. The scheme proposed by Li et al. [18] is a multi-authority scheme for cloud servers and enhances Emura et al.'s [10] CP-ABE scheme with scalable revocation.

A. Access policy

Access policy is the combination of attributes, which allows decryption of a document. Jahid et al.'s [19] scheme use the same tree access structure as used in the Bethencourt et al.'s [7] scheme. Table III shows the comparison of the access policies.

TABLE III. ACCESS POLICY

Scheme	*Access policy used*
Bethencourt et al. [7]	Tree-based Access Structure
Jahid et al. [19]	Tree-based Access Structure
ProSRCC	AND-gates on multi-valued attributes
Li et al. [18]	AND-gates on multi-valued attributes

B. Size of Each Entity

We compare the sizes for various entities such as PK, MK, SK, and ciphertext in terms of the elements of a bilinear group. Table IV illustrates the comparison between the different schemes. Here n is the number of attributes. The ciphertext for Jahid et al.'s [19] scheme depends on the total number of attributes present in the access policy, whereas in the case of the ProSRCC and Li et al.'s [18] schemes the size of the ciphertext is constant. If number of attributes = 9, then size of each value will be as given in Table V.

C. Computational Overhead

Computational overhead is shown in the form of group operation and pairing operation in Table VI. Jahid et al. [19] does more number of group operations and pairing computations as compared to ProSRCC and Li et al. [18] in encryption and decryption.

D. Running Time

We have implemented the schemes and measured the actual time taken by the encryption and decryption processes as given in Table VII. The ProSRCC scheme provides scalable revocation with a constant-sized ciphertext. The encryption times are much less as compared to Jahid et al.'s [19] scheme for the same number of attributes.

E. Comparison of Features Provided by Different Schemes

Different features of the attribute based encryption schemes like- revocation, scalability and size of ciphertext have been compared in Table VIII.

Our scheme is efficient from Jahid et al.'s [19] scheme in that the length of the ciphertext and the costs for decryption does not depend on the number of attributes. Especially, the number of pairing computations is constant. AND-gates on multi-valued attributes makes the access structure, a subset of the access structures presented in [9]. Our scheme is better than the scheme provided by Li et al. [18] because, in this scheme, the user secret key is updated each time attribute-based revocation occurs. However, in our scheme whenever any number of attributes are revoked from any user, it is added to the revoked list and is maintained and taken care by the proxy server.

TABLE IV. SIZE OF EACH ENTITY

Scheme	*PK*	*MK*	*SK*	*Cipher-text*
Jahid et al. [19]	3G1 + GT	Zp + G	(2n+1)G1	(2n+1)G1 + GT
ProS-RCC	(2n+1)G1 + GT	(n+1)Zp	2 G1	2G1 + GT
Li et al. [18]	(2n+1)G1 + GT	(n+1)Zp	(n+1)G1	2G1 + GT

TABLE V. SIZE OF EACH ENTITY WITH NUMBER OF ATTRIBUTES=9

Scheme	*PK*	*MK*	*SK*	*Ciphertext*
Jahid et al. [19]	3G1 + GT	Zp+G	19G1	19G1 + GT
ProSRCC	19G1 + GT	10Zp	2G1	2G1 + GT
Li et al. [18]	19G1 + GT	10Zp	10G1	2G1 + GT

F. Performance graph

The performance graphs in Figures 1, 2 and 3 illustrate the time required by the different schemes by Jahid et. al. [19], Emura et al. [10] CP-ABE and ProSRCC our proposed revocation scheme for key generation, encryption, and decryption respectively. Key-generation time and encryption time for Jahid et al. [19] and the original CP-ABE scheme [7] are almost same. Only decryption time differs from the original CP-ABE scheme. Hence, we compare the performances of Jahid et al.'s [19] PIRATTE scheme, Emura et al.'s [10] scheme without revocation and our revocation scheme ProSRCC.

It is clear from figure 1 that the time taken by Jahid et al. [19] scheme to generate the private key is high as compared to the Emura et al.'s [10] and our proposed schemes. Initially, our scheme is taking less time to generate the private keys as compared to the Emura et al.'s scheme [10]. However, after 6-7 attributes time taken to generate keys is increased. Figure 2 shows that Jahid et al.'s [19] scheme takes more time for encryption as compared to Emura et al.'s [10] and our scheme. In case of decryption initially, Jahid et al. [19] scheme is taking less time as compared to Emura et al. [10] and our scheme. However, after 3-4 attributes time is increasing almost linearly, and it is more as compared to Emura et al.'s [10] and our scheme.

G. Security Features of Our Scheme

Our scheme is secure against following attacks

1) *Collusion resistant:* For every user, their secret key is blinded by a secret number r, so two users can never collude to decrypt a ciphertext.
2) *Chosen ciphertext attack (CCA):* According to the selective security game for CP-ABE, as explained by Emura et al. [10], adversary sends the challenge access structure *W* to the challenger. As a result, the challenger replies with *PK*. Then adversary submits an attribute list L to the challenger, where $L \neq W$. The challenger gives the corresponding secret key. Adversary further submits an encrypted text *C*, for which access structure is *W*. The challenger replies with the decrypted plaintext *M*. After the completion of this phase, adversary now gives *M0* and *M1*, two equal length messages to the challenger. The challenger is free to choose either *M0* or *M1* and then runs the encryption algorithm on the chosen plaintext and gives it to the adversary. Now the adversary can submit multiple keygen queries to get the secret keys related to the various set of the attributes list. Each time, it generates the secret key with a different random number *r*, which blinds the key, so adversary will not be able to guess the secret key even in a brute-force manner. In case of revocation, the problem is still the same, so the adversary will not be able to guess or compute the secret key.
3) *Chosen plaintext attack (CPA):* It is CPA secure because it links each ciphertext with a different secret key *s*. The selective game for CPA security eliminates the decryption queries; rest is same as in the Chosen-ciphertext attack(CCA) secure selective game. The adversary submits the keygen queries and gives the plaintext to encrypt. It repeats the process several times. However, each time it encrypts the ciphertext with a different random number *s*; it blinds the new ciphertext *s*. Moreover, it also blinds each secret key *SK* by a new random number *r*, so the secret key can also not be guessed. As explained in Section IV that finding the value of x in g^x is a computationally hard problem.
4) *Forward secrecy:* It is secure because for each different ciphertext secret key is different, this means that compromise of one message cannot jeopardize others as well, and there is no one secret value for encryption whose acquisition would compromise multiple messages.

TABLE VI. COMPUTATIONAL OVERHEAD

Scheme	*Encryption time*	*Decryption time*
Jahid et al. [19]	(n+1)G1 + nG2 + GT	2GT + nG2
ProSRCC	(n+1)G1 + 2G2	2GT + 2G2
Li et al. [18]	3G1	3GT

TABLE VII. RUNNING TIME

Scheme	*Encryption time*	*Decryption time*
Jahid et al. [19]	0.36sec	0.08sec
ProSRCC	0.0605sec	0.042sec

VII. CASE STUDY: SELECTIVE FOOD TOKEN VENDING MACHINE

As traditional mobile phones have evolved into smart mobile phones, vending machines have also developed into smart vending machines, though at a much slower pace. Newer technologies, such as the Internet connectivity, different types

TABLE VIII. FEATURE COMPARISON

Scheme	*Revocation*	*Scalability*	*Constant Length Ciphertext*
CP-ABE [7]	✗	✗	✗
EMURA [10]	✗	✓	✓
PIRATTE [19]	✓	✗	✗
SPIRC [23]	✓	✓	✗
ProSRCC	✓	✓	✓

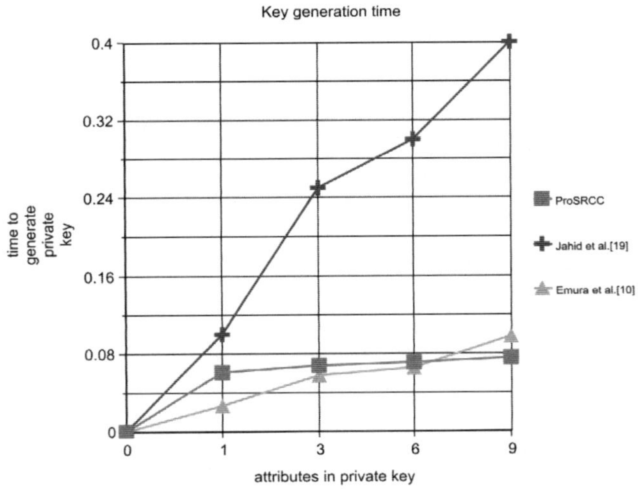

Figure. 1. Key generation time

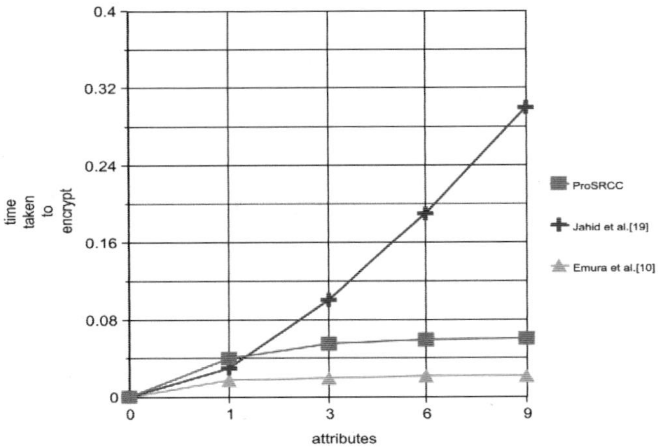

Figure. 2. Encryption time

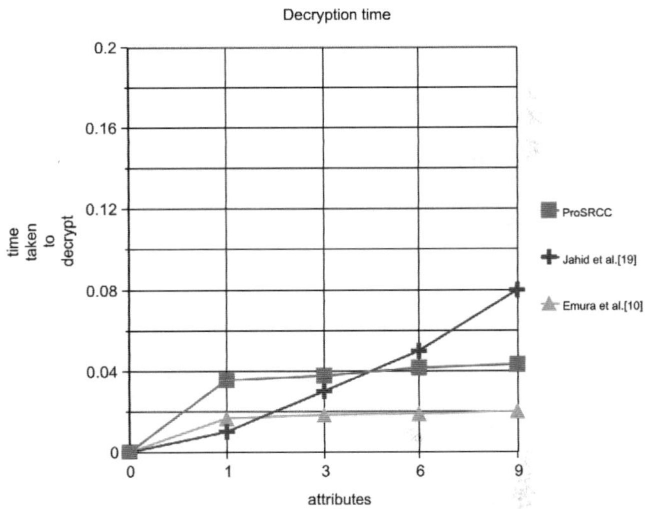

Figure. 3. Decryption time

of cameras and sensors, advanced payment systems, and a wide range of identification technology, such as Near-Field Communication (NFC) and Radio-frequency identification(RFID) [23] [24] have been an important part in this development. Such smart vending machines provide a more user-friendly experience and further reduce the operating costs thus improving the performance of the vending operations using remote manageability and intelligent back-end algorithms. These smart vending machines can be used easily as a selective access control systems.

Consider a token vending machine installed in a company's office as shown in Figure 4. A food token vending machine is such type of machine, which provides the tokens based on the level of an employee. The mode of payment can be coins or smart cards. It provides many types of tokens, e.g., T1, T2, and T3. However, it provides a different type of token for a different level of employee, and there can be a large number of tokens. The food vending machine accepts a smart card/ID card of an employee. Based on their work-level, each employee's card has different attributes, which make their secret key. Once an employee inserts his card to the token vending machine, it reads the secret key. Based on their secret key, a certain menu is shown on the screen. The menu can be reading by partial decryption process on the machine and the proxy server. The proxy then checks its revocation list and computes C_{user_i} and C_{attr_i} elements and passes to the in-built decryption process. Then the decryption process finds the value of *M* (here type of *M* is the type of food token, e.g., *T1*, *T2*, and *T3*). If M matches to any token type value *M*, it provides that type of token. Otherwise, the machine prints an appropriate message on the screen. The vending machine is shared by number of people and provides beverages on a selective basis. The ProSRCC scheme is suitable to encrypt the menu. It is based on Emura et. al's CP-ABE scheme [10] and hence the ciphertext will be constant in size so that minimal storage is required on the vending machine. Also, the ProSRCC scheme provides scalable revocation of users so that the vending machine can be used uninterrupted by other valid users.

The values of *T1*, *T2*, and *T3* are pre-calculated as an encrypted ciphertext. The proxy can communicate with the server having information about the employee and their work-level. Suppose an employee leaves the company, another employee

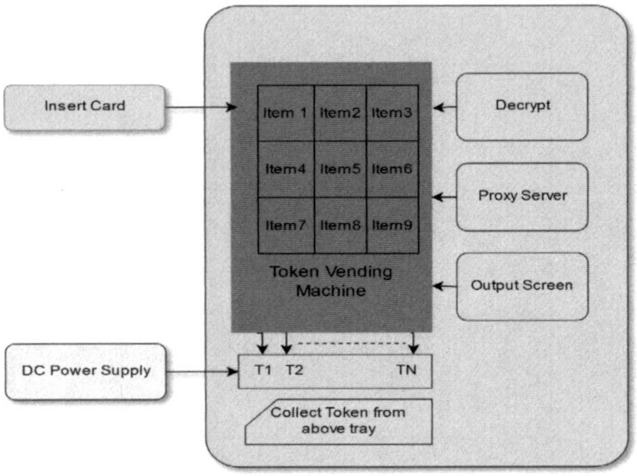

Figure. 4. Selective Food Token Vending Machine

wants to use his card. In this case, the proxy server will deny access because when an employee leaves the company, his id is then added to the revoked user list, resulting in the denial of service. The other non-revoked users can access the vending machine uninterruptedly without any requirement of re-encryption of re-distribution of keys.

Whenever the food items are updated, the food token vending machine also updates itself. Each time an employee is promoted or demoted from his work-level, an update is made in the revocation list by the proxy server. The changes made by the proxy server are reflected while providing the food token to an promoted/demoted employee of the company.

VIII. Conclusion

Revocation mechanism is an important feature of any encryption system to administer the malicious behavior of its users and to provide the selective access to its users based on their attributes. For such a system to work in a resource-constrained device, our scheme ProSRCC provides scalable revocation feature with constant ciphertext length. It is an improvement over Emura et al.'s [10] scheme as their scheme does not provide revocation feature. Li et al. [18] propose a revocation scheme for Emura et al.'s [10] scheme. However, it lacks scalable revocation. The ProSRCC scheme is secure as compared to the other schemes. Our scheme is secure against CPA and CCA attacks, and it is also collusion resistant. It is scalable as compared to Jahid et al.'s [19] PIRATTE scheme because the number of attributes revoked in our scheme is not limited. In the the PIRATTE scheme it is limited to t users(t represents the polynomial's degree used in the scheme). It provides the revocation feature, but ciphertext length is not constant. Thus, ProSRCC can provide selective access from a stationary device used for sharing selective data to multiple users by supporting optimized ciphertext length and scalable revocation feature.

References

[1] D. Boneh and M. K. Franklin, "Identity-based encryption from the Weil pairing," SIAM J. Comput., vol. 32, no. 3, pp. 586-615, 2003.

[2] X. Boyen and B. Waters. "Anonymous hierarchical identity-based encryption (without random oracles),"CRYPTO, pages 290-307, 2006.

[3] R. Canetti, S. Halevi, and J. Katz. "Chosen-ciphertext security from identity-based encryption,"EUROCRYPT, pp. 207-222, 2004.

[4] D. Boneh and B. Waters. "Conjunctive, subset, and range queries on encrypted data,"TCC, pp. 535-554, 2007.

[5] J. Katz, A. Sahai, and B. Waters. "Predicate encryption supporting disjunctions, polynomial equations, and inner products,"EUROCRYPT, pp. 146-162, 2008.

[6] C. Lee, P. Chung, and M. Hwang, "A survey on attribute-based encryption schemes of access control in cloud environments,"International Journal of Network Security, vol-15, no. 4, pp. 231-240, 2013.

[7] J. Bethencourt, A. Sahai, and B. Waters, "Ciphertext-policy attribute-based encryption,"IEEE Symposium on Security and Privacy, pp. 321-334,2007.

[8] L. Cheung and C. Newport, "Provably secure ciphertext-policy ABE,"ACM Conference on Computer and Communications Security, pp. 456-465,2007.

[9] T. Nishide, K. Yoneyama, and K. Ohta, "Attribute-based encryption with partially hidden encryptor-specified access structures,"Springer Applied Cryptography and Network Security, pp. 111-129, 2008.

[10] K. Emura, A. Miyaji, K. Omote, A. Nomura, and M. Soshi, "A ciphertext-policy attribute-based encryption scheme with constant ciphertext length,"International Journal of Applied Cryptography, vol. 2, no. 1, pp. 46-59, 2010.

[11] V. Goyal, A. Jain, O. Pandey, and A. Sahai, "Bounded ciphertext policy attribute-based encryption,"Springer Automata, Languages, and Programming Lecture Notes in Computer Science, vol. 5126, pp. 579-591, 2008.

[12] X. Liang, Z. Cao, H. Lin, and D. Xing, "Provably secure and efficient bounded ciphertext policy attribute-based encryption,"ACM conference of International Symposium on ACM Symposium on Information, Computer and Communications Security, pp. 343-352, 2009.

[13] L. Ibraimi, Q. Tang, P. Hartel, and W. Jonker, "Efficient and provable secure ciphertext-policy attribute-based encryption schemes,"Springer Information Security Practice and Experience, pp. 1-12, 2009.

[14] PBC Library: https://crypto.stanford.edu/pbc/, Last accessed July 29,2018

[15] CP-ABE Toolkit- http://acsc.cs.utexas.edu/cpabe/,Last accessed July 29,2018

[16] L. Pang, J. Yang, and Z. Jiang, "A Survey of Research Progress and Development Tendency of Attribute-Based Encryption," The Scientific World Journal, vol. 2014, 13 pages, 2014.

[17] Software used to create graph https://nces.ed.gov/nceskids/createagraph/default.aspx?ID=6499c61b86e443359920ad4fa9c65166 Last accessed July 29,2018

[18] X. Li, S. Tang, L. Xu, H. Wang, and J. Chen, "Two-Factor Data Access Control With Efficient Revocation for Multi-Authority Cloud Storage Systems,"Journal of IEEE Access, pp. 1-1. 10, 2016.

[19] S. Jahid and N. Borisov. "Piratte: Proxy-based immediate revocation of attribute-based encryption." arXiv preprint arXiv:1208.4877, 2012.

[20] Y. Imine, A. Lounis, and A. Bouabdallah, "Immediate attribute revocation in decentralized attribute-based access control,"IEEE conference of Trustcom/BigDataSE/ICESS, pp. 33-40. IEEE, 2017.

[21] N. Attrapadung and H. Imai, "Attribute-based encryption supporting direct/indirect revocation modes,"Springer International Conference on Cryptography and Coding, pp. 278-300, 2009.

[22] R. Zhang, L. Hui, S. Yiu, X. Yu, Z. Liu, Z. L. Jiang, "A Traceable Outsourcing CP-ABE Scheme with Attribute Revocation,"IEEE conference Trustcom/BigDataSE/ICESS, pp. 363-370, 2017

[23] D. Sethia, H. Saran, and D. Gupta, "CP-ABE for Selective Access with Scalable Revocation: A case study for Mobile-based Healthfolder,"International Journal of Network Security, Vol.20, No.4, pp.689-771, 2018.

[24] V. Coskun, B. Ozdenizci, and K. Ok, "A Survey on Near Field Communication (NFC) Technology," Springer Wireless Personal Communications, Vol.71, No.0, pp.2259-2294, 2013.

[25] The GNU Multiple Precision Arithmetic Library: https://gmplib.org/, Last accessed July 29,2018

A Logic-Based Network Security Zone Modelling Methodology

Sravani Teja Bulusu, Romain Laborde, Ahmad Samer Wazan, Francois Barrère, Abdelmalek Benzekri Authors
IRIT / Université Paul Sabatier, Toulouse, France
sbulusu@irit.fr, laborde@irit.fr, ahmad-samer.wazan@irit.fr, francois.barrere@irit.fr, abdelmalek.benzekri@irit.fr

Abstract— **Network segmentation and security zone modelling is a best practice approach, widely known for minimizing the risks pertaining to the compromise of enterprise networks. In this paper, we propose a security zone modelling methodology, which automates the process of security zone specification using a definite set of formalized rules. It mainly helps to derive network security requirements based on the Clark-Wilson lite formal model. We illustrate our methodology using an example case study of e-commerce enterprise network infrastructure.**

Keywords- Network Security requirements; Security zoning.

I. INTRODUCTION

Over the past years, the growing dependency of the business-critical applications and processes on network technologies and services, has expanded the threat landscape to a large extent. Today, networks constitute the main vector as well as the convenient platform, to launch attacks against organizations. An inadequate network security design can lead to data loss in spite of the monitored traffic, and security incidents handling. In addition adds overhead in terms of time, effort, and costs.

The current practice for eliciting and analyzing early network security requirements is driven by security zoning, a well-known defense in depth strategy for network security design [1]. Security zones constitute the logical grouping of security entities that are identified with similar protection requirements (e.g., data confidentiality and integrity, access control, audit, logging, etc.). Each security zone is identified with different trust levels, which exhibit the rigor of required protection. Determining security zones and respective trust levels is a preliminary step for security architects in capturing other network security requirements (e.g., related to data flows), and later in selecting the right network security controls/mechanisms (such as VPN, IP Firewall, etc.).

In this regard, several works, theories, and best practice approaches are available, explaining on various zone classification schemes and patterns [2]–[4]. Nevertheless, there there exists no standard methodology that can drive the specification of zones for a given infrastructure. In practice, the design of the security zone model is manual and depends on the expertise of the security architects who may forget some details while specifying the zone model. Given this situation, how to How to ensure that the proposed network segmentation is correct and cost-effective? How to ensure that no network security requirement is missing or irrelevant?

In this paper, we propose a security zone modelling methodology, which automates the process of security zones specification using a definite set of formalized rules, thereby leaving less space to any manual errors. It helps in deriving network security requirements based on the Clark-Wilson lite formal security model for integrity. We illustrate our methodology using an example case study of e-commerce enterprise network infrastructure.

The rest of this paper is organized as follows. Section II briefs the literature study on zone modelling. Section III describes the example case study. Section IV details the strategy our zone modelling methodology. Section V includes a discussion of proposed methodology. Finally, Section VI concludes this article.

II. RELATED WORKS

From our literature study, we noticed limited works concerning network security zones in academic sector [5], [6]. Majority of the existing works are found to be from industrial/government sectors [2]–[4], which mainly focus on providing foundational best practice guidelines, and reference modelling patterns, for building secured networks. In this section, we confine our discussion to these reference models. From a broad view, these reference models propose minimum set of zones as well as inter/intra zone interactions rules necessary to be implemented, for achieving basic logical network security design.

For instance, the British Columbia model [4] describes seven zones and allows communication inside the zones and only between adjacent zones. Secure Arc [3] defines eight zones. It also add a parallel cross-zones segmentation concept, called silos, see Figire1. Communications are allowed only between adjacent zones and within the same silo, or between adjacent silos within the same zone. The aim is to limit the interaction between the zones to only dedicated traffic even though they are adjacent to each other. Besides, there exists no restriction on either the number of zones or their category types, as they depend on the size and type of the business. Some of the commonly identified network zones include internet zone, demilitarized zones, etc. Internet zone, by default, is assumed as extremely hostile and least trusted, as it is publicly accessible to everyone including the anonymous threat actors. The Enterprise zone and restricted zone contain the set of security entities (e.g., users, desktops, servers, etc.) that are part of the enterprise. Sensitive assets are confined to highly restricted zones. The demilitarized zone (DMZ) is the intermediate zone that usually sits between the trusted and less trusted zone in order to reduce attacks surfaces. The extranet zone contains trust security entities that belong to an external third-part domain (e.g., external internet service provider). Finally, the management zone constitutes of entities that are involved in security management activities such as monitoring, and administering the zones and their interactions. Likewise, different patterns propose different set of zones and interaction rules for zone interactions. The communication between zones are monitored and controlled by some security measures (e.g., a firewall, a gateway, etc.).

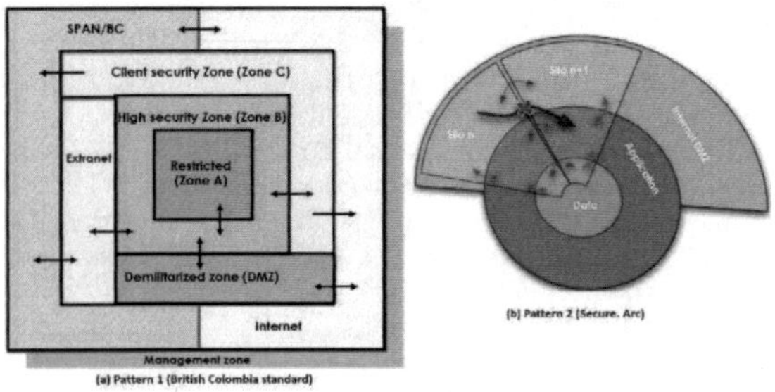

Figure 1. Example zone reference models [3], [4]

In academic sector, *Gontarczyk et al.* [6] proposed a standard blue-print that includes three classes of security zone (no physical measures, limited physical measures, and strong physical measures). It also provides a classifier to guide the deployment of systems/applications. *Ramasamy et al* [5] proposed a bottom-up approach for discovering the security zone classification of devices in an existing enterprise network. However, these documents are only guidelines and must be manually adapted. As a consequence, they exists no rigorous methodology to help security architects in validating their network security requirements.

III. EXAMPLE CASE STUDY

To illustrate our methodology implementation, we consider an e-commerce enterprise network case study [7]. The initial network architecture, as given in Figure 2 (a), consists of server components such as such as WEB server, DNS server, Application server, Database server, and the Accountability server.

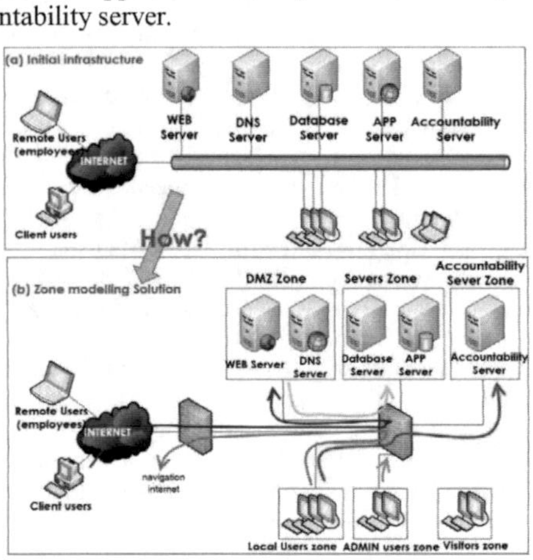

Figure 2. e-commerce example case study [7]

The employees are distinguished as administrators and standard users, who can connect to the network through LAN or WIFI. If the employees are outside the enterprise, they can remotely connect to the enterprise network. The Accountability server is said to be highly critical as it manages the financial information of the company (e.g., salaries of employers). Finally, when the clients visit the enterprise, they are allowed to connect to WEB through WIFI. Figure 2(b) depicts an example of zone modelling solution proposed by the network architects of the enterprise. It is evident that the solution reflects some best practice guidelines by defining some zones such as DMZ zone, user's zones, etc.

For instance, the Accountability server is isolated in a separate zone as it is critical. Comparatively, the application and data base servers are less critical, but cannot be exposed to Internet. Likewise, the arguments can be subjective, referring to the criticality of the assets and their risk impact, if compromised. However, how did the architects arrive to this solution (from the initial architecture in Figure 2(a) to Figure 2(b)? How can security architect demonstrate the correctness of the final security architecture? In this regard, a formal approach justifying the transition from the problem to the solution is required, for a traceable and verifiable security zone specification process.

IV. THE PROPOSED METHODLOGY - STRATEGY

The principle motivation of our work is to propose a generic methodology that can drive the specification of network security zones, with respect to the business interaction needs. The conception of our methodology commenced with an idea of merging the concepts of trust and criticality, using the integrity property. The reason behind choosing integrity is fundamental. According to the oxford dictionary, integrity from computer science perspective is defined as "*Internal consistency or lack of corruption in electronic data*", whereas integrity of humans is defined as the "*The quality of being honest*".

For example, consider that we are reading a scientific article published as a security conference. In this case, we expect the information contained in this article to be scientifically true, because the content of each article is validated by reviewers, who are recognized in the domain of security. Contrarily, we can't have the same expectation for scientific articles published in teenager blogs since there is no content validation. The information available in the blog is not necessarily wrong. It just means that the readers do not have the same level of assurance. Scientific articles published in the security conferences are more trustful than those published in teenager blogs. Integrity is thus related to trust when considering the external or unmanaged systems. Likewise, integrity is also related to risk. A critical system must be consistent, « honest », which means it requires high level of integrity. In addition, systems take decisions based on information (e.g. a program executes an algorithm based on its inputs). If input information is wrong, then decisions can be wrong too. Therefore, we will only permit critical system to consider information with high level of integrity (i.e. high level of assurance). Hence, integrity is a pivot concept between trust and risk.

In practice, there exists several models for integrity such as Biba [8], clark-wilson [9], which propose abstract solutions to preserve the integrity of information flows. These models are widely used in current operating systems for improving the integrity protection of the information flows in inter-process communications (e.g., Microsoft Windows Integrity Mechanism [10]). In our methodology, we propose to integrate these formal integrity security concepts to security zone modelling design principles, for addressing the risks pertaining to traffic flows. We adapt the concepts of Clark-Wilson lite [11] model (lighter version of clark-wilson model), for verifying the integrity property of traffic flows traversing multiple zones. In below, we briefly discuss the underlying concepts of our methodology.

A. *Security domains, security zones and agents*

To facilitate the integration of security zoning concepts to our network requirement analysis context, we mainly consider three elements: domains, zones and agents. A security domain represents the organizational authority, which controls and manages the entities (i.e., servers, software, data, users, etc.) that belong to it. We call these entities as agents. Furthermore, a security domain can be refined into sub-domains highlighting different policies or procedures within the same organization. Agents are categorized into two groups. System agents refer to entities under direct control such as software/hardware systems that are developed and/or maintained by the enterprise. Environment agents are not under direct control and refer to humans, or to some purchased third party software/hardware. Finally, security zones constitute logical grouping of agents with common protection requirements.

B. *Integrity levels*

To facilitate the integration risk analysis concepts to our network requirement analysis context, we consider a unified scale of integrity levels for all the domains, zones and agents which is determined based on risk analysis. Figure 3(b) shows some hypothetical scales, assumed for the case study.

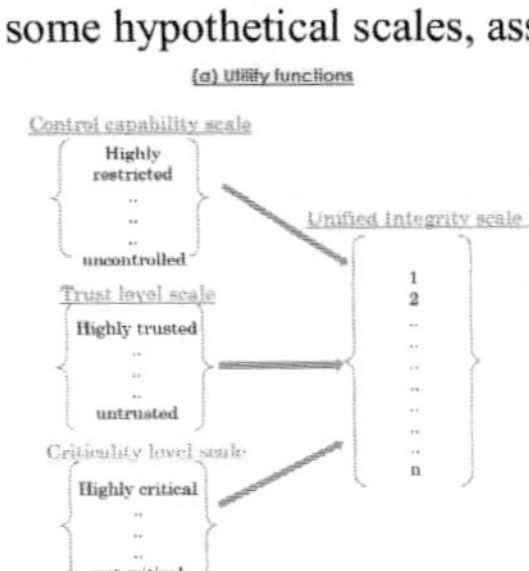

(b) Integrity levels of domains and agents for case study

Domain	Control capability	Integrity
Enterprise internal sub- domain	Highly restricted	5
Enterprise external sub-domain	Less controlled	2
internet	uncontrolled	1
System agents	**Criticality**	**Integrity**
WEB server	Partially critical	3
DNS server	Partially critical	3
APP sever	Partially critical	3
Database server	Critical	4
Accountability server	highly critical	5
Environment agents	**Trust**	**Integrity**
Admin user	highly trusted	4
Local user	trusted	3
visitor	Partially trusted	2
Remote user	Partially trusted	2
Client user	not trusted	1

Figure 3. Integrity values of domains and agents for the example case study

The integrity level of a domain is defined based on its *control capability* that describes the potential of a domain for controlling its agents. For instance, a well-controlled domain means that the security management activity within the domain is mature. In our scenario, the enterprise domain is divided into two sub-domains (see Figure 4). The *internal sub-domain* consists in the assets within enterprise premises and the *external sub-domain* is the remote users. Likewise, the integrity levels of *environment agents* are determined based on their *trust levels*. Trust level in general, specifies the degree of the trustworthiness over the expected behavior of environment agents in a given context. Since remote users are not in controlled domain, remote users are less trusted than local users.

Finally, the integrity level of *system agents* are determined based on their *criticality levels*. Criticality level determines the sensitivity to threats and their risk impact on the overall business. Here, the accountability server being highly critical requires a high level of integrity. On the other hand, the WEB server is considered less critical for business, which means it doesn't require as many as integrity requirements.

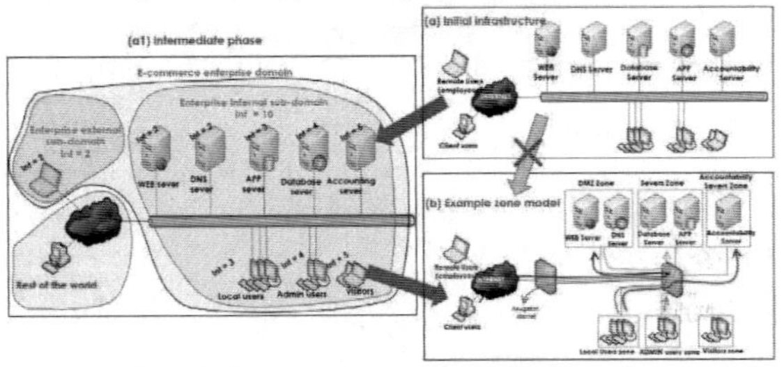

Figure 4. Our methodology conceptual initialization

Furthermore, in our methodology context, we assume the existence of some utility functions (Figure 3(a)) that map the control capability labels of domains, criticality and trust levels of agents into a unified scale of integrity levels. For instance, IEC 61508 [12] defines safety integrity levels (SIL) based on controllability of the system from the risk of failures. Similar, these utility functions must be determined based on business risk impact, which is a pre-requisite to define zone model [4].

C. *The Clark-Wilson lite model*

Finally, to introduce the security verification on data flow, we validate that the integrity of the information flow is respected. According to CW-lite integrity model [11], all information flowing from untrusted subjects to trusteed subjects must be filtered. Here the trust of the subjects are represented with integrity levels. The filter is placed at the receiving subject's side. Figure 5 shows the formal rule.

$$flow(s_i, s, I) \wedge \neg filter(s, I) \rightarrow (int(s_i) \geq int(s))$$

Figure 5. CW-lite security filtering rule [11]

This predicate should be read as follows: "if a subject s receives an information flow from a subject s_i at interface I, then either there is an integrity validation filter at interface I or the integrity level of s_i is greater or equal to the integrity of subject s". Here, the integrity validation filters correspond to security verification procedures (e.g., a WEB application firewall that checks SQL statements or URL formats).

V. PROPOSED METHODOLOGY

Our zone modelling methodology (see Figure 6) is divided into two main steps: (1) Determining the security zones and integrity validation filters and (2) Identifying data flows integrity requirements and flows access control filters.

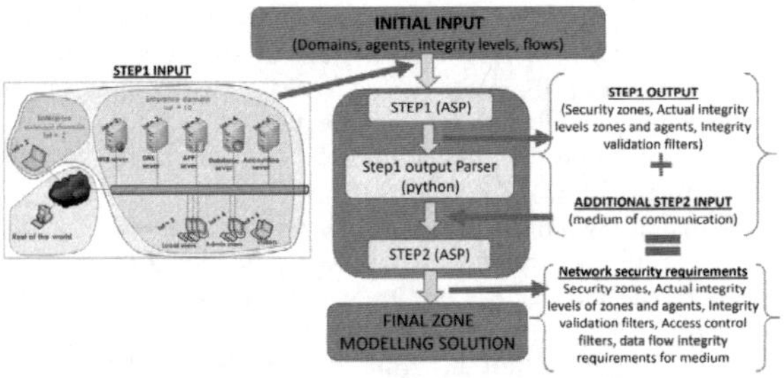

Figure 6. Our methodological approach overview

As shown in Figure 6, at step1, the initial input is the set of security domains, the set of agents, the integrity levels of domains and agents, and the data flows between agents. As a result of step1, our process computes the security zones and the integrity validation filters. In the second step, the designer needs to provide additional information about the media of communication (i.e., the networks). The final result is a set of network security requirements, which are a set security zones, integrity validation filters, agents integrity requirements, access control filters and integrity data flow protection requirements.

In the following, we discuss in detail the modelling rules at step1 and step2.

A. *Specifying zones and filtered flows*

The main goal of this step is to specify zones and identify integrity validation filters. At this step 1, we start with a system as a set of domains (DOMAIN), zones (ZONE) and agents (AGENT). We represent it as follows:

$$S = <\mathrm{DOMAIN}, \mathrm{ZONE}, \mathrm{AGENT}, \mathrm{FLOW}, \mathrm{INSIDE}_Z^D, \mathrm{INSIDE}_A^D, \mathrm{INSIDE}_A^Z, \mathrm{Int}, \mathrm{Int}_{max}, \mathrm{Int}_{min}, \mathrm{Int}_{actual}, \mathrm{Agent}_{server}, \mathrm{Agent}_{client} >$$

Where,

- DOMAIN is the set of security domains.
- ZONE is the set of security zones.
- AGENT is the set of agents, named after entities. $\mathrm{AGENT} = \mathrm{ENV\_AGENT} \cup \mathrm{SYST\_AGENT}$ with ENV_AGENT and SYST_AGENT being the set of environment and system agents such that $\mathrm{ENV\_AGENT} \cup \mathrm{SYST\_AGENT} = \emptyset$.
- Agent_{server} : $\mathrm{AGENT} \rightarrow \{\mathrm{TRUE}, \mathrm{FALSE}\}$ states if agent is a server (e.g., WEB server).
- Agent_{client} : $\mathrm{AGENT} \rightarrow \{\mathrm{TRUE}, \mathrm{FALSE}\}$ states if agent is a client (e.g., browser).
- $\mathrm{FLOW} \subseteq \mathrm{AGENT} \times \mathrm{AGENT}$ is the set of allowed flow of information.
- $\mathrm{INSIDE}_Z^D \subseteq \mathrm{ZONE} \times \mathrm{DOMAIN}$ is a relation that states a zone is in a domain.
- $\mathrm{INSIDE}_A^D \subseteq \mathrm{AGENT} \times \mathrm{DOMAIN}$ is a relation that states an agent is in a domain.
- $\mathrm{INSIDE}_Z^D \subseteq \mathrm{AGENT} \times \mathrm{ZONE}$ is a relation that states an agent is in a zone.
- $\mathrm{Int}: \mathrm{DOMAIN} \rightarrow \mathbb{N}$ returns the integrity level of a security domain which is fixed.
- $\mathrm{Int}_{max}: \mathrm{ZONE} \cup \mathrm{AGENT} \rightarrow \mathbb{N}$ returns the maximum integrity of a zone or an agent. For environment agents, this value is directly derived from their trust label.
- $\mathrm{Int}_{min}: \mathrm{AGENT} \rightarrow \mathbb{N}$ returns the minimum integrity level of an agent. For system agents, this value is directly derived from the criticality label.
- $\mathrm{Int}_{actual}: \mathrm{ZONE} \cup \mathrm{AGENT} \rightarrow \mathbb{N}$ returns the actual integrity of a zone or an agent, which are the final integrity values chosen at the end of the computation.
- integrity-validation-filter(a: AGENT, f: FLOW, val1: Int, val2: Int) states integrity validation requirements such that *integrity-validation-filter(a, f, val1, val2)* describes integrity protection mechanism at agent *a* must sanitize dataflow *f* with an integrity level of *val1* to achieve a data assurance level of *val2*.

In other words, Int, Int_{max} and Int_{min} represent the integrity utility functions in Figure 3. Accordingly, we define the rules of step1 as follows:

RULE1: Every agent is inside a domain.

$$\forall a \in \mathrm{AGENT}, \exists\, d \in \mathrm{DOMAIN} \mid (a, d) \in \mathrm{INSIDE}_A^D$$

RULE2: Every security domain contains at least one security zone.

$$\forall d \in \mathrm{DOMAIN}, \mathrm{card}(\{z \mid z \in \mathrm{ZONE}, (z, d) \in \mathrm{INSIDE}_Z^D\}) \geq 1$$

RULE3: The maximum integrity level of a security zone is equal to the integrity level of the domain. This is because, a domain controls zone and therefore we cannot have more assurance on a zone than that of the domain.

$$\forall d \in \mathrm{DOMAIN}, \forall z \in \mathrm{ZONE}, (d, z) \in \mathrm{INSIDE}_Z^D \quad \mathrm{Int}_{max}(z) = \mathrm{Int}(d)$$

RULE4: Similar to Rule 3, the maximum integrity level of an agent is equal to the integrity level of domain.

$$\forall d \in \mathrm{DOMAIN}, \forall a \in \mathrm{AGENT}, (a, d) \in \mathrm{INSIDE}_A^D \quad \mathrm{Int}_{actual}(a) \leq \mathrm{Int}(d)$$

RULE5: The actual integrity of a zone cannot be greater than its maximum integrity.

$$\forall z \in \mathrm{ZONE}, \mathrm{Int}_{actual}(z) \leq \mathrm{Int}_{max}(z)$$

RULE6: The actual integrity of agents must be between the maximum and the minimum integrity levels of the agents.

$$\forall a \in \mathrm{AGENT}, \mathrm{Int}_{min}(a) \leq \mathrm{Int}_{actual}(a) \leq \mathrm{Int}_{max}(a)$$

RULE7: The actual integrity levels of an agent is same as that of its residing zone.

$$\forall a \in \mathrm{AGENT}, \forall z \in \mathrm{ZONE}, (a, z) \in \mathrm{INSIDE}_A^Z, \quad \mathrm{Int}_{actual}(a) = \mathrm{Int}_{actual}(z)$$

RULE8: The actual integrity levels of the interacting agents must adhere to the CW-lite integrity rule. In this way, an agent doesn't access a lower integrity information.

$$\forall a1, a2 \in \mathrm{AGENT}, (a1, a2) \in \mathrm{FLOW} \wedge \neg\, \text{integrity-validation-filter}(a2, \mathrm{flow}(a1, a2), \mathrm{Int}_{actual}(a1), \mathrm{Int}_{actual}(a2)) \Rightarrow \mathrm{Int}_{actual}(a1) \geq \mathrm{Int}_{actual}(a2)$$

RULE9: Server agents and client agents cannot reside in same zone. Because, as per the zone modelling design principles, intra-zone interactions are usually not analysed.

With reference the security design principle known as complete mediation rule, every access to every object must be checked for authority[13]. By default, this complete mediation rule is checked for client-server models. Therefore, if server and client reside in same zone there will be a conflict.

$$\forall a1, a2 \in AGENT, \forall z1, z2 \in ZONE, (a1, z1) \in INSIDE^{Z}_{A}, (a2, z2) \in INSIDE^{Z}_{A}, Agent_{server}(a1), Agent_{client}(a2) \Rightarrow z1 \neq z2$$

RULE10: Server agents that are not equally accessible to the client agents cannot reside in same zone. This rule refers to least privilege principle [13] that permits only privileged flows. Since the intra-zone interactions are not controlled from network point of view (as mentioned earlier), once an agent connects to a server in zone, then the agent can potentially communicate with other servers within that zone. Therefore, our rule states that, if any two servers reside in a zone and a client is denied flow to one of them, then it will result in a conflict.

$$\forall a1, a2, a \in AGENT, \forall z1, z2 \in ZONE, (a1, z1), (a2, z2) \in INSIDE^{Z}_{A}, (a, z1), (a, z2) \notin INSIDE^{Z}_{A}, Agent_{server}(a1), Agent_{server}(a2), Agent_{client}(a), flow(a1, a), \neg flow(a2, a) \Rightarrow z1 \neq z2$$

B. Step2: Specifying integrity requirements for the communication medium between zones

At the end of step1, we have the set of zones along with the integrity validation filters. In step2, we address the security issues of inter-zone interactions, i.e., we consider the protection of the flow through the network communication medium (e.g., wired/wireless networks, etc.,) that connect zones. The main goal of this step is to protect the integrity of data flows when traversing untrusted media of communication. Suitably, we complete our system model as follows:

$$S = < DOMAIN, ZONE, AGENT, FLOW, MEDIUM, INSIDE^{D}_{Z}, INSIDE^{D}_{A}, INSIDE^{Z}_{A}, INSIDE^{D}_{M}, CONNECT, PATH, Int, Int_{max}, Int_{min}, Int_{actual} >$$

Where:

- MEDIUM is the set of media of communication.
- $INSIDE^{D}_{M} \subseteq MEDIUM \times DOMAIN$ is a relation, which states that a medium of communication is in a domain.
- $CONNECT \subseteq MEDIUM \times ZONE$ is a relation, which states that a zone is connected to a medium of communication.
- $Int_{max}: ZONE \cup AGENT \cup MEDIUM \rightarrow \mathbb{N}$ returns the maximum integrity level of a security zone, agent or medium of communication.
- $Int_{actual}: ZONE \cup AGENT \cup MEDIUM \rightarrow \mathbb{N}$ returns the actual integrity level of a security zone, agent or medium of communication.
- $PATH \subseteq FLOW \times (ZONE \cup MEDIUM) \times (ZONE \cup MEDIUM)$, is a relation that stores where flows are transiting with the constraint that $\forall (f, e1, e2) \in PATH \Rightarrow (e1, e2) \in CONNECT \vee (e1, e2) \in CONNECT$. For instance, $(f,m,z) \in PATH$ means that flow *f* transits between medium *m* to zone *z*.
- access-control-filter(c: CONNECT, f: FLOW states access control requirements such that *access-control-filter(c,f)* means flow *f* must be permitted at connection *c*.
- dataflow-integrity-protection(f: FLOW, e: ZONE∪ MEDIUM, value: INT) states dataflow protection requirements such that *dataflow-integrity-protection(f,e,val)* means some protection mechanism must be applied on dataflow *f* over zone or medium *e* to preserve an integrity level of *val*.

Similar to domains, zones, and agent, the medium of communication m1 has two integrity levels: Int_{min} (m1), and Int_{actual} (m1). Accordingly, we add new rules to include constraints on media of communication:

RULE11: Every zone must be connected to a medium of communication.

$$\forall z \in ZONE, \exists\, m \in MEDIUM, (m, z) \in CONNECT$$

RULE12: At each zone, there must be an access control filter that permits allowed flow of information. Not explicitly allowed flows are denied by default.

$$\forall (f, e1, e2) \in PATH, e1 \in MEDIUM \Rightarrow access\text{-}control\text{-}filter((e1, e2), f)$$

Respectively:

$$\forall (f, e1, e2) \in PATH, e1 \in ZONE \Rightarrow access\text{-}control\text{-}filter((e2, e1), f)$$

RULE13: The actual integrity level of a medium of communication is the minimum value of the integrity level of its domain, the trust on the medium (i.e., its maximum integrity), and the actual integrity levels of the connected zones.

$$\forall m \in MEDIUM, Int_{actual}(m) = \min(\{Int(d) \mid d \in DOMAIN, (m, d) \in INSIDE^{D}_{M}\} \cup \{Int_{max}(m)\} \cup \{Int_{actual}(z) \mid z \in ZONE, (m, z) \in CONNECT\})$$

RULE14: A flow that transits over a medium or a zone, requires an integrity protection, if the integrity level of the medium or the zone is lower than the level of integrity of the flow.

$$\forall (a1, a2) \in FLOW, \forall e1, e2 \in ZONE \cup MEDIUM \mid (flow(a1, a2), e1, e2) \in PATH, (\min(Int_{actual}(a1), Int_{actual}(a2)) > Int_{actual}(e1) \Rightarrow data\text{-}flow\text{-}integrity\text{-}protection(flow(a1, a2), e1, \min(Int_{actual}(a1), Int_{actual}(a2))).$$

Respectively:

$$\forall (a1, a2) \in FLOW, \forall e1, e2 \in ZONE \cup MEDIUM \mid (flow(a1, a2), e1, e2) \in PATH, (\min(Int_{actual}(a1), Int_{actual}(a2)) > Int_{actual}(e2) \Rightarrow data\text{-}flow\text{-}integrity\text{-}protection(flow(a1, a2), e2, \min(Int_{actual}(a1), Int_{actual}(a2))).$$

VI. DISCUSSION

Our zone modelling rules are abstract and design independent therefore does not restrict the design solutions. Therefore, we do yet classify the zone types like DMZ, restricted, etc. We implemented the whole process in ASP using solver Clingo [14] and Python2.7 to automate the security zones computation. Due to space constraints, we do not detail on the tool implementation of the case study. Instead, we limit our discussion to the integrity levels and network security requirements.

The actual integrity levels of zones and agents correspond to the pre-requisite security requirements that ensure the expected behaviour of the agents as well as the expected security management capability of the zones. The future security design implementing these requirements must maintain these integrity levels at minimum. In practice, there already exist formally accepted approaches, which specify the profoundness of security verification required, for varying design assurance levels (known as DALs). DALs are determined from the safety assessment process and hazard analysis by examining the effects of a failure condition in aircraft systems [15]. The higher the DAL is, the higher the assurance activities or verification methods are demanded.

Furthermore, the network security requirements defined by our methodology. Firstly, the integrity validation filters (from RULE9) defined for the filtered flows represent validation processes to be implemented either by the target agent (e.g., by some specific validation code) or some external security mechanisms (e.g., deep inspection mechanisms). For instance, the data flow between the local users and the accountability server must be validated. Let's say their actual integrity values are 3 and 5 respectively. Then as per RULE9, an incoming data flow having an integrity level of 3 must be sanitized in order to conform integrity level 5. Interpretation of such integrity validation requirement, i.e. what means validation to conform integrity level of 5, which can be carried out on the basis of dedicated documents such as the specification for data assurance levels by EUROCONTROL [16]. Suitably, the filter validation can be implemented at the end of accountability server using a security mechanism such as a WEB application firewall that checks for SQL injection. As a result, the refinement of the filtering functionality may give rise to new security verification requirements. However, describing the refinement of the integrity verification filtering requirements is out of the scope of this article.

Secondly, access control filters (from RULE 12) defined at the entry/exit interfaces of each zone describe the need to control all the inter-zone communications. Depending on the security design specifications, these filters may correspond to firewalls, application gateways, etc., depending on the security design specifications. One access control filter may be implemented by one or more access control mechanisms (e.g., firewalls). This depends on the integrity level of the zones. Finally, the integrity flow requirements defined (from RULE14) for the data flow describe the need for security protection mechanism while transiting a medium or a zone.

VII. Conclusion and Perspectives

Network security zone modelling is a well-known approach that contributes to the defense-in-depth strategy from the network security perspective. However, no rigorous approach formally defines this process. To address this issue, we proposed a zone modelling methodology based on Clark-Wilson lite formal model. We provide a set of formal rules as well as the list of initial integrity levels values computed based on risk impact, which makes our methodology approach traceable and verifiable.

As future works, we plan to integrate this work in the process of security requirements engineering. This allows refining business level security objectives into network security requirements. In parallel, we would like to extend our security zone modelling approach to consider the confidentiality and availability requirements as well.

Acknowledgment

This work is part of project IREHDO2 funded by DGA/DGAC. The authors thank all the security experts at Airbus who helped us with their useful comments.

References

[1] SANS, 'Infrastructure Security Architecture for Effective Security Monitoring'. 2015.

[2] Government of Canada, Communications Security Establishment, 'Baseline Security Requirements for Network Security Zones in the Government of Canada'. 2007.

[3] Secure Arc, 'Logical Security Zone Pattern. http://www.securearc.com/wiki/index.php/Logical_Security_Zone_Pattern'.

[4] Province of British Columbia, 'Enterprise IT Security Architecture Security Zones: NETWORK SECURITY ZONE STANDARDS - Office of Chief Info Officer'. 2012.

[5] Ramasamy et al, 'Towards Automated Identification of Security Zone Classification in Enterprise Networks.', in *Hot-ICE*, 2011.

[6] A. Gontarczyk, P. McMillan, and C. Pavlovski, 'Blueprint for Cyber Security Zone Modeling', *Inf. Technol. Ind.*, 2015.

[7] Cybedu, 'Sensibilisation et initiation à la cybersécurité-consortium', 2017.

[8] Biba, 'Integrity considerations for secure computer systems', DTIC, 1977.

[9] D. D. Clark and D. R. Wilson, 'A comparison of commercial and military computer security policies', in *Security and Privacy, IEEE Symposium on*, 1987.

[10] Microsoft, 'Windows Vista integrity mechanism and earlier integrity models'. [Online]. Available: https://msdn.microsoft.com/fr-FR/library/bb625957.aspx.

[11] U. Shankar, T. Jaeger, and R. Sailer, 'Toward Automated Information-Flow Integrity Verification for Security-Critical Applications.', in *NDSS*, 2006.

[12] IEC 61508, 'Functional safety of electrical/electronic safety-related systems - Part 1: General requirements'. 2010.

[13] J. H. Saltzer and M. D. Schroeder, 'The protection of information in computer systems', *Proc. IEEE*, 1975.

[14] M. Gebser, B. Kaufmann, R. Kaminski, M. Ostrowski, T. Schaub, and M. Schneider, 'Potassco: The Potsdam answer set solving collection', vol. 24, pp. 107–124, 2011.

[15] Bieber et al, 'DALculus–theory and tool for development assurance level allocation', in *International Conference on Computer Safety, Reliability, and Security*, 2011.

[16] EUROCONTROL, 'Specification for Data Assurance Levels'. Mar-2012.

Towards a Blockchain-based Identity Provider

Andreas Grüner, Alexander Mühle, Tatiana Gayvoronskaya, Christoph Meinel
Hasso Plattner Institute (HPI)
University of Potsdam, 14482, Potsdam, Germany
Email: {andreas.gruener, alexander.muehle, tatiana.gayvoronskaya, christoph.meinel}@hpi.uni-potsdam.de

Abstract—**The emerging technology blockchain is under way to revolutionize various fields. One significant domain to apply blockchain is identity management. In traditional identity management, a centralized identity provider, representing a trusted third party, supplies digital identities and their attributes. The identity provider controls and owns digital identities instead of the associated subjects and therefore, constitutes a single point of failure and compromise. To overcome the need for this trusted third party, blockchain enables the creation of a decentralized identity provider serving digital identities that are under full control of the associated subject. In this paper, we outline the design and implementation of a decentralized identity provider using an unpermissioned blockchain. Digital identities are partially stored on the blockchain and their attributes are modelled as verifiable claims, consisting of claims and attestations. In addition to that, the identity provider implements the OpenID Connect protocol to promote seamless integration into existing application landscapes. We provide a sample authentication workflow for a user at an online shop to show practical feasibility.**

Keywords–Blockchain; distributed ledger technology; digital identity; self-sovereign identity; Ethereum.

I. Introduction

In 2008, Satoshi Nakamoto published the foundational paper on Bitcoin and started the rise of its underlying blockchain technology [1]. Bitcoin is the first popular digital currency based on a peer-to-peer network without the involvement of a trusted third party. The concept of a decentralized digital currency scheme is generalized by the decentralized execution of additional computations. Bitcoin provides a limited scripting language to enforce requirements on the processing of payments [1]. Beyond this, the Ethereum blockchain comprises a Turing-complete virtual machine for the execution of arbitrary code [2]. This capability allows the implementation of smart contracts [3] to specify complex behaviour for payments or value transfer in general. On top of that, it enables further applications without requiring a centralized entity. Thus, current blockchain technology allows decentralized storage and execution of applications within a network of peers, eliminating the need for a trusted third party [4].

Identity management is concerned with the representation and administration of entities and their attributes as digital identities. Digital identities serve in the identification, authentication and authorization process for applications [5]. The security of an application significantly depends on recognizing users and preventing impersonation attacks of other users. In this regard, secure identification and authentication procedures are fundamental to avoid misuse. Furthermore, authorization ensures that properly authenticated users act within granted privileges. Therefore, identity management is a substantial cornerstone in securing the digital world and in preventing fraud.

A pivotal entity in this domain is an identity provider. The identity provider implements identification, authentication and authorization functions and provides these services to other parties [6]. Traditionally, an identity provider represents a trusted third party and is used within an organization. In addition to that, identity providers that are external to organizations are used in identity federation scenarios. An end user wants to authenticate at a service provider. The service provider redirects the end user to the identity provider for this process. The identity provider confirms a successful login or reports a failed authentication to the service provider. Based on the result, access to the offered service is granted or denied.

A service provider significantly relies on the proper execution of the processes carried out by the identity provider. This trust is mainly derived from contractual obligations, due diligence and reputation of the identity provider. Overall, in traditional identity management, the identity provider is a trusted third party and essential to the security of applications.

The centralized identity provider as the trusted third party has several downsides. First and foremost, the identity provider needs to be trusted due to centralized control and ownership of digital identities and their attributes. The subject of the digital identity is not in possession of its own data. Additionally, the identity provider represents a single point of failure and therefore decreased reliability. As a central entity the identity provider may accumulate a large amount of identity data and becomes a profitable target to attackers, thereby increasing motivation for data theft.

To address these challenges, we have devised a decentralized implementation of an identity provider using an unpermissioned blockchain. The blockchain-based identity provider removes the trusted third party from identity management and remediates centralized control and ownership of the digital identities as well as the single point of failure and compromise. Trust in the decenrally issued identities is derived from the transparency of the blockchain implementation and the attestation issuers, that verify claims. Additionally, the OpenID Connect [7] protocol is implemented to facilitate seamless integration into existing application landscapes and eases the transition from conventional providers.

The remainder of this paper is structured in the following way. In Section 2, we present related work and concepts. The subsequent section provides background on the interrelations between blockchain technology and identity management. We devise our blockchain-based identity provider in Section 4. Section 5 describes a sample authentication workflow using the implemented identity provider. We provide suggestions for future work in Section 6 and conclude the paper in Section 7.

II. Related Work

Numerous practical and academic projects combine blockchain technology and identity management [8]. These projects target either specific parts of identity management or are directly concerned with a self-sovereign identity. Implementation approaches differ between creating specific-purpose blockchains or adding functionality on top of existing blockchains using smart contracts. However, the majority of projects offer only a limited amount of detail regarding the technical implementation. In the following section, we describe uPort and Sovrin due to the sufficient amount of available information and the maturity of the solutions. Additionally, we point out differences to our blockchain-based identity provider.

A comprehensive self-sovereign identity solution is implemented by uPort [9] in the form of smart contracts on the Ethereum blockchain. A digital identity is mainly represented as a controller, proxy, and recovery contract. The address of a proxy contract is the identifier of the digital identity. The controller contract establishes a management function to administrate and use the proxy contract as an identity. This distinction enables the replacement of the controller contract and fosters persistence of the proxy contract address. The restoration of the private key is the intent of the recovery contract. Additionally, a central and user-independent registry contract on the blockchain is used to reflect bindings between identities and claims or attestations. Claims and attestations are stored on InterPlanetary File System (IPFS) [10] or central cloud storages. Besides blockchain-based components of uPort, there are additional elements of the ecosystem. A developer library enables the integration into applications. The uPort mobile app is the key application for the end user to manage the digital identity.

Compared to uPort, our blockchain-based identity provider solution is implemented as dedicated unpermissioned blockchain yielding a benefit on computational efficiency and reduced transaction cost. uPort uses the general execution environment and transaction costs on Ethereum. Our identity provider is directly integrated into a blockchain and uses dedicated transactions. Besides that, our identity provider offers OpenID Connect conformity to seamlessly integrate into existing application landscapes.

Sovrin [11] is a public and permissioned blockchain solution dedicated to providing identity management. Sovrin nodes are distinguished as validator or observer nodes. Validators are specifically chosen nodes that are permissioned to write the next state of the blockchain and include transactions. Observer nodes solely read the blockchain and make the information available for clients. Sovrin is supervised by a complex trust framework with different governance bodies that make decisions on the further development of the blockchain and the admission of new validator nodes. Additionally, participation in the network is liable to contractual agreements issued by the Sovrin Foundation [12]. A digital identity of Sovrin comprises an identifier and attributes are modelled as claims and attestations. Aliases can be linked to the identifier to increase privacy. Several claim types are differentiated that enable, for instance, clear, encrypted and hashed storage on the blockchain. Storage providers can be used to save the data in case the claim is not directly stored on the blockchain.

In contrast to Sovrin and the use of governance bodies, our blockchain-based identity provider utilizes an unpermissioned blockchain to avoid reliance on trusted third parties and to foster the vision of a self-sovereign identity.

III. Blockchain and Identity Management

Considering both domains, blockchain technology and identity management, there is mutual interest and applicability. On the one hand, a permissioned blockchain requires the implementation of identity management and access control to grant privileges on the blockchain layer to eligible participants. A permissioned blockchain comprises predetermined nodes for transaction processing and block creation [13]. The predetermined nodes need to be identified and permissions must be assigned to the respective digital identities.

On the other hand, using blockchain technology to build a distributed execution environment for self-sovereign identities forms a distinct identity provider. Blockchain technology enables the implementation of a decentralized digital identity that is not issued and owned by a trusted third party. This digital identity is under true control of its associated entity. Therefore, a decentralized digital identity adhering to specific characteristics is named a self-sovereign identity. These properties are elaborated by Allen [14] and can be grouped into the categories security, controllability and portability [15]. The cluster security comprises protection, minimisation and persistence. Protection refers to the general precedence of the digital identity's owner rights. Minimisation is concerned with data privacy and the reduction of information disclosure about the subject. Persistence describes the long-term existence of a digital identity. Controllability is the second category in the attribute grouping and encompasses existence, control and consent. Furthermore, persistence is repeatedly indicated. Existence describes, that a digital identity should reflect a physical object. The control of the identity is completely in the possession of the owner and without the consent of the owner no information is revealed. Portability is the last category and comprises interoperability, transparency and access. The digital identity and corresponding identity provider services are interoperable with customers and provider services applying standard protocols. The implementation, operation and actioning of the digital identity is transparent to all involved parties. The owner, or any legitimate party, has easy access to information or attributes of the digital identity. Overall, blockchain technology is able to provide decentralized identity management for other applications in a novel way.

IV. A Blockchain-based Identity Provider

In the following sections, we outline our decentralized identity provider based on blockchain technology. Starting with objectives and requirements that lead to particular design decisions, we subsequently present the overall architecture, theoretic model and implementation of the novel identity provider.

A. Objective

In traditional identity management, digital identities and their attributes are issued by a centralized identity provider that represents a trusted third party. Service providers need to trust the correctness of the identity provider as well as the validity of issued digital identities and their attributes. In addition to that, trust is required in properly performing the authentication process of a subject. Furthermore, the centralized identity provider is in full control and ownership of the digital identity and its attributes. Therefore, the subject needs to trust the identity provider on carefully handling and protecting its data. Besides that, trust in compliant behaviour according to regulation and contracts of the identity provider is required. The subject does not expect arbitrary actions, for instance revoking attributes or the complete digital identity, leaving the subject without access to potential critical resources. An identity provider usually serves numerous subjects and therefore collects and stores an accumulated amount of data being a profitable target for attackers. Overall, a centralized identity provider represents a single point of compromise and control.

To overcome these challenges, blockchain technology enables the implementation of a decentralized identity provider without it being a trusted third party. We devise a novel implementation approach of an identity provider using an unpermissioned blockchain to decentralize identity management and derive trust in digital identities from claims and attestations instead of the identity provider itself. The blockchain-based identity provider applies conventional protocols to seamlessly integrate into existing application landscapes confining required changes on the side of the service provider.

B. Requirements

Besides the general objective, we consider the following requirements as significant for our blockchain-based identity provider.

- Decentralization. Decentralization of the identity provider model is a key factor to foster independence from a central authority. In general, decentralization is enabled by the blockchain model. However, an introduction of concentrated external dependencies needs to be prevented in the blockchain network.
- Standard Protocols. The usage of identity management protocols as standards is necessary to foster a seamless integration and migration from conventional identity providers to the blockchain-based identity provider.
- Efficiency. The identity provider should be cost efficient with regards to transaction fees to foster its usage.

C. Design Decisions

There are different solution approaches to building a blockchain-based identity provider that fulfils the stated objective and implements the listed requirements. We make the subsequent design decisions to achieve an optimal solution.

The identity provider is implemented as a separate blockchain instead of a smart contract-based approach on an existing general purpose blockchain. Using smart contracts on another blockchain affects efficiency in terms of computation and cost. A dedicated identity provider blockchain implements the required components more efficiently compared to an execution on a general purpose distributed virtual machine. Furthermore, relying on a general purpose blockchain implies the adoption of the respective transaction fee cost model. Adjusted transaction costs to identity management yield a cost benefit.

To concentrate on the development of the identity provider, we fork an existing blockchain as the foundation and integrate the identity provider as a core component. We determined

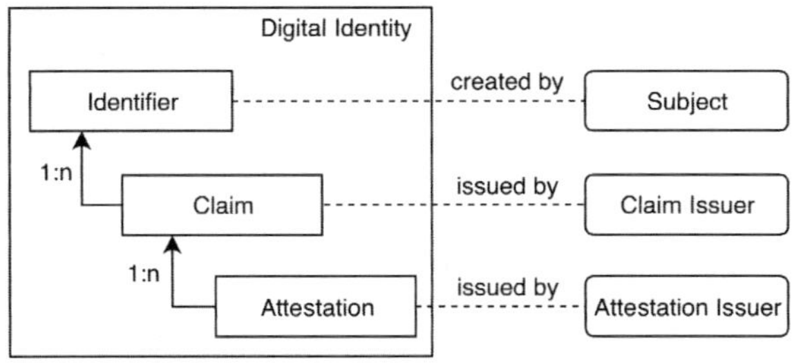

Figure 1. Digital Identity Model and Actors

Ethereum as the most suitable solution for our identity provider based on the broad community, extensive documentation and published source code of the different clients.

Furthermore, we chose the OpenID Connect protocol as integration pattern into existing applications. OpenID Connect specification as an amendment of OAuth 2.0 [16] is developed by major technology companies and has wide adoption. Besides that, identity federation with social networks (e.g. Facebook) are highly used.

D. Digital Identity Model and Actors

The digital identity comprises a unique identifier and attributes. The identifier is chosen arbitrarily by the subject upon creation of the identity. Uniqueness is ensured due to recording and verification on the blockchain network. The attributes of the digital identity are modelled as claims and attestations. A claim is a statement about an attribute of the digital identity. The attestation of a claim is an assertion about the correctness and validity of a claim by a digital identity. See Figure 1 for an overview of the model. The digital identity is created by a subject generally referring to an end user. The claim issuer creates statements about the identity and the attestation issuer asserts these statements. The service provider offers services to end users. To use a service the subject authenticates and potentially authorizes itself to the service provider by using the blockchain-based identity provider. Both end user and service provider can act as claim and attestation issuer.

E. Architecture and Authentication Process

In traditional identity management, the subject, identity provider and service provider represent distinct entities. The subject registers at the identity provider to create a digital identity and potentially provide information about attributes. The service provider forwards the subject to the identity provider during the authentication process. The subject proves with credentials to be in control of the respective digital identity and the identity provider sends the authentication result to the service provider.

Using a blockchain-based identity provider, the distinct entity of an identity provider is replaced by a blockchain network leading to changes in the general architecture and the authentication process. An overview of the architecture is depicted in Figure 2. Subject and service provider each operate a node in the network to establish a connection to the decentralized identity provider. Initially, the subject creates a digital identity by issuing a transaction to the network.
Upon requesting access at a service provider (for instance at an online shop) the service provider forwards the subject to the

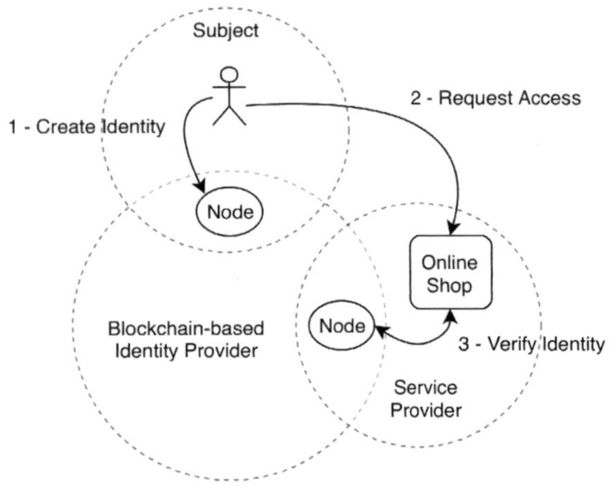

Figure 2. Architecture

local node of the identity provider. Subsequently, the subject proves to be in control of the presented digital identity and the service provider grants access to its portal.

F. Theoretic Model

Our blockchain-based identity provider is based on the Ethereum blockchain. Therefore, we extend the world state of Ethereum as the theoretic model by an additional identity state. The state transition function is modified to embrace changes of the identity state resulting from newly introduced identity transactions that are recognized by the blockchain.

1) World State and Identity State: The entire state is named world state and comprises address to account state associations [2]. We extend the world state to additionally include mappings from addresses to identity states aligned to the account states and formally define it as follows.

$$\sigma = (A, I)$$

A comprises the account states as defined in [2] with $A_{[m]}$ referencing a specific account by address m. We define I as the set of identity states with $I_{[m]}$ referencing the identity state of address m. An identity state contains the following attributes.

- Nonce n. A scalar value matching the changes of the identity. An identity is created with nonce = 1.
- Identifier i. An arbitrary string that references the digital identity.
- Owner o. Owner represents the related account of the identity. This account controls the digital identity.
- Claims c. The attribute comprises a cryptographic hash of a trie that stores the claims of the identity. The data of a claim might be stored on the blockchain or outside the blockchain network. In case the data of the claim is stored at another storage provider a cryptographic hash is added as information of the claim to the blockchain.
- Attestations a. The property contains a cryptographic hash of a trie that stores attestations for the claims of the digital identity. Comparable to claims, the attestations can be stored on the blockchain or on another storage solution having the cryptographic hash on the blockchain.

The identity state is formally defined as follows.

$$I_{[m]} = (n, i, o, c, a)$$

2) Transactions: A transaction is a cryptographically signed message to the blockchain network. There are two types of transactions T: Contract creation transaction T_{con} and message call transaction T_{msg} [2]. These transactions are determined to evolve the account state. We introduce three additional transaction types to facilitate the identity model and allow identity state changes. These transactions are as follows.

- Create Identity T_{cre}. An identity is initially created by specifying the identifier i. The owner o is indirectly set to the account from which the transaction originates.
- Modify Identity T_{mod}. An identity is modified during its lifetime by adding or removing claims and attestations.
- Delete Identity T_{del}. An identity is deactivated by removing the owner as well as clearing claims and attestations. Therefore, the control of the identity is revoked and no further actions are possible.

We extend the definition of a transaction T in [2] to comprise the following fields.

- Type p. The attribute specifies the transaction type and is one of T_{con}, T_{msg}, T_{cre}, T_{mod} or T_{del}.
- Nonce n. The nonce determines the count of transactions generated by the sender that is defined with the attribute from f.
- GasPrice p. Gas is consumed for executing computations of the transaction. Gas price p is the cost for one unit of gas.
- GasLimit g. The field determines the upper bound of gas used for the transaction.
- To t. The property defines the recipient of the transaction.
- From f. The field characterizes the originator of the transaction either being an account itself or an identity.
- Value v. Value v defines the payment transferred to the recipient of the transaction.
- Signature w, r, s. The properties comprise the cryptographic signature of the transaction by the sender as defined in [2].
- Init i. Data used for transaction of type T_{con}.
- Data d. Data used for transaction of type T_{msg} and T_{mod}.

The general validity of a transaction is determined through the verification of the sender's cryptographic signature. A valid transaction containing the sender's address of an account is signed with the corresponding key pair. Additional basic transaction verification steps are defined in [2]. Invalid transactions are not processed.

3) State Transition:
The world state transitions into a new state based on transactions issued to the network. These transactions advance the world state's underlying account [2]. Additionally, identity transactions update the identity states. The mining of the next block of the blockchain persists the included transactions and

```
       did = "did:bbidp:" idstring
  idstring = 1*idchar
    idchar = ALPHA / DIGIT
```

Figure 3. bbIdP DID Method Scheme

advertises the state evolvement to all nodes of the network. The state transition function Υ advances the world state σ to the new world state σ' based on a Transaction T and is formally defined as follows [2].

$$\sigma' = \Upsilon(\sigma, T)$$

We detach account state transitions from identity state transitions and define the following sub functions of Υ.

$$(A, I)' = \Upsilon((A, I), T)$$

$$\Leftrightarrow$$

$$\Upsilon_A(A, T) = \begin{cases} A', & T \in \{T_{con}, T_{msg}\} \\ A, & T \notin \{T_{con}, T_{msg}\} \end{cases}$$

$$\wedge \Upsilon_I(I, T) = \begin{cases} I', & T \in \{T_{cre}, T_{mod}, T_{del}\} \\ I, & T \notin \{T_{cre}, T_{mod}, T_{del}\} \end{cases}$$

The identity state transition function Υ_I is the main function of the blockchain-based identity provider.

G. Implementation

The foundation of our blockchain-based Identity Provider (bbIdP) is the Python client of Ethereum comprising the main libraries pyethapp [17] and pyethereum [18]. We adapted the pyethereum implementation according to the theoretical model to support the newly introduced identity management transactions and to store identity information in a separate identity state. Pyethapp is modified to use the updated pyethereum library accordingly. To fully leverage the identity provider model, pyethapp's service oriented architecture is extended by an OpenID Connect provider based on the pyoidc library [19] to offer respective service and achieve straightforward integration.

The representation of identifier, claims and attestations differentiates an internal and external model. The external model is aligned to standards under development by World Wide Web Consortium (W3C) community working groups [20] [21]. The internal specification is a reduced representation to facilitate a streamlined implementation. The blockchain-based identity provider offers remote procedure calls to retrieve identifier, claims and attestations in the external format. Additionally, the OpenID Connect provider accepts the external representation.

The format of the identifier is aligned to the Decentralized IDentifier (DID) specification [20] and defined as a particular DID method scheme (see Figure 3). The method namespace is bbidp and abbreviates the blockchain-based identity provider proposed in this paper. The portion idstring is a combination of one or more characters or numbers. This identifier is specified during the creation of the digital identity. It is provided in the "To" attribute of the identity creation transaction. To externally reference the identity, the fully qualified decentralized identifier is used. In general, the external structure of a claim follows the credential entity model of the Verifiable Claims [21] community working group. A claim is represented in the JavaScript Object Notation (JSON) [22] format. A sample is shown in Figure 4. Each claim consists of a claim identifier, meta data and a property that contains the actual attribute of the digital identity. A claim is issued in simplified form to the blockchain contained in the data field of the identity modification transaction. Issuer and issue timestamp are implicitly obtained from the respective transaction. The specified attribute of the identity can be issued as a cryptographic hash to increase privacy. Internally, the claim is stored in the claim trie of the appropriate identity. The key is the claim identifier and the value is represented by the remaining attributes. To revoke an existing claim, a transaction is issued containing a claim with the same identifier that has no claim attribute.

```
{
  "id": "identifier"
  "type" : "Smith",
  "claim" : {
    "id" : "did:bbidp:bob"
    "firstname" : Bob
  }
}
```

Figure 4. Sample Claim

The attestation of a claim is a signature of the claim itself by the attestation issuer. It is represented in JSON and internally stored in the attestation trie of the identity. Additionally, the attestation comprises meta data about the issuer, creation time and the referred claim. In contrast to the Verifiable Claims working group, we internally separated the attestation from the claim to allow various attestations of a single claim from different attestation issuers.

The integrated OpenID Connect provider serves a simple web page. Upon re-directing a user from the originating portal for authentication, it provides a random value encoded as Quick Response (QR) code [23]. The provider expects as return value a JSON data structure containing the random value and the identity profile that is signed by the owner account of the digital identity. Subsequently, the provider verifies against the blockchain, that the signature is valid and the used account corresponds to the owner of the digital identity. In case of positive verification, the provider returns a positive message and redirects the user back to the originating portal. In case of authentication failure, an error message is delivered.

V. Sample Workflow

Alice owns an online book shop. To order a book, a customer needs to login to the online shop. The online shop offers the possibility to login with our blockchain-based identity provider (see Figure 5). Bob wants to buy products in Alice's online shop. He creates a digital identity on the blockchain-based identity provider network by issuing an identity creation transaction with the identifier "bob". After selecting products in the online shop, Bob navigates to the sign-in page. Next, the blockchain-based identity provider is chosen as a login method by Bob. Consequently, the identity provider generates a random value and provides it in the form of a QR code to the online shop in an iFrame. Bob signs the random value and the profile of his digital identity related by the identifier "did:bbidp:bob" and sends it to the embedded callback address of the identity provider. Upon successful verification of the return message, Alice's online shop recognises Bob.

Figure 5. Sample Online Shop

VI. Future Work

A future enhancement for our blockchain-based identity provider is the functional extension to utilize claims and attestations for the purpose of authorization in alignment with the OAuth 2.0 protocol. A service provider could add an attestation of a purchased service to the digital identity of a customer. Based on the attested claim, the service provider can grant access to the purchased offering upon return of the customer to the online service. An additional research area is related to the security of the public unpermissioned blockchain, that is used as an identity provider. Remain the security assumptions for a general purpose blockchain valid in case of a dedicated blockchain for identity management.

VII. Conclusion

Blockchain technology enables the creation of a decentralized identity provider without a trusted third party. We presented the design and implementation of a novel blockchain-based identity provider that offers digital identities containing verifiable claims. The blockchain-based identity provider conforms to the OpenID Connect protocol in order to integrate seamlessly in existing authentication processes. The conjunction of the conventional OpenID Connect protocol with the novel blockchain-based identity provider model enables overarching usage of these technologies. Finally, we described a sample authentication workflow to show practical feasibility.

References

[1] S. Nakamoto. Bitcoin: A peer-to-peer electronic cash system. [Online]. Available: https://bitcoin.org/bitcoin.pdf [retrieved: 2018-07-18] (2008)

[2] G. Wood. Ethereum: A secure decentralised generalised transaction ledger. [Online]. Available: https://pdfs.semanticscholar.org/ac15/ea808ef3b17ad754f91d3a00fedc8f96b929.pdf [retrieved: 2018-07-18]

[3] N. Szabo. Smart contracts: Building blocks for digital markets. [Online]. Available: http://www.fon.hum.uva.nl/rob/Courses/InformationInSpeech/CDROM/Literature/LOTwinterschool2006/szabo.best.vwh.net/smart_contracts_2.html [retrieved: 2018-07-18] (1996)

[4] C. Meinel, T. Gayvoronskaya, and M. Schnjakin, "Blockchain: Hype oder innovation," Hasso-Plattner Institute, Prof.-Dr.-Helmert-Strae 2-3, 14482 Potsdam, Germany, 2018.

[5] G. Williamson, D. Yip, I. Sharoni, and K. Spaulding, Identity Management: A Primer. MC Press Online, LP., 2009.

[6] MIT. Information systems & technology website. the knowledge base. idp (identity provider). [Online]. Available: http://kb.mit.edu/confluence/display/glossary/IdP+(Identity+Provider) [retrieved: 2018-07-18]

[7] OpenID Foundation. Openid connect. [Online]. Available: http://openid.net/connect/ [retrieved: 2018-07-18]

[8] Blockchain and identity. [Online]. Available: https://github.com/peacekeeper/blockchain-identity [retrieved: 2018-07-19] (2018)

[9] C. Lundkvist, R. Heck, J. Torstensson, Z. Mitton, and M. Sena. uport: A platform for self-sovereign identity. [Online]. Available: http://blockchainlab.com/pdf/uPort_whitepaper_DRAFT20161020.pdf [retrieved: 2018-07-19] (2016)

[10] J. Benet. Ipfs. content addressed, versioned, p2p file system. [Online]. Available: https://arxiv.org/pdf/1407.3561.pdf [retrieved: 2018-07-19] (2014)

[11] D. Reed, J. Law, and D. Hardman. The technical foundations of sovrin. a white paper from the sovrin foundation. [Online]. Available: https://www.evernym.com/wp-content/uploads/2017/07/The-Technical-Foundations-of-Sovrin.pdf [retrieved: 2018-07-19] (2016)

[12] D. Reed et al. Sovrin provisional trust framework. [Online]. Available: https://sovrin.org/wp-content/uploads/2018/03/Sovrin-Provisional-Trust-Framework-2017-06-28.pdf [Accessed: 2018-07-19] (2017)

[13] BitFury Group. Public versus private blockchains. part 1: Permissioned blockchains. white paper. [Online]. Available: https://bitfury.com/content/downloads/public-vs-private-pt1-1.pdf [retrieved: 2018-07-19] (2015)

[14] C. Allen. The path to self-sovereign identity. [Online]. Available: http://www.lifewithalacrity.com/2016/04/the-path-to-self-soverereign-identity.html/cointelegraph.com/news/first-iteration-of-ethereum-metropolis-hard-fork-to-appear-monday [retrieved: 2018-07-18] (2016)

[15] A. Tobin and D. Reed. The inevitable rise of self-sovereign identity. a white paper from the sovrin foundation. [Online]. Available: https://sovrin.org/wp-content/uploads/2017/06/The-Inevitable-Rise-of-Self-Sovereign-Identity.pdf [retrieved: 2017-07-19] (2017)

[16] Internet Engineering Task Force. Request for comments: 6749. the oauth 2.0 authorization framework. [Online]. Available: https://tools.ietf.org/html/rfc6749 [retrieved: 2017-07-19] (2012)

[17] Pyethapp. [Online]. Available: https://github.com/ethereum/pyethapp [retrieved: 2018-07-18]

[18] Pyethereum. [Online]. Available: https://github.com/ethereum/pyethereum [retrieved: 2018-07-19]

[19] Pyoidc. [Online]. Available: https://github.com/OpenIDC/pyoidc [retrieved: 2018-07-16]

[20] D. Reed et al. W3c community group draft report. decentralized identifiers (dids) v0.9. data model and syntaxes for decentralized identifiers (dids). [Online]. Available: https://w3c-ccg.github.io/did-spec/ [retrieved: 2018-07-18] (2018)

[21] M. Sporny and D. Longley. W3c community group draft report. verifiable claims data model and representations 1.0. [Online]. Available: https://www.w3.org/2017/05/vc-data-model/CGFR/2017-05-01/ [retrieved: 2018-06-15] (2018)

[22] Internet Engineering Task Force. Request for comments: 7159. the javascript object notation (json) data interchange format. [Online]. Available: https://tools.ietf.org/html/rfc7159 [retrieved: 2018-07-20] (2014)

[23] International Standardization Organization. Iso/iec 18004:2000. information technology - automatic identification and data capture techniques - bar code symbology - qr code. [Online]. Available: https://tools.ietf.org/html/rfc7159 [retrieved: 2018-07-20] (2000)

Enhancement of Usability of Information Security Systems

Gwang-Il Ju
Dept. of Scienct and Technology Cyber Security Center
Korea Institute of Science and Technology Information
Daejeon, Korea
e-mail: kiju@kisti.re.kr

Hark-Soo Park
Dept. of Scienct and Technology Cyber Security Center
Korea Institute of Science and Technology Information
Daejeon, Korea
e-mail: hspark@kisti.re.kr

Abstract—**An information security system can be divided into the administrator mode and the user mode, in terms of its interface. This research can provide a way to achieve effective results in terms of compliance with security policies through division. In this paper, we propose a human-centric security system which is based on user-centered security (User eXperience) interface. In particular, this study divides the user layer by profiling using the UX methodology's personalization method. Based on this, we apply the information security system on a scenario-by-scene basis, and prepare the factors that could cause difficulties in advance. The information security system was able to confirm the increase of the management level in terms of security policy compliance at the user side, resulting in insight from various HCI (Human Computer Interaction)s standpoints. This can lead to meaningful results that future users can reference in information security systems that they can directly control.**

Keywords- Usability; Compliance; Information Security System.

I. INTRODUCTION

With the performance improvement in computing infrastructure and the increase in its complexity, there have been numerous studies on how to solve the difficulties users face in HCI (Human Computer Interaction) and the need for a solution to the complexity from the perspective of the human factor. A security system officer needs to pursue user-personal security and help users feel comfortable with security. According to the 'Psychology of Security for the Home Computer User' released at the IEEE Symposium [1], the current approach to security is not appropriate because it overlooks the ease of use. In addition, the paper 'The Weakest Link Revisited [2]' written on IEEE Security & Privacy read that the weakest point from a corporate security standpoint is the user. In other words, making security more convenient for users can significantly upgrade a corporate security level.

In this way, information security is approaching the service concept for user's efficient business performance from the aspect of enterprise business. This study aims to present the direction of an effective information security system by analyzing the result when the user improves usability through information security as a service concept.

II. RELATED WORK

In terms of a study on HCI approach from the perspective of information security, the NIST [3] has developed a framework which can reduce user errors in a control system from the usability standpoint. The framework provides a common language and mechanism for organizations to: (1) describe current cybersecurity status; (2) describe their target state for cybersecurity; (3) identify and prioritize opportunities for improvement within the context of risk management; (4) assess progress towards the target state; (5) foster communications among internal and external stakeholders.

L. Jean Camp [4] suggested the privacy and mental model for security (Figure 1). This model is used for the effective communication regarding the environmental aspects of risks and is operated to handle misinterpretations for complicated risks. It cannot take care of everything, but can help users have a better understanding using a certain model. It is applicable to physical security, medical infections, criminal behavior, economics failure and warfare.

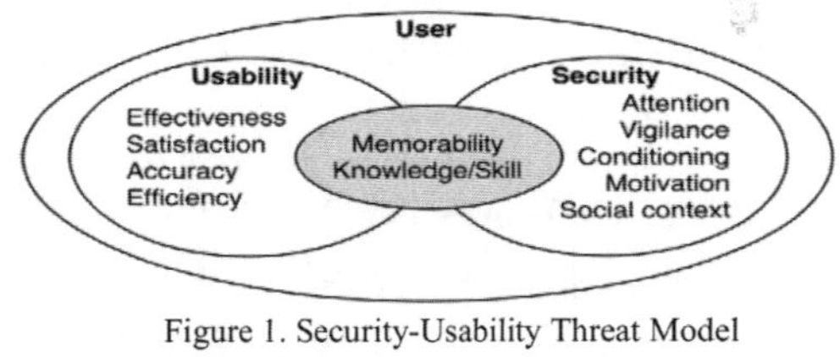

Figure 1. Security-Usability Threat Model

HCI security has evolved in a way to strengthen the usability of user application from the perspective of information security. Ronald [5] proposed the Security-usability Threat Model (Figure 1) in consideration of HCI extension in security. This study attempted to discuss its application which can reinforce the usability of a security system based on the HCI user methodology.

D. D. Woods [6] studied information processing by humans in HCI and applied it to system design with a goal of maximizing productivity. It applied organizational information security policy through profiling techniques based on demographic characteristics. This study aimes at classifying users through demographic profiling and then categorizing the effects of information security policy.

In this study, we construct a map by grouping users through user profile and interviewing the subjects, and analyzing key points where users can experience difficulties based on them. Based on this, we formulate the problems that users face and draw the conclusion that a more user friendly information system is needed by applying the solution system.

III. METHOD

A. Information System Profiling

This study attempted to apply the HCI approach based on the diagnosis of the parts which would be handled by users in person in the past from the perspective of user interface in a security system. In particular, it analyzes security system services through profiling and journey maps which can specify target users in terms of user experience.

One obvious approach to synthesizing usability engineering and securing systems is to apply established procedures for enhancing usability to developing on existing secure systems. Techniques for enhancing the usability of software cover a wide range of fields and sophistication [8].

Contextual Design [9] uses in-depth studies of potential users' work habits and needs to determine initial product goals.

Contextual Inquiry [9] provides usability testing on a deployed product, where real users using the system in their daily chores allow observers to record this use.

This study performs a classification through user profiling before launching a case study and then categorizes the type of security users. 'K' is a professional IT research agency in which most users have a high level of knowledge about IT. The age range varied widely. Then, the data was divided into age and amount of information in a 2X2 format and profiled. TABLE I divides the users into the understanding of occupation and IT and the tendency of each. Through this, we aim to utilize the users more sophisticatedly to track the direction they pursue.

TABLE I. INFORMATION SECURITY USER PROFILING

Type	Age	IT Understanding	Security Observance Tendency
Type A	Researcher in his/her 30s	Fast approach to new technology (early adopter), quick to keep pace with current IT trends, with a high level of IT knowledge	Strong resistance against security policy, but no disagreement regarding institutional security policy
Type B	Administrator in his/her 30s	Repetitive tasks, source of a large amount of information	High observance of information security policy
Type C	Researcher in his/her 40-50s	Relatively poor understanding of IT	Hard to apply it to security policy due to multiple work experiences
Type D	Administrator in his/her 40-50s	Very poor understanding of IT	Hard to apply it to security policy due to multiple work experiences

B. Information System Journey Map

A journey map [7] (Figure 2) has been widely used in diverse fields as an analysis technique of user behavior along with scenario mapping. To derive user pain points, it is executed in the following procedure.

While there is no standardized approach or methodology for customer journey mapping, a survey of current practitioners and an evaluation of surrounding literature revealed four universal traits: (1) a team-oriented execution, (2) a highly visual, nonlinear nature, (3) the use of touch-points, and (4) an emphasis on real customers and consumers.

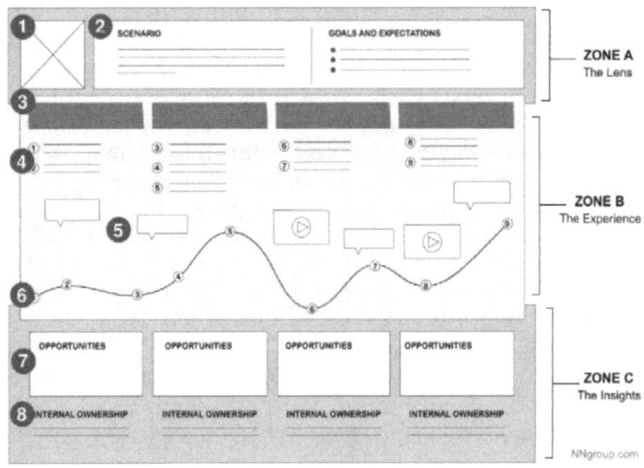

Figure 2. Journey Map (NN Group)

In this study, we made an IS Journey map for the security system (Figure 3) based on the NN group map. As a result, based on interviews with users, we found a point where we can identify their difficulties.

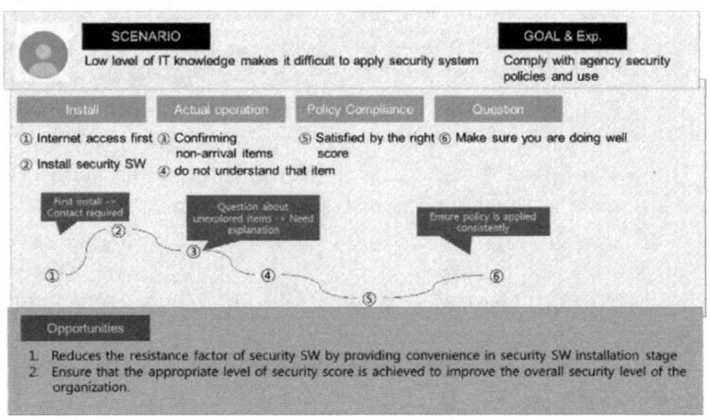

Figure 3. IS Journey Map (for Security System)

C. Change of institutional Security Policy to Journey Map

'K' agency has performed security management in terms of managerial security and technical security. From the perspective of technical security, a centralized security check solution had been applied. In 2015, however, such policy improved in a way for users to be able to check security indicators in person [10]. This change is significant in two aspects: i) performance improvement after the replacement of old facilities, ii) shift of a security system, allowing a user to control the system in person. See TABLE II.

TABLE II. SECURITY INSPECTION SOLUTIONS

Category	Previous	Now
Manufacturer	'N'	'C'
Year Introduced	2009	2015
Feature	Centralized	User check

Such security policy indicators were applied, focusing on the matters which are directly or indirectly checked by the government bureau during the security inspection period, and the details are in TABLE III.

TABLE III. INFORMATION SECURITY INDICATORS BY CATEGORY

No.	Description
1	Windows login account password
2	Screensaver password
3	Time of screensaver activation (min.)
4	Anti-virus installed
5	Firewalls set
6	Shared folder set
7	Shared folder password
8	Windows security update
9	Local system set
10	Conditions of the unused ActiveX

'K' agency's security policy is organized in a top-down structure in which national and government-led security policies are collectively delivered from the top to the bottom. Therefore, the agencies at the bottom are always under the influence of those on top. To increase the flexibility of institutional security policies, a separate guideline has been prepared to guide the users.

Users were positioned, as shown in Figure 4, to check PC security vulnerability. First, vulnerability was assessed through scores (out of 100 points). It was designed for a central manager to set a target score and make users reach the goal.

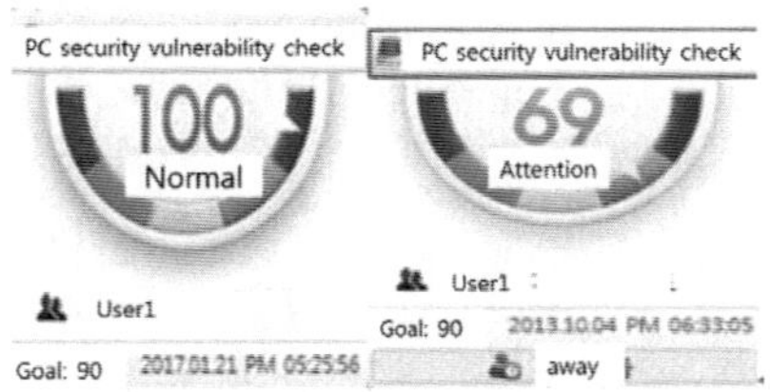

Figure 4. Check on PC Security Vulnerability by Scores

In addition, the level of PC security vulnerability was classified by color to draw more attention from users. The indicators in each sector were designed to be fixed in person and applied as shown in Figure 4. In the case of interface security, which is simply a change of screen, there is a case of studying an efficient method for real-time monitoring of security control [11]. However, below we show examples of user-centered actual measurement and performance.

IV. EXPERIMENTAL RESULTS

According to the application of a new security system, the security policy of 'K' agency has brought the following results in comparison to conventional policies (out of 100 points). While a security level (scores) was low in conventional systems, the related indicators have improved as stated in TABLE IV through the improvement of a security system and provision of user-centered security services.

Score acquisition status was classified by the integration score before (2015), the application year (2016), and the operation (2017) for 1 year after application of security system.

TABLE IV. ACQUISITIONS BY SECURITY INDICATOR

Level	Before	Apply	After
1	76	77	86
2	45	94	98
3*	47	98	99
4	71	99	99
5	88	98	99
6	79	94	98
7*	79	98	99
8	77	100	100
9*	87	91	91
10	56	65	77
Mean	70.5	91.4	94.6

After the replacement of the security system, the scores improved for most indicators. Until now, the policies have gradually improved. According to the significantly improved indicators, compliance rates have increased, focusing on the indicators which can be applied by users in person after simple settings such as 'screen saver setting'. Then, most indicators were close to a perfect score. Finally, complete content and organizational editing is done before formatting.

The reason why the new system can acquire high scores is that the integration score (Figure 4) can be checked directly, and the user has provided convenience for confirming and taking security measures directly.

Based on the findings above, the following results were obtained:

1) An easy-to-execute security policy was applied with the application of policies by security of user group (profiling).

2) Compliance rates increased after a shift from the conventional centralized policy transferred from a little understanding of security policies to a way for users to check them in person.

3) The difficulties in applying security policies through a journey map were supported in man-to-man format to make them applied more easily.

A security system gains significant improvements after analyzing user experience factors from a security service perspective and applying profiling and user journey map as a way of service methodology. As a result, it was able to derive the following implications on the endpoint of future security systems:

1) Realization of efficient security policies through classification of major risks and vulnerability factors in a collective application of security policies by a policy indicator

2) Shift from the conventional centralized security policy transfer to user-centered security service

3) Better understanding of users with the application of service methodology.

V. Conclusion

With the recent increase in security breaches due to the vulnerability of user security, the importance of internal security control aside from an outside attack has become increasingly important [12]. Therefore, this study attempted to derive the applications of a more efficient security system through a better understanding of the users from a security service perspective and service-methodology approach. Escaping from conventional studies which focused on how to reduce user errors from a human factor perspective, this study discussed a way to increase the understanding of end-users.

As a result, it is anticipated that the study results would be useful in analyzing the end users' intention to observe security policies and establish a turning point with the intention to reduce a security system manager's workload. In this paper, we propose to expand the scope of research into a more specific security system by establishing a larger scale and a standard in future research although it is limited in the subject and scale of user profiling. In addition, there might be further studies on the extension of a study scope with more types of specific security systems (user vaccination) or a behavioral analysis on the users' security awareness to provide customized security services by user.

Acknowledgment

This research was supported by Korea Institute of Science and Technology Information (KISTI).

References

[1] B. Payne and W. Edwards, "A Brief Introduction to Usable Security", IEEE Computer Society, May, 2008, doi: 10.1109/MIC.2008.50

[2] I. Arce, "The Weakest Link Revisited", IEEE Security & Privacy, April, pp.72-76, 2003, doi: 10.1109/MSECP.2003.1193216

[3] NIST, "Discussion Draft of the Preliminary Cybersecurity Framework", Aug. 2013

[4] L. Camp, "Mental models of privacy and security", IEEE Society on Social Implications of Technology, Vol 28(3), Sep. 2009, doi: 10.1109/MTS.2009.934142

[5] R. Kainda, I. Flechais, and A.W. Roscoe, "Security and Usability:Analysis and Evaluation", International Conference on Availability , Reliability and Security, Feb. 2010, doi: 10.1109/ARES.2010.77

[6] D. D. Woods and E. M. Roth, "Cognitive Engineering: Human Problem Solving with Tools", Human Factors: The Journal of the Human Factors and Ergonomics Society, pp.415-430, 1988

[7] Nielsen Norman Group, "Customer Journey Map", https://www.nngroup.com/articles/customer-journey-mapping/

[8] S. Faily, J. Lyle, Ivan, and A. Simpson, "Usability and security by design: a case study in research and development", Internet Society NDSS symposium, Feb 2015

[9] D. Wixcon, K. Holzblatt, and S. Knox, "Contextual Design: An Emergent View of System Design", in CHI'90 Conference Proceedings, April pp.329-336, 1990

[10] G. Ju, J. Park, W. Heo, J. Gil, and H. Park, "A Study of the Factors Influencing Information Security Policy Compliance", Advanced Multimedia and Ubiquitous Engineering, May, pp. 720-728, 2017

[11] J. Park, S. Kim, S. Ahn, C. Lim, and K. Kim, "A Study on Interface Security Enhancement", KIPS Transactions on Computer and Communication Systems, Vol. 4, pp.171-176, 2015

[12] Ponemon Institute, "Risky Business: How Company Insiders Put High Value Information at Risk", June 2016

Information Security Resilience for Public Sector

HarkSoo Park
Dept. of Science and Technology Cyber Security Center
Korea Institute of Science and Technology Information
Daejeon, Korea
e-mail: hspark@kisti.re.kr

Gwangil Ju
Dept. of Science and Technology Cyber Security Center
Korea Institute of Science and Technology Information
Daejeon, Korea
e-mail: kiju@kisti.re.kr

***Abstract*— Recently, rapid changes in IT environment have shifted the security paradigm from data protection to protection of people. As a result, IT-related government policies have also changed. In terms of IT compliance, government bureau have suggested diverse laws and guidelines. Under these circumstances, this study attempts to determine IT compliance issues from the perspective of IT security personnel in a public agency and derive the related issues from the information security standpoint. Furthermore, it targets to address how to develop the IT security compliance in a progressive manner, focusing on the case of the public authority 'K Agency' after checking current IT security compliance issues.**

Keywords-component; Information Security System; Resilience; Compliance.

I. INTRODUCTION

Security Resilience refers to the ability to continuously deliver the intended outcome despite adverse cyber events. [1]. According to the National Information Protection White Book [2], the government passed the 'National Cyber Security Bill' during the National Assembly due to the continued threats to national security by North Korea and other serious cyber security issues on January 3, 2017. In a public sector, for the establishment of cloud security policy, an Act on the Development of Cloud Computing and Protection of its Users was put into effect in September 2015. In case of the Personal Information Protection Act, in addition, privacy protection has been stricter every year. In fact, many public agencies have made a lot of effort to examine and implement IT security compliance requests whenever they occur.

As a result, the security officers at various levels of the organizations are continuously spending administrative expenses to implement IT security compliance for the public sector in Korea and abroad. In addition, there is the burden of the implementation.

II. IT SECURITY COMPLIANCE IN KOREA

Domestic compliance has been proposed starting from 2009 with the focus on the financial sector. Since IT compliance is an information technology related to internal control, it is closely related to information security and IT systems of each organization are met with the requirements of government policies and guidelines, as well as to establish information systems in the direction that they can achieve.

According to Financial Security Institute (FSI) [3], it has reviewed and analyzed domestic and international laws & standards and industrial standards for IT system security management and published the compliance (2000). Then, the guidelines (2015) have been provided to each financial institution [4].

In the public sector, an FSI guide-level promotion system is not available yet. The administrative body 'Ministry of the Interior and Safety' and professional agency 'Korea Internet & Security Agency' have promoted IT security-related compliance. The major IT compliances are listed in TABLE I.

TABLE. I IT COMPLIANCE STATUES IN PUBLIC SECTOR

Category	Description
Public Sector IT Compliance (Domestic Law)	- National Information Framework Act - Act on Information Network Promotion and Information Protection, etc. - Information Communication Infrastructure Protection Act - E-government Act - Privacy Act - Act on Promotion of Information Protection Industry - Development of laws Concerning Development of Cloud Computing and Protection of Users
Other Domestic Laws	- Electronic document and electronic trading Act - Electronic Signature Act - Communication Confidentiality Protection Act - Copyright law - Industrial Technology Protection Act - Act on Protection and Utilization of Location Information, etc.
Global	GDPR
Standard/Certification	ISO27001, ISMS, PIMS, ePrivacy

Public sector IT compliance major issues can be divided into information security, privacy, and informatization. The Ministry of Public Administration and Security is promoting related policies to establish information system and information management system for the public sector based on the National Informatization Basic Law and the Personal Information Protection Act. The Information Security Division is responsible for assessing the level of information security at various levels of the National Intelligence Service (NIS), which acts as the National Cyber Security Control Tower, and has designated and managed major information and communication infrastructure.

In particular, the national information security management system is structured for the NIS to handle the national information security planning and coordination, as stated in Figure 1 (defined by Kim [5]). This management system is handled separately from the informatization and privacy protection which is done by the Ministry of the Interior and Safety. Therefore, the information security manager from a public agency is required to respond to each compliance issue by informatization, information security and privacy protection individually.

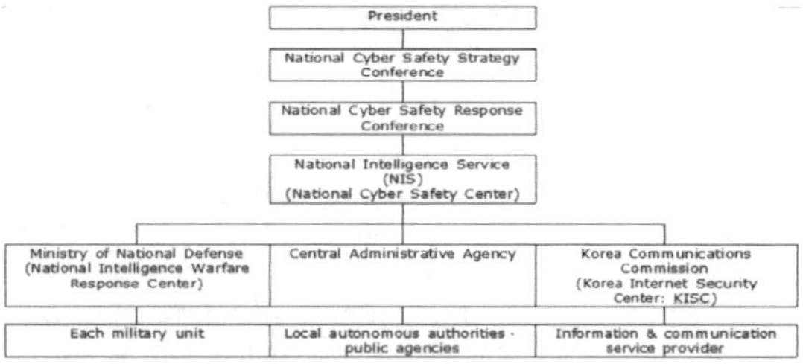

Figure. 1. National Information Security Management

III. CASE STUDY : 'K' AGENCY'S IT SECURITY COMPLIANCE

The 'K' agency affiliated with the Ministry of Science and Technology is a government-funded research institute in the IT infrastructure field of science and technology, and operates more than 100 information systems. To operate on many information systems and informatization projects, the information security system of 'K' agency was divided into information security governance (Figure 2) and the following information security management system (Figure 3) was drawn as follows [6]:

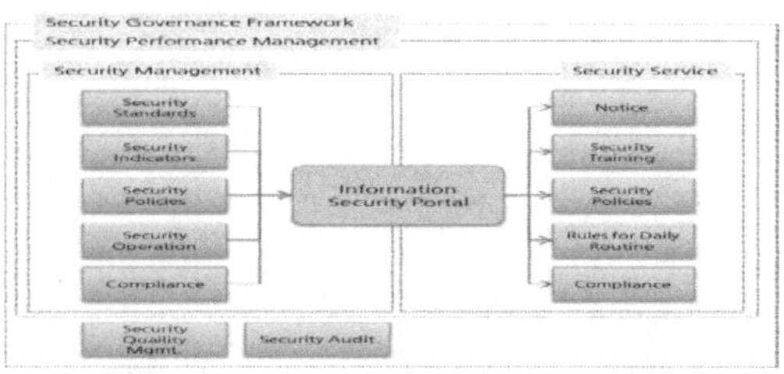

Figure. 2. Information Security Governance

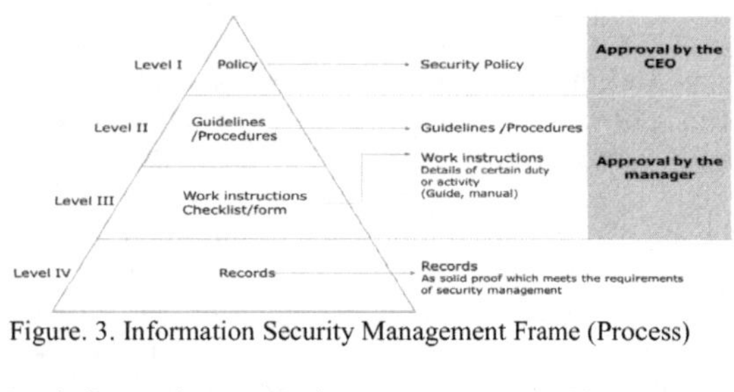

Figure. 3. Information Security Management Frame (Process)

In information security governance, 'K' agency has responded to the related information and compliance issues in real-time through the information security portal. In 2017, the security management was integrated with the intranet and provided in an electronic payment format (11 duties in total). As a result, the duties of security managers from each department and agency became more convenient (TABLE II).

TABLE II. APPLICATION EXAMPLE OF IT BUSINESS INTEGRATION

Category	Related Work Process
Informatization	- Enable / Change / Terminate DNS - LAN / Telephone Installation Request - Review of Equipment Installation - VPN Request - Review of RFP(Informatization Project) - Review of Output(Informatization Project)
Information Security	- Review of Information Security - Review of Security Level - External Access Permission / Blocking
IT Asset	- Import Asset(RFID connection) - Export Asset(RFID connection)

IV. CONCLUSION

In order to secure resilience, close implementation of government policy should be preceded. The government-level IT compliance has been performed in accordance with its related laws. Under some laws, a fine is charged on the un-fulfillment. Under these circumstances, IT departments can fulfill their role provided that there is close implementation with government compliance, and the related duties in the agencies are efficiently integrated. Then, the tasks should be promoted to improve the management level in each category (informatization, information security, personal information).

For this purpose, it is necessary to take active role in ensuring the information security dedicated organization and actively participate in the project in terms of the working organization, the management, the staff, and the auditing, and public relations activities of the government IT compliance are the most important.

This study approached what should be fulfilled first from the IT security compliance's perspective in a public sector. It is anticipated that it would suggest specific guidelines for the public sector and make a contribution to the improvement of the information security management level in a public sector.

REFERENCE

[1] B. Fredrik et al, "Cyber Resilience Fundamentals for a Definition", Advances in Intelligent System & Computing, 2015.

[2] National Intelligence Agency, National Information Protection White Book in 2017, 2017.

[3] Financial Security Institute, Financial Compliance Analysis Report, 2009

[4] Financial Security Institute, Financial Security Governance Guideline, 2015

[5] J. Kim, "National Information Security Agenda and Policies", Digital Policy Studies, Vol. 10, 2012

[6] G. Ju et al, A study of the factors that influence the information security compliance, Lecture Notes in Electrical Engineering, 2017, Vol. 448, p.720-728.

Cyber Security Threats Targeting CPS Systems: A Novel Approach Using Honeypot

Sameera Almulla[1], Elias Bou-Harb[2], Claude Fachkha[1,3]

College of IT and Engineering
[1] University of Dubai, Dubai, United Arab Emirates
[2] Cyber Threat Intelligence Laboratory, Florida Atlantic University, Florida, United States
[3] Steppa Cyber Inc., Canada
e-mail: {salmulla,cfachkha}@ud.ac.ae, ebouharb@fau.edu

***Abstract*—Supervisory Control and Data Acquisition (SCADA) systems are quite prominent for use in industrial, utility, and facility-based processes. While such technology continues to evolve in the context of Cyber-Physical Systems (CPS), and new paradigms such as the Internet-of-Things (IoT) arise, the threat of such systems remains relatively obscure, especially from the operational cyber security perspective. Various obstacles hinder the cyber security analysis of such systems, including the lack of (malicious) empirical data in addition to numerous logistic, privacy and reputation concerns. In this paper, we draw upon large-scale empirical data that was uniquely captured and analyzed from a recently deployed, Internet-scale CPS-specific honeynet. The aim is to shed light on misdemeanors and malicious activities targeting such CPS honeypots for threat inference, characterization and attribution. In addition, this aims at (1) collecting rare empirical data targeting such systems for further forensic investigations and sharing with the research community and (2) contributing to generating CPS-tailored empirical attack models to aid in effective CPS resiliency. The results identify and attribute the top sources of such suspicious and unauthorized SCADA activities and highlight a number of targeted threats. Furthermore, we uncover undocumented abuse against CPS services operating in building automation systems as well as factory environments.**

Keywords*–*SCADA System; CPS Security; CPS honeypots; Threat characterization.

I. INTRODUCTION

The Internet today continues to experience constant attacks targeting Cyber-Physical System (CPS). Such systems are defined by the National Institute of Standard and Technology (NIST) [1] as a set of inter-connected and distributed physical processes which control and monitor industrial control sectors such as utilities (i.e., electric, water, oil, natural gas), transportation, and building automation systems.

Several factors are affecting CPS security. First, in an ideal situation, the isolation of a CPS network from the external unsecured network (e.g., Internet) is a common practice. However, this is not the case, as there is a necessity to access such systems remotely using external devices. Second, support, consultants and vendors who connect their devices to the CPS network for various purposes create potential CPS security risks [2]. Third, replacing original parts in the CPS network with low-quality equipment to reduce the cost has recently triggered critical security against CPS systems by generating a plethora of 0-day vulnerabilities [3] [4]. Last but not least, the modernization of smart cities, inter-connected devices and IoT will obviously scale the threat vector against SCADA systems. According to the Industrial Control System Computer Emergency Response Team (ICS-CERT) [5], the assessment teams have identified hundreds of vulnerabilities within CPS architectural design. The rise of attacks on CPS compared to 2016 was attributed to the widespread adoption of the IoT technology.

Given the scarcity of CPS-specific tailored cyber threat intelligence, the contributions of this paper could be summarized as follows:

- deploying distributed SCADA monitors (i.e., honeypots) in various countries,
- analyzing and characterizing one month of unsolicited and suspicious SCADA communications, and
- measuring and validating the severity impact of such SCADA activities.

The remainder of this paper is organized as follows. Section II provides an overview of the related work. Section III presents the approach used to profile CPS cyber activities. Section IV elaborates the derived results based on the analyzed one-month period of SCADA data. Section V puts forward a few limitation points and its limitation. Finally, Section VI summaries and concludes this paper.

II. RELATED WORK

The literature review could be divided into mainly two parts, namely, probing analysis and CPS analysis.

A. Probing Analysis

Since probing activities is an important topic in cyber security and Internet measurements, it has been the focus of attention in many contributions. In [6], the authors provided an extensive survey in which they categorize the scanning topics based on their nature, strategy, and approach. Leonard *et al.* [7] performed stochastic derivation of a number of relations in order to propose an optimal stealth distribution scanning activity based on the probability of detection. The authors undertook the attackers' perspective (and not the measurement point of view) in order to significantly minimize the probability of detection. In [8] [9], the authors studied probing activities towards a large campus network using netflow data. They attempted to find different probing strategies and study their harmfulness. They analyzed the scanning behaviors by introducing the notion of gray IP space and techniques to detect potential scanners. Pryadkin *et al.* [10] performed an empirical evaluation of cyber space to infer the occupancy of IP addresses. In addition, J. Heidemann *et al.* [11] was one of the first works to survey the edge hosts in the public Internet. Cui *et al.* [12] analyzed a wide-area scan and presented a quantitative lower bound on the number of vulnerable embedded devices on a global scale. Further, in [13], the authors analyzed data from a large darknet composed of 5.5 million addresses to study Internet-wide probing activities. They detected probing events as large spikes generated by unique sources.

Furthermore, in [14], we have proposed a hybrid approach based on time-series analysis and context triggered piecewise hashing as applied to passive darknet dataset to infer, characterize and cluster probing activities targeting CPS protocols. Our work is complementary to the aforementioned contributions by focusing only on probes targeting CPS honeypots.

B. CPS Traffic Analysis

CPS network traffic monitoring and analysis can be divided in two main categories, namely, interactive monitoring and passive monitoring. On one hand, honeypots are an example of low- to high-interactive trap-based monitoring systems [2]. The first CPS honeypot, known as the SCADA HoneyNet Project, was designed and deployed in 2004 by Cisco Systems [15]. Digital Bond, a company that specializes in CPS cyber-security, deployed two SCADA honeypots in 2006 [16]. The release of Conpot in 2013 has greatly facilitated the deployment and management of CPS honeypots [17]. In order to evaluate the strength of a given honeypot in deceiving the attackers, Sysman *et al.* [18] introduced the notion of "Indicators of Deception", where some of the most popular low and medium interaction honeypots were examined. An indicator of deception is an action performed by the honeypot that may alert the attackers to identify that they are interacting with a honeypot. For example, Artillery [19] honeypot, by default blocks any malicious activities trying to connect with the services they emulate. Therefore, such honeypot is easy to be identified only due to their default action. Therefore, the deployed conpot was carefully configured to deceive the intruders without being noticed.

On the other hand, in terms of passive analysis, such methods include the study of network telescope traffic to generate statistics and trends related to various inferred CPS misdemeanors. The first limited reported network telescope study which addressed the security of CPS protocols was conducted in 2008 by Team Cymru [20]. Their report included coarse statistics on scans targeting commonly used CPS protocols, such as Distributed Network Protocol (DNP3) [21], Modbus [22] and Rockwell-encap [23]. Vasilomanolakis *et al.* [24] propsed a multi-stage attack detection system based on the attack signature analysis with CPS honeypot. The authors introduced a mobile device based CPS honeypot that monitors incoming probing activities, in general. Unlike the work presented in [24], our proposed methodology presents the first large-scale experimentation of the deployment and operation of a CPS-specific attacks by leveraging existing CPS honeypot that performs the essential analytics on attacks targeting CPS services on a darknet.

In contrast to current practices, in this work, we intend to establish a large-scale honeynet infrastructure to collect and curate CPS data from a plethora of systems and configurations. While the utilization of honeypots in cyber security tasks is definitely not new, their use cases tended to be ad hoc, independent and non-CPS focused. Thus, we propose a systematic and collaborative approach to harvest Internet-scale CPS honeypot data in a planned/staged manner.

III. Methodology

The proposed methodology consists of three phases: (1) data monitoring, which includes data collection; (2) data analytics, which provides statistics and information on the collected data; and (3) result's validation, which proves and affirms the obtained results.

In a nutshell, the monitored Internet activities are amalgamated into a centralized database for analysis and insights generation. Finally, the results are validated via trusted third party data-sets. Figure 1 provides an overview of our methodology. The deployed infrastructure is composed of 32 hosts distributed in 8 countries. In this setup, we were able to monitor activities originating from more than 40 countries targeting countries where the monitors are deployed.

First, in the data monitoring phase, every host is assigned an Internet public IP address to attract any unauthorized SCADA activity. Subsequently, we leverage three types of sensors that run simultaneously on the incoming traffic. We describe each of the sensors below:

- Generic sensors, which are configured to collect data from various communication protocols, SCADA and non-SCADA. Such sensors aim at (1) collecting all activities for through network investigation; and 2) helping in differentiating between random and focused SCADA activities. Please note that the deployed infrastructure mimics the internal dynamics of CPS systems, where the external vantage point has been protected by basic configuration of iptables.
- Network Intrusion Detection System (NIDS) sensors, which are Network based Intrusion Detection System, are used to identify threats that target the generic sensors as well as SCADA sensors. Such sensors provide more insights on the intention of the captured network activity. In this work, we have leveraged Snort [25] engine, an open-source NIDS, to detect and classify intrusions.
- SCADA sensors, which are typical SCADA honeypots which have been setup in interactive mode. SCADA sensors have been configured to monitor incoming traffic targeting SCADA protocols, namely, Modbus and Distributed Network Protocol (DNP3) as per their default setup [2]. Typical CPS dynamics (i.e., control and communications) provided by Modbus on port TCP 502 and Siemens on port TCP 102 have been emulated. Please note that the honeypots have been configured with public IP addresses but have not been advertised publically to prevent their immediate exploitation.

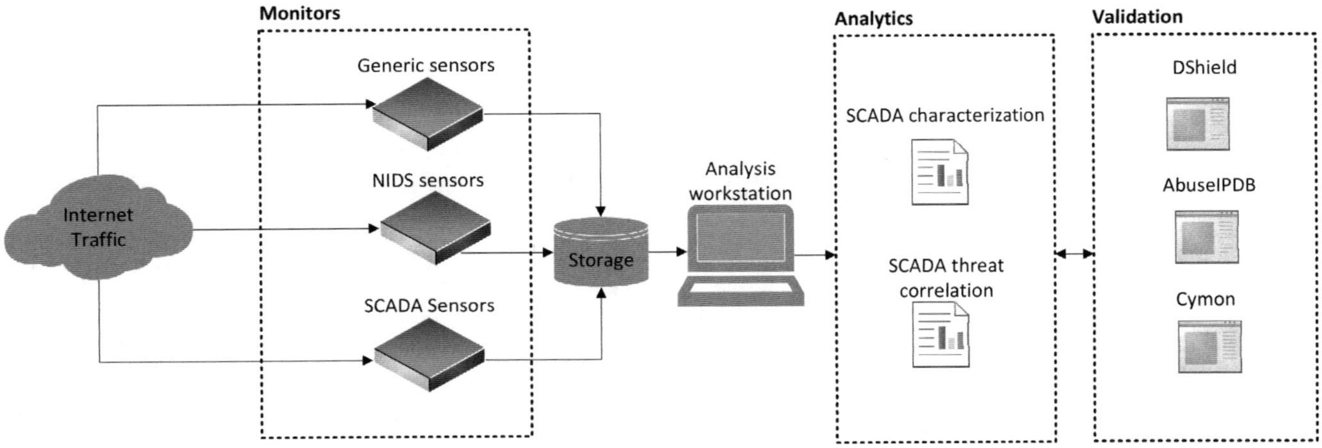

Figure 1. Methodology Overview

Second, in the analysis phase, the collected data from the monitors are pushed into an un-relational database for further analysis. In this context, we leverage several open source tools (e.g., whois [26]) to characterize the SCADA activities and identify the countries, cities, and Autonomous System (AS) names involved. Furthermore, the amalgamation in the previous phase allows us to correlate between the generic sensors and NIDS sensors data with the SCADA sensors data. For instance, we were able to tell the percentage of SCADA communication compared to generic ones and the types of threats affiliated to SCADA activities.

Last but not least, in order to validate our findings, reduce false positives and assess our methodology in identifying unreported (potential 0-days) attempts, we leverage three other trusted third-party datasets, namely, DShield [27], AbuseIPDB [28] and Cymon [29]. Such datasets provide rich insights on suspicious Internet activities such as types of threats and reputations of IP addresses. In the next section, we list our results based on this proposed multi-phase approach.

IV. Preliminary Results

The aim of this section is to provide an overview of our results based on our proposed approach. This section is divided into three parts. On one hand, the first part provides a characterization based on the overall data collected from our generic sensors. The latter collects generic network flow information which might include conventional Internet communications including SCADA activities. In fact, even if we setup a SCADA sensor, as long as it is publicly available, adversaries' activities can target SCADA services, in addition to any other services (ports) available on this sensor. On the other hand, the second part provides more detailed analysis based on SCADA sensors only. These sensors are dedicated to imitate SCADA hosts.

We have setup the SCADA sensor as per the open source deployment in [2]. We run the sensor in default mode, which emulates the basic SCADA host on the following services: Siemens S7-200 [30] Central Processing Unit (CPU) with 2 slaves, Modbus on port 502 Transmission Control Protocol (TCP), S7 Communication (S7Comm) [31] on port 102 TCP, HTTP on port 80 TCP, and Simple Network Management Protocol (SNMP) on port 161 User Datagram Protocol (UDP). Finally, the last part provides an overview of the threats associated to such SCADA activities. Such inference can help us understand the impact of these activities and the intention of the user, who is originating the cyber activity.

A. Data Overview

As mentioned earlier, this section provides an overview of any Internet activities or network traffic targeting the deployed sensors.

Overall, Figure 2 provides an overview of: 1) the number of identified flows, where a flow is defined as a collection of packets originating from one source IP address to one or multiple destination IP addresses; 2) total unique IP counts; 3) total number of scanning activities in all flows; and 4) alerts and intrusions associated to these flows.

The number of alerts and intrusions identified via network-based monitoring systems [25] is relatively high due to the fact that one source IP address within a flow might generate multiple threats on multiple sensors. Further discussion will be elaborated in Section IV-B. It is important to mention that our data is based on one-month period, namely, March 2018.

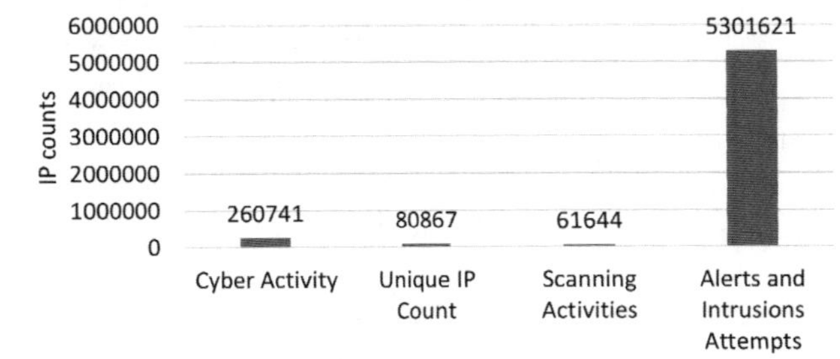

Figure 2. CPS Traffic Behavior Characterization

We have proceeded with the process of data characterization by identifying the top source countries, which initiated unsolicited cyber activities targeting our sensors. Figure 3 provides the top 10 source countries. United States is leading in terms of activities, followed by China then Brazil and Russia. Note that the United States generated around 44,500 flows, which is almost 38% of the global top countries. It is noteworthy to mention the surprising appearance of small countries in Asia, such as Vietnam and Indonesia, which have generated a relatively large number (almost 30%) of activities.

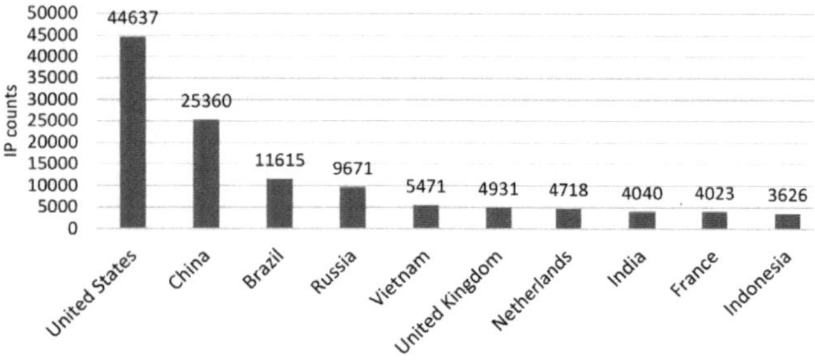

Figure 3. Top 10 Source Countries - Generic Sensors

We further classify the network traffic based on the initiating Autonomous Systems (AS). An AS number can uniquely identify Internet Service Providers (ISPs).

In Figure 4, we list the top 10 AS numbers, as per the traffic targeting our generic sensors. It is worth mentioning that, given that United States is identified as the highest country generating Internet traffic, however, based on AS classifications, Brazil is identified as the highest with 22.6% of the total traffic. This means that more network flows are originated from one single Brazilian AS number as compared to the United States, where more distributed flows are originated from various AS numbers. It is noteworthy to mention that Chinese ASes, which are ranked second and third, have generated together around 35% of the top ASes' traffic.

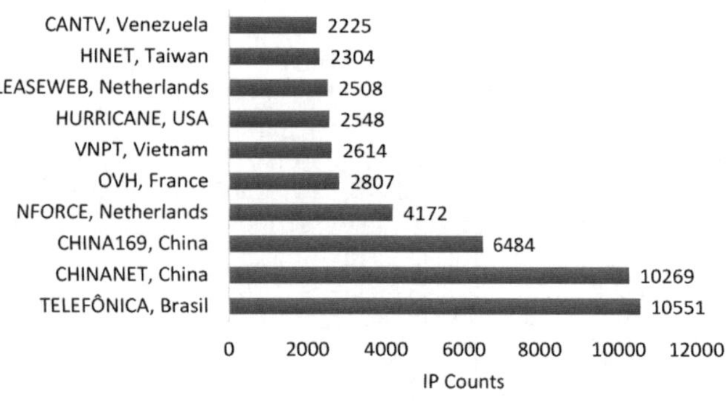

Figure 4. Top 10 Source AS Numbers - Generic Sensors

B. *SCADA-Specific Cyber Activities*

In this section, we aim at inferring probing events targeting main SCADA communication and control protocols as per the deployment of sensors in [2]. Using this deployment, we identified 54,511 SCADA cyber activities, in which 1,173 unique IP address are involved. This number of activities represents almost 21% of the total 260,741 generic cyber events, which were identified in the previous section (IV-A).

As shown in Figure 5, almost half (48.4%) of the top SCADA activities is generated from the United States. Furthermore, as per the AS name representation in Figure 6, the United States ASes are dominating with CariNet on top of the list. In light of the findings in Figure 6, we can further categorize probing events based on ASes associated services. For example, the purpose of probing can be to conduct scientific research [32] such as University of Michigan (UMICH in US), or the malicious probing activities got generated using a leased host from external service providers such as Linode [33] and Leasweb [34].

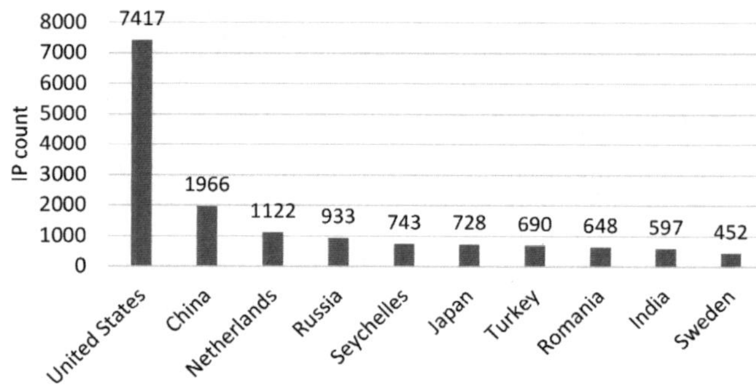

Figure 5. Top Source Countries - SCADA Activities

It is noteworthy to mention Seychelles among the top 5 source countries with 743 activities. Note that Seychelles, among many other islands, is a good location for abusers who find countries with weak or absent cyber security policies. In general, such islands can be easily set for botnet, Command and Control C&C servers and repositories of stolen information.

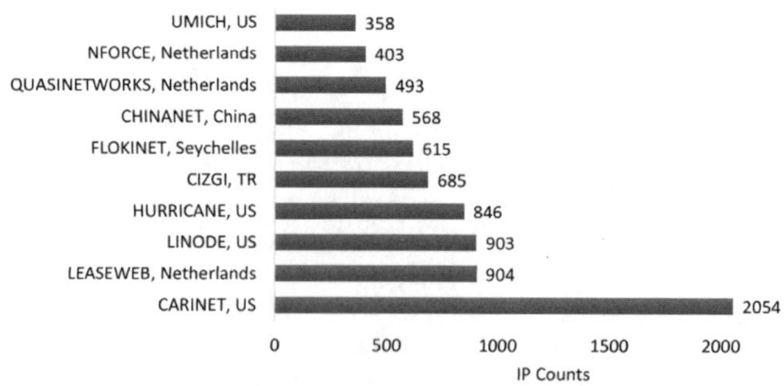

Figure 6. Top Source AS Names - SCADA Activities

In order to assess the severity of such SCADA activities, we have classified the traffic as per Table I. In a nutshell, our classification, which is motivated by [2], flags the network severity as medium, once a session is created, high if a request or response is generated, and critical if messages are transferred or communicated among the deployed monitors and the source IP addresses. Since the monitoring sensors are set on unused IP addresses, any traffic targeting them is deemed to be suspicious and/or unauthorized, or at least misconfigured.

As per the aforementioned approach, the investigation revealed that 13% of SCADA cyber activities are of medium severity, 64% of highly severity and 23% of critical severity.

TABLE I. CPS Probing Activities Severity Rating

Probing Activity Type	Severity Level
Session	Medium
Request/Response	High
Traffic/Connection	Critical

This result is shown in Figure 7.

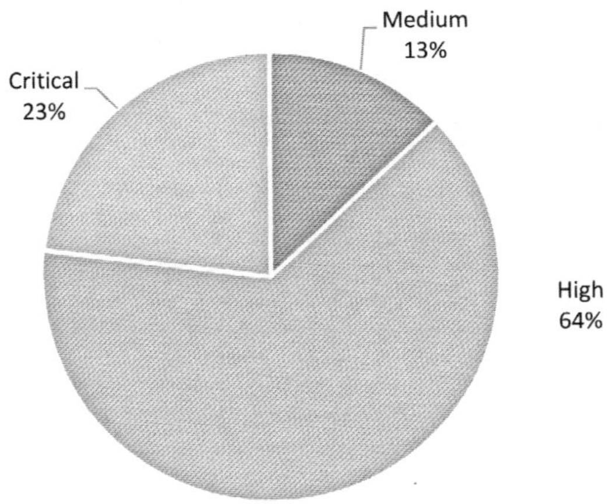

Figure 7. The Severity of SCADA Cyber Activities

In order to achieve a better accuracy and understanding as per the abused services, next, we characterize the communication per the targeted ports, which represent specific operated services. Figure 8 visualizes the distribution of abused services for those of critical severity only. This means that such activities have not just probed requested connection or a session to the deployed monitors, but also have shared data, after the connection setup.

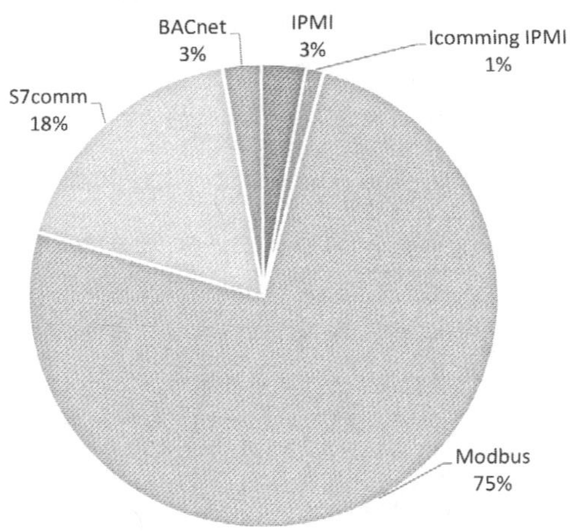

Figure 8. Top Critical Abused SCADA Services

It is not very surprising to identify that Modbus is the most (75%) critically abused SCADA service. Such result is not new for security researchers [14], who have already found similar results based on the analysis of passive monitoring sensors. It is also important to mention that Modbus is the most widely used SCADA service today. In addition to S7comm and BACnet, which came second and third after Modbus respectively, the Intelligent Platform Management Interface (IPMI) has been also found but with very minimal numbers (total of 4%).

C. Validation

In an attempt to validate our findings, we adopt the approach used in [14], where publicly available online databases namely DShield, AbuseIPDB, and Cymon are used. Undoubtedly, the integration and synergy of the findings from multiple online databases will lead to better validation of the obtained results.

DShield is a community-based firewall log correlation system that holds records on reported suspicious IP addresses. Furthermore, the online database returns the risk scale, targeted attacks and a total number of the report counts. DShield reports the speciousness of a reported IP address on a scale from 0% (lowest) to 100% (highest)

As stated earlier, we validated the source IP addresses of the SCADA network communication activities. Our findings revealed that 100% of the worldwide source IP addresses were found in DShield, with an average risk scale of 53%. Among the highly risky malicious sources of SCADA communication, where the risk scale was either 90% or 100%, the maximum attack counts are 2,946 and 53,215 report counts. Overall, the average attack counts of the detected source IP addresses is 1,199, while the average reported malicious IP addresses were 22,016. DShield findings summary are listed in Table II.

TABLE II. Validation Summary

	Dshield			AbuseIPDB
	Risk Scale	Attacks Count	Report Count	Abuse Confidence Rate
Minimum	0%	133	3000	15%
Maximum	100%	2946	65158	100 %
Average	53%	1199	22016	67%

To measure the abuse confidence rate of the detected SCADA activities, we used the AbuseIPDB's online repository which indexes Internet-scale specious IP addresses as reported by the service providers and backbone network operators. Our investigation revealed that the average abuse confidence rate of the unsolicited interaction is 67.4%, with a maximum of 100% abuse confidence rate and the minimum of 15%. A summary of the validation results are listed in Table II.

In an effort to map the results obtained from AbuseIPDB to DShield, we observed that despite the high-risk scale of the source of SCADA traffic, the abuse confidence rate varied from 15% to 57%. This implies that there are abuse cases reported for those IP addresses in DShield and that have not been reported in AbuseIPDB.

Next, we will correlate threats generated from such activities. To identify the type of the network traffic activities, we levereged Cymon's [29] online repository. Cymon is a largest open source tracker of malware, botnets, spams, etc. Based on our findings, 66.6% of malicious activities were e-mail attacks, and 50% of the following types: WEB attacks, Internet Message Access Protocol (IMAP) attacks, Secure Shell (SSH) attacks, and File Transfer Protocol (FTP) attacks. In addition to the attacks, 16.6% of scanning activities were detected, such as Domain Name Service (DNS) attacks, password disclosure attempts, telnet scans and Remote Desktop Protocol (RDP) scans.

V. Discussion

In this section, we interpret and describe the significance of our findings in light of the proposed methodology.

Vantage Points: Our contribution is limited to the number of deployed monitors. Although this study covers 32 monitors across 8 countries, we cannot identify SCADA activities targeting networks beyond such vantage points. However, we believe that this work is a step forward for building a more distributed network of monitors at large-scale.

Internal SCADA Dynamics: Our model covers the CPS communication targeting SCADA hosts from an Internet perspective. However, this contribution does not cover the security or monitoring of communications within SCADA systems (e.g., inside a power plant), neither hardware devices (e.g., physical smart grid). Our approach complements on-site SCADA security mechanisms such as network isolation SCADA security systems.

VI. Conclusion and Future Work

Conducting research on SCADA data is challenging due to the restrictions on physically accessing critical infrastructure sites. In this paper, we have analyzed SCADA data independently of the infrastructure, via SCADA sensors deployed on the Internet. Our contribution is unique in terms of the following items: 1) our dataset which is collected from more than 32 deployments in 8 countries and (2) our analysis which correlates conventional data with SCADA data and associated threats. Our analysis uncovers unsolicited traffic originating from various countries and AS names. Our future work involves fully-automating the detection and analysis models at a large scale and in real-time. Furthermore, we are developing algorithms to provide insights on the intention of the scans (i.e., benign vs malicious). The purpose is to produce threat intelligence data and sharing in addition to generating notifications for awareness and mitigation of threats against SCADA systems.

Acknowledgment

The dataset used in this research was provided by Steppa Cyber Inc (steppa.ca). The authors would like to thank all the research team at Steppa. Furthermore, the authors would like to thank our colleagues from Dubai Electronic Security Agency (DESC), who provided insight and expertise that assisted this research.

References

[1] S. Keith, P. Victoria, L. Suzanne, A. Marshall, and H. Adam, "Guide to Supervisory Control and Data Acquisition (SCADA) and Industrial Control Systems Security," [Online]: https://nvlpubs.nist.gov/nistpubs/SpecialPublications/NIST.SP.800-82r2.pdf, 2015, retrieved: August, 2018.

[2] C. Scott and R. Carbone, "Designing and implementing a honeypot for a scada network," The SANS Institute Reading Room., vol. 22, 2014, p. 2016.

[3] M. Burmester, E. Magkos, and V. Chrissikopoulos, "Modeling security in cyber–physical systems," International journal of critical infrastructure protection, vol. 5, no. 3-4, 2012, pp. 118–126.

[4] E. Bou-Harb, M. Debbabi, and C. Assi, "A statistical approach for fingerprinting probing activities," in Availability, Reliability and Security (ARES), 2013 Eighth International Conference on. IEEE, 2013, pp. 21–30.

[5] Department of Homeland Security (DHS), "ICS-CERT Monitor Newsletter," [Online]: https://ics-cert.us-cert.gov/sites/default/files/Monitors/ICS-CERT_Monitor_Nov-Dec2017_S508C.pdf, 2017, retrieved: August, 2018.

[6] E. Bou-Harb, M. Debbabi, and C. Assi, "Cyber scanning: a comprehensive survey," IEEE Communications Surveys & Tutorials, vol. 16, no. 3, 2014, pp. 1496–1519.

[7] X. W. D. Leonard, Z. Yao and D. Loguinov, "Stochastic analysis of horizontal ip scanning," in INFOCOM, 2012 Proceedings IEEE. IEEE, 2012, pp. 2077–2085.

[8] Y. Jin, Z.-L. Zhang, K. Xu, F. Cao, and S. Sahu, "Identifying and tracking suspicious activities through ip gray space analysis," in Proceedings of the 3rd annual ACM workshop on Mining network data. ACM, 2007, pp. 7–12.

[9] Y. Jin, G. Simon, K. Xu, Z. Zhang, and V. Kumar, "Grays anatomy: Dissecting scanning activities using ip gray space analysis," SysML07, 2007.

[10] Y. Pryadkin, R. Lindell, J. Bannister, and R. Govindan, "An empirical evaluation of ip address space occupancy," USC/ISI, Tech. Rep. ISI-TR-2004-598, 2004.

[11] J. Heidemann, Y. Pradkin, R. Govindan, C. Papadopoulos, G. Bartlett, and J. Bannister, "Census and survey of the visible internet," in Proceedings of the 8th ACM SIGCOMM conference on Internet measurement. ACM, 2008, pp. 169–182.

[12] A. Cui and S. Stolfo, "A quantitative analysis of the insecurity of embedded network devices: results of a wide-area scan," in Proceedings of the 26th Annual Computer Security Applications Conference. ACM, 2010, pp. 97–106.

[13] Z. Durumeric, M. Bailey, and J. A. Halderman, "An internet-wide view of internet-wide scanning." in USENIX Security Symposium, 2014, pp. 65–78.

[14] C. Fachkha, E. Bou-Harb, A. Keliris, N. Memon, and M. Ahamad, "Internet-scale probing of CPS: Inference, characterization and orchestration analysis," in Network and Distributed System Security Symposium (NDSS), 2017.

[15] V. Pothamsetty and M. Franz, "Scada honeynet project: Building honeypots for industrial networks," 2008.

[16] Digital Bond, "SCADA Honeynet," [Online]: http://www.digitalbond.com/tools/scada-honeynet/, retrieved: August, 2018.

[17] HoneyNet Project, "CONPOT ICS/SCADA Honeypot," [Online]: http://conpot.org/, retrieved: August, 2018.

[18] D. Sysman, G. Evron, and I. Sher, "Breaking honeypots for fun and profit," in BLACKHAT, 2015.

[19] Project Artillery, "SCADA Honeynet," [Online]: https://blog.binarydefense.com/project-artillery-now-a-binary-defense-project, retrieved: August, 2018.

[20] Team CYMRU, "Who is looking for your SCADA infrastructure?" [Online]: https://www.team-cymru.com/ReadingRoom/Whitepapers/2009/scada.pdf, 2008, retrieved: August, 2018.

[21] DNP, "Overview of the DNP3 Protocol," [Online]: https://www.dnp.org/Pages/AboutDefault.aspx, 2011, retrieved: August, 2018.

[22] Modicon, "Modbus," [Online]: http://www.modbus.org/, 2018, retrieved: August, 2018.

[23] Rockwell, "Rockwell Automation," [Online]: https://www.rockwellautomation.com/site-selection.html, 2018, retrieved: August, 2018.

[24] E. Vasilomanolakis, S. Srinivasa, C. G. Cordero, and M. Mhlhuser, "Multi-stage attack detection and signature generation with ics hon-

eypots," in NOMS 2016 - 2016 IEEE/IFIP Network Operations and Management Symposium, 2016, pp. 1227–1232.

[25] M. Roesch, "Snort: Lightweight intrusion detection for networks." in Lisa, vol. 99, no. 1, 1999, pp. 229–238.

[26] "Whois," [Online]: https://www.whois.net/, 2018, retrieved: August, 2018.

[27] Internet Storm Center, "DShield," [Online]: https://www.dshield.org/, retrieved: August, 2018.

[28] Digital Ocean, "AbuseIP DB," [Online]: https://www.abuseipdb.com/, retrieved: August, 2018.

[29] Open Threat Intelligence, "Cymon," [Online]: https://cymon.io/, retrieved: August, 2018.

[30] Siemens, "Programmable Controller System Manual," [Online]: https://cache.industry.siemens.com/dl/files/582/1109582/att_22063/v1/s7200_system_manual_en-US.pdf, 2018, retrieved: August, 2018.

[31] ——, "S7 Communication (S7comm)," [Online]: https://wiki.wireshark.org/S7comm, 2018, retrieved: August, 2018.

[32] M. Bailey, E. Cooke, F. Jahanian, A. Myrick, and S. Sinha, "Practical darknet measurement," in Information Sciences and Systems, 2006 40th Annual Conference on, 2006, pp. 1496–1501.

[33] Linode, "Linode Cloud Hosting Service," [Online]: https://welcome.linode.com/features-1gb/?gclid=EAIaIQobChMIt_2Rgbym3QIVVTPTCh1ACALZEAAYASAAEgLH2_D_BwE, 2018, retrieved: August, 2018.

[34] Leaseweb, "Global Hosted Infrastructure (IaaS) and Cloud Solutions," [Online]: https://www.leaseweb.com/, 2018, retrieved: August, 2018.

Metrics for Continuous Active Defence

George O.M. Yee
Computer Research Lab, Aptusinnova Inc., Ottawa, Canada
Dept. of Systems and Computer Engineering, Carleton University, Ottawa, Canada
email: george@aptusinnova.com, gmyee@sce.carleton.ca

***Abstract*—As a sign of the times, headlines today are full of attacks against an organization's computing infrastructure, resulting in the theft of sensitive data. In response, the organization applies security measures (e.g., encryption) to secure its vulnerabilities. However, these measures are often only applied once, with the assumption that the organization is then protected and no further action is needed. Unfortunately, attackers continuously probe for vulnerabilities and change their attacks accordingly. This means that an organization must also continuously check for new vulnerabilities and secure them, to continuously and actively defend against the attacks. This paper derives metrics that characterize the security level of an organization at any point in time, based on the number of vulnerabilities secured and the effectiveness of the securing measures. The paper then shows how an organization can apply the metrics for continuous active defence.**

Keywords- sensitive data; vulnerability; security measure; security level; metrics; continuous defence.

I. INTRODUCTION

Headlines today are full of news of attacks against computing infrastructure, resulting in sensitive data being compromised. These attacks have devastated the victim organizations. The losses have not only been financial (e.g., theft of credit card information), but perhaps more importantly, have damaged the organizations' reputation. Consider, for example, the following data breaches that occurred in 2017 [1]:

- March, 2017, Dun & Bradstreet: This business services company found its marketing database with over 33 million corporate contacts shared across the web. The company claimed that the breach occurred to businesses, numbering in the thousands, that had bought its 52 GB database. The leak may have included full names, work email addresses, phone numbers, and other business-related data from millions of employees of organizations such as the US Department of Defence, the US Postal Service, AT&T, Walmart, and CVS Health.
- September, 2017, Equifax: This is one of the three largest credit agencies in the US. It announced a breach that may have affected 143 million customers, one of the worst breaches ever due to the sensitivity of the data stolen. The compromised data included social security numbers, driver's license numbers, full names, addresses, birth dates, credit card numbers, and other personal information. Hackers had access to the company's system from mid-May to July by exploiting a vulnerability in website software. Equifax discovered the breach on July 29, 2017.

There were many more breaches in 2017, and in fact, no year can be said to have been breach-free. Moreover, the problem appears to be getting worst, as 2017 has been mentioned [2] as a "record-breaking year" for data breaches: a total of 5,207 breaches and 7.89 billion information records compromised.

In response to attacks, such as the ones described above, organizations determine their computer system vulnerabilities and secure them using security measures. Typical measures include firewalls, intrusion detection systems, two-factor authentication, encryption, and training for employees on identifying and resisting social engineering. However, once the security measures have been implemented, organizations tend to believe that they are safe and that no further actions are needed. Unfortunately, attackers do not give up just because the organization has secured its known computer vulnerabilities. Rather, the attackers will continuously probe the organization's computer system for new vulnerabilities that they can exploit. This means that the organization must continuously analyze its computer system vulnerabilities and secure any new ones that it discovers. In order to do this effectively, it is useful to have quantitative metrics of the security level at any particular point in time, based on the number of vulnerabilities secured and the effectiveness of the security measures, at that point in time. An acceptable security level can be set, so that if the security level falls below this acceptable level due to new vulnerabilities, the latter can be secured to bring the security level back to the acceptable level. This work derives such metrics and shows how to apply them for continuous active defence, i.e., continuous vulnerabilities evaluation and follow up.

The objectives of this work are: i) derive straightforward, clear metrics of the resultant protection level obtained by an organization at any point in time, based on the use of security measures to secure vulnerabilities and the effectiveness of the measures, ii) show how these metrics can be calculated, iii) show how the metrics can be applied for continuous active defence. We seek straightforward, easy to understand metrics since complicated, difficult to understand ones tend not to be used or tend to be misapplied. We base these metrics on securing vulnerabilities since this has been and continues to be the method organizations use to secure their computer infrastructure.

The rest of this paper is organized as follows. Section II discusses sensitive data, attacks, and vulnerabilities. Section III derives the metrics and presents various aspects of the metrics, including some of their strengths, weaknesses, and limitations. Section IV explains how to apply the metrics for continuous active defence. Section V discusses related work and Section VI gives conclusions and future research.

II. SENSITIVE DATA, ATTACKS, AND VULNERABILITIES

Sensitive data is data that needs protection and must not fall into the wrong hands. It includes private or personal information [3], which is information about an individual, can identify that individual, and is owned by that individual. For example, an individual's height, weight, or credit card number can all be used to identify the individual and are considered as personal information or personal sensitive data. Sensitive data also includes non-personal information that may compromise the competitiveness of the organization if divulged, such as trade secrets or proprietary algorithms and formulas. For government organizations, non-personal sensitive data may include information that is vital for the security of the country for which the government organization is responsible.

DEFINITION 1: *Sensitive data* (SD) is information that must be protected from unauthorized access in order to safeguard the privacy of an individual, the well-being or expected operation of an organization, or the well-being or expected functioning of an entity for which the organization has responsibility.

DEFINITION 2: An *attack* is any action carried out against an organization's computer system that, if successful, compromises the system or the SD held by the system.

An attack that compromises a computer system is Distributed Denial of Service (DDoS). One that compromises the SD held by the system is a Trojan horse attack in which malicious software (the Trojan) is planted inside the system to steal SD. Attacks can come from an organization's employees, in which case the attack is an *inside attack*. For example, a disgruntled employee secretly keeps a copy of a SD backup and sells it on the "dark web".

DEFINITION 3: A *vulnerability* of a computer system is any weakness in the system that can be targeted by an attack with some expectation of success. A vulnerability can be secured to become a *secured vulnerability* through the application of a security measure.

An example of a vulnerability is a communication channel that is used to convey sensitive data in the clear. This vulnerability can be targeted by a Man-in-the-Middle attack with reasonable success of stealing the sensitive data. This vulnerability can become a secured vulnerability by encrypting the sensitive data that the communication channel carries.

A computer system can undergo upgrades, downgrades, and other modifications over time that changes its number of secured and unsecured vulnerabilities. It is thus necessary to specify a time *t* when referring to vulnerabilities. Clearly, the number of secured and unsecured vulnerabilities of a computer system at time *t* is directly related to the security level of the system at time *t*. This idea is formalized in the next definition.

DEFINITION 4: A computer system's security level (SL) at time t, or SL(t), is the degree of protection from attacks that results from having q(t) secured vulnerabilities, and p(t) unsecured vulnerabilities, where the system has a total of N(t) = p(t)+q(t) secured and unsecured vulnerabilities. SL(t) is uniquely represented by the pair (p(t), q(t)).

Clearly SL(t) increases with increasing q(t) and decreases with increasing p(t). Figure 1 shows 3 SL(t) points on the (p(t), q(t)) plane for N(t)=100.

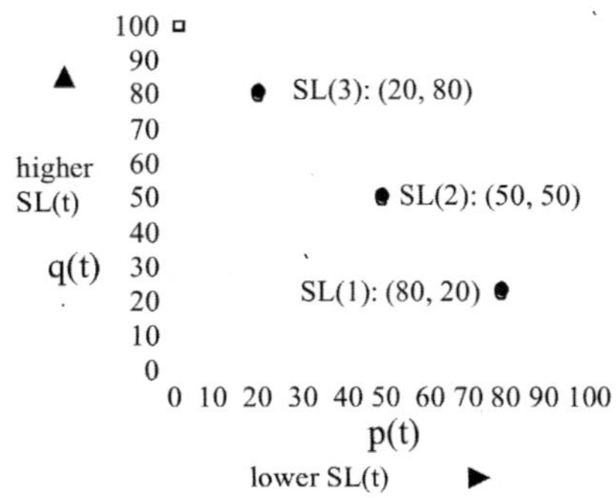

Figure 1. SL(t) points corresponding to a computer system with N(t)=100. SL(3) is higher security than SL(2), which is higher security than SL(1).

In Figure 1, the higher values of q(t) correspond to higher security levels, and the higher values of p(t) correspond to lower security levels.

III. METRICS FOR CONTINUOUS ACTIVE DEFENCE

While the pair (p(t), q(t)) uniquely represents SL(t), it cannot be used to calculate the value of SL(t), which would be useful in tracking the security of a system over time as its vulnerabilities change. In this section, we derive two metrics for the value of SL(t), one assuming that the measures securing vulnerabilities are totally reliable; the other with the measures only partly reliable. Both metrics are applied right after the vulnerabilities have been determined, and possibly before any of them have actually been secured. Determining vulnerabilities is discussed in Section III.C below.

A. Metric with Totally Reliable Securing Measures

We seek a metric STRM(t) (STRM is an acronym for "SL with Totally Reliable Measures") for a computer system's SL(t), where all securing measures are totally reliable. Suppose that p(t) and q(t) are as in Definition 4. Let $P_t(e)$ represent the probability of event e at time t. Let "exploit" mean a successful attack on a vulnerability. Let "all exploits" mean exploits on 1 or more vulnerabilities. Let $U_k(t)$ denote an unsecured vulnerability k at time t. We have

$$SL(t) = P_t(\text{no exploits}) = 1\text{-}P_t(\text{all exploits}) \quad (1)$$

However, the only exploitable vulnerabilities are the unsecured vulnerabilities since the securing measures are totally reliable. Therefore

$$P_t(\text{all exploits}) = \Sigma_k\, [P_t(\text{exploit of } U_k(t))]$$

by applying the additive rule for the union of probabilities, assuming that 2 or more exploits do not occur simultaneously. Let $u_k(t)$ be a real number with $0 < u_k(t) \leq p(t)$ and $\Sigma_k u_k(t) = p(t)$. Set

$$P_t(\text{exploit of } U_k(t)) \approx u_k(t)/(p(t)+q(t)) \quad (2)$$

By substitution using (2)

$$P_t(\text{all exploits}) \approx \Sigma_k\, [u_k(t)/(p(t)+q(t))]$$
$$= \Sigma_k u_k(t)/(p(t)+q(t))$$
$$= p(t)/(p(t)+q(t)) \quad (3)$$

The condition $0 < u_k(t) \leq p(t)$ is needed to ensure that there is some probability for an unsecured vulnerability to be exploited. The condition $\Sigma_k u_k(t) = p(t)$ is necessary in order for $P_t(\text{all exploits}) \leq 1$. Expression (2) gives a way of assigning values for $P_t(\text{exploit of } U_k(t))$ based on a risk analysis [3]. However, expression (3) ensures that such assignment is not needed for calculating STRM(t). In other words, the fact that some vulnerabilities are more likely to be exploited than others does not affect the value of STRM(t).

Substituting (3) into (1) gives

$$SL(t) \approx 1\text{-}[p(t)/(p(t)+q(t))]$$
$$= q(t)/(p(t)+q(t)) \quad \text{if } p(t)+q(t) > 0$$
$$= 1 \quad \text{if } p(t)+q(t) = 0$$

We obtain STRM(t) by assigning as follows:

$$\mathbf{STRM(t) = q(t)/(p(t)+q(t)) \quad if\ p(t)+q(t) > 0} \quad (4)$$
$$\mathbf{= 1 \quad if\ p(t)+q(t) = 0} \quad (5)$$

We see from (4) that $0 \leq STRM(t) \leq 1$ if $p(t)+q(t) > 0$ and has value 0 if $q(t)=0$ (the system has no secured vulnerabilities) and 1 if $p(t)=0$ (all of its vulnerabilities are secured). We see from (5) that STRM(t)=1 if $p(t)+q(t)=0$ (no vulnerabilities, which is unlikely). The values of the metric are therefore as expected.

B. *Metric with Partially Reliable Securing Measures*

Here, we seek a metric SPRM(t) (SPRM is an acronym for "SL with Partially Reliable Measures") for a computer system's SL(t) where the measures securing the vulnerabilities are only partially reliable.

Let $V_k(t)$ denote a secured vulnerability k at time t. The reliability $r_k(t)$ of the measure securing $V_k(t)$ can be defined as the probability that the measure remains operating from time zero to time t, given that it was operating at time zero [4]. The unreliability of the measure is then $1\text{-}r_k(t)$. We have the events

[exploit of $V_k(t)$] if and only if [$V_k(t)$ selected for exploit] AND [measure securing $V_k(t)$ unreliable]

Since the two right-hand side events are independent,

$$P_t(\text{exploit of } V_k(t)) = P_t(V_k(t) \text{ selected for exploit}) \times P_t(\text{measure securing } V_k(t) \text{ unreliable})$$

Set

$$P_t(V_k(t) \text{ selected for exploit}) \approx 1/(p(t)+q(t)) \quad (6)$$

since attackers will have no preference to attack one secured vulnerability over another secured vulnerability (they should not even see them as vulnerabilities). Again, applying the additive rule for the union of probabilities,

$$P_t(\text{all } V_k(t) \text{ exploits}) = \Sigma_k[P_t(V_k(t) \text{ selected for exploit}) \times P_t(\text{measure securing } V_k(t) \text{ unreliable})]$$
$$= \Sigma_k\, [(1/(p(t)+q(t)))(1\text{-}r_k(t))]$$
$$= [\Sigma_k(1\text{-}r_k(t)]/[p(t) + q(t)]$$
$$= [q(t)\text{-}\Sigma_k r_k(t)]/[p(t) + q(t)]$$
$$=[q(t)/(p(t)+q(t))]\text{-}\Sigma_k r_k(t)/(p(t) + q(t)) \quad (7)$$

Now, since both $U_k(t)$ and $V_k(t)$ can be exploited,

$$P_t(\text{all exploits})=P_t(\text{all } U_k(t) \text{ exploits}) + P_t(\text{all } V_k(t) \text{ exploits})$$
$$\approx [p(t)/(p(t)+q(t))] + [q(t)/(p(t)+q(t))]\text{-}\Sigma_k r_k(t)/(p(t) + q(t))$$
$$= 1 - \Sigma_k r_k(t)/(p(t) + q(t)) \quad (8)$$

by substitution using (3) and (7), where (3) is $P_t(\text{all } U_k(t) \text{ exploits})$. Finally, by substitution using (1) and (8),

$$SL(t) \approx 1 - 1 + \Sigma_k r_k(t)/(p(t) + q(t))$$
$$= \Sigma_k r_k(t)/(p(t) + q(t)) \quad \text{if } p(t) \geq 0,\ q(t) > 0$$
$$= 1 \quad \text{if } p(t)+q(t) = 0$$
$$= 0 \quad \text{if } p(t)>0,\ q(t) = 0$$

We obtain SPRM(t) by assigning as follows:

$$\mathbf{SPRM(t) = \Sigma_k r_k(t)/(p(t)+q(t)) \quad if\ p(t) \geq 0,\ q(t) > 0} \quad (9)$$
$$\mathbf{= 1 \quad if\ p(t)+q(t) = 0} \quad (10)$$
$$\mathbf{= 0 \quad if\ p(t)>0,\ q(t)=0} \quad (11)$$

We see from (9) that $0 < SPRM(t) < 1$ for $p(t) \geq 0$, $q(t) > 0$ (all vulnerabilities may or may not be secured), and from (10) that SPRM(t) = 1 for $p(t)+q(t) = 0$ (no vulnerabilities, which is unlikely). We see from (11) that SPRM(t) = 0 for $p(t)>0$, $q(t) = 0$ (no secured vulnerabilities). We also see that for $r_k(t) = 1$, SPRM(t) is the same as STRM(t). The values of the metric are therefore as expected.

C. *Calculating the Metrics*

Calculating STRM(t) requires the values of p(t) and q(t) at a series of time points of interest. SPRM(t) requires the values of p(t), q(t), and the reliability value for each measure used to secure the vulnerabilities.

To obtain the values of p(t) and q(t), an organization may perform a threat analysis of vulnerabilities in the organization's computer system that could allow attacks to occur. Threat analysis or threat modeling is a method for systematically assessing and documenting the security risks associated with a system (Salter et al. [5]). Threat modeling involves understanding the adversary's goals in attacking the system based on the system's assets of interest. It is predicated on that fact that an adversary cannot attack a system without a way of supplying it with data or otherwise accessing it. In addition, an adversary will only attack a system if it has some assets of interest. The method of threat analysis given in [5] or any other method of threat analysis will yield the total number N(t) of vulnerabilities to attacks at time t. Once this number is known, the organization can select which vulnerabilities to secure and which security measures to use, based on a prioritization of the vulnerabilities and the amount of budget it has to spend. A way to optimally select which vulnerabilities to secure is described in [6]. Once vulnerabilities have been selected to be secured, we have q(t). Then p(t) = N(t) – q(t). The threat analysis may be carried out by a project team consisting of the system's design manager, a security and privacy analyst, and a project leader acting as facilitator. In addition to having security expertise, the analyst must also be very familiar with the organization's computer system. Further discussion on threat analysis is outside the scope of this paper. More details on threat modeling can be found in [6]. Vulnerabilities may be prioritized using the method in [3], which describes prioritizing privacy risks.

The reliability values for hardware measures used to secure the selected vulnerabilities may be obtained from the hardware's manufacturers (e.g., hardware firewall). Reliability values for software and algorithmic measures are more difficult to obtain (e.g., encryption algorithm). For these, it may be necessary to estimate the reliability values based on the rate of progress of technology. For example, one could estimate the reliability of an encryption algorithm based on estimates of the computer resources that attackers have at their disposal. If they have access to a super computer, an older encryption algorithm may not be sufficiently reliable. One could also opt to be pessimistic and assign low reliability values, which would have the net effect of boosting security by securing more vulnerabilities, in order to meet a certain SL(t) level (see Section IV). Reliability values for security measures represent a topic for future research.

It is important to note that at each time point where the metrics are calculated, the values of p(t) and q(t) are generated anew. Vulnerabilities secured previously with totally reliable measures would not appear again as vulnerabilities. On the other hand, vulnerabilities secured with only partially reliable measures should be identified again as vulnerabilities. Further, it is not necessary to have actually implemented the securing measures before calculating the metrics.

D. Graphing the Metrics

The metrics STRM(t) and SPRM(t) are both functions of p(t), q(t), and t. Figure 2 shows a 3-dimensional graph of these metrics with axes for STRM(t)/SPRM(t), p(t), and q(t). Time is not shown explicitly as an axis since we would need 4 dimensions, but is instead represented as time period displacements of the metrics' values.

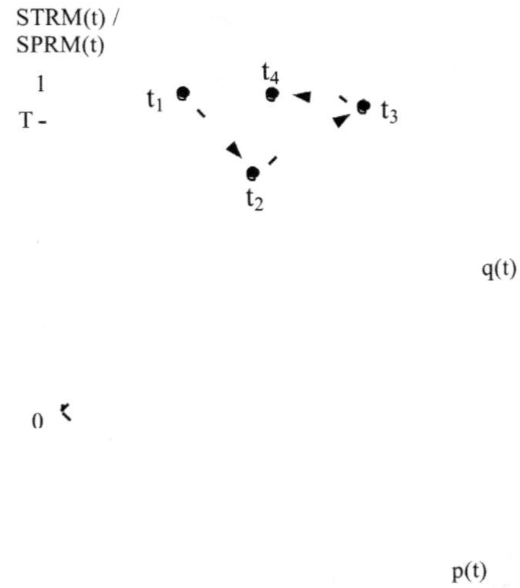

Figure 2. STRM(t)/SPRM(t) values at times $t_1 < t_2 < t_3 < t_4$.

Figure 2 shows 4 values of one of the metrics, labeled according to the times it was evaluated, namely t_1, t_2, t_3, and t_4 where $t_1 < t_2 < t_3 < t_4$. The intervals between these times may be 1 week or 1 month, for example. T is a threshold, below which the metric values should not drop (see Section IV.A). At t_1, one of the metrics was evaluated producing the value shown. At t_2, the metric was again evaluated, but this time the value was found to be much lower than at t_1, and in fact, the value dropped below T. The reason for this was that new vulnerabilities were found that had not been secured. The organization decides to secure the additional vulnerabilities. At t_3, another evaluation was carried out, and this time, the metric had improved, reaching above T. The organization finds some surplus money in its budget and decides to secure 2 other vulnerabilities. An evaluation of the metric at t_4 finds the value a little higher than at t_3, due to the 2 additional vulnerabilities secured. It is thus seen that the security level of a computer system changes over time, in accordance with the system's number of secured and unsecured vulnerabilities.

E. Strengths, Weaknesses, and Limitations

Some strengths of the metrics are: a) conceptually straightforward, and easily explainable to management, and b) flexible and powerful, i.e., they have many application areas, as described in Section IV.

Some weaknesses are: a) threat modeling to determine the vulnerabilities is time consuming and subjective, and b) the SL may involve more factors than vulnerabilities and secured vulnerabilities. For weakness a), it may be possible to automate or semi-automate the threat modeling. Related works [13] and [19] are good starting points for further research. For weakness b), it may be argued that the metrics as presented are sufficient for their envisaged application when other sources of error are considered (e.g., it is difficult to tell where an attacker will strike or how he will strike), and that adding more factors would only make the metrics unnecessarily more cumbersome and time consuming to evaluate with little additional benefit.

Some limitations of the metrics follow. First of all, the metrics are only estimates of the security level, not the security level itself. This was indicated in assigning the probabilities as approximate in expressions (2) and (6) of Section III. Second, as noted in Section III, it makes no difference to the values of the metrics whether one unsecured vulnerability is more likely to be exploited than another. This may be due to the fact that the metrics are estimating the total security of the computer system, and therefore the total number of exploitable vulnerabilities is what's important, not the order in which they are exploited. Third, we applied the additive rule for the union of probabilities in Section III, requiring that 2 or more exploits do not occur simultaneously. This condition holds in general but if it is violated, the metrics will be inaccurate. Other limitations may be that there are vulnerabilities that have not been identified, and a secured vulnerability may not in reality be secured because the attacker has a secret way of defeating the securing measure. However, these other limitations are true of other security methods as well.

IV. Application Areas

In this section, we present some applications for the metrics. In Section IV.A, we discuss how they can be used for continuous active defence of a computer system. In Section IV.B, we present other application areas, such as critical infrastructure and defence.

A. Continuous Active Defence

Attackers do not attack once, and finding that you are well protected, go away. Rather, they continuously probe your defences in order to find new vulnerabilities to exploit. It is thus necessary to continuously evaluate the computer system's vulnerabilities using threat modeling, and add additional security by securing new vulnerabilities when necessary. We call this "Continuous Active Defence" or CAD. How do we know when it is necessary to add more security? This is where the metrics can be applied. Continuous Active Defence involves the following steps:

1. Decide on a threshold for SL(t) below which the values of the metrics should not drop.
2. Decide on the frequency with which to perform threat modeling, e.g., every week, every month, exceptions.
3. Begin Continuous Active Defence by carrying out the threat modeling at the frequency decided above. After each threat modeling exercise, calculate either STRM(t) (if reliability data is not available) or SPRM(t) (if reliability data is available). If the value of the metric falls below T (see Figure 2), secure additional vulnerabilities until the value is above T.
4. If there has been a change to the system, such as new equipment or new software, do an immediate threat analysis, calculate one of the metrics, and add security if necessary based on T. Then, proceed with the frequency for threat modeling decided above.

The value of T and the frequency of threat modeling can be determined by the same threat analysis team mentioned above. The values would depend on the following:

- The potential value of the sensitive data – the more valuable the data is to a thief, a malicious entity, or a competitor, the higher the threshold and frequency should be.
- The damages to the organization that would result, if the sensitive data were compromised – of course, the higher the damages, the higher the threshold and frequency.
- The current and likely future attack climate – consider the volume of attacks and the nature of the victims, say over the last 6 months; if the organization's sector or industry has sustained a large number of recent attacks, then the threshold and frequency need to be higher.
- Consider also potential attacks by nation states as a result of the political climate; attacks by individual hacktivist groups such as Anonymous or WikiLeaks may also warrant attention.

In general, a computer system should be as secure as possible. Therefore, T above 80% and a frequency of weekly would not be uncommon. However, whatever the threshold and frequency, the organization must find them acceptable after considering the above factors. The financial budget available for securing vulnerabilities also plays an important role here, since higher thresholds call for securing more vulnerabilities, which means more financial resources will be needed.

B. Other CAD Application Areas

CAD may also be applied to a specific type of vulnerabilities. An example of this application is dealing with inside attacks. If the organization is particularly susceptible to inside attacks, it can decide to apply CAD to vulnerabilities that can be exploited for inside attacks. In this case, some of the vulnerabilities may be weaknesses of the organization itself, e.g., ineffective screening of job applicants, and the securing measures may not be technological, e.g., having an ombudsman for employee concerns. A list of questions that can be used to identify vulnerabilities to inside attack is given in [6].

CAD can be applied to a specific subset of vulnerabilities that the organization deems are crucial to its mission. For example, a cloud service provider would deem the protection of clients' data crucial to its mission. It can choose to apply CAD to vulnerabilities that are specific to its data storage capabilities, and also apply CAD to its computer system as a whole.

CAD may also be applied to code level vulnerabilities. In this case, the frequency of application will depend on how often the code is changed, due to patching and the addition or deletion of functionality. The threat modeling would have to be tailored to code and would be more of a code inspection exercise.

Finally, CAD may be applied to protect critical infrastructure and defence systems. The power grid is an example of critical infrastructure. The development of the metrics only considers vulnerabilities and reliabilities, which are also found in critical infrastructure and defence systems. However, the threat analyses would involve different types of threats, and the securing measures, would of course, need to be appropriate for the vulnerability. For example, the vulnerability of transformer sabotage in a power grid may need to be secured by the use of intrusion alarms. As another example, the vulnerability of a retaliatory missile site being preemptively destroyed may need to be secured by putting the missile on a mobile platform. The application of CAD to protect critical infrastructure and defence systems is a subject of future research.

V. RELATED WORK

Related work found in the literature includes attack surface metrics, risk and vulnerabilities assessment, vulnerabilities classification, threat analysis, other, and this author's previous work.

A system's attack surface is related to a SL; it is proportional to the inverse of a SL since the lower the attack surface, the higher the SL. Stuckman and Purtilo [7] present a framework for formalizing code-level attack surface metrics and describe activities that can be carried out during application deployment to reduce the application's attack surface. They also describe a tool for determining the attack surface of a web application, together with a method for evaluating an attack surface metric over a number of known vulnerabilities. Munaiah and Meneely [8] propose function and file level attack surface metrics that allow fine-grained risk assessment. They claim that their metrics are flexible in terms of granularity, perform better than comparable metrics in the literature, and are tunable to specific products to better assess risk.

In terms of risk and vulnerabilities assessment, Islam et al. [9] present a risk assessment framework that starts with a threat analysis followed by a risk assessment to estimate the threat level and the impact level. This leads to an estimate of a security level for formulating high-level security requirements. The security level is qualitative, such as "low", "medium", and "high". Vanciu et al. [10] compare an architectural-level approach with a code-level approach in terms of the effectiveness of finding security vulnerabilities. Wang et al. [11] discuss their work on temporal metrics for software vulnerabilities based on the Common Vulnerability Scoring System (CVSS) 2.0. They use a mathematical model to calculate the severity and risk of a vulnerability, which is time dependent as in this work. Gawron et al. [12] investigate the detection of vulnerabilities in computer systems and computer networks. They use a logical representation of preconditions and post conditions of vulnerabilities, with the aim of providing security advisories and enhanced diagnostics for the system. Wu and Wang [13] present a dashboard for assessing enterprise level vulnerabilities that incorporates a multi-layer tree-based model to describe the vulnerability topology. Vulnerability information is gathered from enterprise resources for display automatically. Farnan and Nurse [14] describe a structured approach to assessing low-level infrastructure vulnerability in networks. The approach emphasizes a controls-based evaluation rather than a vulnerability-based evaluation. Instead of looking for vulnerabilities in infrastructure, they assume that the network is insecure, and determine its vulnerability based on the controls that have or have not been implemented. Neuhaus et al. [15] present an investigation into predicting vulnerable software components. Using a tool that mines existing vulnerability databases and version archives, mapping past vulnerabilities to current software components, they were able to come up with a predictor that correctly identifies about half of all vulnerable components, with two thirds of the predictions being correct. Roumani et al. [16] consider modeling of vulnerabilities using time series. According to these researchers, time series models provide a good fit to vulnerability datasets and can be used for vulnerability prediction. They also suggest that the level of the time series is the best estimator for prediction.

With regard to vulnerabilities classification, Spanos et al. [17] look at ways to improve CVSS. They propose a new vulnerability scoring system called the Weighted Impact Vulnerability Scoring System (WIVSS) that incorporates the different impact of vulnerability characteristics. In addition, the MITRE Corporation [18] maintains the Common Vulnerability and Exposures (CVE) list of vulnerabilities and exposures, standardized to facilitate information sharing.

In terms of threat analysis, Schaad and Borozdin [19] present an approach for automated threat analysis of software architecture diagrams. Their work gives an example of automated threat analysis. Sokolowski and Banks [20] describe the implementation of an agent-based simulation model designed to capture insider threat behavior, given a set of assumptions governing agent behavior that pre-disposes an agent to becoming a threat. Sanzgiri and Dasgupta [21] present a taxonomy and classification of insider threat detection techniques based on strategies used for detection.

The following publications fall into the other category. Kotenko and Doynikova [22] investigate the selection of countermeasures for ongoing network attacks. They suggest a selection technique based on the countermeasure model in open standards. The technique incorporates a level of countermeasure effectiveness that is related to the reliability of measures securing vulnerabilities, used in the SPRM(t) metric proposed in this work. Ganin et al. [23] present a review of probabilistic and risk-based decision-making techniques applied to cyber systems. They propose a decision-analysis-based approach that quantifies threat, vulnerability, and consequences through a set of criteria designed to assess the overall utility of cybersecurity management alternatives.

This author's directly related work includes [24] and [6], where the latter is an expanded version of the former. This work improves on these previous works by adding a) time dependency, together with the notion that an organization's security level needs to be continuously evaluated, b) a new metric incorporating the reliability of the securing measures, and c) a description of new application areas.

VI. CONCLUSIONS AND FUTURE RESEARCH

Since attackers continuously probe for new vulnerabilities to exploit, an organization cannot afford to assess its computer system's vulnerabilities once, secure some of the vulnerabilities, and then do nothing further. Rather, the organization needs to assess and secure its vulnerabilities on a continuous basis, i.e., perform CAD. This work has proposed two conceptually clear SL metrics that can be used to evaluate a computer system's security level at any point in time for CAD. One metric assumes that the measures securing vulnerabilities are totally reliable; the other considers the measures to be only partially reliable. CAD may be applied to specific types of vulnerabilities (e.g., vulnerabilities to insider attack), groupings of vulnerabilities that require special attention, specific application areas such as critical infrastructure and defence, and even at the code level.

There are many security metrics in the literature, as seen in Section V. The metrics in this work have the advantages of being easy to understand, and easy to calculate, which may be needed to convince management to provide the necessary resources required for CAD.

Future research includes formulations of other security metrics, the application of security metrics to critical infrastructure and defence, improving the methods for threat modeling, and exploring how this work may complement work in the literature and in the standardization community.

REFERENCES

[1] Identity Force, "2017 Data breaches – the worst so far," retrieved: July, 2018. https://www.identityforce.com/blog/2017-data-breaches

[2] Dark Reading, "2017 Smashed world's records for most data breaches, exposed information," retrieved: July, 2018. https://www.darkreading.com/attacks-breaches/2017-smashed-worlds-records-for-most-data-breaches-exposed-information/d/d-id/1330987?elq_mid=83109&elq_cid=1734282&_mc=NL_DR_EDT_DR_weekly_20180208&cid=NL_DR_EDT_DR_weekly_20180208&elqTrackId=700ff20d23ce4d3f984a1cfd31cb11f6&elq=5c10e9117ca04ba0ad984c11a7dfa14b&elqaid=83109&elqat=1&elqCampaignId=29666

[3] G. Yee, "Visualization and prioritization of privacy risks in software systems," International Journal on Advances in Security, issn 1942-2636, vol. 10, no. 1&2, pp. 14-25, 2017.

[4] ITEM Software Inc.,"Reliability prediction basics", retrieved: July, 2018. http://www.reliabilityeducation.com/ReliabilityPredictionBasics.pdf

[5] C. Salter, O. Saydjari, B. Schneier, and J. Wallner, "Towards a secure system engineering methodology," Proc. New Security Paradigms Workshop, pp. 2-10, 1998.

[6] G. Yee, "Optimal security protection for sensitive data," International Journal on Advances in Security, vol. 11, no. 1&2, pp. 80-90, 2018.

[7] J. Stuckman and J. Purtilo, "Comparing and applying attack surface metrics," Proceedings of the 4th International Workshop on Security Measurements and Metrics (MetriSec '12), pp. 3-6, Sept. 2012.

[8] N. Munaiah and A. Meneely, "Beyond the attack surface," Proceedings of the 2016 ACM Workshop on Software Protection (SPRO '16), pp. 3-14, October 2016.

[9] M. Islam, A. Lautenbach, C. Sandberg, and T. Olovsson, "A risk assessment framework for automotive embedded systems," Proc. 2nd ACM International Workshop on Cyber-Physical System Security (CPSS '16), pp. 3-14, 2016.

[10] R. Vanciu, E. Khalaj, and M. Abi-Antoun, "Comparative evaluation of architectural and code-level approaches for finding security vulnerabilities," Proceedings of the 2014 ACM Workshop on Security Information Workers (SIW '14), pp. 27-34, Nov. 2014.

[11] J. A. Wang, F. Zhang, and M. Xia, "Temporal metrics for software vulnerabilities," retrieved: July, 2018. http://www.cs.wayne.edu/fengwei/paper/wang-csiirw08.pdf

[12] M. Gawron, A. Amirkhanyan, F. Cheng, and C. Meinel, "Automatic vulnerability detection for weakness visualization and advisory creation," Proc. 8th International Conference on Security of Information and Networks (SIN '15), pp. 229-236, 2015.

[13] B. Wu and A. Wang, "A multi-layer tree model for enterprise vulnerability management," Proceedings of the 2011 Conference on Information Technology Education (SIGITE '11), pp. 257-262, October 2011.

[14] O. Farnan and J. Nurse, "Exploring a controls-based assessment of infrastructure vulnerability," Proc. International Conference on Risks and Security of Internet and Systems (CRiSIS 2015), pp. 144-159, 2015.

[15] S. Neuhaus, T. Zimmermann, C. Holler, and A. Zeller, "Predicting vulnerable software components," Proc. 14th ACM Conference on Computer and Communications Security (CCS '07), pp. 529-540, 2007.

[16] Y. Roumani, J. Nwankpa, and Y. Roumani, "Time series modeling of vulnerabilities," Computers and Security, Vol. 51 Issue C, pp. 32-40, June 2015.

[17] G. Spanos, A. Sioziou, and L. Angelis, "WIVSS: A new methodology for scoring information system vulnerabilities," Proc. 17th Panhellenic Conference on Informatics, pp. 83-90, 2013.

[18] MITRE, "Common vulnerabilities and exposures", retrieved: July, 2018. https://cve.mitre.org/

[19] A. Schaad and M. Borozdin, "TAM2: Automated threat analysis," Proc. 27th Annual ACM Symposium on Applied Computing (SAC '12), pp. 1103-1108, 2012.

[20] J. Sokolowski and C. Banks, "An agent-based approach to modeling insider threat," Proc. Symposium on Agent-Directed Simulation (ADS '15), pp. 36-41, 2015.

[21] A. Sanzgiri and D. Dasgupta, "Classification of insider threat detection techniques," Proc. 11th Annual Cyber and Information Security Research Conference (CISRC '16), article no. 25, pp. 1-4, 2016.

[22] I. Kotenko and E. Doynikova, "Dynamical calculation of security metrics for countermeasure selection in computer networks," Proc. 2016 24th Euromicro International Conference on Parallel, Distributed, and Network-Based Processing, pp. 558-565, 2016.

[23] A. Ganin, P. Quach, M. Panwar, Z. A. Collier, J. M. Keisler, D. Marchese, and I. Linkov, "Multicriteria decision framework for cybersecurity risk assessment and management," Risk Analysis, pp. 1-17, 2017.

[24] G. Yee, "Assessing security protection for sensitive data," Proc. Eleventh International Conference on Emerging Security Information, Systems and Technologies (SECURWARE 2017), pp. 111-116, 2017.

The Probable Cyber Attack Concept Exploiting Interrupt Vulnerability in Nuclear Power Plants

Taehee Kim, Soomin Lim, and Sangwoo Kim
Cyber Security Division
Korea Institute of Nuclear Nonproliferations and Control
Daejeon, Korea
email: {kimtaehee, s2min, kjoey}@kinac.re.kr

Abstract—**So far, cyber threats to nuclear power plants have remained an unexplored area. No single cyber attack has been reported that successfully degraded the safety function of a nuclear power plant. However, it is not guaranteed that nuclear power plants are completely safe from cyber attacks. This paper proposes a probable attack concept, which can disrupt the real-time and deterministic nature of instrumentation and control systems.**

Keywords-nuclear power plant; cyber threat; cyber attack; I&C system; preemptive OS; interrupt.

I. INTRODUCTION

Conventionally, Instrumentation and Control (I&C) systems are designed to protect nuclear power plants in terms of safety. This design concept has been implemented at the early stage of nuclear power plants and reinforced for decades. Sometimes, lessons are also learned from accidents [1][2] and they are fed to the design as improvements. As a result, I&C systems can protect the plants from various events, such as failures, errors, and even disasters.

Recently, cyber threats to nuclear power plants have received increased attention. The threats include hacking, viruses, Distributed Denial of Service (DDoS) attacks [3] and they are well-known in general Information Technology (IT) environments. No single cyber attack, however, has been reported that successfully disrupted the safety control of a nuclear power plant. The well-known Stuxnet [4] succeeded to attack the Iran uranium enrichment plant, not nuclear power plants. The feasibility of a successful attack and appropriate countermeasures still remain uncertain in nuclear power plants. Despite this uncertainty, the participants in the nuclear power industry take an optimistic view about the safety of nuclear power plants. They believe detection methods for safety events must be effective for cyber attacks. Actually, the periodic Cyclic Redundancy Checking (CRC) [5] used for detecting memory errors may be useful for detecting the fuzzing attacks [6] messing up the memory.

During a survey on the detection methods for cyber attacks, the usage of I&C systems have attracted our attention. The usage is a factor for reflecting how busy an Operating System (OS) is and it is usually disseminated to the OS itself and surrounding I&C systems. The usage can also be utilised for detecting cyber attacks; a malicious task injected into an OS may increase the usage value. We, however, found a vulnerability that can be invoked by interrupts.

This paper is structured as follows. In Section II, we describe the background: assumptions that need to be described for further discussion. Section III proposes the probable attack concept derived by our research. The difference between the proposed concept and the similar safety event, that is the busy OS case, is given in Section IV. Then, the precautions that may protect the I&C system from the proposed attack and their limits is also given in Section V. Finally, this paper is concluded with conclusions and future works in Section VI.

II. ASSUMPTIONS

This section provides assumptions for further discussion. Although we name this assumptions, we believe the given assumptions are based on the common nature of I&C systems for nuclear power plants.

A. Relatively Low Performance

Reliability is the most expected virtue of I&C systems in the nuclear power industry. One of the typical methodologies to calculate reliability is analyzing each components as we can see in MIL-HDBK-217F [7]. The application history, however, is the most powerful proof of reliability. The proven I&C systems in the actual nuclear power plants will be preferred in other plants.

Therefore, most nuclear power plants tend to adopt proven I&C systems, although they have relatively low performance. Having a long application history means that I&C systems had been adopted and developed for a long time. On occasion, the systems may have been developed several decades ago, and their CPUs are operated at a low speed of few MHz. In general, the CPUs are slower than personal computers or even cell phones.

B. Preemptive Operating System

The safety controls of nuclear power plants should handle safety events timely, that is, real-time, and deterministic manner.

"Real-time" means that safety controls always respond within the requested time limit. A safety control with time limit of n milliseconds should respond within n milliseconds. "Deterministic" means that responding of safety controls are always predictable. Decision factors that may change responds of the safety controls should be known in advance. Different or random outputs from a same safety control are not permitted if decision factors are not changed.

I&C systems with a preemptive OS can support real-time and deterministic nature [8][9] of the safety controls. The preemptive OS periodically scans all tasks and stops current task on executing if urgent task is waiting to be executed. The urgent task does not wait the termination of the other non-urgent tasks, and gets the right to be executed although the other non-urgent tasks are waiting. These periodic scans and exchanges of tasks are called as context switches. By these context switches, time limit is met and we can predict the execution order of tasks.

C. *Interrputs*

An interrupt is one of the well-known methodologies for data exchange between a CPU and peripherals. With an interrupt manner, a CPU executes tasks and does not care peripherals before they inform the CPU. On the other hand, with a polling manner, a CPU periodically stops executing tasks to check peripherals whether they want to exchange data with the CPU.

By their nature, an interrupt is more efficient method than a polling. Time to check peripherals caused by polling is wasted if the peripherals do not have data to exchange. Therefore, most digital systems, such as personal computers adopt an interrupt manner for exchanging data with peripherals. A mouse and a keyboard are representative examples.

Inside of I&C systems used for nuclear power industry, interrupts are preferred methods for data exchange, such as urgent switchover between redundant CPU modules for seamless operation and asynchronous serial communication for downloading tasks.

In this paper, we assume that I&C systems support several interrupts with their own priority.

D. *Interfaces*

The main purpose of I&C systems is to receive inputs from field devices, to process inputs, and to send outputs to where they are needed at. For this reason, I&C systems essentially have various interfaces; analog and digital, input and output.

Serial interfaces for Human and Machine Interfaces (HMIs), and Engineering Work Stations (EWSs) are representative examples in nuclear power plants. Basically I&C systems can execute their tasks of themselves, but they still need HMIs for observing operational values and manipulating configuration settings, and EWSs for managing control logics.

III. Attack Concept

In this section, we propose the probable attack concept that exploits the interrupt vulnerability of I&C systems.

The attack concept is simple: to break the real-time and deterministic nature of I&C systems. In other words, disrupting tasks to be executed within time limits is the proposed attack concept. The following is a summary of how the tasks can be disrupted.

The I&C systems we assume in this paper have various interfaces. In general, these interfaces work in an asynchronous manner for a safety purpose. Unused devices are not connected with interfaces because the devices might be touched by an operator accidentally and then send unintended instructions to I&C systems. Electrical surges from unused devices might also cause malfunctions in I&C systems. This asynchronous nature means that interfaces are based on an interrupt manner. This asynchronous nature brings two implications. The first implication is interfaces are not occupied and are waiting devices. The second implication is that interfaces are driven with an interrupt manner.

The first step for the attack is connecting devices to those unoccupied and interrupt-driven interfaces. For any device, it is possible to enable continuous interrupts. Typical example is a bad USB device. A pair of a dongle and the laptop with software having ability to send serial data automatically is another example.

The second step is enabling interrupts with high priorities continuously to the targeted I&C system through the connected interface. Data contents and an application layer protocol for enabling interrupts do not matter. Every data will be delivered to interrupt handlers whether they are valid or not. An interrupt is a just hardware-level signal used for informing an OS and it cannot interpret data contents. Therefore, even invalid data cannot be filtered and should be delivered to interrupt handlers. These interrupt handlers will consume precious time and disrupt other interrupts with lower priorities.

At the final step, a time tick, that is a kind of interrupt, is delayed by interrupts enabled by the attack. The main purposes of a time tick is measuring the time flow and calling context switches periodically. Therefore, delayed time ticks cause delayed context switches. It means time limits of tasks cannot be met and we cannot predict the execution order of tasks in advance, as written in Section II.B. Finally, the I&C system with delayed time ticks will not work in a timely and deterministic manner.

IV. The Blind Spot of The Usage

The busy OS case given in Section IV.A may be confused with the proposed attack because tasks suffer from delays in that case. However, it is totally different from the proposed attack concept in terms of intention. The proposed attack is a hostile action with intention, while the busy OS case occurs with no intention. It is basically closer to programming errors, such as infinite loops or congestions, not filtered during tests. Based on this difference, the busy OS case can be detected by the usage and thus it is detectable while the proposed attack concept cannot be detectable.

To explain the difference above mentioned, the usage calculation process is described in Section IV.B. Then, it is followed by Section IV.C which describes the blind spot hiding the proposed attack from the detection.

A. Busy OS Case

Tasks executed by I&C systems have various branches and each branch has its own work flows. Some branches may have simple operations while other branches have heavy operations. For example, a task may just observe a certain value before it exceeds thresholds, but the task may write the trend of the value on a slow flash memory with very dense interval time for a future audit. Depend on which branch is being executed, a CPU may be busy or not busy.

If the busyness of an OS, or the usage, reaches 100%, the I&C system cannot afford additional work imposed by a task jumping to a heavy branch. In this case, the safety controls supported by I&C systems cannot work in a timely and deterministic manner. In other words, they are compromised.

B. The Usage Calculation Process

I&C systems keep their own value called the usage, to detect compromised I&C systems by the busy OS case. The usage is the factor reflecting the busyness of an OS. Nested I&C systems observe the usage of each other and I&C systems with a high usage value will be regarded as compromised.

The usage can be calculated by measuring how long time the idle task is executed within the given time. This calculation can be implemented as follows.

1) Calculating G: In initializing phase, an OS does nothing except increasing a variable whthin the given time T and keeps it at the global variable G.

2) Start the OS: After the OS completes initializing phase, a local variable L in the idle task is set to zero and scheduling is started in earnest.

3) Calcuating L: For the given time T, L is continuously increased when the idle task is on execution, while it is not increased when the other tasks are on execution.

4) Comparing L and G: After the given time T, by comparing G and L, the OS can know how long time the idle task was executed within given time. Then L is reset to zero.

5) Repeat: the OS repeats 2) ~ 4).

The above calculation can be expressed by

$$\text{Usage for } T = (1 - (L / G)) \times 100. \qquad (1)$$

The usage value will stay low, if the idle task is executed longer, while it will become high, if the idle task is executed shorter. When it is 100%, a I&C system is fully busy and cannot afford additional work.

C. Blind Spot of Usage

The calculation given in Section IV.B seems quite reasonable and clear. The serious trap, however, is lying on (1) because T cannot be measured. T stands for actual and absolute time, but the OS does not have the tool to measure such time in general. Instead, the OS counts time ticks to measure T. According to this, P is pre-calculated by (2) and hard-coded into the OS.

$$P = T / \text{Interval Time between Time Ticks} \qquad (2)$$

Then, (1) should be updated by

$$T' = \text{Interval Time between Time Ticks} \times P, \qquad (3)$$

$$\text{Usage for } T' = (1 - (L / G)) \times 100. \qquad (4)$$

The proposed attack concept given in Section III extends the interval time among time ticks and makes T' longer by (3). The extended length is same with time spent by the interrupt handlers called by the attack. L and G stay same regardless of attack, because L is not increased in interrupt handler and G is calculated before attack. As a result, the usage value becomes lower than the actual busyness of the OS by (4). This is the obvious blind spot of the usage.

More seriously, nested I&C systems described in Section IV.B cannot detect compromised I&C systems because the usage value will stay low due the blind spot.

V. Precautions and Limits

In this section, a few existing precautions are given. These precautions may be useful to protect I&C system from the proposed attack. They, however, cannot provide complete protection.

A. Blocking Interrupt

In the attack steps given in Section III, the time spent by interrupt handlers may be short in well-designed I&C systems. Furthermore, continuous invalid data received in a short period may be considered as noises or attacks. Then, they will be discarded without an interpretation. This may help to mitigate the attack but cannot provide the complete protection.

The only complete solution is to block the interrupt channel connected with the interface is being attacked. However, it may also block the other essential devices for operation and a future forensic procedure. Once they have been blocked, the targeted I&C systems may need factory reset, which initializes inside of I&C systems and destroys evidences

B. Watchdog

A watchdog [10] is a kind of timer for increasing reliability. It waits to be kicked (to receive a signal from outside) for the pre-defined time limit. If it is not kicked within the time limit, it releases the warning signal. A watchdog is driven by the inside time source and independent from time ticks and interrupts.

In terms of response time, however, a watchdog cannot provide the complete protection. The I&C systems we assume are operated by a preemptive OS, which works in "within time" manner, not "on time". It means that the time limit of a watchdog should have enough margin.

Furthermore, attacks may be designed to delay time tick by *n-1* milliseconds, when a watchdog is set to wait *n* milliseconds.

C. Real-time Clock Component

I&C systems may have other common time sources, such as real-time clock components [11]. It can measure actual time flow independently with time ticks.

Nevertheless, they cannot provide the complete protection because their time scale, that is hour, minute, and second, is not precise enough for context switches in a preemptive OS. The time scale should to be few milliseconds at minimum for efficient tasks scheduling. Because of this, real-time clock components are preferred for displaying the current time.

D. Physical Acess Control for Interfaces

Well-known regulations [12][13] compel nuclear power plants to protect interfaces from unauthorized accesses. The actual protection strategy, however, is implemented by periodic security audits rather than technical security controls. This strategy is inevitable for many legacy systems in nuclear power plants because they were not designed with security considerations. Therefore, interfaces are left to be attacked between audits.

VI. Conclusions and Future Works

In this paper, we proposed the probable attack concept exploiting interrupt vulnerability. The proposed attack delays time ticks first, and then context switches of a preemptive OS. As a result, the real-time and deterministic nature of I&C system are not guaranteed. Furthermore, nested I&C systems for safety controls cannot detect the attack even if the targeted I&C systems are compromised due to the usage blind spot. Existing precautions and their limit analyses were also given.

This paper does not include actual experiments and the feasibility is not proven. However, we believe that nuclear power plants should be protected from any possibility to degrade the safety level.

In the future, we will perform experiments on our test bed. If it is observed that the proposed attack has any influence on the test bed, we will try to find mitigating measures.

References

[1] United States of America, Nuclear Regulatory Commision, *Backgrounder on the Three Mile Island Accident*, 2013. [Oline]. Available from: https://www.nrc.gov. [Accessed: Jul. 2018].

[2] United States of America, Nuclear Regulatory Commision, *Backgrounder on NRC Response to Lessons Learned from Fukushima*, 2015. [Oline]. Available from: https://www.nrc.gov. [Accessed: Jul. 2018].

[3] S. T. Zargar, J. Joshi, and D. Tipper, "A Survey of Defence Mechanisms Against Distributed Denial of Service Flooding Attacks," IEEE Communications Surveys & Tutorials, vol. 15, issue. 4, pp. 2046-2069, 2013.

[4] R. Langner, "Stuxnet: Dissecting a Cyberwarfare Weapon," IEEE Security & Privacy, vol. 9, issue. 3, pp. 49-51, 2011.

[5] A. B. Marton and T. K. Frambs, "A Cyclic Redundancy Checking Algorithm," *Honeywell Computer Journal,* vol. 5, no. 3, 1971.

[6] M. Sutton, A. Greene, and P.amini, Fuzzing: Brute Force Vulnerability Discovery, United States: Addison-Wesley Professional, 2007.

[7] J. W. Harms, "Revision of MIL-HDBK-217, Relaibility Prediction of Electronic Equipment," Proc. IEEE Symp. Annual Reliablity and Maintainability, IEEE Press, 2010, dio:10.1109/RAMS.2010.5448046

[8] International Electrotechnical Commision, *Nuclear power plants – Instumentation and control systems important to safety – Software aspects for computer-based systems performing category A functions*, 2006.

[9] Institute of Electrical and Electronics Engineers, *IEEE Standard Criteria for Programmable Digital Devices in Safety Systems of Nuclear Power Generating Stations*, 2016.

[10] Maxim Integrated, "MAX6814 5-Pin Watchdog Timer Cuircuit," 2014. [Online]. Available from: https://www.maximintegrated.com. [Accessed: Jul. 2018].

[11] Maxim Integrated, "DS1685/DS1687 3V/5V Real-Time Clocks," 2012. [Online]. Available from: https://www.maximintegrated.com. [Accessed: Jul. 2018].

[12] United States of America, Nuclear Regulatory Commision, *Reguatory Guide 5.71: Cyber Security Programs for Nuclear Facilities*, 2010. [Oline]. Available from: https://www.nrc.gov. [Accessed: Jul. 2018].

[13] Republic of Korea, Korea Institue of Nuclear Nonproliferations and Control, *Reguatory Standard – Security for Computer and Information System of Nuclear Facilities*, 2016

Secure Cooperation of Untrusted Components

Roland Wismüller and Damian Ludwig
University of Siegen, Germany
E-Mail: {roland.wismueller, damian.ludwig}@uni-siegen.de

***Abstract*—A growing number of computing systems, e.g., smart phones or web applications, allow to compose their software of components from untrusted sources. For security reasons, such a system should grant a component just the permissions it really requires, which implies that permissions must be sufficiently fine-grained. This leads to two questions: How to know and to specify the required permissions, and how to enforce access control in a flexible and efficient way? We suggest a novel approach based on the object capability paradigm with access control at the level of individual methods, which exploits two fundamental ideas: we simply use a component's published interface as a specification of its required permissions, and extend interfaces with optional methods, allowing to specify permissions which are not strictly necessary, but desired for a better service level. These ideas can be realized within a static type system, where interfaces specify both the availability of methods, as well as the permission to use them. In addition, we support deep attenuation of rights with automatic creation of membranes, where necessary. Thus, our access control mechanisms are easy to use and also efficient, since in most cases permissions can be checked when the component is deployed, rather than at run-time.**

***Keywords*—Software-components; security; typesystems.**

I. Introduction

In today's computer based systems, the software environment is often composed of components developed by an open community. Prominent examples are web applications, and smart phones with their app stores. A major problem in such systems is the fact that the component's sources and thus, the components themselves may not be trusted [1]. In order to ensure security in systems composed of untrusted components, the *Principle Of Least Authority* (POLA) should be obeyed, i.e., each component should receive just the permissions it needs to fulfill its intended purpose [2]. The term 'authority' denotes the effects, which a subject can cause. These effects can be restricted via permissions, which control the subject's ability to perform actions. An appealing and popular approach to implement POLA is the use of the object capability model [3,4], where unforgeable object references are used as a capability allowing to use the referenced object.

A good introduction to the object capability model and POLA is provided in [5]. The general properties of capability systems, as well as some common misconceptions about capabilities are pointed out in [6], where the authors also show that capabilities have strong advantages over access control lists and can support both confinement and revocation. Murray [4] discusses several common object capability patterns, including membranes, which allow a deep attenuation of rights.

Based on the object-capability paradigm, several secure languages have been devised. A pioneer in this area is the work of Mark Miller [3] on the E language, which points out the prerequisites for secure languages: memory safety, object encapsulation, no ambient authority, no static mutable state, and an API without security leaks. In addition to these features, E provides method level access control, but requires the programmer to manually implement security-enforcing abstractions, like membranes. Based on E, Joe-E [7] restricts Java such that access to objects is only possible via capabilities that have been explicitly passed to a component. Joe-E also supports immutable interfaces allowing to implement secure plug-ins. It uses compile-time checking and secure libraries to disable insecure features of Java like, e.g., reflection and ambient authority. In a similar spirit, Emily [8] is a secure subset of OCaml, whereas Maffeis et al. [1] specifically address the problem of mutual isolation of (third-party) web applications written in JavaScript. These language-based approaches share two fundamental problems: Since they restrict the programming language, they not only confine interactions between components, but also limit the programmer's capabilities within a component. Another drawback is that security can only be guaranteed, if all components are distributed at the source code level, which in practice is infeasible for reasons of protecting intellectual property rights.

A feasible solution for the second problem is the use of a Virtual Machine (VM) that enforces security. An example for such an approach is Oviedo3, which includes a secure VM implementing capability-based access control at the granularity of methods [9]–[11]. However, Oviedo3 only provides basic mechanisms for the management of access rights, i.e., adding and removing the permission to execute a single method for a single object reference, and must check all these permissions at run-time. Thus, Oviedo3 is neither easy to use nor efficient.

To overcome the drawbacks of existing approaches, the goal of our work is to provide a VM that

- allows components to be distributed and deployed in binary form while still providing security,
- enables fine-grained access control without putting a relevant annotation or implementation burden on the components' programmers,
- minimizes the number of required run-time checks by performing most checks when a component is deployed.

In this paper, we suggest an easy to use approach that eliminates the shortcomings of existing capability systems and secure high-level languages, and addresses the special needs for the secure cooperation of untrusted components. In Section II, we present a component model, where each component specifies its minimal and desired permissions in a natural way using interfaces. We then outline the basics of a type system that allows fine-grained access restrictions and optional methods (Section III). Finally, we introduce concepts for a virtual machine and a secure, strongly-typed byte code, that allows static type checking at deployment time and the automatic creation of membranes (Section IV). We conclude the paper by giving an outlook to our future work (Section V).

II. COMPONENT MODEL

Our work is based on the established definition of a software component, as given by Szyperski: "*A software component is a unit of composition with contractually specified interfaces and explicit context dependencies only. A software component can be deployed independently and is subject to composition by third parties*" [12]. We assume that components are distributed as compiled byte code for a VM, rather than source code. Their internal structure is not relevant, however, we require that a component defines a purely object oriented interface, i.e., to its environment it appears to be composed of classes. One of these classes, the *principal class*, is the starting point for defining the component's interface.

Under these conditions, at run-time a component can be viewed as a collection of objects. Thus, secure interaction between components can be implemented by an extended object capability model, where the type of a reference imposes additional access restrictions.

In this run-time model, we can exactly determine the interface that a component C requires from its environment (by determining the types of all references and values that C can receive), as well as the interface it provides to the environment (i.e., the types of all references and values that C returns) by just examining the type of C's principal class. Now, a central idea of our approach is to view these interfaces also as a specification of the required (requested) and provided (granted) permissions of a component. E.g., if a method m is in C's required interface, then C requires the permission to invoke m. As an extension, we also allow optional methods in component interfaces. In this way, the type of the principal class explicitly defines

- $\mathcal{T}_{\text{in}}$: the minimum and maximum permissions that C requests from its environment, where C will use optional methods, if they are available, but does not require them for its correct operation, and
- $\mathcal{T}_{\text{out}}$: the minimum and maximum permissions that C grants to its environment, where for each optional method, C may decide at run-time whether or not to provide it.

As an example, consider a calendar component that holds objects implementing an interface `Appointment`. Users can create new appointments or get a list of all stored ones. The public interface of this component could look like shown in Listing 1 (assuming `String` is a built-in type).

As the component has no input (we omitted the parameters of `createAppointment()` for simplicity), `Calendar` does not request any permissions from its environment, so $\mathcal{T}_{\text{in}} = \emptyset$. In contrast, it grants permission to use the stored

LISTING 1. CALENDAR INTERFACE

```
component interface Calendar {
  interface Appointment {
    int startTime();
    int endTime();
    String location();
    String subject();
  }
  void createAppointment(...);
  Appointment[] getAppointments();
}
```

appointments via the `Appointment` interface, which results in $\mathcal{T}_{\text{out}} = \{\texttt{Calendar}, \texttt{Appointment}\}$.

A calendar client displaying the appointments stored in a calendar may have a component interface similar to Listing 2.

LISTING 2. CALENDAR CLIENT INTERFACE

```
component interface CalendarClient {
  interface CalendarProvider {
    Event[] getAppointments();
  }
  interface Event {
    int startTime();
    int endTime();
    optional String subject();
  }
  void displayEvents();
  void setProvider(CalendarProvider c);
}
```

This interface specifies the permissions the client needs from a `CalendarProvider`: it must be able to call the `getAppointments()` method, which returns an array of objects of type `Event`. On an `Event`, the client must be able to call `startTime()` and `endTime()`, and it will use `subject()`, if available. Thus, for the calendar client component we have $\mathcal{T}_{\text{out}} = \{\texttt{CalendarClient}\}$ and $\mathcal{T}_{\text{in}} = \{\texttt{CalendarProvider}, \texttt{Event}\}$. Since we use structural typing for component interfaces, a reference to the `Calendar` component can be passed to `setProvider()`, as `Appointment` provides all the methods required by `Event`.

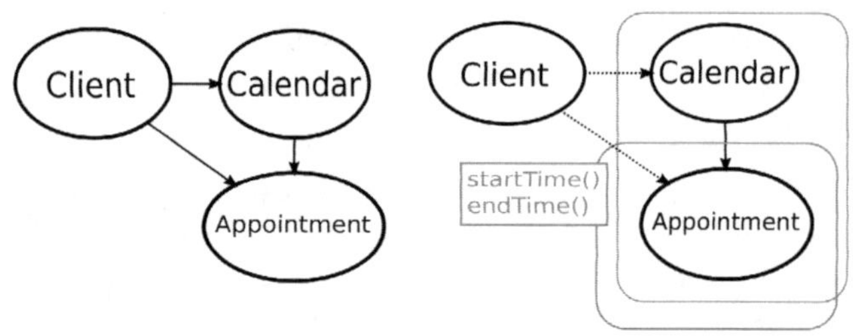

Figure 1. Full access to `Appointment` (left) versus restricted permissions (right).

In this example, the calendar client will not be able to

TABLE I. INTENDED SEMANTICS OF COMPONENT INTERFACE TYPES.

Status of method m in interface type T	Assertion that referenced object has method m	Permission to call method m
m is not in T	no	no
m is optional in T	no	yes
m is required T	yes	yes

call the `location()` method on events received from any `CalendarProvider`, because it is not part of the `Event` interface. Formally, a component C can invoke method m on an object o from another component, only if o can be assigned to a reference of some type $T \in \mathcal{T}_{\text{in}}(C)$, which allows to call m. Especially, a component can only execute the operations explicitly specified in its published interface. This means that everything the component can do is explicitly visible in its published interface, so the user can decide not to install the component or to only provide it with a reference to a restricted calendar object. Traditionally, this requires to manually program a membrane for the `Calendar` component, such that the objects returned by `getAppointments()` do not have a `subject()` method (see Figure 1). In our model, the same effect can be achieved by just casting the `Calendar` reference to a more restricted interface, where the `subject()` method is missing. In Figure 1, the client has access to `Calendar` through a membrane. The calendar membrane's `getAppointments()` method in turn returns membranes for the `Appointment` objects, that only allow two methods to be called.

In principle, if the `Calendar` component declared the `subject()` method in `Appointment` as optional, it also could decide at runtime whether or not to expose this method to the client invoking `getAppointments()`, based, e.g., on some authentication procedure. However, we believe that this decision should be left to the user assembling the components.

Note that a component's published interface (what it pretends to do) may differ from its actually implemented interface, e.g., a component may try to call a method not declared in its published interface. However, because the component will always be *used* via its published interface, such a deviation will result in a type error at run-time. We will briefly present our type system in the next section.

III. TYPE SYSTEM

As outlined before, we interpret a component's interface type as a specification of access permissions for methods. In addition, we retain the traditional interpretation, which asserts that all objects implementing the interface will offer the specified methods. We achieve both goals by using optional methods, as shown in Table I.

As the main goal of our type system is security, it must enforce the access restrictions given in Table I in such a way that no component can amplify its rights by type conversions, i.e., down-casting. Whenever possible, we ensure this property statically, i.e., at the time a component is deployed, rather than by using run-time checks. In addition, we avoid delayed type failures: once a component C is deployed and a reference to C's primary object has successfully been assigned to a variable of some component interface type I, all methods in I can be invoked without type errors. Finally, the type system supports an easy attenuation of rights by just up-casting a reference, without the need to manually code a membrane.

For safety and security reasons, we allow the VM to load a component, only if the component's code is *well-typed.* According to Cardelli [13], this means that the code will not exhibit any unchecked run-time errors (although controlled exceptions are allowed). The main question in this context is: when can we allow to assign a reference from a variable r of type S to a variable r' of type T, when at least one of these types is a component interface type? The important restriction here is that we must not allow r' to gain more permissions than r via down-casting.

Assume that there exists a method m that is optional in S, but required in T. Table I shows that there are no security concerns in this situation, since both S and T allow to call m. However, since T asserts that the referenced object has method m, we must check this condition at run-time when assigning r to r'. We can assign $r : S$ to $r' : T$ *without* a run-time type check, if and only if

- there is no optional method in S that is requred in T,
- each required method of T is also present in S,
- each method of S can be assigned to its corresponding method in T without run-time check, i.e., all its arguments and results can be assigned without check (this avoids delayed type failures).

A different situation arises if there exists a method m that is optional in T, but is not present in S. In this case, Table I shows that T actually allows to call m (if the referenced object o provides that method), while S does not. Thus, we actually can assign $r : S$ to $r' : T$, if after this assignment r' references an object that does *not* provide m. We ensure this by using a coercion semantics, where the result of the assignment is a reference to a membrane for o that does not provide method m. Vice versa, this means that we can assign $r : S$ to $r' : T$ *without* introducing a membrane, if and only if

- each method of T is also declared in S, and
- all methods of S can be assigned to the corresponding method of T without a need for a membrane.

This type systems enables the construction of a secure VM, which can decide at deployment time for which assignments in a component's code a run-time check is required and/or a membrane must be introduced.

IV. COSMA

The *Component Oriented Secure Machine Architecture* (COSMA) is a secure VM based on the outlined type system. It comes with a specification for an object oriented byte code, called *Component Intermediate Language*. The structure of this byte code reflects that of a component: The entry point for a component's code always is its principal class, which logically contains all other classes. Method implementations are structured into basic blocks. Such a block is a sequence of instructions and is the only admissible target of a branch instruction. Instructions do not allow direct access to the memory. Instead, they use typed operands to access abstract storage locations. There is also no visible call stack, but a high-level method call instruction, where lists of operands are passed for arguments and results. This ensures that a malicious program cannot forge references (e.g., by abusing an untyped stack), which is the major requirement for a secure object-capability system. Since the byte code does not contain any names except the obligatory method names for component interfaces, it also protects the component developer's intellectual property rights.

We need a secured byte code, since secure high-level languages "*can still be attacked from below*" [14]. In order to prevent such attacks, we must use "*computers on which only capability-secure programs are allowed*" [14]. Thus, new programs can only be loaded into COSMA as components represented in our byte code.

When a component is deployed into the VM, it is associated with a new context that serves as a trust (or protection) unit. Within this context, the component's principal class is instantiated, and a reference (capability) to this *principal object* is returned and gets casted to the component's published interface. Initially, this reference is the only way to interact with the component. When an object in a context X creates another object, the new object also is associated with X. Thus, a context comprises all objects that are (transitively) created by the principal object of a loaded component. COSMA ensures that references can point to objects in a different context, only if they have a component interface type and thus are subject to the security restrictions outlined in Section III. References with "normal" class or interface types are also supported, but can only point to objects in the local context. Thus, we do not restrict the code's expressiveness within a component.

During deployment, a component's complete byte code is checked for consistency, which includes type checking. Since the byte code does not allow any untyped data accesses, this can be done on a per-instruction basis, without a need for a complex verification of instruction sequences, as it is necessary, e.g., in Java byte-code [15]. Based on the type information available in the component's code, COSMA automatically generates the code for all required membranes, relieving the programmer from this burden. At run-time, membranes are automatically inserted via coercion semantics when permissions are "casted away". Thus security constraints are enforced mainly statically, leaving only a few run-time checks.

V. Conclusion and Future Work

In this paper, we propose a new concept for the secure cooperation of untrusted components. This involves a component model, where each component declares its required and granted permissions via a self-explanatory public interface. This interface can then be used to connect it to other components. Components are distributed in a secure byte code with high-level instructions that preserves typing information, but still protects intellectual property rights. The corresponding VM implements a type system ensuring that a component cannot gain more permissions than those explicitly mentioned in its public interface. Type checking is done at deployment time, with some additional run-time checks, where necessary. Coercion semantics is used to automatically insert membranes.

At present we have a fully operational implementation of the type system and the VM, as well as a compiler translating a minimalistic language into our byte code. A formal specification of the type system, including subtyping and coercion, is also available, along with the semantics of the implemented instructions and a formal proof that no instruction sequence can amplify a component's permissions.

In the current implementation all components are executed by the same VM, thus, security of the connections is not an issue. In the future, the model can be extended to distributed systems using remote method invocation, provided that the communication link between the VMs uses a secure protocol ensuring authentication and integrity.

We are currently working on another compiler for a more mature, Java-like programming language, that enables us to execute more realistic programs. This will allow us to compare our implementation to other approaches. Especially, we will evaluate its performance against plain Java, so we can assess the costs for the run-time checks and the indirection caused by the use of membranes. Our long term goal is to provide a complete programming system that can be used to develop and deploy component-based software in an easy and secure way.

References

[1] S. Maffeis, J. C. Mitchell, and A. Taly, "Object Capabilities and Isolation of Untrusted Web Applications," in *Proc. of IEEE Symp. Security and Privacy*. Oakland, CA, USA: IEEE, May 2010, pp. 125–140.

[2] M. S. Miller and J. S. Shapiro, "Paradigm Regained: Abstraction Mechanisms for Access Control," in *Advances in Computing Science - ASIAN 2003. Progamming Languages and Distributed Computation*, ser. LNCS, vol. 2896. Springer, 2003, pp. 224–242.

[3] M. S. Miller, "Robust composition: Towards a unified approach to access control and concurrency control," Ph.D. Thesis, Johns Hopkins University, Baltimore, Maryland, May 2006.

[4] T. Murray, "Analysing object-capability security," in *Proc. of the Joint Workshop on Foundations of Computer Security, Automated Reasoning for Security Protocol Analysis and Issues in the Theory of Security*, Pittsburgh, PA, USA, Jun. 2008, pp. 177–194.

[5] M. S. Miller, B. Tulloh, and J. S. Shapiro, "The Structure of Authority: Why Security Is not a Separable Concern," in *Proc. 2nd Intl. Conf. on Multiparadigm Programming in Mozart/Oz*. Charleroi, Belgium: Springer, 2004, pp. 2–20.

[6] M. S. Miller, K. P. Yee, and J. Shapiro, "Capability Myths Demolished," Systems Research Laboratory, Johns Hopkins University, Technical Report SRL2003-02, 2003, http://srl.cs.jhu.edu/pubs/SRL2003-02.pdf [retrieved: 7, 2018].

[7] A. Mettler, D. Wagner, and T. Close, "Joe-E: A Security-Oriented Subset of Java," in *Network and Distributed Systems Symposium*. Internet Society, Jan. 2010, pp. 357–374.

[8] M. Stiegler, "Emily: A High Performance Language for Enabling Secure Cooperation," in *Fifth Intl. Conf. on Creating, Connecting and Collaborating through Computing C5'07*. Kyoto, Japan: IEEE, Jan. 2007, pp. 163–169.

[9] D. A. Gutierrez *et al.*, "An Object-Oriented Abstract Machine as the Substrate for an Object-Oriented Operating System," in *Object-Oriented Technology ECOOP, Workshop Reader*, ser. LNCS, vol. 1357. Jyvskyl, Finland: Springer, Jun. 1997, pp. 537–544.

[10] M. A. D. Fondon, D. A. Gutierrez, L. T. Martinez, F. A. Garcia, and J. M. C. Lovelle, "Capability-based protection for integral object-oriented systems," in *Proc. Computer Software and Applications Conference COMPSAC '98*. Vienna, Austria: IEEE, Aug. 1998, pp. 344–349.
[11] M. A. D. Fondon *et al.*, "Integrating capabilities into the object model to protect distributed object systems," in *Proc. Intl. Symp. on Distributed Objects and Applications*. Edinburgh, GB: IEEE, Sep. 1999, pp. 374–383. [Online]. Available: http://dx.doi.org/10.1109/DOA.1999.794067
[12] C. Szyperski, *Component Software: Beyond Object-Oriented Programming*, 2nd ed. Boston, MA, USA: Addison-Wesley, 2002.
[13] L. Cardelli, "Typeful Programming," in *Formal Description of Programming Concepts*, E. Neuhold and M. Paul, Eds. Springer, 1991, pp. 431–507.
[14] M. Stiegler, "The E Language in a Walnut," 2000, http://www.skyhunter.com/marcs/ewalnut.html [accessed: 7, 2018].
[15] X. Leroy, "Java bytecode verification: Algorithms and formalizations," *Journal of Automated Reasoning*, vol. 30, no. 3, pp. 235–269, May 2003. [Online]. Available: https://doi.org/10.1023/A:1025055424017

Implementation of Eavesdropping Protection Method over MPTCP Using Data Scrambling and Path Dispersion

Toshihiko Kato[1)2)], Shihan Cheng[1)], Ryo Yamamoto[1)], Satoshi Ohzahata[1)] and Nobuo Suzuki[2)]
1) University of Electro-Communications, Tokyo, Japan
2) Advanced Telecommunication Research Institute International, Kyoto, Japan
e-mail: kato@net.lab.uec.ac.jp, chengshihan@net.lab.uec.ac.jp, ryo_yamamoto@net.lab.uec.ac.jp, ohzahata@net.lab.uec.ac.jp, nu-suzuki@atr.jp

Abstract—**In order to utilize multiple communication interfaces installed mobile terminals, Multipath Transmission Control Protocol (MPTCP) has been introduced recently. It can establish an MPTCP connection that transmits data segments over the multiple interfaces, such as 4G and Wireless Local Area Network (WLAN), in parallel. However, it is possible that some interfaces are connected to untrusted networks and that data transferred over them is observed in an unauthorized way. In order to avoid this situation, we proposed a method to improve privacy against eavesdropping using the data dispersion by exploiting the multipath nature of MPTCP. The proposed method takes an approach that, if an attacker cannot observe the data on *every* path, he cannot observe the traffic on *any* path. The fundamental techniques of this method is a per-byte data scrambling and path dispersion. In this paper, we present the result of implementing the proposed method within the Linux operating system and its performance evaluation.**

Keywords- Multipath TCP; Eavesdropping; Data Dispersion; Data Scrambling.

I. INTRODUCTION

Recent mobile terminals are equipped with multiple interfaces. For example, most smart phones have interfaces for 4G Long Term Evolution (LTE) and WLAN. In the next generation (5G) network, it is studied that multiple communication paths provided multiple network operators are commonly involved [1]. In this case, mobile terminals will have more than two interfaces.

However, the traditional TCP establishes a connection between a single IP address at one end, and so it cannot utilize multiple interfaces at the same time. In order to cope with this issue, MPTCP [2] is being introduced in several operating systems, such as Linux, Apple OS/iOS [3] and Android [4]. MPTCP is an extension of TCP. Conventional TCP applications can use MPTCP as if they were working over traditional TCP and are provided with multiple byte streams through different interfaces.

MPTCP is defined in three Request for Comments (RFC) documents by the Internet Engineering Task Force. RFC 6182 [5] outlines architecture guidelines. RFC 6824 [6] presents the details of extensions to support multipath operation, including the maintenance of an MPTCP connection and subflows (TCP connections associated with an MPTCP connection), and the data transfer over an MPTCP connection. RFC 6356 [7] presents a congestion control algorithm that couples the congestion control algorithms running on different subflows.

When a mobile terminal uses multiple paths, some of them may be unsafe such that an attacker is able to observe data over them in an unauthorized way. For example, a WLAN interface is connected to a public WLAN access point, data transferred over this WLAN may be disposed to other nodes connected to it. One way to prevent the eavesdropping is the Transport Layer Security (TLS). Although TLS can be applied to various applications including web access, e-mail, and ftp, however, it requires at least one end to maintain a public key certificate, and so it will not be used in some kind of communication, such as private server access and peer to peer communication.

As an alternative scheme, we proposed a method to improve confidentiality against eavesdropping by exploiting the multipath nature of MPTCP [8][9]. Even if an unsafe WLAN path is used, another path may be safe, such as LTE supported by a trusted network operator. So, the proposed method is based on an idea that, if an attacker cannot observe the data on *every* path, he cannot observe the traffic on *any* path [10]. In order to realize this idea, we adopted a byte based data scrambling for data segments sent over multiple subflows. This mixes up data to avoid its recognition through illegal monitoring over an unsafe path. Although there are some proposals to use multiple TCP connections to protect eavesdropping [11]-[14], all of them depend on the encryption techniques. The proposed method is dependent on the exclusive OR (XOR) calculation that is much lighter in terms of processing overhead.

In this paper, we show the result of implementation of the proposed method and the result of performance evaluation. We adopted a kernel debugging mechanism in the Linux operating system so as to modify the Linux kernel as least as possible. We conducted performance evaluation through Ethernet and WLAN using off-the-shelf PCs and access point.

The rest of this paper is organized as follows. Section II explains the details of the proposed method. Section III shows how to implement the proposed method within the MPTCP software in the Linux operating system. Section IV gives the results of the performance evaluation. In the end, Section V concludes this paper.

II. DETAILS OF PROPOSED METHOD

Figure 1 shows the overview of the proposed method. When an application sends data, it is stored in the send socket buffer in the beginning. The proposed method scrambles the data by calculating XOR of a byte with its preceding 64 bytes in the sending byte stream. Then, the scrambled data is sent through multiple subflows associated with the MPTCP connection. Since some data segments are transmitted through trusted subflows, an attacker monitoring only a part of data segments cannot obtain all of sent data and so cannot descramble any of them. When receiving data segments, they are reordered in the receive socket buffer by MPTCP. The proposed method descrambles them in a byte-by-byte basis just before an application reads the received data.

Figure 2 shows the details of data scrambling. In order to realize this scrambling, the data scrambling module maintains

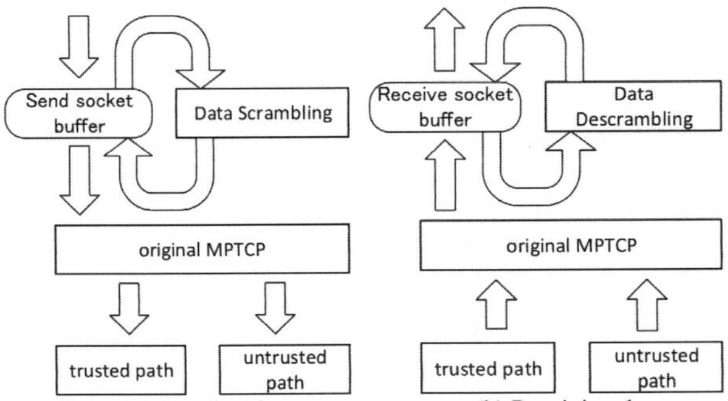

(a) Sending data (b) Receiving data

Figure 1. Overview of proposed method [8].

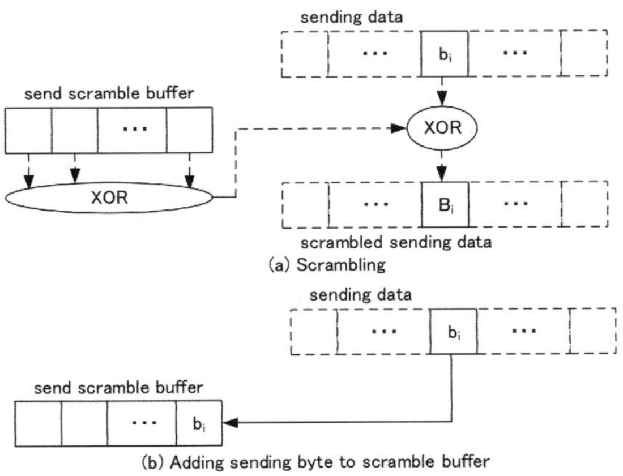

Figure 2. Processing of data scrambling [8].

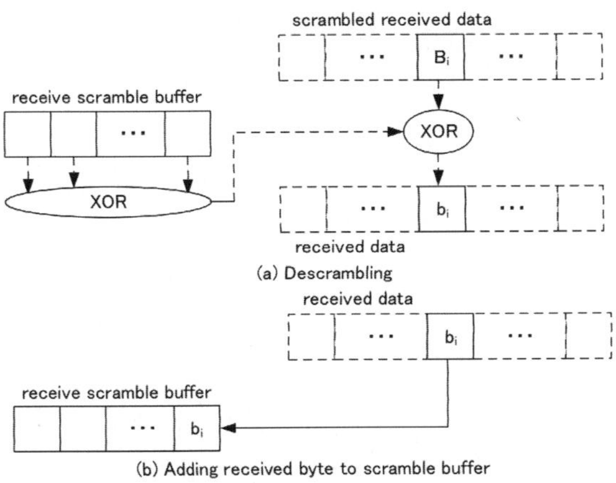

Figure 3. Processing of data descrambling [8].

the *send scrambling buffer*, whose length is 64 bytes. It is a shift buffer and its initial value is HMAC of the key of this side, with higher bytes set to zero. The key used here is one of the MPTCP parameters, exchanged in the first stage of MPTCP connection establishment. When a data comes from an application, each byte (b_i in the figure) is XORed with the result of XOR of all the bytes in the send scrambling buffer. The obtained byte (B_i) is the corresponding sending byte. After calculating the sending byte, the original byte (b_i) is added to the send scramble buffer, forcing out the oldest (highest) byte from the buffer. The send scrambling buffer holds recent 64 original bytes given from an application. By using 64 byte buffer, the access to the original data is protected even if there are well-known byte patterns (up to 63 bytes) in application protocol data.

Figure 3 shows the details of data descrambling, which is similar with data scrambling. The data scrambling module also maintains the receive scramble buffer whose length is 64 bytes. Its initial value is HMAC of the key of the remote side. When an in-sequence data is stored in the receive socket buffer, a byte (B_i that is scrambled) is applied to XOR calculation with the XOR result of all the bytes in the receive scramble buffer. The result is the descrambled byte (b_i), which is added to the receive scramble buffer.

By using the byte-wise scrambling and descrambling, the proposed method does not increase the length of exchanged data at all. The separate send and receive control enables two way data exchanges to be handled independently. Moreover the proposed method introduces only a few modification to the original MPTCP.

III. IMPLEMENTATION

A. *Use of Kernel Probes*

Since MPTCP is implemented inside the Linux operating system, the proposed method also needs to be realized by modifying operating system kernel. However, modifying an operating system kernel is a hard task, and so we decided to use a debugging mechanism for the Linux kernel, called kernel probes [15].

Among kernel probes methods, we use a way called "JProbe" [9]. JProbe is used to get access to a kernel function's arguments at runtime. It introduces a JProbe handler with the same prototype as that of the function whose arguments are to be accessed. When the probed function is executed, the control is first transferred to the user-defined JProbe handler. After the user-defined handler returns, the control is transferred to the original function [15].

In order to make this mechanism work, a user needs to prepare the following;

- registering the entry by `struct jprobe` and
- defining the init and exit modules by functions `register_jprobe()` and `unregister_jprobe()` [16].

In the Linux kernel, function `tcp_sendmsg()` is called when an application sends data to MPTPCP (actually TCP, too) [17]. As stated in Section II, the scrambling will be done at the beginning of this function. So, we define a JProbe handler for function `tcp_sendmsg()` for scrambling data to be transferred.

In order for an application to read received data, it calls function `tcp_recvmsg()` in MPTCP. In contrast to data scrambling, the descrambling procedure needs to be done at the end of this function. So, we introduce a dummy kernel function and export its symbol just before the returning points of function `tcp_recvmsg()`. We then define a JProbe handler for descrambling in this dummy function.

By adopting this approach, we can program and debug scrambling/descrambling independently of the Linux kernel itself.

B. Modification of Linux opeating system

We modified the source code of the Linux operating system in the following way. We believe that this is a very slight modification that requires to us to rebuild the kernel only once.

- *Introduce a dummy function in* `tcp_recvmsg()`.

As described above, we defined a dummy function named `dummy_recvmsg()`. It is defined in the source file "`net/ipv4/tcp.c`" as shown in Figure 4. It is a function just returning and inserted before function `tcp_recvmsg()` releases the socket control. The prototype declaration is done in the source file "`include/net/tcp.h`".

- *Maintain control variables within socket data structure.*

In order to perform the scrambling/descrambling, the control variables, such as a scramble buffer, need to be installed within the Linux kernel. The TCP software in the kernel uses a socket data structure to maintain internal control data on an individual TCP / MPTCP connection [17]. This is controlled by the following variable, as shown in Figure 4.

```
struct tcp_sock *tp = tcp_sk(sk);
```

This structure includes the MPTCP related parameters, such as keys and tokens. The parameters are packed in an element given blow.

```
int tcp_recvmsg(struct sock *sk, struct msghdr *msg,
      size_t len, int nonblock,int flags, int *addr_len) {
   struct tcp_sock *tp = tcp_sk(sk);
   . . . .
   dummy_recvmsg(sk, msg, len, nonblack, flags, addr_len);
   release_sock(sk);
   return copied;
   . . . .
} // dummy_recvmsg() inserted
EXPORT_SYMBOL(tcp_recvmsg);

void dummy_recvmsg(struct sock *sk, struct msghdr *msg,
      size_t len, int nonblock, int flags, int *addr_len)
{
   return;
} // Defining dummy_recvmsg()
EXPORT_SYMBOL(dummy_recvmsg);
```

Figure 4. Dummy function in `tcp_recvmsg()`.

```
struct mptcp_cb {
  . . . .
  unsigned char sScrBuf[64], rScrBuf[64];
  unsigned char sXor, rXor;
  int sIndex, rIndex, sNotFirst, rNotFirst;
};
```

Figure 5. Control variables for data scrambling/descrambling.

```
struct mptcp_cb *mpcb;
```

So, we added the control variables for data scrambling in this data structure. Figure 5 shows the control variables. The details of those variables are given in the following.

- `sScrBuf[64]` and `rScrBuf[64]`: the send and receive scramble buffers, used as ring buffers.
- `sXor` and `rXor`: the results of calculation of XOR for all the bytes in the send and receive scramble buffers.
- `sIndex` and `rIndex`: the index of the last (newest) element in `sScrBuf[64]` and `rScrBuf[64]`.
- `sNotFirst` and `rNotFirst`: the flags indicating whether the scrambling and descrambling are invoked for the first time in the MPTCP connection, or not.

C. Implementation of scrambling

(1) Framework of JProbe handler

Figure 6 shows the framework of JProbe hander defined for `tcp_sendmsg()`. Function `jtcp_sendmsg()` is a main body of the JProbe hander. The arguments need to be exactly the same with the hooked kernel function `tcp_sendmsg()`, and it calls `jprobe_return()` just before its returning. Data structure `struct jprobe mptcp_jprobe` specifies its details.

Function `mptcp_scramble_init()` is the initialization function invoked when the relevant kernel module is inserted. In the beginning, it confirm that the hander has the same prototype with the hooked function. Then it defines the entry point and registers the JProbe handler. Function `mptcp_scramble_exit()` is called when the relevant kernel module is removed. It removes the entry point and unregisters the hander from the kernel.

(2) Flowchart of data scrambling

The data scrambling procedure is implemented in `jtcp_sendmsg()`. Figure 7 shows the flowchart for this

```
static const char procname[] = "mptcp_scramble"
int jtcp_sendmsg(struct sock *sk, struct msghdr *msg,
        size_t size) {
  struct tcp_sock *tp = tcp_sk(sk);
  . . .
  jprobe_return();
  return 0;
} // (i) JProbe handler

static struct jprobe mptcp_jprobe = {
  .kp = {.symbol_name = "tcp_sendmsg",},
        .entry = jtcp_sendmsg,
}; // (ii) Register entry

static __init int mptcp_scramble_init(void) {
  int ret = -ENOMEM;
  BUILD_BUG_ON(__same_type(tcp_sendmsg, jtcp_sendmsg) == 0);
  if(!proc_create(procname, S_IRUSR, init_net.proc_net, 0))
    return ret;
  ret = register_jprobe(&mptcp_jprobe);
  if (ret) {
    remove_proc_entry(procname, init_net.proc._net);
    retrun ret;
  }
  return 0;
} // (iii) Init function
module_init(mptcp_scramble_init);

static __exit void mptcp_scramble_exit(void) {
  remove_proc_entry(procname, init_net.proc._net);
  unregister_jprobe(&mptcp_jprobe);
} // (iv) Exit function
module_exit(mptcp_scramble_exit);
```

Figure 6. JProbe hander definition for `tcp_sendmsg()`.

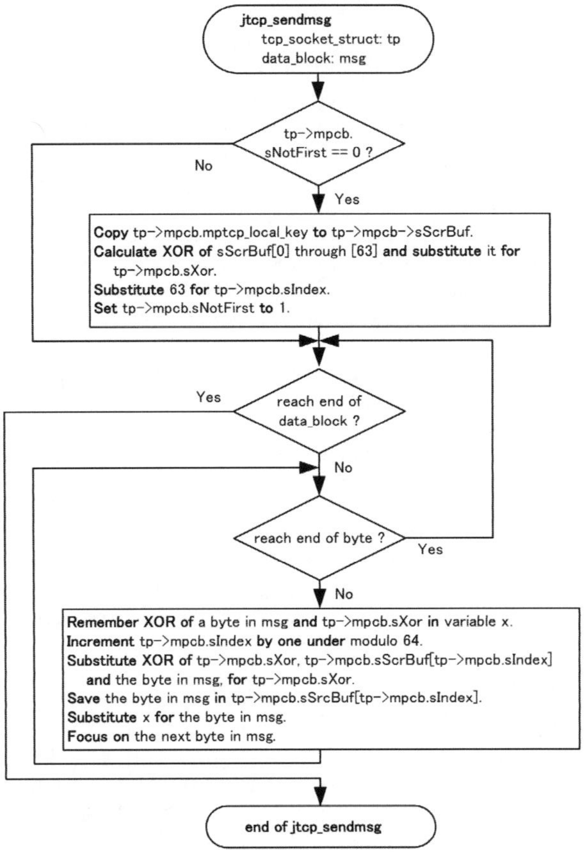

Figure 7. Flowchart of data scrambling.

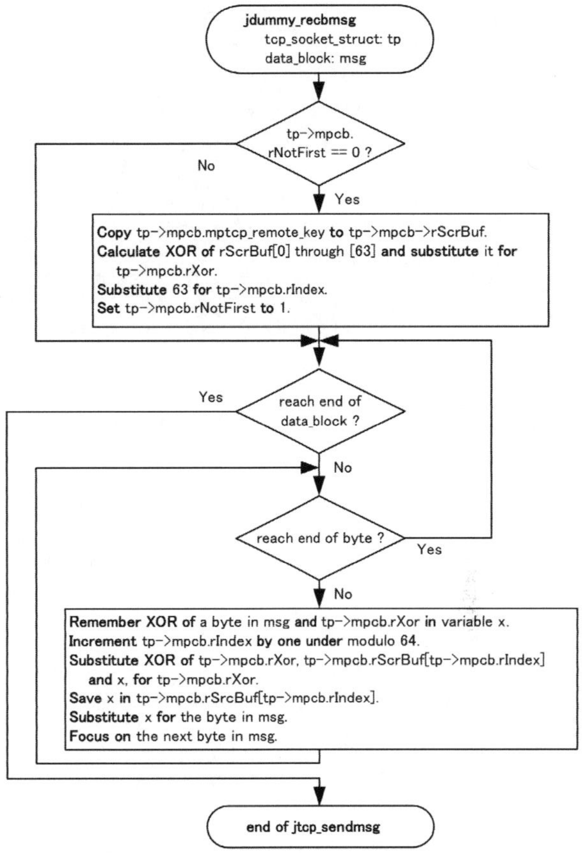

Figure 8. Flowchart of data descrambling.

procedure. When `jtcp_sendmsg()` is called, it is checked whether this function is invoked for the first time or not. If it is the first invocation over a specific MPTCP connection, `sScrBuf[]` is initialized to the value of the local key maintained in the `struct mptcp_cb` structure. Then, XOR of all the bytes in `sScrBuf[]` is calculated and saved in `sXor`, and `sIndex` is set to 63.

The argument containing data (`msg`) is a list of data blocks, and so individual blocks are handled sequentially. For each data block, a byte-by-byte basis calculation is performed in the following way. First, the XOR of the focused byte and `sXor` is saved in temporal variable `x`. Then, `sIndex` is advanced by one under modulo 64. Thirdly, the XOR of `sXor`, `sScrBuf[sIndex]` and the original byte are calculated and saved in sXor. It should be noted that the value in `sScrBuf[sIndex]` at this stage is the oldest value in the send scramble buffer. Fourthly, the original byte is stored in `sScrBuf[sIndex]`,which means that the send scramble buffer is updated. At last, the byte in the message block is replaced by the value of `x`.

D. Implementation of descrambling

The data descrambling is implemented similarly with scrambling. We developed the JProbe handler for function `dummy_recvmsg()` in the same way with the approach given in Figure 6. The flowchart of descrambling procedure is shown in Figure 8. This is similar with the flowchart shown in Figure 7. In the first part of the flowchart, it should be noted that `rScrBuf[]` is set to the remote key, which is the local key in the sender side. In this case, the data block is a descrambled data. Therefore, in the byte-by-byte basis part, the original value (`x` in the figure) is used to calculate `rXor` and is stored in `rSrcBuf[rIndex]`.

IV. EXPERIMENT

We implemented the proposed method over the Linux operating system (Ubuntu 16.04 LTS). We evaluated it in the experimental configuration shown in Figure 9. Two Panasonic Let's note PCs are used as a client and a server. The processor types are Intel UPU U1300 with 1.06GHz and Intel Pentium M with 1.50 GHz. The client PC is connected with an access point (Buffalo Air Station G54) through WLAN and Ethernet. On the other hand, the server PC is connected with the access point through Ethernet. We used 802.11g with 2.4 GHz as WLAN and 100base-T as Ethernet. The WLAN interface does not use any encryption. We suppose that the Ethernet link is a trusted network and the WLAN link without any encryption is an untrusted network. A MacBook Air with macOS High Sierra is used as an attacker. It runs Wireshark to capture packets sent over WLAN.

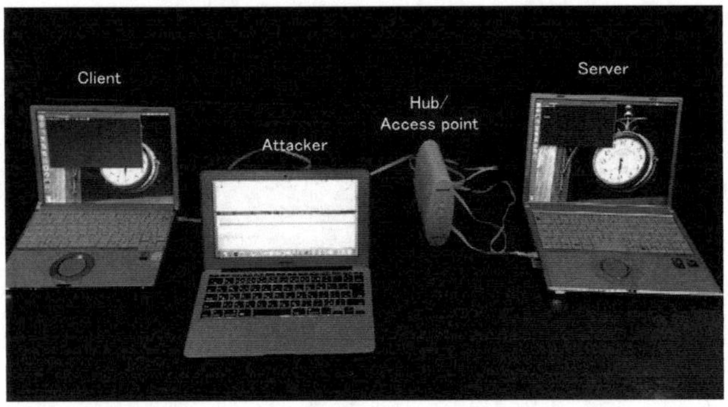

Figure 9. Experiment configuration.

The network setting is as follows.

- Since the access point works as a bridge, the client and the server are connected to the same subnetwork, 192.168.0.0/24.
- The Ethernet and WLAN interfaces in the client are assigned with IP addresses 192.160.0.1 and 192.168.0.3, respectively. The Ethernet interface in the server is assigned with IP address 192.168.0.2. The ESSID of the WLAN is "MPTCP-AP."
- In order to use two interfaces at the client, the IP routing tables are set for individual interfaces, by use of the ip command in the following way (for the Ethernet interface `enp4s1`).
  - `ip rule add from 192.168.0.1 table 1`
  - `ip route add 192.168.0.0/24 dev enp4s1 scope link table 1`
- The JProbe handlers for `jtcp_sendmsg()` and `jdummy_recvmsg()` are built as kernel modules. They are inserted and removed using `insmod` and `rmmod` Linux commands without rebooting the system.
- In the experiment, we used `iperf` for sending data from the client to the server, using Ethernet and WLAN.
- In the attacker, the Wireshark network analyzer is invoked for monitoring a WLAN interface with the monitor mode set to effective.

Figure 10 shows a result of the attacker's monitoring of iperf communication over WLAN in the conventional communication. In the iperf communication, an ASCII digit sequence "0123456789" is sent repeatedly. If the attacker can monitor the WLAN, the content is disposed as shown in this figure. Figure 11 shows a monitoring result by the attacker over the WLAN link when the data scrambling is performed. This figure shows the monitoring result for the first data segment over the WLAN link, which is the same with Figure 10. The original data is a repetition of "0123456789" but the data is scrambled in the result here. So, it can be said that the attacker cannot understand the content, even the WLAN link is not encrypted.

As for the throughput of iperf communication, we executed ten times evaluation runs. The results are as follows.
Without scrambling: 89.92 Mbps average, 1.19 Mbps STD.
With scrambling: 86.04 Mbps average, 1.69 Mbps STD.
Since the processor types used in the experiment are rather old, the processing of scrambling and descrambling provided some overhead. But we believe that the throughput reduction is small.

V. Conclusions

This paper described the results of implementation and evaluation of a method to improve privacy against eavesdropping over MPTCP communications, which we proposed in the previous papers. The proposed method here is based on the not-every-not-any protection principle, that is, *if an attacker cannot observe the data over trusted path such as an LTE network, he cannot observe the traffic on any path.* Specifically, the proposed method uses the byte oriented data scrambling and the data dispersion over multiple paths.

In the implementation of the proposed method, we took an approach to avoid the modification of the Linux kernel as much as possible. The modification is as follows. The control

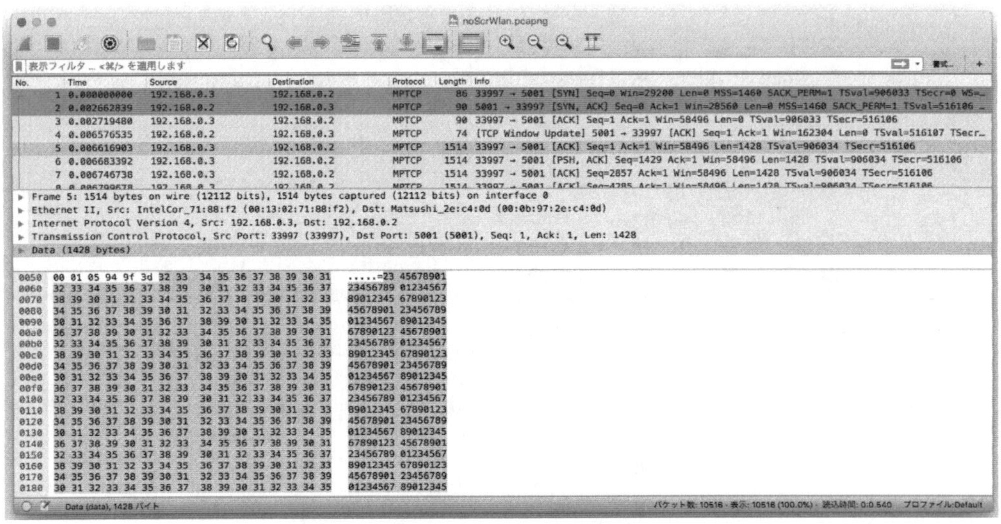

Figure 10. Capturing result when no scrambling is performed.

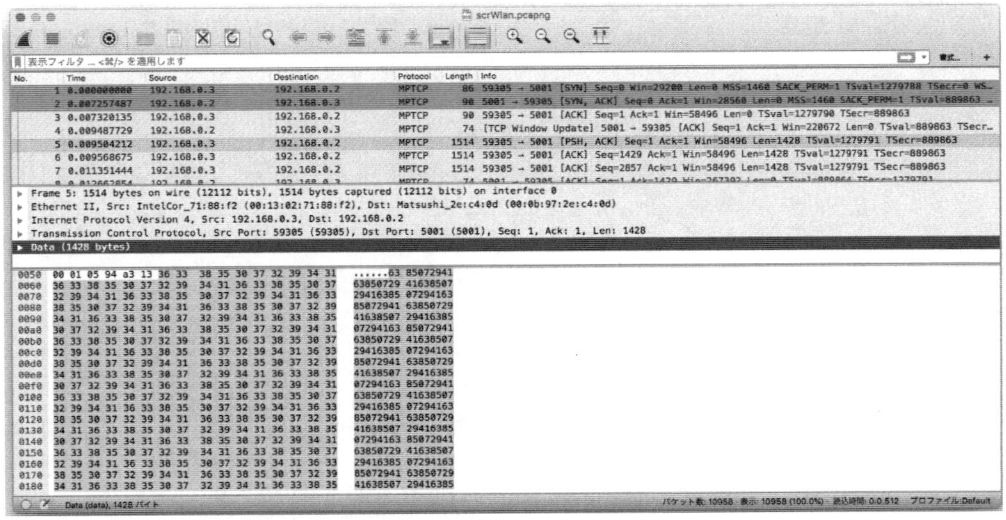

Figure 11. Capturing result when scrambling is performed.

parameters are inserted in the socket data structure, and the dummy function for the last part of `tcp_recvmsg()` function. The main part of scrambling and descrambling is implemented by use of the kernel debugging routine called JProbe handler, which is independent of the kernel.

Through the experiment, we confirmed that the data transferred over unencrypted WLAN link cannot be recognized when the data scrambling is performed. As for the performance, the throughput of the scrambled communication is just a little smaller than the conventional communication exposed to unauthorized access.

ACKNOWLEDGMENT

This research was performed under the research contract of "Research and Development on control schemes for utilizations of multiple mobile communication networks," for the Ministry of Internal Affairs and Communications, Japan.

REFERENCES

[1] NGNM Alliance, "NGMN 5G White Paper," https://www.ngmn.org/fileadmin/ngmn/content/downloads/Technical/2015/NGMN_5G_White_Paper_V1_0.pdf, Feb. 2015, [retrieved: Jul., 2018].

[2] C. Paasch and O. Bonaventure, "Multipath TCP," Communications of the ACM, vol. 57, no. 4, pp. 51-57, Apr. 2014.

[3] AppleInsider Staff, "Apple found to be using advanced Multipath TCP networking in iOS 7," http://appleinsider.com/articles/13/09/20/apple-found-to-be-using-advanced-multipath-tcp-networking-in-ios-7, [retrieved: Jul, 2018].

[4] icteam, "MultiPath TCP – Linux Kernel implementation, Users:: Android," https://multipath-tcp.org/pmwiki.php/Users/Android, [retrieved: Jul., 2018].

[5] A. Ford, C.Raiciu, M. Handley, S. Barre, and J. Iyengar, "Architectural Guidelines for Multipath TCP Development," IETF RFC 6182, Mar. 2011.

[6] A. Ford, C. Raiciu, M. Handley, and O. Bonaventure, "TCP Extensions for Multipath Operation with Multiple Addresses," IETF RFC 6824, Jan. 2013.

[7] C. Raiciu, M. Handley, and D. Wischik, "Coupled Congestion Control for Multipath Transport Protocols," IETF RFC 6356, Oct. 2011.

[8] T. Kato, S. Cheng, R. Yamamoto, S. Ohzahata, and N. Suzuki, "Protecting Eavesdropping over Multipath TCP Communication Based on Not-Every-Not-Any Protection," in Proc. SECURWARE 2017, pp. 82-87, Sep. 2017.

[9] T. Kato, S. Cheng, R. Yamamoto, S. Ohzahata, and N. Suzuki, "Proposal and Study on Implementation of Data Eavesdropping Protection Method over Multipath TCP Communication Using Data Scrambling and Path Dispersion," International Journal On Advances in Security, 2018 no. 1&2, pp. 1-9, Jul., 2018.

[10] C. Pearce and S. Zeadally, "Ancillary Impacts of Multipath TCP on Current and Future Network Security," IEEE Internet Computing, vol. 19, iss. 5, pp. 58-65, Sept.-Oct. 2015.

[11] J. Yang and S. Papavassiliou, "Improving Network Security by Multipath Traffic Dispersion," in Proc. MILCOM 2001, pp. 34-38, Oct. 2001.

[12] M. Nacher, C. Calafate, J. Cano, and P. Manzoni, "Evaluation of the Impact of Multipath Data Dispersion for Anonymous TCP Connections," In Proc. SecureWare 2007, pp. 24-29, Oct. 2007.

[13] A. Gurtov and T. Polishchuk, "Secure Multipath Transport For Legacy Internet Applications," In Proc. BROADNETS 2009, pp. 1-8, Sep. 2009.

[14] L. Apiecionek, W. Makowski, M. Sobczak, and T. Vince, "Multi Path Transmission Control Protocols as a security solution," in Proc. 2015 IEEE 13th International Scientific Conference on Informatics, pp. 27-31, Nov. 2015.

[15] LWN.net, "An introduction to KProbes," https://lwn.net/Articles/132196/, [retreieved: Jul., 2018].

[16] GitHubGist, "jprobes example: dzeban / jprobe_etn_io.c," https://gist.github.com/dzeban/a19c711d6b6b1d72e594, [retreieved: Jul., 2018].

[17] S. Seth and M. Venkatesulu, "TCP/IP Architecture, Desgn, and Implementation in Linux," John Wiley & Sons, 2009.

Deployment Enforcement Rules for TOSCA-based Applications

Michael Zimmermann, Uwe Breitenbücher, Christoph Krieger, and Frank Leymann

Institute of Architecture of Application Systems, University of Stuttgart,
70569 Stuttgart, Germany
Email: {lastname}@iaas.uni-stuttgart.de

***Abstract*—In the context of Industry 4.0, gathering sensor data and using data analysis software can lead to actionable insights, for example, enabling predictive maintenance. Since developing these data analysis software requires some special expert knowledge, often external data scientist are charged for that. However, often the data to be analyzed is of vital importance and thus, must not leave the company. Therefore, applications developed and modeled as deployment models by third-parties have to be enforced to be executed in the local company's network. However, manually adapting a lot of these deployment models in order to meet the company's requirements is cumbersome, time consuming and error-prone. Furthermore, some kind of enforcement mechanism is required to really ensure that these data security and privacy requirements are fulfilled. Thus, in this paper, we present an approach considering these issues during the deployment time of the application. The presented approach is based on the Topology and Orchestration Specification for Cloud Applications (TOSCA), an OASIS standard enabling the description of cloud applications as well as their deployment. The approach enables the specification as well as the enforcement of reoccurring and generic requirements and restrictions of TOSCA-based declarative deployment models, without the need to adapt or modify these deployment models. The practical feasibility of the presented approach is validated by extending our open-source prototype OpenTOSCA, which provides a modeling tool, a TOSCA Runtime, as well as a self-service portal for TOSCA.**

***Keywords*–Cloud Computing; Application Provisioning; Automation; TOSCA; Security.**

I. Introduction

In the area of Internet of Things [1] and Industry 4.0 [2], the gathering of sensor data can lead to actionable insights by utilizing data analysis software, for instance, enabling predictive maintenance of cyber-physical manufacturing systems. However, the development of such analysis software for analyzing the gathered data requires special expert knowledge, for example, about implementing machine learning algorithms [3]. But, since companies often do not have this kind of knowledge and expertise for implementing such complex and domain-specific analysis software by themselves, they typically charge external data scientists to build the required software for them. Unfortunately, because of data security and privacy reasons as well as different company requirements and policies, often the gathered data to be analyzed is of vital importance for the company and must not leave the company and thus, can not be provided to third-parties, as for example, the data scientists [4]. Therefore, data scientists have to provide their developed software in a way, that enables the companies to automatically install and configure the analysis software, required middleware, and dependencies as well as to execute and link the software with the sensor data in their local company's infrastructure [5].

However, the data security and privacy requirements and policies as well as infrastructure information can differ from company to company or might be kept secretly as well. Therefore, third-party companies and data scientists can not always take these requirements and policies into account when developing the analysis software and creating the deployment models enabling the automated provisioning. Thus, the deployment models need to provide some configuration capabilities in order to be easily adaptable to the local infrastructure and environment of the respective company. Furthermore, with modern applications consisting of complex and heterogeneous components, it can become difficult to comply security requirements, especially when different deployment technologies are used [6] [7]. However, the enforcement of the defined security requirements needs to be ensured under all circumstances in order to secure the data. Regardless of whether the deployment model is created by a third-party company, an external data scientist, or even internally. Therefore, some possibility to easily specify such reoccurring requirements reflecting the company's policies as well as an automated enforcement mechanism are required. However, in a way that separates the modeling of requirements from the modeling of deployment models, since this again is a complex task and requires expert knowledge.

In this paper, we tackle the aforementioned issues. We present our concept of *Deployment Enforcement Rules* in order to specify reusable requirements and restrictions for TOSCA-based declarative deployment models. Furthermore, our approach ensures the enforcement of these requirements and restrictions during the provisioning of an application. Our approach is based on the Topology and Orchestration Specification for Cloud Applications (TOSCA), an OASIS standard enabling the description of cloud applications as well as their deployment [8]. By extending an existing deployment technology, our approach enables the fully automated deployment of cloud and IoT applications, while enforcing security requirements. Our approach is validated by a prototypical implementation based on the OpenTOSCA Ecosystem [9] [10].

The remainder of this paper is structured as follows:
In Section II, the fundamental concepts of the standard TOSCA are explained. TOSCA is used within our approach as a cloud and IoT application modeling language. Afterward, in Section III our approach is motivated by illustrating a TOSCA-based Industry 4.0 scenario. In Section IV, our approach of Deployment Enforcement Rules for declarative deployment models based on TOSCA are explained. In Section V, our approach is validated by presenting a prototypical implementation based on the OpenTOSCA Ecosystem. In Section VI, an overview of related work is given. Finally, Section VII concludes this paper and presents an outlook on future work.

II. Topology and Orchestration Specification for Cloud Applications

Since our work is based on TOSCA, in this section, the OASIS standard TOSCA is explained. The TOSCA standard enables the automated deployment, as well as management of cloud and IoT applications. In this section, we only briefly describe the fundamental concepts of TOSCA required to understand our presented approach. A detailed overview of TOSCA can be found in the TOSCA Specifications [8] [11], the TOSCA Primer [12] and an overview by Binz et al. [13].

A. Nodes, Relationships, Types, and Templates

Using TOSCA, the components of an application – software components as well as infrastructure components – and their relationships to each other can be described in a standardized and portable manner. The modeled structure of an application is defined by so-called *Topology Templates*. A Topology Template is a directed graph and consists of nodes and directed edges. The nodes represent the components of the application and are called *Node Templates*. A Node Template could be, for example, an Apache Tomcat, an Ubuntu virtual machine, or an OpenStack hypervisor. The Node Templates are connected by the edges, which are called *Relationship Templates* and specify the relations between the Node Templates. A Relationship Template could define, for example, a "hostedOn", "dependsOn", or "connectsTo" relation between two Node Templates. Thus, Relationship Templates are specifying the structure of an application. In order to enable reusability, the semantics of Node Templates and Relationship Templates are defined by *Node Types* and *Relationship Types*. Node Types as well as Relationship Types are reusable entities allowing to define *Properties*, as well as *Management Operations*. A NodeType "OpenStack", for example, may have defined Properties for specifying the URL required for accessing a running OpenStack instance as well as credential information, such as a username or a password. The Management Operations defined by a Node Type can be bundled in interfaces and can be invoked in order to manage the instances of this component. For example, an "Apache Tomcat" Node Type may define a Management Operation "install" in order to install the component itself as well as a Management Operation "deployApplication" in order to deploy an application on it. Furthermore, a cloud provider or hypervisor Node Type typically provides Management Operations in order to create virtual machines ("createVM") as well as to terminate virtual machines ("terminateVM").

B. Implementation Artifacts and Deployment Artifacts

Two kinds of artifacts are defined by TOSCA: (i) *Implementation Artifacts (IAs)*, as well as (ii) *Deployment Artifacts (DAs)*. The Management Operations defined by Node Types are implemented by IAs. An IA itself can be implemented using various technologies, for instance, as a Web Services Description Language (WSDL)-based web service, a shell script, or by using configuration management technologies, such as Ansible [14] or Chef [15]. Generally, three kinds of IAs can be distinguished, dependent on the way they are processed: (i) IAs, that are copied to the target environment of the application and are executed there, for example, shell scripts. (ii) IAs, that are deployed and also executed in the *TOSCA Runtime* environment (cf. Section II-E), for example, SOAP-based web services. These IAs typically use remote access protocols, for instance SSH or SFTP in order to manipulate components, perform operations on it, and to transfer files on a virtual machine for example. (iii) IAs, that are just referred within a Topology Template, since the modeled component is already running somewhere. Such IAs are, for example, a web service API of a cloud provider or a hypervisor, such as OpenStack.

The TOSCA standard also defines so-called Deployment Artifacts. In contrast to IAs, DAs implement the business functionality of a Node Template. For example, the DA of a PHP application node could be a *.ZIP file, which contains the PHP files, images, and all other files required for provisioning the PHP application. Another example of a DA would be a *.WAR file, implementing the java web application of a node. Deployment Artifacts are typed and may define additional information, such as the location of the corresponding binary.

C. Management Plans

In order to create or terminate an instance of a modeled TOSCA-based application or to automate the management, so-called *Management Plans* are used. A Management Plan defines all tasks as well as the order in which these tasks need to be executed in order to fulfill a specific management functionality, for example, to provision a new instance of the modeled application. Therefore, the Management Operations which are specified by Node Types and are implemented by the corresponding Implementation Artifacts are invoked by Management Plans. The TOSCA standard allows to use any arbitrary process modeling language, but recommends to use workflow languages such as the *Business Process Execution Language (BPEL)* [16] or the *Business Process Model and Notation (BPMN)* [17]. There is also a BPMN extension called *BPMN4TOSCA* [18], [19], which is explicitly tailored for describing TOSCA-based deployment and management plans.

D. Cloud Service Archives

The TOSCA specification also defines a portable as well as self-contained packaging format, so-called *Cloud Service Archive (CSAR)*. A CSAR enables to package all aforementioned artifacts, templates, type definitions, plans, and all other additionally required files together into one archive, which technically is a .zip file. Therefore, a CSAR contains everything required for enabling the automated provisioning and management of the modeled application. Moreover, because of the mentioned characteristics, CSARs also enable to easily share and distribute such modeled TOSCA-based applications, for example, between colleagues, project partners, or to customers.

E. TOSCA Runtimes

The processing and execution of CSARs is done by standard-compliant TOSCA Runtimes. However, there are two different approaches for provisioning a TOSCA-based application: (i) declaratively as well as (ii) imperatively [20]. Therefore, there are also two types of TOSCA Runtimes. A TOSCA Runtime can either process a Topology Template (i) declaratively by interpreting and deriving the actions required to provision the modeled application directly from the Topology Template itself. In this case, no Management Plan is required. Furthermore, a TOSCA Runtime can also process a TOSCA-modeled application (ii) imperatively by using Management Plans associated with a Topology Template, specifying which Management Operations need to be executed in which order.

III. Motivating Scenario

In this section, a TOSCA-based motivation scenario is described. This motivation scenario is used throughout the entire paper for explaining and demonstrating our approach. Figure 1 illustrates the motivation scenario as a TOSCA Topology Template. The modeled application abstractly depicts an exemplary Industry 4.0 scenario with a data analytics stack on the left side (*PredictionService*) and the data to be analyzed on the right side (*MySQLDB*) of the illustrated topology.

In Industry 4.0, for example, manufacturing data gathered during the production process can be analyzed in order to enable predictive maintenance of cyber-physical manufacturing systems. The analytics stack in Figure 1 consists of an *Apache Flink* Node Template, which is hosted on (specified by using a "hostedOn" Relationship Template) an *Ubuntu* virtual machine Node Template. The virtual machine is managed by the hypervisor OpenStack, which should be operated locally in the infrastructure of the company. In general, Apache Flink is an analytics platform with batch as well as stream processing capabilities enabling the integration, processing, and analyzing of data sources, such as MySQL databases. In our motivation scenario, the MySQL database used to store the generated analysis data is also running on an Ubuntu virtual machine, which is hosted on the same OpenStack instance as the Prediction Service. Since, the Prediction Service needs to establish a connection to the MySQL database in order to access and analyze the data, both Node Templates are connected using a "connectsTo" Relationship Template. Furthermore, required credentials, for instance, the username ("DBMSUsername") or password ("DBMSPassword") of the database are provided as Properties. In oder to instantiate an Ubuntu virtual machine, the OpenStack Node Template exposes Management Operations, like for example "createVM". Management Operations can use Properties, predefined during the modeling time, as input in order to customize the specification of a component, for example, the amount of RAM or hard disk capacity in case of a virtual machine. But also during the provisioning time, the modeled application can still be customized. This can be achieved by setting the value of any arbitrary Property to "getInput()". The values of such defined Properties are requested when the provisioning is instantiated. The advantage of this is that a parameterizable CSAR containing the Topology Template and all other required files can be distributed among business partner or customers. In Figure 1, for example, the username ("HUsername"), the password ("HPassword"), as well as the endpoint ("Endpoint") are defined as "getInput()" in order to enable the adaption of these Properties according to the company's respective infrastructure. Due to the fact, that the data to be analyzed can contain business-critical information that has to be protected and must not leave the company, the OpenStack needs to be operated within the local environment of the company. Therefore, in our scenario the credentials and the endpoint of the local OpenStack are not predefined and need to be provided during provisioning time of the application.

However, the enforcement of the local deployment needs to be ensured under all circumstances in order to secure the data. Regardless of whether the Properties are provided manually when the provisioning of the application is instantiated or are already predefined in the deployment model. Therefore, some possibility to specify such requirements and restrictions regarding the deployment model as well as an enforcement mechanism are required to achieve that. Of course, besides the requirement to restrict the physical location of the provisioning of the application, other requirements are imaginable as well. For example, a requirement specifying that some components are only allowed to be hosted on specific operating systems, because they might provide some special security features. Using TOSCA, it is possible to specify such non-functional requirements, for example, by defining corresponding *Policy Types* and *Policy Templates*. However, they need to be modeled directly within the Topology Template and are attached to Node Templates for which the policy needs to be fulfilled. Therefore, in order to meet the respective requirements, for every CSAR the Topology Model respectively the TOSCA definition files must be adapted according to the company's business requirements and policies. However, manually adapting a lot of CSARs in order to meet the same requirements is cumbersome, time consuming and error-prone. Therefore, an alternative option enabling the easily specification as well as enforcement of these reoccurring and generic requirements is required. The defined requirements should be appendable to a CSAR without adapting TOSCA definition files, but just by adding additional files defining the requirements. Also, besides *Whitelisting Rules*, defining what is allowed, also *Blacklisting Rules*, defining what is forbidden should be supported. In the following section we explain our idea of generic and reusable *Deployment Enforcement Rules* tackling these issues in detail.

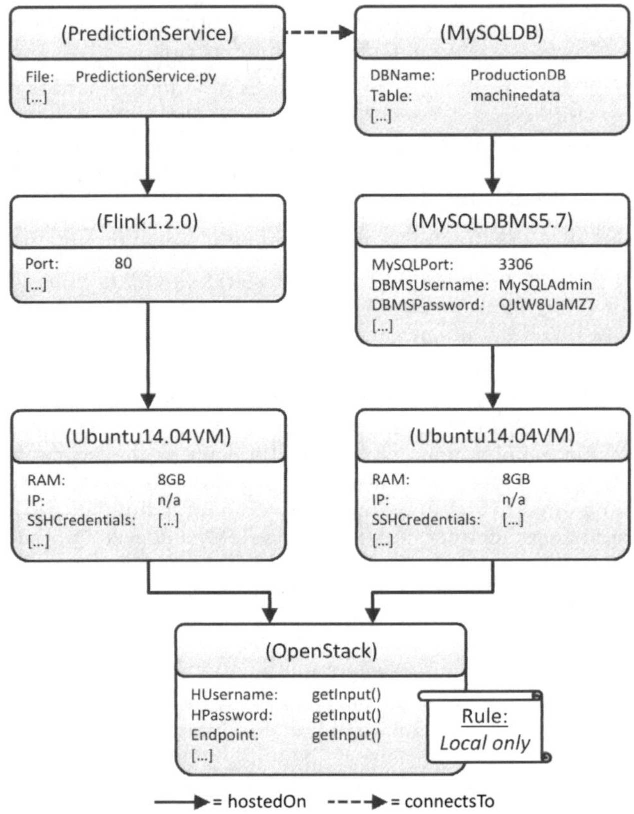

Figure 1. Analytics functionality as well as the database containing the dataset to be analyzed should be hosted on the local infrastructure of the company due to data security and privacy requirements.

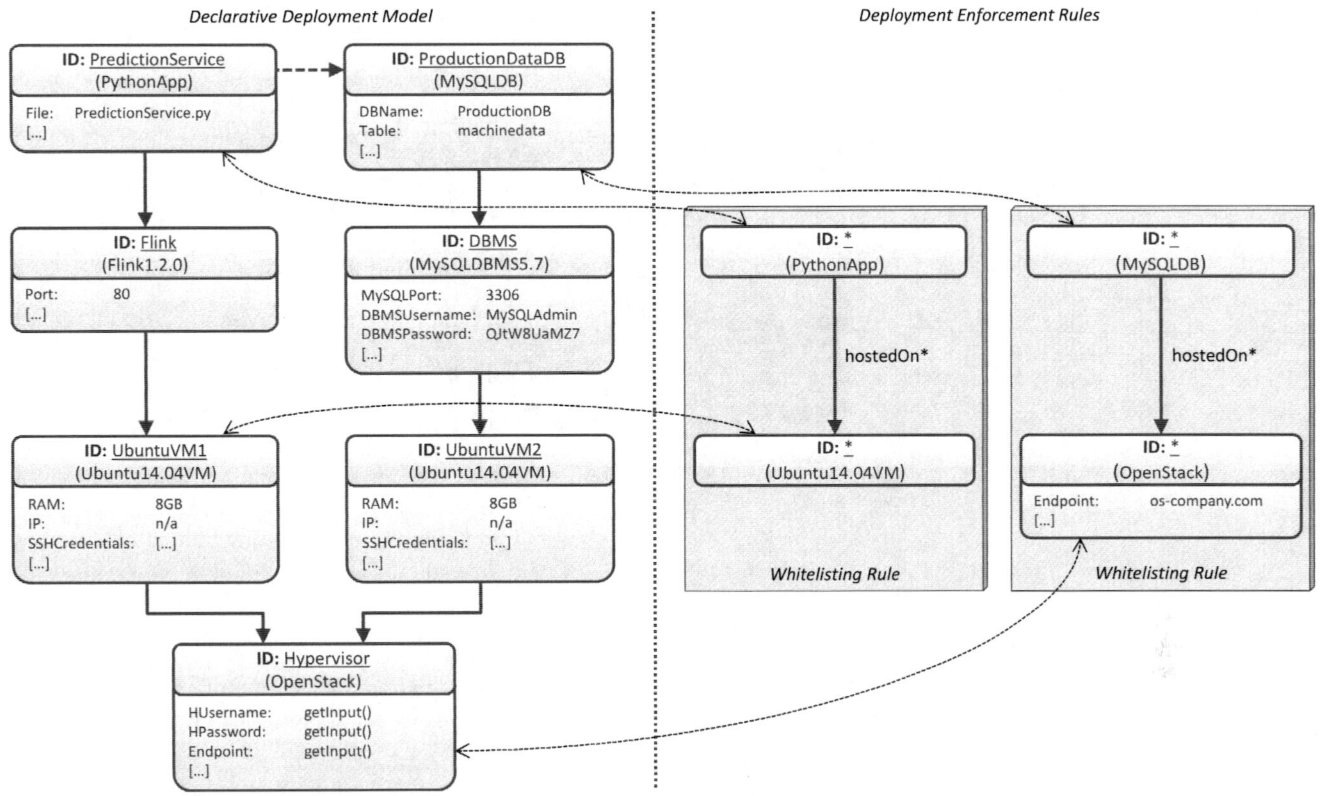

Figure 2. Concept of Deployment Enforcement Rules for defining requirements for declarative deployment models that have to be fulfilled to deployment time.

IV. Deployment Enforcement Rules

In this section, our approach of *Deployment Enforcement Rules* for specifying requirements regarding the deployment model are explained. First, an overall presentation of the Deployment Enforcement Rules concept is given, following the TOSCA-based motivation scenario described in the previous section. After that, the full potential of the approach is shown by combining *Whitelisting Rules* together with *Blacklisting Rules* in order to define more complex requirements and restrictions.

The main goal of our Deployment Enforcement Rules approach is to enable the creation of generic and reusable rules for automatically ensuring the fulfillment of specified requirements and restrictions regarding the deployment model of an application. For example, requirements restricting the physical location where an application is allowed to be provisioned or requirements restricting that just specific operating systems are allowed to be used or are forbidden. Furthermore, the Deployment Enforcement Rules should be specified separately from the deployment models in order to be easily appendable to the existing deployment model, but without the need to adapt or modify the respective deployment models. Thus, no expertise about the deployment model, the contained components, or the used deployment technologies are required in order to make the deployment models compliant to the company's security policies. Only the requirements and restrictions that should be taken into account when provisioning the modeled application must be known for defining the Deployment Enforcement Rules. Once defined, these rules can be reused over and over again.

A. Overview of the Approach

The concept of our approach is illustrated in Figure 2, following the motivation scenario introduced in Section III. On the left side of the figure, the declarative deployment model for provisioning the analysis software as well as the database containing the data to be analyzed is shown. The deployment model is the same as already described in the previous section, however now also providing the IDs of the components, such as "Hypervisor" or "UbuntuVM1". The Node Types are defined within the brackets, e.g., "OpenStack" or "Ubuntu14.04VM". On the right side of the figure, two exemplary Deployment Enforcement Rules are illustrated. Since both rules explicitly are defining what is allowed instead of what is forbidden, both shown rules are Whitelisting Rules. In the shown example, the left rule defines, that a component of the type "PythonApp" is only allowed to be installed on a virtual machine running Ubuntu 14.04., because this might be the stablest and securest Ubuntu version available. The rule on the right side defines, that a MySQL database must be hosted on an OpenStack instance running on the specified "Endpoint" *os-company.com*, because this is the endpoint where the company's local OpenStack instance is running. Therefore, the database containing the data can only be hosted within the company's local infrastructure and thus, the data is not leaving the company's sovereignty. In both rules, the ID of the components is not defined, which means that in these cases only the Node Types are taken into account for deciding if the rules are fulfilled or not, independently of the ID of the specific Node Template in the deployment model.

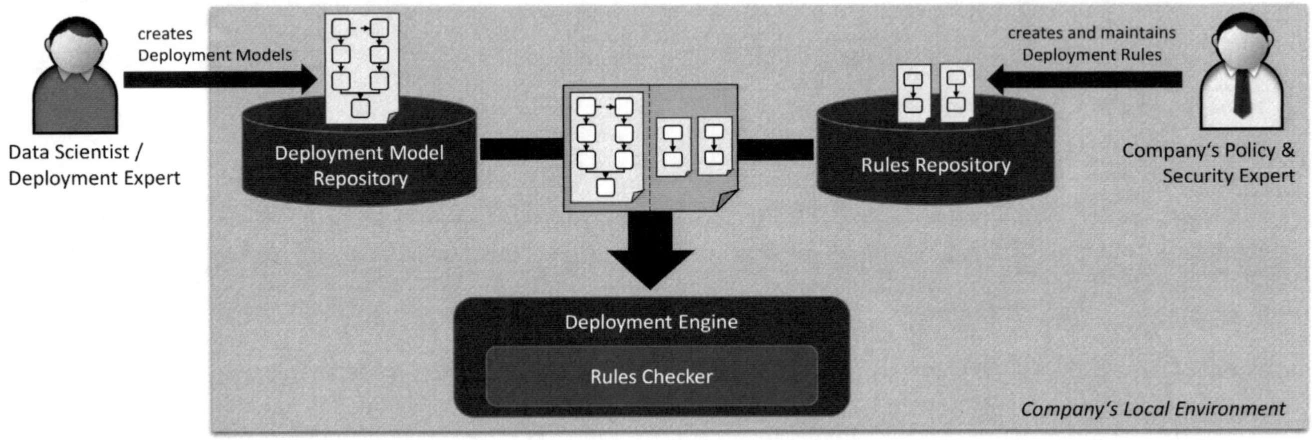

Figure 3. Overview of the Deployment Enforcement Rules approach, showing involved roles, models, and components.

Both Deployment Enforcement Rules shown in Figure 2 are defined using a transitive relation ("hostedOn*"). Since the middleware, dependencies, and other required components are not necessarily important for the fulfillment of security requirements, using the transitive relation enables to only specify the relevant components in order to define the Deployment Rules. Regarding the deployment model shown in Figure 2, after matching the "MySQLDB" node in the Deployment Enforcement Rule with the "ProductionDataDB" in the deployment model, the "hostedOn" relations in the deployment model are traced downwards the modeled stack until the "OpenStack" node is found – or no further "hostedOn" relation can be found. When the "OpenStack" node is found, it is checked whether the value of the "Endpoint" property defined in the Deployment Enforcement Rule is matching the actual value of the "Endpoint" property in the deployment model or not. Since properties can already be predefined in the deployment model (cf. "MySQLPort" in node "DBMS" of Figure 2) or are only provided when the provisioning is instantiated (cf. "Endpoint" in node "Hypervisor" of Figure 2), the rules need to be checked for fulfilling to deployment time, thus, they are called Deployment Enforcement Rules. To sum up, the use of transitive relations enable to specify only the components relevant for a specific Deployment Enforcement Rule and therefore, ease the creation of Deployment Enforcement Rules as well as increase the reusability of already existing Deployment Enforcement Rules.

The involved roles, models, and components of the approach are shown in Figure 3. On the left side, a possibly external data scientist or deployment expert is shown. This person is responsible for implementing the application and creating the deployment model. Possessed deployment models can be stored within the company's local environment using the *Deployment Model Repository*. On the right side a company's internal policy and security expert is shown, which is responsible for creating and maintaining the Deployment Enforcement Rules according to the company's polices and restrictions. Again, the created rules can be persistently stored in a local *Rules Repository*. Deployment models and Deployment Enforcement Rules are combined beforehand the deployment in order to ensure the enforcement of the security policies of the company. Therefore, the *Deployment Engine* contains a *Rules Checker* for checking if the specified Deployment Enforcement Rules are fulfilled.

B. Further Examples, Blacklisting Rules, and Inheritance

In this subsection two more exemplary Deployment Enforcement Rules are presented. While on the left side of Figure 4 another Whitelisting Rule is illustrated, on the right side a Blacklisting Rule is shown. Furthermore, the support of inheritance for Deployment Enforcement Rules is demonstrated.

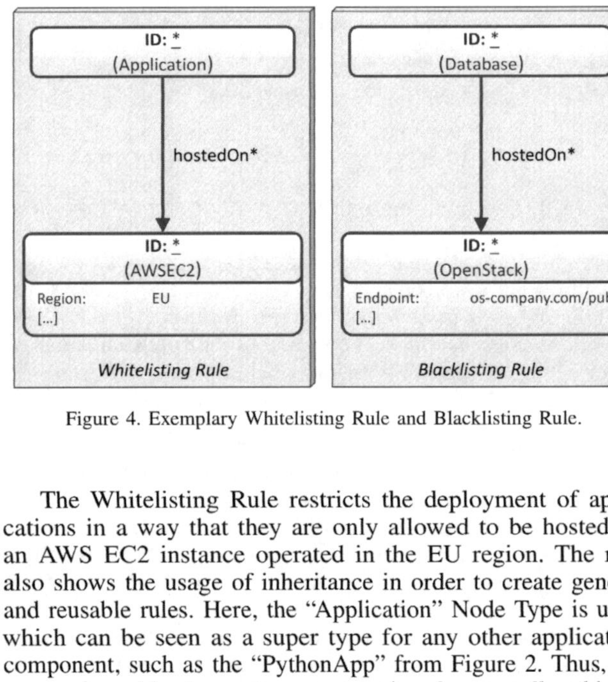

Figure 4. Exemplary Whitelisting Rule and Blacklisting Rule.

The Whitelisting Rule restricts the deployment of applications in a way that they are only allowed to be hosted on an AWS EC2 instance operated in the EU region. The rule also shows the usage of inheritance in order to create generic and reusable rules. Here, the "Application" Node Type is used, which can be seen as a super type for any other application component, such as the "PythonApp" from Figure 2. Thus, the approach enables to create very generic rules as well as highly unique rules, for example, by defining the specific Node Type as well as providing the ID of the component to be checked. The Blacklisting Rule on the right side forbids that any database is hosted on the OpenStack instance running on the "Endpoint" *os-company.com/pub*, since this might be an OpenStack instance accessible from outside the company's infrastructure and thus, the data would not be secure there. As shown in this subsection, depending on the concrete requirement, our approach enables to define and use Whitelisting as well as Blacklisting Rules.

V. Validation & Prototype

In this section, we present our implemented prototype supporting the modeling and enforcing of Deployment Enforcement Rules. The prototype validates the practical feasibility of our proposed approach presented in the previous section. While in the first subsection, the general architecture as well as the components of the prototype are introduced, in the second subsection details of the concrete implementation are presented.

A. System Architecture

A conceptual architecture of our prototype is illustrated in Figure 5. The prototype consists of four main components: (i) the *modeling tool*, (ii) the *repository*, (iii) the *self-service portal*, and (iv) the *deployment engine*. By using the modeling tool, a user can graphically create and maintain deployment models as well as required reusable elements, such as relations and component types. Furthermore, the modeling tool also enables to define and maintain Deployment Enforcement Rules. The modeling tool is connected with the repository. In the repository, the created deployment models, relations, component types, as well as Deployment Enforcement Rules can be persistently stored. The self-service portal is used to chose an available deployment model of an application and to instantiate the deployment of it. Therefore, the self-service portal has access to the repository. Furthermore, not yet specified property values (cf. Section III) can be provided here. The deployment engine consumes deployment models in order to deploy the defined applications. Moreover, the deployment engine contains the *rules checker* component, which is responsible for checking whether the Deployment Enforcement Rules are fulfilled for the processed deployment models during the deployment time.

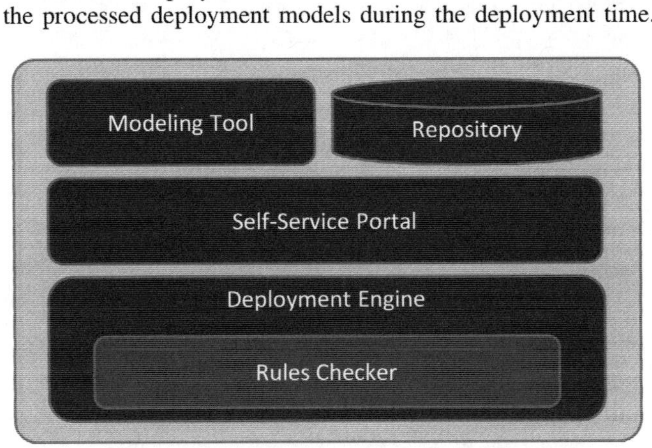

Figure 5. Architectural overview of the prototype.

B. Prototypical Implementation

Our prototype is based on the *OpenTOSCA Ecosystem* and extends the *OpenTOSCA Container* [9] component. OpenTOSCA is a standards-based TOSCA Runtime Environment, consisting of three main components: (i) *Winery* [10], (ii) *Vinothek* [21], and (iii) OpenTOSCA Container. Winery is a graphical tool for modeling and managing TOSCA Topology Templates as well as Node Types, Relationship Types and so on. Furthermore, Winery enables to package the topology as well as all required files into a CSAR and export it. Technically, Winery is implemented using Java 1.8 and is available as Web Application Archive (WAR). From an architectural perspective, Winery is split into two components: (i) *Topology Modeler*, the graphical front end for modeling the topologies and (ii) *Winery Repository*, which is the back end of Winery and enables the persistently storing of all files. Furthermore, since the same elements of the TOSCA standard are required for modeling Deployment Enforcement Rules as for modeling TOSCA Topology Templates, such as Node Template and Relationship Templates, Winery can also be used to model, store, as well as to export Deployment Enforcement Rules.

OpenTOSCA Container is the deployment engine of our prototype. It processes the exported CSARs from Winery, interprets the contained TOSCA deployment models, deploys Implementation Artifacts as well as Management Plans, and provisions the modeled application. In order to validate the practical feasibility of our proposed approach, we implemented the *Rules Checker* as an additional component of the OpenTOSCA Container. The Rules Checker component is responsible for checking if the Deployment Enforcement Rules presented in this paper are fulfilled or not. Therefore, the nodes, relations, properties, as well as the overall structure of the specified Deployment Enforcement Rules are checked against the Topology Template that should be provisioned. If the Deployment Enforcement Rules are fulfilled, the deployment of the modeled application can be continued. However, if the Deployment Enforcement Rules are unfulfilled, e.g., due to not matching endpoint properties in case of a Whitelisting Rule, the deployment is terminated and a corresponding error message is displayed. Afterwards, in case of not matching properties, these properties breaking the rules can be adapted in order to fulfill the rules and the deployment can be initiated again. Technically, the OpenTOSCA container as well as the Rules Checker component are implemented using Java 1.8 and are based on the OSGi Framework Equinox [22], a Java-based runtime environment enabling to build modular applications.

Vinothek is a self-service portal, providing a graphical user interface for enabling the end user to choose an available application and start the provisioning of it. If information are missing, such as required endpoint properties, a username, or a password, the user initiating the provisioning can insert this missing information here. Vinothek is also implemented using Java Server Pages (JSPs) and packaged as a WAR and thus, can be easily deployed on a web container such as Tomcat.

To sum up, we implemented our concepts within the OpenTOSCA Ecosystem, which already was able to process TOSCA Topology Templates and provision the modeled applications. In this work, we further extended the prototype by adding the additional Rules Checker component to also support the provisioning under consideration of security-related requirements and restrictions by supporting Deployment Enforcement Rules. All three mentioned OpenTOSCA components are open-source and can be obtained from GitHub (https://github.com/OpenTOSCA).

VI. Related Work

In this section, we present related work on our approach of enforcing company defined data security and privacy requirements during the deployment time of an application.

Walraven et al. [23] present PaaSHopper, which is a policy-driven middleware platform for developing and deploying multi-tenant SaaS applications in multi-PaaS environments. Based on the current context of stakeholder defined properties the middleware decides, on which parts in a multi-cloud a given request is processed or data will be stored. To achieve policy-awareness, PaasHopper middleware includes a policy-driven execution layer consisting of the two main components, the *Dispatcher* and the *Policy Engine*. Driven by the current context of defined policies, the *Dispatcher* selects an adequate component in a multi-cloud on which a request is processed or data will be stored. To do so, the dispatcher uses the *Policy Engine* to select a component instance that complies with the current context of policies. Contrary to our approach, modeling and enforcing data security and privacy requirements are restricted to applications that are deployed on PaaS solutions. Moreover, the restrictions that can be defined are limited to processing and storage of data, whereas our approach enables the specification of various requirements and restrictions.

Képes et al. [24] present an approach of enforcing specified non-functional security requirements during the provisioning phase of applications. For example, access restrictions or secure password requirements. These requirements are specified in form of policies that are attached to the Node Templates of a TOSCA Topology Template. Subsequent a Policy-Aware Provisioning Plan Generator transforms a given template into an executable policy-aware provisioning plan. In order to provide the required technical activities for the policy-aware provisioning, the Plan Generator provides a plugin system for implementing reusable policy aware-deployment logic. In difference to our loosely coupled deployment rules, their generated policy-aware provisioning plans are tightly coupled with the TOSCA Topology Templates they are generated from.

A similar approach to define non-functional security restrictions is presented by Blehm et al [25]. They also define security restrictions by means of policies attached to TOSCA Topology Templates. In addition they implemented policy specific services to ensure that the security restrictions are adhered. Again, the main difference to our approach is that the non-functional requirements are not separated from the deployment model but are directly attached to it. Thus, the deployment models need to be manually adapted to meet the company‘s requirements.

Waizenegger et al. [26] present the *IA-Approach* and the *P-Approach* to implement TOSCA-based security policy enforcement. The IA-Approach extends IAs by implementing the already existing Management Operations again with additional policy enforcing steps. The P-Approach extends the Plan required for provisioning the application with additional policy enforcing activities. Unlike to our approach, in their approach the policy enforcing elements are not separated from the deployment model but are directly attached to IAs or Plans.

Fischer et al. [27] present an approach to ensure compliance of application deployment models during their design time on the basis of the TOSCA standard. Similar to our approach, they aim to separate concerns about the knowledge base of a company's compliance requirements and the technical expertise of modeling applications, so that compliance experts can define compliance rules that can then be used to ensure compliance in deployment models. To achieve this, they introduce the concept of *Deployment Compliance Rules* which provide a means to ensure that deployment structures are conform with a company's compliance requirements. A deployment compliance rule consists of an Identifier graph to identify a compliance-relevant area in application deployment models and a Required Structure graph to define the allowed structure for the given compliance-relevant area. Unlike to our approach, the compliance checking of the deployment model is done during their design time. Moreover, Deployment Compliance Rules only allow to model allowed deployment structures and do not provide a means to define structures that are explicitly not allowed in a deployment model. Furthermore, the concept of transitive relations to ensure high reusability as well as faster modeling of the rules is not supported in their approach.

There are different approaches to specify and enforce certain requirements and restrictions in business process models. Fellmann and Zasada [28] conduct a literature review to provide an overview of the state-of-the-art approaches for mapping a company's compliance rules to business process models. Koetter et al. [29] present the concept of a Compliance Descriptor that links laws, regulations, and company intern restrictions to their technical implementation. Thereby, a Compliance Descriptor provides a means to consider the phases design-time, deployment and run-time of a business process life cycle. Depending on the phase different technologies are used for the technical implementation of the compliance requirements. Linear temporal logic (LTL) is used for design-time rules, TOSCA for requirements during the deployment phase and ProGoalML for run-time monitoring. Schleicher et al. [30] introduce the concept of *Compliance Domains* which can be used to model data restrictions for runtime infrastructures, such as different types of cloud environments or local data centers. In their approach, areas of business processes, modeled in Business Process Model and Notation (BPMN), can be marked by compliance experts with Compliance Domains that contain certain service level agreements and compliance rules that needs to be met. Based on this information, a graphical business process modeling tool can enforce the defined requirements during design time and notify the modeler if a selected runtime environment or data that enters a compliance domain violates them. For the most part, their work focuses on the restriction of data flows on the level of business process models, while our approach provides a method for enforcing security and privacy requirements on the level of declarative deployment models.

VII. Conclusion and Future Work

In this paper, we presented our approach of Deployment Enforcement Rules enabling the specification as well as the automated enforcement of reoccurring requirements and restrictions of declarative deployment models. For demonstrating the approach we used the OASIS standard Topology and Orchestration Specification for Cloud Applications (TOSCA). The approach allows to specify the Deployment Enforcement Rules separately from the deployment models and without the need to adapt or modify any deployment model at all. We showed, that by using transitive relations, only the relevant components need to be specified within a rule, which results in a high reuseability of the Deployment Enforcement Rules. Furthermore, we showed that the approach enables to define Whitelisting Rules, which specify what is allowed as well as Blacklisting Rules, which specify what is forbidden. Thus, depending on the requirements and circumstances the rules can be used very flexible. A validation of our approach is provided by a prototypical TOSCA-based implementation. In the future, we plan to extend our Deployment Enforcement Rules approach by also taking other TOSCA-elements into account, e.g., Deployment Artifacts attached to Node Templates.

ACKNOWLEDGMENT

This work was partially funded by the project SePiA.Pro (01MD16013F) of the BMWi program Smart Service World and the German Research Foundation (DFG) project ADDCompliance (314720630).

REFERENCES

[1] L. Atzori, A. Iera, and G. Morabito, "The Internet of Things: A Survey," Computer Networks, vol. 54, no. 15, 2010, pp. 2787–2805.

[2] M. Hermann, T. Pentek, and B. Otto, "Design Principles for Industrie 4.0 Scenarios," in Proceedings of the 49th Hawaii International Conference on System Sciences (HICSS). IEEE, 2016, pp. 3928–3937.

[3] G. A. Susto, A. Schirru, S. Pampuri, S. McLoone, and A. Beghi, "Machine Learning for Predictive Maintenance: A Multiple Classifier Approach," Transactions on Industrial Informatics, vol. 11, no. 3, 2015, pp. 812–820.

[4] M. Falkenthal et al., "Towards Function and Data Shipping in Manufacturing Environments: How Cloud Technologies leverage the 4th Industrial Revolution," in Proceedings of the 10th Advanced Summer School on Service Oriented Computing, ser. IBM Research Report. IBM Research Report, Sep. 2016, pp. 16–25.

[5] M. Zimmermann, U. Breitenbücher, M. Falkenthal, F. Leymann, and K. Saatkamp, "Standards-based function shipping how to use tosca for shipping and executing data analytics software in remote manufacturing environments," in Proceedings of the 2017 IEEE 21st International Enterprise Distributed Object Computing Conference (EDOC 2017), 2017, pp. 50–60.

[6] U. Breitenbücher, T. Binz, O. Kopp, F. Leymann, and M. Wieland, "Policy-Aware Provisioning of Cloud Applications," in Proceedings of the Seventh International Conference on Emerging Security Information, Systems and Technologies (SECURWARE 2013). Xpert Publishing Services, Aug. 2013, pp. 86–95.

[7] U. Breitenbücher et al., "Policy-Aware Provisioning and Management of Cloud Applications," International Journal On Advances in Security, vol. 7, no. 1&2, 2014, pp. 15–36.

[8] OASIS, Topology and Orchestration Specification for Cloud Applications (TOSCA) Version 1.0, Organization for the Advancement of Structured Information Standards (OASIS), 2013.

[9] T. Binz et al., "OpenTOSCA – A Runtime for TOSCA-based Cloud Applications," in Proceedings of the 11th International Conference on Service-Oriented Computing (ICSOC 2013). Springer, Dec. 2013, pp. 692–695.

[10] O. Kopp, T. Binz, U. Breitenbücher, and F. Leymann, "Winery – A Modeling Tool for TOSCA-based Cloud Applications," in Proceedings of the 11th International Conference on Service-Oriented Computing (ICSOC 2013). Springer, Dec. 2013, pp. 700–704.

[11] OASIS, TOSCA Simple Profile in YAML Version 1.0, Organization for the Advancement of Structured Information Standards (OASIS), 2015.

[12] OASIS, Topology and Orchestration Specification for Cloud Applications (TOSCA) Primer Version 1.0, Organization for the Advancement of Structured Information Standards (OASIS), 2013.

[13] T. Binz, U. Breitenbücher, O. Kopp, and F. Leymann, TOSCA: Portable Automated Deployment and Management of Cloud Applications, ser. Advanced Web Services. Springer, Jan. 2014, pp. 527–549.

[14] Red Hat, Inc., "Ansible Official Site." [Online]. Available: https://www.ansible.com [retrieved: July, 2018]

[15] Opscode, Inc., "Chef Official Site." [Online]. Available: http://www.opscode.com/chef [retrieved: July, 2018]

[16] OASIS, Web Services Business Process Execution Language (WS-BPEL) Version 2.0, Organization for the Advancement of Structured Information Standards (OASIS), 2007.

[17] OMG, Business Process Model and Notation (BPMN) Version 2.0, Object Management Group (OMG), 2011.

[18] O. Kopp, T. Binz, U. Breitenbücher, and F. Leymann, "BPMN4TOSCA: A Domain-Specific Language to Model Management Plans for Composite Applications," in Proceedings of the 4th International Workshop on the Business Process Model and Notation (BPMN 2012). Springer, Sep. 2012, pp. 38–52.

[19] O. Kopp, T. Binz, U. Breitenbücher, F. Leymann, and T. Michelbach, "A Domain-Specific Modeling Tool to Model Management Plans for Composite Applications," in Proceedings of the 7th Central European Workshop on Services and their Composition, ZEUS 2015. CEUR Workshop Proceedings, May 2015, pp. 51–54.

[20] U. Breitenbücher et al., "Combining Declarative and Imperative Cloud Application Provisioning based on TOSCA," in International Conference on Cloud Engineering (IC2E 2014). IEEE, Mar. 2014, pp. 87–96.

[21] U. Breitenbücher, T. Binz, O. Kopp, and F. Leymann, "Vinothek - A Self-Service Portal for TOSCA," in Proceedings of the 6th Central-European Workshop on Services and their Composition (ZEUS 2014). CEUR-WS.org, Feb. 2014, Demonstration, pp. 69–72.

[22] Eclipse Foundation, Inc., "Equinox — The Eclipse Foundation." [Online]. Available: http://www.eclipse.org/equinox/ [retrieved: July, 2018]

[23] S. Walraven, D. Van Landuyt, A. Rafique, B. Lagaisse, and W. Joosen, "Paashopper: Policy-driven middleware for multi-paas environments," Journal of Internet Services and Applications, vol. 6, no. 1, 2015, p. 2.

[24] K. Képes, U. Breitenbücher, M. P. Fischer, F. Leymann, and M. Zimmermann, "Policy-Aware Provisioning Plan Generation for TOSCA-based Applications," in Proceedings of The Eleventh International Conference on Emerging Security Information, Systems and Technologies (SECURWARE). XpertPublishing Services, September 2017, pp. 142–149.

[25] A. Blehm et al., "Policy-Framework-Eine Methode zur Umsetzung von Sicherheits-Policies im Cloud-Computing." in GI-Jahrestagung, 2014, pp. 277–288.

[26] T. Waizenegger et al., "Policy4TOSCA: A Policy-Aware Cloud Service Provisioning Approach to Enable Secure Cloud Computing," in On the Move to Meaningful Internet Systems: OTM 2013 Conferences. Springer, Sep. 2013, pp. 360–376.

[27] M. P. Fischer, U. Breitenbücher, K. Képes, and F. Leymann, "Towards an Approach for Automatically Checking Compliance Rules in Deployment Models," in Proceedings of The Eleventh International Conference on Emerging Security Information, Systems and Technologies (SECURWARE). Xpert Publishing Services (XPS), 2017, pp. 150–153.

[28] M. Fellmann and A. Zasada, "State-of-the-art of business process compliance approaches," in 22nd European Conference on Information Systems, (ECIS), June 2014, pp. 1–17.

[29] F. Koetter, M. Kochanowski, A. Weisbecker, C. Fehling, and F. Leymann, "Integrating Compliance Requirements across Business and IT," in Enterprise Distributed Object Computing Conference (EDOC), 2014 IEEE 18th International. IEEE, 2014, pp. 218–225.

[30] D. Schleicher et al., "Compliance Domains: A Means to Model Data-Restrictions in Cloud Environments," in Enterprise Distributed Object Computing Conference (EDOC), 2011 15th European Conference on Information Systems IEEE International. IEEE, 2011, pp. 257–266.

A Botnet Detection System Based on Machine-Learning using Flow-Based Features

Chien-Hau Hung, Hung-Min Sun
Department of Computer Science
National Tsing Hua University
Hsinchu, Taiwan 30013
e-mails: dars2106@gmail.com, hmsun@cs.nthu.edu.tw

Abstract—**Botnets have always been a formidable cyber security threat. Internet of Things (IoT) has become an important technique and the number of internet-connected smart devices has been increasing by more than 15% every year. It is for this reason that botnets are growing rapidly. Although the antivirus on Personal Computer (PC) has being applied for a long time, the threats from the botnets still cannot be eliminated. Smart devices and IOT are still in their initial stages, hence there are uncertainties about the security issues. In the foreseeable future, more devices will become victims of botnets. In this paper, we propose a system for detecting potential botnets by analyzing their flows on the Internet. The system classifies similar flow traffic into groups, and then extracts the behavior patterns of each group for machine learning. The system not only can analyze P2P botnets, but also extracts the patterns to application layer and can analyze botnets using HTTP protocols.**

Keywords- botnet; machine learning; feature selection; J48.

I. INTRODUCTION

Victims of botnets, along with smart devices, have grown substantially in number. According to IoT Online Store [1], there are 22.9 billion devices around the globe being connected to the Internet and being used for multiple purposes. The number of smart devices is estimated to be more than 50 billion by 2020. However, smart devices, such as PC, smart phones and other devices are not as safe as we think. They could be infected by malicious software without any abnormal symptoms until they are needed to act as bots. The bots are controlled by a botmaster through Command and Control (C&C) channels using different kinds of communication protocols.

Over the last decade, a lot of research has been done on the detection of different bot families. Most of the research is based on machine learning, of which the performance mainly depends on the features selected for the classifier. Therefore, selecting proper features for the classification model is important. However, there is a trade-off between achieving high detection accuracy and spending huge computation time on constructing a large classification model. On one hand, using all features to build a classification model leads to a significant overhead. On the other hand, using improper or too few features may cause the accuracy rate to decrease.

Motivation. As the number of botnet attacks has been increasing [2], it is very difficult to find devices without any vulnerability, not to mention the fact that common users do not patch their devices on time. Hence, there is a need for a botnet detection system to verify if the botnets are within the devices.

Our Contribution. We develop a system that can classify the botnets' flow by using machine learning. Users can input the pcap file and automatically generate the report. For the classification model of each botnet family, we select the appropriate sets of features.

In this paper, Section II describes different kinds of botnets and the machine learning technique we apply to detect botnets. In Section III, we discuss several ways to detect botnet. In Sections IV and V, we explain our framework and implementation in detail. Section VI shows the evaluation of our work. Conclusions are given in the last section.

II. BACKGROUND

A. Botnet

The word botnet is a combination of the words robot and network. A botnet consists of a botmaster, bots and usually a C&C server. Botnets can be used to perform various kinds of attacks, e.g., to launch a Distributed Denial of Service Attack (DDoS), to steal data, to send spam, and to function as a backdoor.

Client-Server Botnet. Botnets were originally constructed and operated using a Client-Server model. The infected clients connect to an infected server awaiting commands from the botmaster. Once the botmaster sends commands to the infected server, each client retrieves and executes those commands and reports back their results of actions to the infected server.

P2P Botnet. The problem with client-server botnets is the single point of failure. Therefore, to avoid this issue, new botnets fully operate over Peer-to-Peer (P2P) networks, where each peer acts simultaneously both as a client and as a server. Despite this kind of structure, which operates without a centralized point that makes it hard to be blocked by IP address, botnets are still blockable by ports. Therefore, a combination of HTTP and P2P botnet is used, called HTTP2P botnet, which uses HTTP as the communication protocol and often employs port 80, a method that makes it impossible to be blocked by ports.

Internet of Things with Botnet. With the booming of IoT and promotion of IPv6, there is an increase in the number of Internet-Connected devices. In [3], Y.Feng gives botnets a lots of potential bots to infect, which could result in large scale botnets. Also, the P2P network topology is more sophisticated which makes it easier for botmasters to hide and larger attacks might happen.

B. *Machine Learning*

There are three major classifications of machine learning algorithm: supervised, unsupervised and semi-supervised. Waikato Environment for Knowledge Analysis (WEKA) [6], which was developed by University of Wakato in New Zealand, is a Java language tool with a collection of machine learning algorithms for data mining.

Flow-Based. Open Systems Interconnection (OSI) model [4] defined network architecture into seven layers, with different protocols. The network layer uses protocols like Internet Protocol (IP) [4], Internet Control Message Protocol (ICMP) [4], Internet Group Management Protocol (IGMP) [4] and Internetwork Packet Exchange (IPX) [4]. The transport layer's protocols are TCP, UDP, and svice port addressing. A flow is a network connection with five properties: Source IP, Destination IP, Source Port, Destination Port and Protocol.

As a classifier, we use the J48 Decision Tree [5]. In classification, a classifier uses features to build up a model and classifies the inputs into groups in accordance with their respective features. Among the various classifiers, the decision tree classifier [5], which as the name implies is built in a tree shape, serves as one of the major algorithms. Features of the input data go through the nodes, which are rules of the tree, when fitted, until they reach the leaves of the tree, where the classification is done. While being an open source, J48 is implemented by JAVA based on C4.5 decision tree algorithm.

C4.5 Algorithm [6]. We employ the C4.5 algorithm, developed by Ross Quinlan, to generate a decision tree for the purpose of classification. It became popular after being ranked No.1 in a paper entitled "Top 10 Algorithms in Data Mining" published by Springer Lecture Notes in Computer Science (LNCS) in 2008 [1]. C4.5, which is written based on the Iterative Dichotomiser 3 (ID3) algorithm, uses a training data sets to build a decision tree in a similar way as ID3, except C4.5 utilizes the concept of gain ratio to overcome the problem of biased information entropy. The attribute of the maximum gain ratio is selected as the node to split the tree. The detailed process is explained below.

Feature Selection. The purpose of feature selection is to reduce the number of features. This reduces the training time of the learning model and helps with over-fitting problems. We use Consistency Subset Evaluation as our features selection algorithm. It is a greedy algorithm, which will try 77*(total number of features)^5, each time randomly choosing a subset from the total feature set, then calculating the inconsistency. Finally, result will be one set of features with the smallest inconsistency [8].

III. RELATED WORK

The authors of [9] utilize the flow-based features of existing botnets and select 21 features from 16 botnet families for machine learning. The outcome of the average detection rate is 75%. Q. Yan et al. [10] present a system named PeerClean that detects P2P botnets in real time only by using features extracted from higher layer of OSI network model in the C&C network flow traffic. T. Cai and F. Zou [11] present some features of HTTP Botnet and design a new method for detection. In [12], F. V. Alejandre detects botnets with machine learning algorithms and use genetic method to select features of botnets.

IV. SYSTEM ARCHITECTURE AND DESIGN

A. *Goals*

We propose a system to analyze and predict botnets' behavior by using machine learning tools: WEKA. Furthermore, we hope to provide a system that is feasible, expansible and user-friendly, easy to implement for system managers.

B. *System Framework*

Figure 1 shows the overall system flow, which consists of five parts, namely, "Input Pcap file", "Preprocess", "Machine learning", "Trained Model" and "Report".

1. Record the network flow and save it into pcap format, in this step we can use some tools (e.g., wireshark) to record packet over the network interface. Then input it to the preprocess program.
2. The preprocess program accepts the pcap file then process it into features described in section 4.3. The outcome result of each pcap file will be two arff format files. Then input them into machine learning tools (e.g., WEKA).
3. Supply training sets and test sets and use selected features to build a well performed model.
4. Input a Well-trained model to predict the files from process (B).
5. The output prediction from process (D) along with other model's result then form a prediction report.

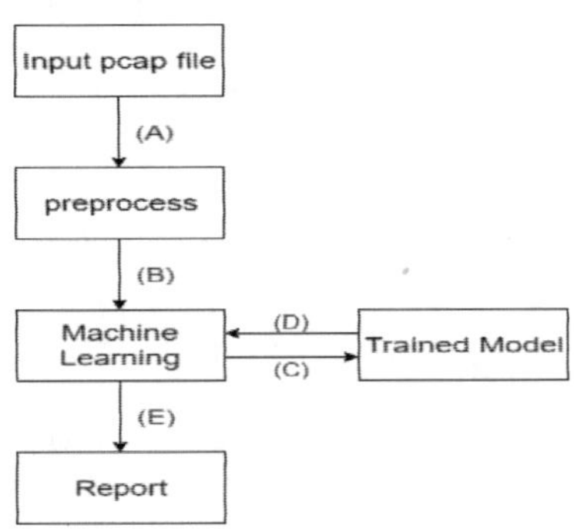

Figure. 1. System Flow

C. *Features*

There are many flow-based features, from which our system selects some. In this section, we will describe some features output from our system.

- Source and Destination port: This is a feature that is often used in detection of botnet traffic, especially port 80 for HTTP and port 443 for HTTPS. These two ports are often used by normal users. Therefore, it is likely that HTTP-based botnets hide their traffic inside.
- Protocol: these features are often used in classifying different traffic. It would look strange when some seldom used protocols appeared in traffic. For example, botnets using UDP protocol will stand out in the network traffic because normal users do not use UDP protocol to communicate. Instead, they often use HTTP or HTTPS, which are using TCP in the transport layer.
- Duration: It means the total time of the connection from beginning to the end. It has been used a lot in detecting potential botnets. It may vary depending on different kind of botnets, but certain types of botnets are known to be chatty. This feature may be useful for some types of botnets.
- First packet length (FPS): First packet length is the length of first packet transferred in the connection, in some situations is similar to duration feature. First packet transferred in the flow reveals some characteristics, which may be useful in detecting specific botnets.
- Flow size features

  — Total number of bytes (TBT) is the total number of bytes transferred and received in the flow. This feature is used to get similarities out of botnet traffic, such as fixed length commands.

  — Average payload packet length (APL) is the average payload of all packet in the flow. This feature is used to get similarities out of botnet traffic.

  — Total number of packets with the same length over the total number of packets (DPL) is the number of same size packets in the flow. This feature is used to get similarities out of botnet traffic.

  — Standard deviation of payload packet length (PV) is the standard deviation of every packets' payload in the flow. This feature is used to get similarities out of botnet traffic.

The reason for using these features is based on the assumption that the traffic generated by bots is more uniform than traffic generated by normal users. For instance, if botnets use fixed length commands, using these features to detect them is more feasible.

- Ratio between the number of incoming packets over the number of outgoing packets (IOPR): Many studies suggest that there should be some difference between the input and output traffic for different kind of protocols. Although there is no evidence indicating any relation between the feature and botnet behavior, this feature still gives ratio between incoming and outgoing traffic for detection of some potential botnet behavior.
- Packet exchange: There is an assumption that botmaster needs to manage all bots, so to keep their connections alive communicating with each bot is necessary. Number of packets exchanged might be useful to identify this behavior.
- Reconnect: In botnet detection, it is common to analyze communication and other features with accurate captured flows. Hence, a simple strategy to prevent detection is by randomly reconnecting as an established connection. Therefore, this feature can be controlled by setting up a specific time window to detect reconnection.
- Number and percentage of small/null packets exchanged: It is widely known that botnets use small packets to maintain communication between bots and C&C servers. However, recent researches haven't seen botnets using null packets. Despite of that, small or null packets were tested in recent researches.
- The features below are used to get similarities in botnets' traffic.

  — average bits-per-second (BS) is the average transferred and received bits per second.

  — average packets-per-second(PPS) is the average transferred and received packets per second.

  — average inter arrival time of packets (AIT) is the average inter arrival time of packets received.

- HTTP method: It is a part of header from HTTP protocol, which indicates the desired action to be performed for a given resource. Botnets use HTTP method [13] to disguise their communication flows among other HTTP flows. However, botnets might still be detectable if a combination of HTTP method and other features is employed.
- HTTP request: HTTP request is spited into three parts: total added weight, length weight and average weight. These three features together can be used to detect potential botnets if botnets use fixed length commands.

V. IMPLEMENTATION

A. *Data Set*

To build and test the detect module, we prepared 3 families of botnet data set: Zeus, Waledac and Virut. The size of each data set is 104MB, 1024MB and 138.77MB. Figure 2 depicts the properties of these three families. PeerRush [14] published their journal and data about detecting P2P botnet. Czech technical university [15] made their records of botnet behavior pcap file public. The fourth botnet data is the testing data from ISOT. This data set is only used to test our model for comparison.

To simulate real world traffic, we record three users' behavior and collect over 120GB data. There are many kinds of different behavior, like using different browsers for various activities. Types of application also vary, e.g., games, communication, SSH and so on.

Botnet	Hosts	Size(MB)	Transport	Protocol	From
Zeus	1	104	UDP	-	PeerRush
Waledac	3	1028	TCP	-	PeerRush
Virut	1	139	TCP	HTTP	CTU
Waledac	2	24	TCP	-	ISOT

Figure. 2. Botnet data set properties

B. Preprocess

Parsing packets. Firstly, we read every packet from the stored pcap file, then we separate each layer, from data link layer to transport layer, and we also took a look at the application layer if the bot uses HTTP protocol. After parsing step, we retrieve twelve properties from packets.

Construct Flow and Conversation. Secondly, we use the flow based analysis. However, we believe flow based features are not enough to distinguish bots from normal users, hence we set a threshold of 2000 seconds to split conversation. After that, we calculate more properties from previous step and get two lists at the end: list of flow and list of conversation. The content blocks of both lists contain nineteen properties.

Calculate Features for Machine Learning. Finally, we employ the thirty-one properties from the above two steps to build up features for machine learning tools [16]. Lots of computation is involved in this step, and numpy library was very helpful. For the testing purpose, we add some noise to payload, inter arrival time and features related to these two features to make sure the model performs well.

- source port
- destination port
- protocol
- total number of packets exchanged
- number of null packets exchanged
- number of small packets exchanged
- percentage of small packets exchanged
- ratio between the number of incoming packets over the number of outgoing packets
- number of re-connection
- flow duration
- length of the first packet
- total number of bytes
- average payload
- average payload sent
- average payload received
- total number of packets with the same length over the total number of packets
- standard deviation of payload packet length
- average bits-per-second
- average inter arrival time of packets
- average inter arrival time of packets sent
- average inter arrival time of packets received
- average packets-per-second
- median inter arrival time of packets
- median inter arrival time of packets sent
- median inter arrival time of packets received
- variance packet size
- variance packet size sent
- variance packet size received
- max packet size
- HTTP method
- HTTP uniform resource locator (URL) total weight
- HTTP uniform resource locator (URL) length
- HTTP uniform resource locator (URL) average weight

Noise Algorithm. To verify if our model is robust enough, we added some noise on the features. The add noise algorithm [10] formula is shown in figure 3, in which X represents the feature to which noise is going to be added. 'Var' is the integer randomly chosen in the range of -1 to 1. Noise stands for the scale of noise going to be added. In this case, we adopt the noise at half to one-third the scale of the original data. Noise will be added in payload, inter arrival time and features related to these two, e.g., median inter arrival time of packets, average inter arrival time of packets, average payload and other similar features.

$$X' = X + Var*Noise*X$$

X = feature need to add noise

Var = random [-1,1]

Noise = random [25,33] / 100

Figure. 3. Add noise algorithm

VI. EVALUATION

A. Experimental Design

Purpose. Our basic purpose is to analyze the behavior of each family of botnets. That is, when botnets infect any Internet-connected devices, they should be detected through recording every packet over the Internet. Our system can further identify which device might have been infected.

Experimental Process. This process aims to find normal data affection to the model we built. Firstly, reduce the instances of normal data to about 50% to make the characteristics of infected data more obvious. Secondly, increase the percentage of normal data over infected data to make it closer to the real situation. Finally, we add different level noise into testing data sets in payload and inter arrival time and some other related features to evaluate the model.

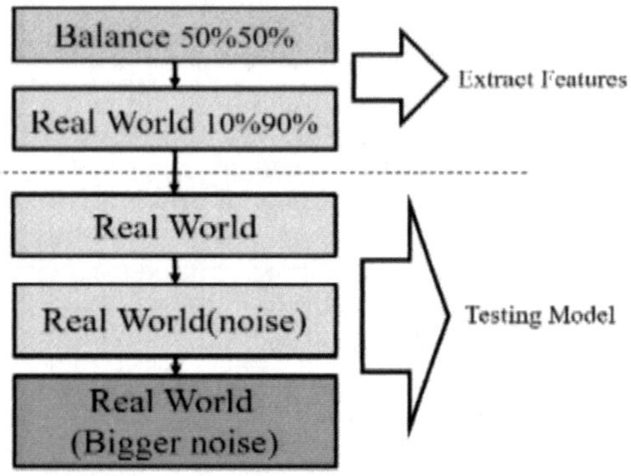

Figure. 4. Work flow of experiment process

B. Evaluation

Figure 5 shows the data sets for each step. To avoid obvious characteristics, we remove destination and source ports before selecting features to build J48 tree.

	Balance		Real World				Real World (noise)		Real World (bigger noise)	
	Feature selection		Feature selection + Train		Test		Test		Test	
	Infected	Healthy	Infected	Healthy	Infected	Healthy	Infected	Healthy	Infected	Healthy
Zeus	6,020	6,906	6,020	42,761	6,098	45,619	6,098	45,619	6,098	45,619
Virut	1,717	1,732	1,717	29,196	186	29,593	186	29,593	186	29,593
Waledac	20,437	21,323	8,276	59,301	9,957	71,135	9,957	71,135	9,957	71,135

Figure. 5. Data set of each process

Figure 6 shows the feature selecting result while evaluating Balance data set, we choose features scoring over 8 points as the feature set. As the results show, normal data and virut using HTTP protocol, so the HTTP feature of virut got high score. Figure 7 shows the feature selecting result while evaluating Real World data set. We also choose features scoring over 8 points as the feature set. As shown by the result, with the increase of normal data, the HTTP feature of every botnet family got higher score.

	protocol	PX	NNP	PSP	IOPR	Reconnect	Duration	FPS	TBT	avg_payload	avg_payload_sent	avg_payload_received	DPL	PV	BS
Zeus	4	10	0	10	5	0	6	9	10	0	0	0	0	0	1
Virut	5	10	0	7	9	10	0	1	9	10	0	10	0	3	0
Waledac	10	6	0	10	2	10	9	0	10	3	8	10	0	0	0

	avg_iat	avg_iat_sent	avg_iat_received	PPS	median_iat	median_iat_sent	median_iat_received	var_pkt_size	var_pkt_size_sent	var_pkt_size_received	max_pkt_size	HTTP_method	URL_total_weight	URL_len	URL_average_weight
Zeus	10	5	0	0	0	1	0	0	0	0	4	0	1	0	6
Virut	0	0	0	0	10	6	2	3	0	0	10	7	2	9	8
Waledac	0	0	2	0	5	10	0	2	0	0	8	0	0	0	4

Figure. 6. Balance feature selection

	protocol	PX	NNP	PSP	IOPR	Reconnect	Duration	FPS	TBT	avg_payload	avg_payload_sent	avg_payload_received	DPL	PV	BS
Zeus	1	10	0	10	6	0	10	9	10	0	0	0	0	0	1
Virut	2	10	0	4	9	10	0	1	10	7	0	10	0	2	0
Waledac	10	5	0	10	3	10	9	0	10	3	8	6	0	1	0

	avg_iat	avg_iat_sent	avg_iat_received	PPS	median_iat	median_iat_sent	median_iat_received	var_pkt_size	var_pkt_size_sent	var_pkt_size_received	max_pkt_size	HTTP_method	URL_total_weight	URL_len	URL_average_weight
Zeus	10	8	5	0	0	0	2	0	0	0	4	1	10	5	9
Virut	0	0	0	0	10	10	4	5	0	0	10	9	3	10	9
Waledac	0	0	2	0	5	9	0	0	0	0	10	0	9	3	10

Figure. 7. Real world feature selection

Zeus	PX	PSP	Duration	FPS	TBT	avg_iat	avg_iat_sent	URL_total_weight	URL_average_weight			
Virut	PX	IOPR	Reconnect	TBT	avg_payload	avg_payload_received	median_iat	median_iat_sent	max_pkt_size	HTTP_method	URL_len	URL_average_weight
Waledac	protocol	PSP	Reconnect	Duration	TBT	avg_payload_sent	avg_payload_received	median_iat_sent	max_pkt_size	URL_total_weight	URL_average_weight	

Figure. 8. Feature selection for each family

Figure 8 shows the three models and the features they are built upon to perform well in the simulation.

	TPR	TNR	FPR	FNR	Accuracy	Precision	Recall
	Real World						
Zeus	0.978	0.987	0.013	0.022	0.9855	0.939	0.978
Virut	0.903	0.998	0.002	0.097	0.9973	0.730	0.903
Waledac	0.994	0.996	0.004	0.006	0.9952	0.995	0.994
	Real World (noise 25~33%)						
Zeus	0.971	0.987	0.013	0.029	0.9843	0.939	0.971
Virut	0.892	0.998	0.002	0.108	0.9972	0.728	0.892
Waledac	0.960	0.996	0.004	0.040	0.9804	0.994	0.960
	Real World (bigger noise 33~50%)						
Zeus	0.963	0.987	0.013	0.037	0.9829	0.938	0.963
Virut	0.872	0.998	0.002	0.128	0.9972	0.726	0.872
Waledac	0.945	0.996	0.004	0.055	0.9735	0.994	0.945

Figure. 9. Result of each botnet family with different noise level

While evaluating each model we built, we add noise in test data set. First, testing with pure data Zeus and Waledac perform well, although Virut only performs 90% but it is still a good model. Second, we add 25% to 33% noise in test data set. Adding noise causes the TPR of our model to decrease, but overall the result is acceptable. Finally, we add a bigger noise range from 33% to 50% in the test data set. As we can see from Figure 9, the TPR of our model decrease a bit, but it is still a good result. We think it is because of using a higher level features.

C. Comparison

We implement the system in [9] and use the same data set that we test on our system. Figure 10 shows the tested result of our work and the system in [9].

	Our system Real World							Beigi et al 's system Real World						
	TPR	TNR	FPR	FNR	ACC.	PRE.	Recall	TPR	TNR	FPR	FNR	ACC.	PRE.	Recall
Zeus	0.978	0.987	0.013	0.022	0.9855	0.939	0.978	0.954	0.996	0.004	0.046	0.9890	0.982	0.954
Virut	0.903	0.998	0.002	0.097	0.9973	0.730	0.903	0.839	0.998	0.002	0.161	0.9968	0.712	0.839
Waledac	0.994	0.996	0.004	0.006	0.9952	0.995	0.994	0.972	0.992	0.008	0.028	0.9891	0.956	0.972

Figure. 10. Comparison without adding noise

	Our system Real World (25~33% noise)							Beigi et al 's system Real World (25~33% noise)						
	TPR	TNR	FPR	FNR	ACC.	PRE.	Recall	TPR	TNR	FPR	FNR	ACC.	PRE.	Recall
Zeus	0.971	0.987	0.013	0.029	0.9843	0.939	0.971	0.941	0.996	0.004	0.059	0.9868	0.982	0.941
Virut	0.892	0.998	0.002	0.108	0.9972	0.728	0.892	0.226	0.998	0.002	0.774	0.993	0.40	0.226
Waledac	0.960	0.996	0.004	0.040	0.9804	0.994	0.960	0.688	0.996	0.008	0.312	0.8615	0.992	0.688

Figure. 11. Comparison after adding 25% to 33% noise

	Our system Real World (33~50% noise)							Beigi et al 's system Real World(33~50% noise)						
	TPR	TNR	FPR	FNR	ACC.	PRE.	Recall	TPR	TNR	FPR	FNR	ACC.	PRE.	Recall
Zeus	0.963	0.987	0.013	0.037	0.9829	0.938	0.963	0.934	0.996	0.004	0.066	0.9857	0.981	0.934
Virut	0.872	0.998	0.002	0.128	0.9972	0.726	0.872	0.247	0.998	0.002	0.753	0.3087	0.422	0.247
Waledac	0.945	0.996	0.004	0.055	0.9735	0.994	0.945	0.553	0.995	0.008	0.447	0.8027	0.99	0.553

Figure. 12. Comparison after adding 33% to 50% noise

As shown in Figures 11 and Figure 12, our model can resist more noise compared to the system in [9]. Under this context, we add features to higher layer like HTTP features and it indeed helps in separating healthy data from infected data since normal users use HTTP and HTTPS more often nowadays.

VII. CONCLUSION

We propose a system for detecting potential infected bots by using machine learning and flow based detecting techniques. As the result shows, our model can clearly recognize normal users from all packets. On top of that, we retrieve features from data link layer to app layer. Although botnets do not necessarily employ HTTP, HTTP features, at least it could help to learn normal users' behavior and thus improve our accuracy rate to higher than the average accuracy rate in the paper "Towards Effective Feature Selection in Machine Learning-Based Botnet Detection Approaches" [9]. System managers can easily use our system by simply recording the network flow into pcap format, and our system will process it into machine learning format and output the results in a report.

ACKNOWLEDGMENT

This research was supported in part by the Ministry of Science and Technology, Taiwan, under the Grant MOST 107-2218-E-007-030.

REFERENCES

[1] "IoT Online Store's report of IoT device number," http://www.iotonlinestore.com/. [Dec., 2016]

[2] "Highest botnet flow increasing by year," http://www.ithome.com.tw/news/111220. [Jan., 2017]

[3] Y. Feng, "How to fight against botnets in IoT," http://staff.cs.kyushu-u.ac.jp/data/event/2016/02/160107_Yaokai_Feng.pdf. [Feb., 2016]

[4] "ISO-OSI-layer-model-tcpip-model," http://programmerhelp404.blogspot.tw/2014/01/iso-osi-layer-model-tcpip-model.html. [Jan., 2014]

[5] "WEKA classifiers trees j48," http://weka.sourceforge.net/doc.dev/weka/classifiers/trees/J48.html.

[6] " C4.5 algorithm," https://en.wikipedia.org/wiki/C4.5_algorithm. [Jul., 2018]

[7] X. Wu et al., "Top 10 algorithms in data mining," Knowledge and information systems, vol. 14, no. 1, pp. 1–37, 2008.

[8] H. Liu, R. Setiono, "A probabilistic approach to feature selection-a filter solution," in ICML, vol. 96, 1996, pp. 319–327.

[9] E. B. Beigi, H. H. Jazi, N. Stakhanova, and A. A. Ghorbani, "Towards effective feature selection in machine learning-based botnet detection approaches," in Communications and Network Security (CNS), 2014 IEEE Conference on. IEEE, 2014, pp. 247–255.

[10] Q. Yan, Y. Zheng, T. Jiang, W. Lou, and Y. T. Hou, "Peerclean: Unveiling peer-to-peer botnets through dynamic group behavior analysis," in Computer Communications (INFOCOM), 2015 IEEE Conference on. IEEE, 2015, pp. 316–324.

[11] T. Cai and F. Zou, "Detecting http botnet with clustering network traffic," in School of Information Security Engineering Shanghai Jiao Tong University, 2012, pp. 1–6.

[12] F. V. Alejandre, N. C. Cortés, and E. A. Anaya, "Feature selection to detect botnets using machine learning algorithms," in Electronics, Communications and Computers (CONIELE- COMP), 2017 International Conference on. IEEE, 2017, pp. 1–7.

[13] "Hypertext transfer protocol," https://en.wikipedia.org/wiki/Hypertext_Transfer_Protocol. [Jul., 2018]

[14] B. Rahbarinia, R. Perdisci, A. Lanzi, and K. Li, "Peerrush: mining for unwanted p2p traffic," in International Conference on Detection of Intrusions and Malware, and Vulnerability Assessment. Springer, 2013, pp. 62–82.

[15] C. R. CTU University, "The ctu-13 dataset. a labeled dataset with botnet, normal and background traffic," 2013.

[16] E. Alparslan, A. Karahoca, and D. Karahoca, "Botnet detection: Enhancing analysis by using data mining techniques," in Advances in Data Mining Knowledge Discovery and Applications. InTech, 2012.

Enhanced Software Implementation of a Chaos-Based Stream Cipher

Guillaume Gautier*, Safwan El Assad†, Olivier Deforges*,
Sylvain Guilley‡, Adrien Facon‡, Wassim Hamidouche*
* Univ Rennes, INSA Rennes, CNRS, IETR - UMR 6164, F-35000 Rennes, France
Email: guillaume.gautier@insa-rennes.fr, olivier.deforges@insa-rennes.fr, wassim.hamidouche@insa-rennes.fr
†Polytech Nantes, CNRS, IETR - UMR 6164, F-44000 Nantes, France
Email: safwan.elassad@univ-nantes.fr
‡ Secure-IC SAS, F-35510 Cesson-Sévigné, France
Email: sylvain.guilley@secure-ic.com, adrien.facon@secure-ic.com

***Abstract*—Cipher algorithms have been created a long time ago to protect sensitive information. With the evolution of technology, particularly the increase of computational power, the multiplication of devices, the interconnection of those devices, ciphers need to be created and/or enhanced to match challenges brought by this new environment. In general, chaos-based stream ciphers have three shortcomings: their implementation is not constant-time, they have weak keys, and are not portable. We show in this paper how to overcome those three limitations in the case of our stream cipher. The stream cipher performance including statistical analysis and computational performance are carried out and compared to state-of-the-art algorithms: Advanced Encryption Standard (AES)-CounTeR (CTR), HC-128 and Rabbit.**

Keywords*—*Chaos-based stream ciphers; Constant time; Statistical analysis; Computational performance.

I. INTRODUCTION

The need of encryption methods has nearly always existed to protect sensitive information. The number of connected devices is constantly and rapidly increasing. Those devices are communicating between each other through multiple channels exchanging information, such as sensor readings or orders to control other devices. In this context, the protection of sensitive data exchanged over networks is necessary. For this purpose, a secure cryptography that can be embedded into as many devices and architectures is, now more than ever, required. This means that algorithms are required to have the lowest complexity, and implementations have to reduce the energy consumption, the code size and the Random-Access Memory (RAM) without compromising security.

Stream ciphers are commonly used to encrypt data in real time applications like, for example, in selective video encryption [1][2]. It consists in performing an eXclusive OR (XOR) operation between a plain text and the output of a deterministic random generator. In the literature, multiple stream ciphers exist, the eSTREAM project was promoting the design of efficient and compact stream cipher such as HC-128 [3] or Rabbit [4], but according to [5], eSTREAM ciphers are not all secured.

The chaos theory is used in cryptography for its natural property of deterministic randomness. Indeed, chaos-based ciphers generally use chaotic maps for their combination of security and relatively low complexity.

This paper shows the different enhancements, in terms of both secure and embedded implementation, of the chaos-based stream cipher designed in [6][7] and implemented in [8][9].

The main contributions of this paper are the following.

- Remove the vulnerabilities to time-attack analysis, consisting in analysing execution time of secret-dependent operations in order to retrieve the secret key for example, a constant-time implementation is proposed.
- Propose a fixed-point implementation whereas the original stream cipher [8][9] uses a floating-point number representation [10] to widen the range of architectures able to embed the stream cipher.
- A new solution is proposed to correct the minor vulnerability inherent to the reduction operation.

The rest of this paper is organized as follows. In Section II, a functional presentation of the stream cipher and the associated generator is introduced. Then, Section III presents the enhancements brought to the previous implementation along the expected results. The stream cipher performance (statistical analysis and computational performance) are carried out and compared to AES-CTR, HC-128 and Rabbit algorithms in Section IV. Finally, Section V concludes this paper.

II. ORIGINAL CHAOS-BASED STREAM CIPHER

A. The Stream Cipher

The original stream cipher, based on a Pseudo-Chaotic Number Generator (PCNG), has been implemented in C [8][9]. As illustrated in Figure 1a, in order to obtain a ciphered text (C), the plain text (P) is encrypted using a XOR operation between the plain text and the PCNG output (X_g). The PCNG is initialized with a secret key (K) of length between 200 and 456 bits, depending on the number of internal delays, and a 64-bit-long Initial Vector (IV).

B. Pseudo-Chaotic Number Generator (PCNG)

The PCNG uses a couple of chaotic maps, the skew tent and the PieceWise Linear Chaotic (PWLC) map, to produce N-bit samples, with $N = 32$, at each instant n. The two maps are encapsulated in two different cells and the output cells ($X_s(n)$ and $X_p(n)$) are paired using a XOR operation as illustrated in Figure 1b.

Figure 1c shows the block diagram of a cell where $X(n)$ can be $X_s(n)$ for Skew Tent map, or $X_p(n)$ for PWLC map,

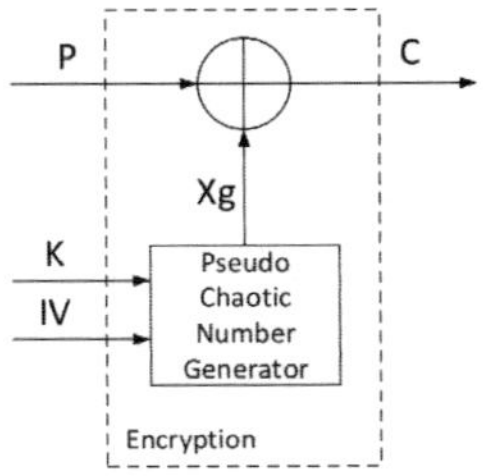

(a) Stream cipher block diagram

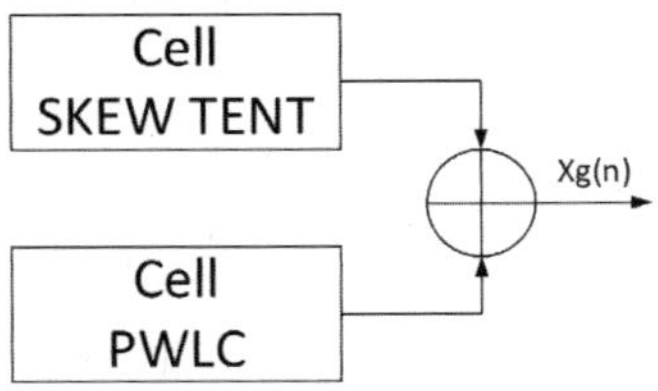

(b) Association of the two PCNG cells

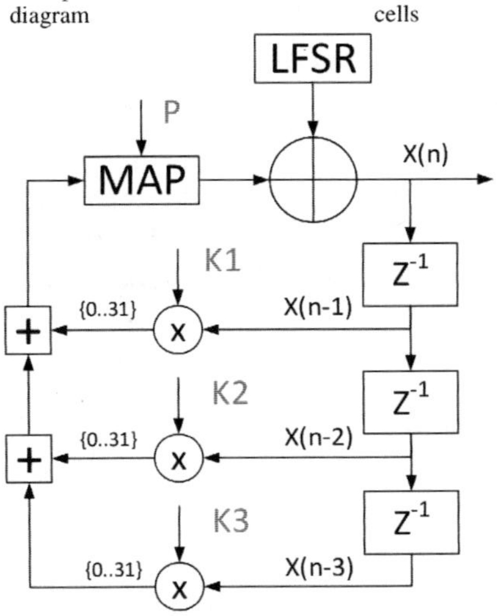

(c) Generic block diagram of a cell

Figure 1. Block diagram of the chaos-based stream cipher

P can be P_s or P_p and $K1$, $K2$, $K3$ can be $K1_s$, $K2_s$, $K3_s$ or $K1_p$, $K2_p$, $K3_p$, respectively.

Each cell in Figure 1c is composed of its own chaotic map. One cell is using the Skew Tent map defined by (1) and the other is using the PWLC map defined by (2).

$$X_s(n) = STmap(X_s(n-1), P_s) = \begin{cases} \left\lfloor 2^N \times \frac{X_s}{P_s} \right\rfloor & \text{if } 0 < X_s < P_s \\ \left\lfloor 2^N \times \frac{2^N - X_s}{2^N - P_s} \right\rfloor & \text{if } P_s < X_s < 2^N \\ 2^N - 1 & \text{otherwise} \end{cases} \quad (1)$$

$$X_p(n) = PLWCmap(X_p(n-1), P_p) = \begin{cases} \left\lfloor 2^N \times \frac{X_p}{P_p} \right\rfloor & \text{if } 0 < X_p < P_p \\ \left\lfloor 2^N \times \frac{X_p - P}{2^{N-1} - P_p} \right\rfloor & \text{if } P_p < X_p < 2^{N-1} \\ \left\lfloor 2^N \times \frac{2^N - P_p - X_p}{2^{N-1} - P_p} \right\rfloor & \text{if } 2^{N-1} < X_p < 2^N - P_p \\ \left\lfloor 2^N \times \frac{2^N - X_p}{P_p} \right\rfloor & \text{if } 2^N - P_p < X_p < 2^N \\ 2^N - 1 & \text{otherwise} \end{cases} \quad (2)$$

The map outputs are periodically perturbed using a Linear Feedback Shift Register (LFSR) [9] and are encapsulated inside an Infinite Impulse Response (IIR) filter with a variable order (1 to 3) (see Figure 1c). Increasing the filters' order will improve the statistical performance significantly.

In the cell Skew Tent, the parameter $P_s \in]0, 2^{32}[$ and the coefficients of the IIR filter $K1_s$, $K2_s$, $K3_s \in]0, 2^{32}[$ are part of the secret key, for PWLC, the parameter $P_p \in]0, 2^{31}[$ and $K1_p$, $K2_p$, $K3_p \in]0, 2^{32}[$, respectively.

C. Secret key and IV set-up

The first iteration is computed according to the following equations:

$$Xin_s = \left(MSB(IV) + \sum_{i=1}^{nbDelay} Xi_s \times Ki_s \right) mod\ 2^N$$
$$X_s(0) = STmap\left[Xin_s, P_s\right] \quad (3)$$

$$Xin_p = \left(LSB(IV) + \sum_{i=1}^{nbDelay} Xi_p \times Ki_p \right) mod\ 2^N$$
$$X_p(0) = PLWCmap\left[Xin_p, P_p\right] \quad (4)$$

where the values Xi_s and Xi_p are parameters of the key.

As shown in Equations (3) and (4), the 32 Most Significant Bits (MSB) of the IV are fed to the Skew Tent map and respectively the 32 Less Significant Bits (LSB) to the PWLC map.

III. ENHANCED SOFTWARE IMPLEMENTATION

A. Constant-Time Implementation

The implementation introduced in [8][9] showed secret-dependent timings. Indeed, the implementation profiling shows that the maps' computation is not constant since a branching is used to compare elements of the secret key and the complexity of each branch is different, resulting in different execution times. Branching is done by comparing X_s to P_s or X_p to P_p, as shown in Figure 2 for PWLC map given as an example.

Require: $X_p \in]0; 2^{32}[$ and $P_p \in]0; 2^{31}[$
  if $0 < X_p < P_p$ **then**
    $X_p \leftarrow X_p \times ratio3$
  else if $(P_p < X_p < M_2)$ **then**
    $X_p \leftarrow (X_p - P_p) \times ratio4$
  else if $M_2 < X_p < (M_1 - P_p)$ **then**
    $X_p \leftarrow (M_1 - P_p - X_p) \times ratio4$
  else if $(M_1 - P_p) < X_p < M_1$ **then**
    $X_p \leftarrow (M_1 - X_p) \times ratio3$
  else
    $X_p \leftarrow M_1 - 1$
  end if
  return X_p
where $M_1 = 2^{32}$, $M_2 = 2^{31}$ and ratios are defined in (5).

Figure 2. Calculate $X_p(n) = PLWCmap(X_p(n-1), P_p)$

Having secret-dependent timings is a vulnerability that an attacker can exploit to retrieve elements of the secret key. To overcome this problem, the proposed solution is detailed, as pseudo-code, in Figure 3. In order to achieve the same computational time and complexity for each sample, the maps compute, first, all the flags B_1 to B_5 used to determine which case should be selected. Then, the maps compute all the cases and masks them to select the correct output value. Similar modifications are applied to $STmap()$.

Require: $X_p \in]0; 2^{32}[$ and $P_p \in [0; 2^{31}[$
$B_1 \leftarrow 0 < X_p < P_p$
$B_2 \leftarrow P_p < X_p < M_2$
$B_3 \leftarrow M_2 < X_p < (M_1 - P_p)$
$B_4 \leftarrow (M1 - P_p) < X_p < M_1$
$B_5 \leftarrow (B_1 + B_2 + B_3 + B_4) = 0$
$X_1 \leftarrow (X_p \times ratio3)\&\text{mask}(B_1);$
$X_2 \leftarrow ((X_p - P_p) \times ratio4))\&\text{mask}(B_2)$
$X_3 \leftarrow ((M_1 - P_p - X_p) \times ratio4))\&\text{mask}(B_3)$
$X_4 \leftarrow ((M_1 - X_p) \times ratio3))\&\text{mask}(B_4)$
return $(X_1 + X_2 + X_3 + X_4 + ((M_1 - 1)\&\text{mask}(B_5))$
where $M_1 = 2^{32}$, $M_2 = 2^{31}$, ratios are defined in (5) and mask(B_X) returns 0xFFFFFFFF if $B_X = 1$, otherwise 0.

Figure 3. Calculate $X_p(n) = PLWCmap(X_p(n-1), P_p)$

B. Fixed-Point Implementation

In the C implementation of [8][9], the maps were computed using double-precision floating-point number representation [10], which cannot always be computed on embedded systems. The other drawback is the computational power required to perform such operation.

The software pre-calculates ratios for each maps. These ratios depend on the parameters P_s and P_p contained in the secret key and are defined as follows:

$$ratio1 = \frac{2^{32}}{P_s}; \quad ratio2 = \frac{2^{32}}{2^{32} - P_s}; \qquad ratio3 = \frac{2^{32}}{P_p}; \quad ratio4 = \frac{2^{32}}{2^{31} - P_p} \tag{5}$$

To match the double-precision floating-point standard [10] previously used, the 12.52 format is taken as the fixed point representation.

Due to the precision required to perform this computation of the maps, using the fixed-point ratio, at least 96-bit number is required. The computation consists in adding/subtracting 32-bit input, multiply it by the 64-bit ratio and then shift the result by 52 to obtain the result on 32 bits. The targeted platform (i.e., x86-64 Central Processing Unit (CPU)) computation is done on 128-bit words. The implementation of the fixed point ratios is described in Figures 4 and 5. Figure 4 shows how the pre-calculation of the ratio is performed and Figure 5 presents the implementation of the PWLC map, the same thinking is applied to the Skew Tent map.

$ratio1 \leftarrow (M_1 << 52)/P_s$
$ratio2 \leftarrow (M_1 << 52)/(M_1 - P_s)$
$ratio3 \leftarrow (M_1 << 52)/P_p$
$ratio4 \leftarrow (M_1 << 52)/(M_2 - P_p)$
where $M_1 = 2^{32}$ and $M_2 = 2^{31}$.

Figure 4. Computation of the ration using a fixed-point representation 12.52

Require: $X_p \in]0; 2^{32}[$ and $P_p \in [0; 2^{31}[$
$B_1 \leftarrow 0 < X_p < P_p$
$B_2 \leftarrow P_p < X_p < M_2$
$B_3 \leftarrow M_2 < X_p < (M_1 - P_p)$
$B_4 \leftarrow (M1 - P_p) < X_p < M_1$
$B_5 \leftarrow (B_1 + B_2 + B_3 + B_4) = 0$
$X_1 \leftarrow ((X_p \times ratio3) >> 52)\&\text{mask}(B_1);$
$X_2 \leftarrow (((X_p - P_p) \times ratio4) >> 52)\&\text{mask}(B_2)$
$X_3 \leftarrow (((M_1 - P_p - X_p) \times ratio4) >> 52)\&\text{mask}(B_3)$
$X_4 \leftarrow (((M_1 - X_p) \times ratio3) >> 52)\&\text{mask}(B_4)$
return $(X_1 + X_2 + X_3 + X_4 + ((M_1 - 1)\&\text{mask}(B_5))$
where $M_1 = 2^{32}$, $M_2 = 2^{31}$, ratios are defined in (5) and mask(B_X) returns 0xFFFFFFFF if $B_X = 1$, otherwise 0.

Figure 5. Calculate $X_p(n) = PLWCmap(X_p(n-1), P_p)$ using a fixed-point representation 12.52

C. Uniqueness of reduced products

Uniqueness of reduced products inside the IIR filter is primary. Indeed, the filter initialization being based on the secret key, filter output needs to be different for each keys, otherwise the generated sequence is the same. Two solutions are possible, the key space can be reduced to remove the weak keys or, as proposed below, to shift the result before the reduction to N bits, where N is the internal resolution of the chaotic maps, here $N = 32$.

Let $q = P(C = C')$ be the probability of having $C = C'$ with $C = A \times B$, $C' = A' \times B'$ and A, A', B, B' being four distinct unsigned integers defined on N bits. Equation (6) presents the probability of having q in different cases. In our case, the generator is included in the second case, i.e., $q \neq 0$. The proposed solution aims to minimize the probability q.

$$\begin{cases} q = 0 & \text{if } C \text{ or } C' \text{ is defined on 2N-bits} \\ q \neq 0 & \text{if } C \text{ and } C' \text{ are defined on } M,\ M' \text{ bits,} \\ & \text{with } M,\ M' < 2N \end{cases} \tag{6}$$

Let $\epsilon(j)$ be equal to $1 << j$ with $\{j \in \mathbb{N} \mid j < N\}$ and let i be an integer in $[0; N-1]$ where i number of right shifts executed before the reduction to N bits. In the worst case, i.e., $A' = A$, $B' = B \oplus \epsilon(j)$ or $A' = A \oplus \epsilon(j)$, $B' = B$, the probability q is equal to:

$$\begin{aligned} q_N(i) = \; & P((A \times B) >> i = (A \times (B \oplus \epsilon(N-1))) >> i) \\ & + P((A \times B) >> i = (A \times (B \oplus \epsilon(0))) >> i) \\ = \; & 2^{-(i+1)} + 2^{-(N-i)} \end{aligned}$$

Figure 6 shows the value of q_N depending on the value i for $N = 32$. Minimum of q_{32} is obtained for $i = 15$ and $i = 16$. In the rest of the paper, we consider the value $i = 16$. The new generic block diagram of a cell using shifting is presented in Figure 7.

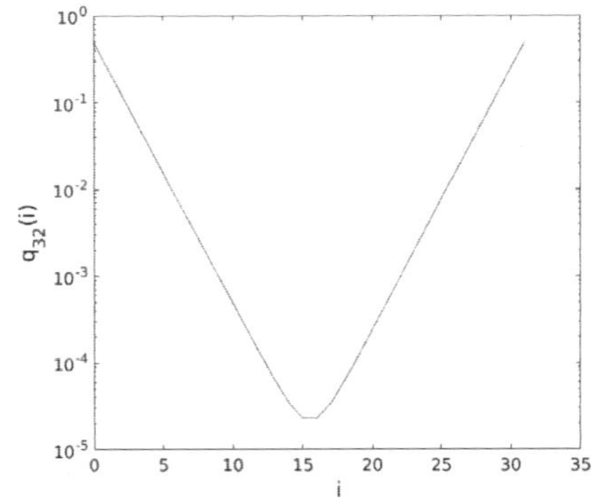

Figure 6. Probability $q_N(i)$ of having $A \times B = A' \times B'$ being four distinct unsigned integers defined on N bits, for $N = 32$

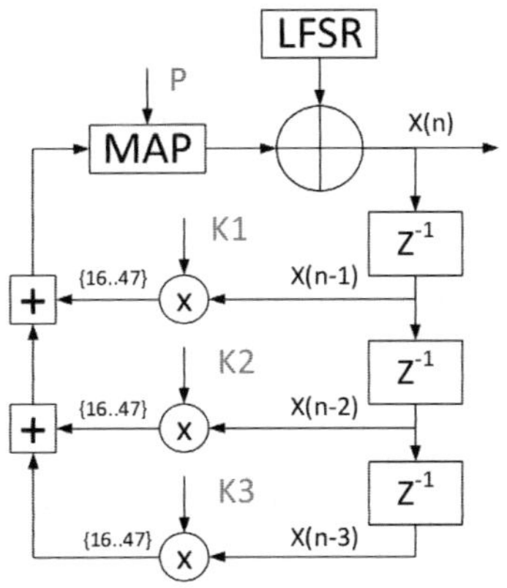

Figure 7. New generic block diagram of a cell using shifts

IV. Results and Discussions

In this section, multiple versions of the cipher are implemented and tested.

- V0: this version corresponds to the initial version presented in [8][9].
- Shifting: this version is V0 that includes the enhancement presented in Section III-C.
- Fixed-Point: this version is V0 that includes the enhancement presented in Section III-B.
- Shifting + Fixed-Point: this version is the combination of the two previous versions.
- Constant time (CT): this version is the Shifting + Fixed-Point version with constant-time implementation presented in Section III-A.

A. Statistical Tests

To ensure the robustness of the enhanced implementations against statistical attacks, we perform the following statistical tests. The statistical tests are only run on the constant-time version. Similar results are obtained for all considered versions.

1) NIST Statistical Tests Suite (STS) SP 800-22: National Institute of Standards and Technology (NIST) STS [11] the popular test suite for investigating the randomness of binary data is applied. The suite contains 188 tests and sub-tests that assess the randomness of arbitrarily long binary sequences. These tests focus on a variety of different types of non-randomness that could exist in a sequence.

To perform the different tests, 100 sequences of 31250 32-bit samples (i.e., 1 million bits per sequence) are generated using 100 different secret keys. All 188 tests and sub-tests of the suite are run. For each test, a set of 100 P_{value} is produced and a sequence passes a test whenever the $P_{value} \geq \alpha = 0.01$, where α is the level of significance of the test. A value of α = 0.01 means that 1% of the 100 sequences are expected to fail. The proportion of sequences passing a test is equal to the number of $P_{value} \geq \alpha$ divided by 100.

Table I presents the NIST STS's results of the constant-time version. The P_{values} of all the tests are strictly over 0.01, meaning that the cipher passed all the tests. Passing this test is necessary, but not sufficient to affirm that generated sequences are random.

TABLE I. NIST STS RESULTS OF THE 3-DELAY CONSTANT-TIME STREAM CIPHER

Tests	P Value	Proportion of passed keys(%)
Frequency	0.51412	100.00
LinearComplexity	0.51412	99.00
LongestRun	0.16261	100.00
OverlappingTemplate	0.92408	98.00
RandomExcursions	0.21822	99.58
Rank	0.94631	100.00
BlockFrequency	0.00463	99.00
NonOverlappingTemplate	0.51879	98.96
ApproximateEntropy	0.22482	99.00
CumulativeSums	0.89412	100.00
Serial	0.21070	99.50
Universal	0.19169	99.00
Runs	0.07572	98.00
FFT	0.17187	98.00
RandomExcursionsVariant	0.40488	98.40

2) Correlation - Hamming Distance (HD): These tests show the non-similarity of two generated streams from two different keys.

The correlation coefficient is computed using the binary representation of the sequences where $1 \rightarrow 1$ and $0 \rightarrow -1$. The expected value of the correlation coefficient ρ_{ij}, for two completely random sequences, should be equal to 0.

Figure 8a shows the obtained correlation coefficients between two-by-two different sequences. As we can see, all correlation coefficients are centred around 0 and maximum and minimum values are bounded by $3,94 \times 10^{-3}$, result expected for non-correlated sequences.

The average HD is defined in (7), where S_x is the generated sequence of size L, x is the index of a key inside an array of 100 random keys. The expected value, for two completely random sequences, should be equal to $\frac{1}{2}$.

$$HD_{ij} = \left\{ \frac{1}{L} \times \sum_{k=1}^{L} S_i(k) \oplus S_j(k) \quad \text{if } i \neq j \right. \qquad (7)$$

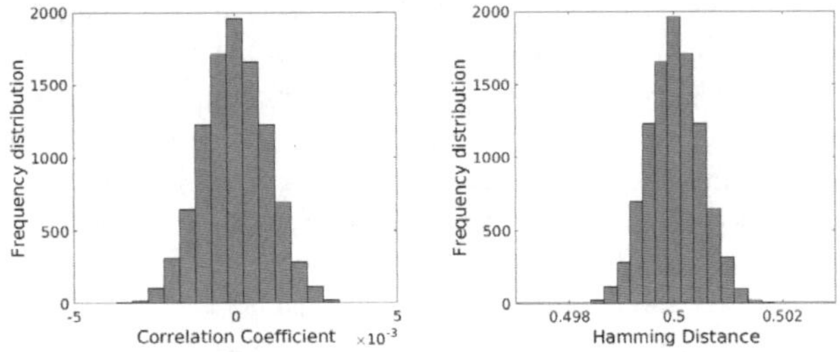

(a) (b)

Figure 8. Frequency distribution of the correlation coefficients (a) and hamming distances (b) of the 3-delay stream cipher

Figure 8b shows HDs centred around $\frac{1}{2}$, and maximum deviation is bound by $1,97 \times 10^{-3}$, meaning there is equal chance to generate a 0 or 1.

3) Histogram distribution: The aim of this test is to determine if the histogram distribution is uniform. To assert that, the χ^2 test is used. If a generated sequence verifies (8), the key associated passes the χ^2 test.

$$\sum_{i=0}^{C} \frac{(V_{observed}(i) - V_{expected})^2}{V_{expected}} < V_{critical} \quad (8)$$

This test is run on our algorithms, and some reference algorithms. The test conditions are the following.

- The test is run independently over 1000 randomly generated keys, and IVs.
- Samples are unsigned 32-bit integers.
- 10^8 samples are generated per sequence.
- $C = 1000$ classes are used.
- $V_{expected} = \frac{10^8}{C} = 10^5$
- $V_{critical}$ is computed using the inverse of the chi-square cumulative distribution function as defined in [12][13]. For this paper, $V_{critical} = 1073.6$.

Table II shows the percentage of keys passing the χ^2 test with a set of 1000 random keys and different algorithms.

The performance of literature algorithms is close to 95%. The initial version is only presenting 88,1% passing keys, but 94.6% keys for the enhanced version pass the test and is close to standard algorithms.

TABLE II. HISTOGRAM PERFORMANCE

Algorithm	Key passing χ^2 test
V0 - 3 delays	88.1%
Constant Time - 3 delays	94.6%
AES	94.9%
HC-128	95.4%
Rabbit	95.5%

B. constant time measurement

To check if the algorithmic meets with the constant time requirement, the Kalray Multi-Purpose Processing Array (MPPA®) manycore architecture [14] and a x86 platform are used.

a) On Kalray MPPA® processor: the MPPA® architecture is designed to achieve high energy efficiency, and deterministic response times for compute-intensive embedded applications.

The MPPA® processor , code-named Bostan, integrates 256 Very Long Instruction Word (VLIW) application cores and 32 VLIW management cores (288 cores in total) which can operate from 400 MHz to 600 MHz on a single chip and delivers more than 691.2 Giga FLOPS single-precision for a typical power consumption of 12 W. The 288 cores of the MPPA® processor are grouped in 16 Compute Clusters (CC) and implement two Input/Output Subsystems (IO) to communicate with the external world through high-speed interfaces via the PCIe Gen3 and Ethernet 10 Gbits/s.

MPPA® platforms integrate a register that counts the number of CPU cycles elapsed since the start of the machine. Indeed, it allows to measure a precise complexity of any algorithm ran on this architecture. To measure this complexity, a simple difference of two register readings, one before starting the encryption and one after, is performed.

The number of cycles measured is normalized to have the Number of Cycles per Byte (NCpB) (Equation (9)).

$$NCpB = \frac{C}{M \times K} \quad (9)$$

where C is the number of cycles elapsed since the start of the encryption, K is the number of keys used and M is the size, in bytes, of the message.

b) On INTEL® x86 processor: similar measurement method exists for INTEL® x86 processor, using Time Stamp Counter (TSC) register [15], but is not as precise. The reading of the TSC register returns the number of ticks elapsed since the start of the machine. The Number of Ticks per Byte (NTpB) is the unit used to compare the two implementations and is defined in (10).

$$NTpB = \frac{T}{M \times K} \quad (10)$$

where T is the number of ticks elapsed since the start of the encryption, measured using TSC register, K is the number of keys used and M is the size, in bytes, of the message.

c) Results and discussions: to check the time stability of the constant-time version, 100 encryptions of a same 125000-byte-long message using 100 random keys are started on two different architectures, MPPA® processor (Figure 9a) and on x86 processor (Figure 9b).

As illustrated by Figures 9a and 9b, the number of cycles/ticks necessary to encrypt a byte in the initial version clearly depends on the key used, no matter which architecture is used. Oppositely, in the constant-time implementation, the NCpB/NTpB is constant, consequently removes the vulnerabilities to timing attacks.

C. Time performances

Time measurements are done on an Intel Core i7-6700 CPU @3.40GHz. The test environment is set as follows:

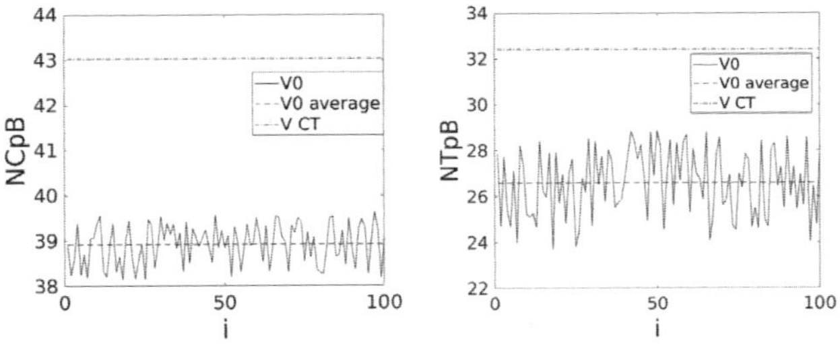

(a) on MPPA® Processor (b) on x86 Processor

Figure 9. NCpB/NTpB = f(Key[i]) of the initial version(V0) and the constant time(CT) version

- CPU frequencies are fixed at 3.00 GHz.
- Hyper-Threading is disabled.
- Pre-fetching is disabled.
- Process is assigned to a core using *taskset* command.

The function *gettimeofday()* is used to measure the time elapsed between the beginning and the end of the encryption. The message to encrypt is 125000 bytes long.

The metric used in this paper is defined as follows.

$$NCpB = \frac{F \times t}{M \times K} \quad (11)$$

where t is the time measured, K is the number of keys used, M is the size, in bytes, of the message and F is the frequency of the CPU. In this paper:

- $F = 3.00$ GHz.
- $M = 125000$ Bytes.
- $K = 100$ Keys.

Table III presents timing performance for different implementations of our cipher and some standard encryption methods. As shown in Table III, the constant-time version is a bit slower than other versions, but close to AES-CTR. HC-128 and Rabbit present better performance, however, these algorithms manifest some weaknesses against some attacks such as injection and side-channel attacks mentioned in [5].

V. Conclusion and Future Work

In this paper, we have proposed different enhancements for the original stream cipher implementation. The problem generated by product reductions is resolved by the patch presented in Section III-C. To secure the cipher against time attacks, one type of side-channel attack, we realized a constant-time implementation including all achieved enhancements.

The next step of this work would be to perform algebraic, side-channel and injection attacks for the initial and the constant-time versions to demonstrate the robustness of the cipher and its implementations. Then, a measurement of the energy consumption, the code size and the RAM needed for the cipher execution should be done to determine if the cipher can be categorized as lightweight.

Also, the initial and the constant-time versions will be implemented on embedded FPGA platform.

TABLE III. TIMING OF THE DIFFERENT CIPHER VERSIONS COMPARED TO STANDARD CIPHERS

Cipher version	delay	NCpB
V0	1	20.86
	2	22.11
	3	22.59
Shifting	1	20.82
	2	22.54
	3	23.43
fixed point	1	21.21
	2	22.24
	3	22.72
shifting + fixed-point	1	21.68
	2	22.79
	3	23.65
Constant-Time	1	24.46
	2	26.04
	3	27.06
HC-128		2.35
Rabbit		5.82
AES CTR		24.38

References

[1] S. Lian, J. Sun, J. Wang, and Z. Wang, "A chaotic stream cipher and the usage in video protection," *Chaos, Solitons and Fractals*, vol. 34, no. 3, pp. 851 – 859, 2007.

[2] W. Hamidouche, M. Farajallah, N. Sidaty, S. E. Assad, and O. Deforges, "Real-time selective video encryption based on the chaos system in scalable hevc extension," *Signal Processing: Image Communication*, vol. 58, pp. 73 – 86, 2017.

[3] H. Wu, "New stream cipher designs," M. Robshaw and O. Billet, Eds. Berlin, Heidelberg: Springer-Verlag, 2008, ch. The Stream Cipher HC-128, pp. 39–47.

[4] M. Boesgaard, M. Vesterager, and E. Zenner, *The Rabbit Stream Cipher*. Springer Berlin Heidelberg, 2008, pp. 69–83.

[5] C. Manifavas, G. Hatzivasilis, K. Fysarakis, and Y. Papaefstathiou, "A survey of lightweight stream ciphers for embedded systems," *Security and Communication Networks*, vol. 9, no. 10, pp. 1226–1246, dec 2015.

[6] S. El Assad, H. Noura, and I. Taralova, "Design and analyses of efficient chaotic generators for crypto-systems," vol. 0, pp. 3–12, 10 2008.

[7] S. El Assad and H. Noura, "Generator of chaotic sequences and corresponding generating system," Patent WO2011121218, Oct., 2011, extension internationale Brevets France n° FR20100059361 et FR20100052288. WO2011121218 (A1) 6/10/2011 CN103124955 (A) 29/05/2013 JP2013524271 (A) 17/06/2013 US2013170641 (A1) 3/07/2013.

[8] A. Arlicot, "Sequences Generator Based on Chaotic Maps," Université de Nantes, Tech. Rep., February 2014.

[9] M. A. Taha, S. E. Assad, A. Queudet, and O. Deforges, "Design and efficient implementation of a chaos-based stream cipher," *International Journal of Internet Technology and Secured Transactions*, vol. 7, no. 2, p. 89, 2017.

[10] "IEEE Standard for Floating-Point Arithmetic," *IEEE Std 754-2008*, pp. 1–70, Aug 2008.

[11] L. E. Bassham et al., "A statistical test suite for random and pseudorandom number generators for cryptographic applications," National Institute of Standards and Technology(NIST), Tech. Rep., 2010.

[12] M. Abramowitz and I. A. Stegun, *Handbook of mathematical functions: with formulas, graphs, and mathematical tables*. Government Printing Office, 1964, vol. 55.

[13] E. Kreyszig, *"Introductory Mathematical Statistics"*. John Wiley, 1970.

[14] B. D. de Dinechin, "Kalray MPPA®: Massively parallel processor array: Revisiting DSP acceleration with the Kalray MPPA Manycore processor," in *Hot Chips 27 Symposium (HCS), 2015 IEEE*. IEEE, 2015, pp. 1–27.

[15] Intel Corporation, "Intel 64 and IA-32 Architectures Software Developer's Manual Volume 2B: Instruction Set Reference, M-Z," Tech. Rep., 2016.

Adopting an ISMS based Model for better ITSM in Financial Institutions

Zidiegha Seiyaboh, Mohammed Bahja
School of Computer Science and Technology
University of Bedfordshire
Luton, Bedfordshire, UK
Email: Zidiegha.seiyaboh@study.beds.ac.uk, Mohammed.bahja@beds.ac.uk

Abstract—**In recent times, the day-to-day business operations in financial institutions have shown dependence on information systems and Information Technology (IT). IT service management systems have helped in managing the complexity of IT service delivery for delivering financial institutions' critical business. IT service management systems have become fully integrated into IT organizational arrangements as a micro part of financial institutions. However, the emergence and ever-increasing information security challenges have become a source of worry not only for financial institutions, but all other organizations. Despite this, limited attention has been given to the improvement of IT service management. The purpose of this research-in-progress is to investigate Information Security Management Systems (ISMS) in terms of their capability of improving Information Technology Service Management (ITSM) in financial institutions using International Organization for Standardization (ISO) 27001 standards as a guideline.**

Keywords- Information Security Management System; Information Technology Service Management; ISO Standards; IT services; Service Operation.

I. INTRODUCTION

Information has been identified as a very important aspect of information technology in recent years, such that most organizations and businesses are now focusing on the service-oriented economy rather than a goods-based one as was always the case in the past [1]. The huge rise in threats and cybersecurity breaches across industries including financial institutions has brought about a substantial financial loss and failure of IT service availability. This has led to an increased focus on information security in the sector [2]. One of the effective ways of strengthening an organization's cybersecurity is the implementation and periodic auditing of efficient Information Security Management System (ISMS). [3] stated that ISMS is a management system that embodies policies, processes and procedures that consider the fundamentals of cybersecurity, which are confidentiality, integrity and the availability of IT services and business information [3].

Information Technology Service Management (ITSM) has long been considered a key player for integrating business and IT services. IT service availability and continuity management are part of IT service delivery. Downtime and service failures occur, because of poor IT service availability management systems, which can adversely affect an enterprise's business prospects [4]. Given that the business activities and IT services of an organization are greatly dependent on information security, it is essential that an ISMS ISO based model guided by international standards and frameworks be adopted [5]. To ascertain clearly the relationship between information security and IT service availability, for this research, a detailed analysis of the ITIL 2011 for an ITSM framework, a systematic review of the ISO/IEC 20000 – 1:2011 being a Service Management System (SMS) standard [6] and an investigation into the top ISMS standards, such as ISO 27001, CIS 20 and NIST SP 800-53 will be carried out.

The structure of the paper is in sections. In Section II, a critical review of existing literature is done. In Section III, the possible benefits of ITSM are highlighted. Section IV explains the research methodology to be followed. In Section V, the components of ITIL are discussed. Section VI discusses some of the ISO 27001 controls and their relevance to ITSM. We conclude in Section VII with the findings from related research and an online survey.

II. LITERATURE REVIEW AND RELATED WORK

Recent research has shown that the finance sector has completely embraced the adoption of Information Technology for the enhancement of organizational performance and efficiency [2] but has brought with it many challenges to the sector [7]. Business continuity has been noted to be one of the key business values often identified with the banking industry [7]. Some of the valuable drivers of financial banking, service availability and business continuity are the integration of ITSM to the business operations of these financial institutions. [2]. Thomas Peltier described good security as protecting the assets of an organization and at the same time meeting the objectives and goals of the business [8].

There is a gap in the management and adoption of relevant standards to improve the efficiency of ITSM. This research proposes the adoption of an ISO driven ISMS based model that will bring about a change in the management of IT services and infrastructure.

ITSM is a key player in the process of integrating business and IT services [9]. In a bid to increase the business gains of financial organizations, material resources, human resources, management policies and objectives are being connected through the sharing of information [10]. This linkage has led to the potential for more serious attacks on information and the systems that are used for communicating and processing it than previously [11]. The security and protection of these valuable information assets is now one of the highest priorities for many organizations in the finance sector [12]. Whilst there are some approaches and technologies that have been developed to bring about information security, however none of these can guarantee watertight security [13]. The London Stock Exchange system failure that happened in 2008 is an example of the huge financial loss that can be caused by insufficient protection in the use of IT due to the conflicting interests of stakeholders [14]. Given the potential for big losses, professionals in the industry have started investigating IT related risks intensively [15].

While IT infrastructure failure is classified as an operational risk, it can also be identified as an availability failure from the service delivery management perspective [2]. If ITSM is to deliver its core objectives, an acceptable level of security must be attained, and hence, the need for robust ISMS standards being devised and followed, thereby ensuring the best security practices [16].

ITSM is considered part of the service sciences focusing on IT operations [17]. Specifically, it can be defined as a combination of processes established to ensure quality IT services, in accordance with levels pre-agreed with the customers [18]. Manuel Mora et al (2015) hold that ITSM centers on defining and delivering IT services that support business' goals whilst meeting customer needs [19]. It involves a systematic approach to the management of IT services, covering design, execution, operation, process and review aimed at providing improvement on a continual basis. Moreover, it focuses on the alignment of services and functions rendered by IT within an establishment as much as on the technical aspects of IT. Whilst cost effectiveness is one of the main aspects of the IT services management, it also concerns the whole lifecycle of all IT services [20].

There are various ITSM frameworks with the most common one being the Information Technology Infrastructure Library ITIL, which is the basic standard for most IT service providers [21]. ITIL has been deployed by Hewlett-Packard (HP), IBM and in the Microsoft Operation Framework (MOF) [22]. Microsoft's Operation Framework (MOF) also mirrors the provisions of ITIL standard [23]. ITIL 2011 being the most recent update of version 3, was published in May 2007. There are 26 sections, which are part of the five lifecycle phases, these being: Service Strategy, Service Design, Service Transition, Service Operation and Continual Service Improvement. There is a great difference between the current and previous versions. That is, the previous version, Version 2 comprised a total of ten processes in just two main domains, namely: Service Support and Service Delivery [24] [25].

III. EXPLORING THE IMPACT OF IT SERVICE MANAGEMENT

Jantti et al. highlighted how IT organizations globally have begun to take their service management processes to a higher level based on the adoption of best practice frameworks, like (ITIL). However, many of these companies have yet to demonstrate positive impact from the adoption of such as ITIL as a framework for ITSM [26]. This has stimulated the current investigation that addresses the questions: Has the IT service management process experienced any improvement? What are the factors that could be responsible for poor efficiency of ITSM?

The cardinal objective of this work is to capture the best practices of adopting ISMS frameworks and to identify the factors that will enhance the expected efficiency and improvement of ITSM. Some studies have highlighted the possible benefits of ITSM. For instance, Mauricio and Kolbe identified six benefits from its implementation, internal processes improvement, customer satisfaction, service quality improvement, processes standardization, efficiency increment, and improvement in return on investment (ROI) [27]. Organizations that have implemented ITIL in organizational change projects, have ultimately improved the quality of their services through better IT service management processes. In sum, modelling IT assets that form the IT business process has been identified as the key to IT service management improvement [28].

IV. RESEARCH METHODOLOGY

This exploratory research is a work in progress and is being conducted following the Design Science Research (DSR) methodology [29]. DSR is basically a methodology that encourages the researcher to understand the various aspects of the Information System (IS) being researched and the subsequent creation of new knowledge in the form of a theoretical model.

The steps involved in DSR are:

- Awareness of the problem (This was done through system literature review and conduction of an online survey)
- Suggestion (Adoption of an ISO based ISMS model to improve the efficiency of ITSM)
- Development (Design a framework for the implementation of ISO 27001 as an adopted ISMS model)

- Evaluation (Evaluation to be done using expert judgement)
- Conclusion

In the light of this, there will be two primary iterations, the first to understand the concepts of ITSM and ISMS. The second iteration involves focusing on the designing of a theoretical model [29]. The realization of the artefact of this research work is centered on precise problems, data quantification and a data gathering technique in the form of an online survey questionnaire sent to IT professionals in different financial institutions. Questions 2 - 9 of which inquire about the components of ITSM, while questions 10 - 32 the relevance of ISMS to its efficiency. Before the creation of the theoretical model, in financial Institutions, it is important that the components of ITSM and ISMS be defined.

V. COMPONENTS OF ITIL

As aforementioned, ITIL is one of the widely accepted ITSM frameworks that describes the best practices for managing IT services. It was developed in the early eighties by the Central Computer and Telecommunications Agency (CCTA) following a serious economic downturn, to reduce cost and to manage IT service delivery better. CCTA merged later with the Office of Government Commerce (OGC) and since then, ITIL has been constantly reviewed and updated by the OGC as a service management standard library dealing with information technology (IT). The current version is ITIL 2011, which aims at providing high quality IT services that focus more on the customer and effective IT governance than previously [30]. Most financial organizations have adopted the ITIL framework, because it provides a systematic way of managing their IT services which can enhance customer satisfaction at a much-reduced cost [31].

The life cycle stage of ITSM is the IT operation and maintenance, which is referred to as the "service operation" in ITIL. It functions basically to ensure the normal operation of daily business activities and handles all events and incidents that occur during the information system operations and maintenance process. ITIL service operation consists of five processes namely Incident Management, Problem Management, Event Management, Request Fulfilment, Access Management and four functions - Service Desk, Technical Management, IT Operations Management, and Application Management [32].

VI. ISO 27001 CONTROLS

ISO 27001 is structured into two divisions, which are: ISMS requirements and reference control objectives [33]. It has 14 clauses and 35 domains which include 114 controls. Some of these controls will be focused on in this project, because they are detailed enough to form the basis for an ISMS that will lead to improvement in the efficiency of ITSM in financial Institutions.

Table 1 shows the ISO 27001 controls that will be referenced for this research.

TABLE I. SOME ISO CONTROLS AND THEIR RELEVANCE TO ITSM

S/N	Control No.	Control Statement	Relevance to ITSM
1	A.6.1.1	"All information security responsibilities shall be defined and allocated"	IT Access Management, IT Technical Management, IT Event Management
2	A.6.1.2	"Conflicting duties and areas of responsibility shall be segregated to reduce opportunities for unauthorized or unintentional modification or misuse of the organization's assets"	IT Access Management, IT Technical Management, IT Event Management
3	A.7.2.2	"All employees of the organization and, where relevant, contractors shall receive appropriate awareness education and training and regular updates in organizational policies and procedures, as relevant for their job function"	IT Access Management, IT Technical Management, IT Event Management,

ISO 27001 is the most adopted ISMS standard that allows freedom in implementation. All the controls are classified into one of the following: Data, software, hardware, network and people. The classification of the controls help in evaluating the performance of the standard.

VII. CONCLUSION

The findings from related research and a conducted online survey have shown that financial organizations rely heavily on IT systems to create value for customers and to maximize IT service delivery. The management and adoption of relevant standards and best practice frameworks in the sector is a critical issue in the day to day management of IT services but has received limited attention. For this research, the adoption of an ISO driven ISMS based model that will bring about a change in the management of IT services and infrastructure is proposed. Further research and results from the survey will allow for the development of a theoretical model that it is anticipated will have a positive impact on the efficiency and offerings of ITSM.

REFERENCES

[1] K. Gopinath and R. Vinod, "IT service management automation and its impact to IT industry," in *2017 International Conference on Computational Intelligence in Data Science(ICCIDS)*, India, 2017.

[2] O. Shirley, Yang. Carol, S. HSU. Suprateek and S. L. Allen, "Enabling Effective Operational Risk Management in a Financial Institution: An Action Research Study," *Journal of Management Information Systems,* vol. 34, no. 3, pp. 727 - 753, 1 July 2017.

[3] P. Sanghyun and L. Kyungho, "Advanced Approach to Information Security Management System Model for Industrial Control System," *The Scientific World Journal,* vol. 2014, no. 348305, pp. 1 - 13, 21 July 2014.

[4] A. Sahid, M. Yassine and B. Mustapha, "An Agile Framework for ITS Management in Organizations:," Morocco, 2017.

[5] S. Abbass, H. Parvaneh and K. Hourieh, "A Practical Implementation of ISMS," in *7th International Conference on e-Commerce in Developing Countries:with focus on e-Security*, Iran, 2013.

[6] IEEE, "Adoption of ISO/IEC 20000-1:2011, Information technology—Service management," *IEEE Software & Systems Engineering Standards Committee,* p. 48, 3 June 2013.

[7] R. Choudhary and B. Kunal, "Business Continuity Planning: A Study of Frameworks, Standards and Guidelines for Banks IT Services," vol. 5, no. 8, August 2016.

[8] R. T. Peltier, Information Security Polices, Procedures and Standards: Guidelines for Effective Information Security Management, 2 ed., Florida: Auerbach Publications, 2016.

[9] M. Muhammed, "The Impact of Adopting IT Service Management Processes," 2015. [Online]. Available: http://www.diva-portal.org/smash/record.jsf?pid=diva2%3A1118287&dswid=5844. [Accessed 16 April 2018].

[10] A. A. Simplice, "Improving Financial Access: Insights from Information Sharing and Financial Sector Development," *Development Finance Agenda (DEFA),* vol. 3, no. 3, pp. 14 - 16, 2017.

[11] H. Chang, "Is ISMS for Financial Organizations effective on their business?," *Mathematical and Computer Modelling,* vol. 58, no. 1 - 2, pp. 79 - 84, July 2013.

[12] W. Jingguo, M. Gupta and H. R. Rao, "Insider Threats in a Financial Institution: Analysis of Attack-Proneness of Information Systems Applications," *MIS Quaterly,* vol. 31, no. 1, pp. 91 - 112, 2015.

[13] A. Zahoor, M. Soomro, S. Hussain and A. Javed, "Information Security Management needs more holistic approach: A literature review," *International Journal of Information Management,* vol. 36, no. 2, pp. 215 - 225, 2016.

[14] P. Gary, H. Ray and L. P. Shan, "Information Systems Implementation Failure: Insights from Prism," *International Journal of Information Management,* vol. 28, no. 4, pp. 259 - 269, 2008.

[15] A. Juhani and J. Kari, "Challenges of the Comprehensive and Integrated Information Security Management," China, 2017.

[16] S. Heru, N. A. Mohammad and C. T. Yong, "Information Security Management System Standards: A Comparative Study of the Big Five," *International Journal of Electrical & Computer Sciences,* vol. 11, no. 5, pp. 23 - 29, 2011.

[17] L. A. Mary, "Introducing ITIL Best Practices for IT Service Management," April 2015. [Online]. Available: https://www.nysforum.org/events/4_30_2015/Final.pdf. [Accessed 16 April 2018].

[18] P. Armanda, N. Pratama, N. R. Jefri, P. W. Aji and D.

A. Tinton, "IT Service Management based on service dorminant logic:," in *2017 3rd International Conference on Science in Information Technology*, Indonesia, 2017.

[19] M. Manuel, M. G. Jorge, O. Rory, R. Mahesh and G. Ovsei, "An Extensive Review of IT Service Design in Seven International ITSM Processes Frameworks: Part II," *International Journal of Information Technologies and Systems Approach,* vol. 8, no. 1, pp. 69 - 90, 2015.

[20] R. Wijesinghe, S. Helana and M. Stuart, "Defining the optimal level of business benefits within IS/IT projects: Insights from benefit identification practices adopted in an IT Service Management (ITSM) project," Australia, 2015.

[21] S. Mcloughlin, H. Scheepers and R. Wijesinghe, "Benefit Planning Management for ITSM: Evaluating Benefit Realization Frameworks," New Zealand, 2014.

[22] IBM, "An Integrated Process Model as a Foundation for ITSM," 22 January 2007. [Online]. Available: https://www.bcs.org/upload/pdf/integrated-process-model.pdf. [Accessed 17 April 2018].

[23] P. David, H. Claire and L. Paul, Microsoft Operations Framework 4.0, Norwich: Van Haren Publishing, 2008.

[24] J. Roman, K. Lukáš, Ž. Roman and K. Alena, "Differences between ITIL V2 and ITIL V3 with respect to Service Transition and Service Operation," 2015.

[25] L. Rick, "A Comparison of Best Practice Frameworks: Silos to Lifecycle," Office of Government Commerce, US, 2002.

[26] M. Jantti, T. Rout, L. Wen, S. Heikkinen and A. Cater-Steel, "Exploring the Impact of IT Service Management Process Improvement Initiatives: A case study approach," Australia, 2013.

[27] M. Marrone and M. K. Lutz, "Impact of IT Service Management Frameworks on the IT Organization," *Business Information Systems Engineering,* vol. 3, no. 1, pp. 5 - 18, 2011.

[28] M. Lepmets, C.-S. Aileen, G. Francis and R. Eric, "Extending the IT Service Quality Measurement Framework through a Systematic Literature Review," *Journal of Service Science Research,* vol. 4, no. 1, pp. 7 - 47, 2012.

[29] V. Vaishnavi, K. Bill and P. Stacie, "Design Science Research in Information Systems," 20 December 2004/17. [Online]. Available: http://www.desrist.org/design-research-in-information-systems/. [Accessed 21 April 2018].

[30] N. Ahmad, A. N. Tarek, F. Qutaifan and A. Alhilali, "Technology adoption model and a road map to successful implementation of ITIL," *Journal of Ent. Info. Management,* vol. 26, no. 5, pp. 553 - 576, 2013.

[31] K. V. Jiten and J. F. Nicholas, "Approaches to IT Service Management in improving IT Management in the Banking Sector," Malaysia, 2016.

[32] I. InnoTrain, "IT Service Management Methods and Frameworks Systematization," 2010. [Online]. Available: http://www.central2013.eu/fileadmin/user_upload/Downloads/outputlib/Innotrain_Systematization_2011_04_05_FINAL.PDF. [Accessed 22 April 2018].

[33] S. Bahareh and S. Iman, "Evaluating the effectiveness of ISO 27001:2013 based on Annex A," in *2014 Ninth International Conference on Availability, Reliability and Security (ARES) (2014)*, Switzerland, 2014.

Authentic Quantum Nonces

Stefan Rass, Peter Schartner and Jasmin Wachter
Department of Applied Informatics, System Security Group
Universität Klagenfurt, Universitätsstrasse 65-67
9020 Klagenfurt, Austria
email: {stefan.rass, peter.schartner, jasmin.wachter}@aau.at

Abstract—**Random numbers are an important ingredient in cryptographic applications, whose importance is often underestimated. For example, various protocols hinge on the requirement of using numbers only once and never again (most prominently, the one-time pad), or rest on a certain minimal entropy of a random quantity. Quantum random number generators can help fulfilling such requirements, however, they may as well be subject to attacks. Here, we consider what we coin a *randomness substitution attack*, in which the adversary replaces a good randomness source by another one, which produces duplicate values (over time) and perhaps numbers of low entropy. A binding between a random number and its origin is thus a certificate of quality and security, when upper level applications rest on the good properties of quantum randomness.**

Keywords–Quantum Cryptography; Randomness Substitution Attack; Random Number Generation; Security; Authentication.

I. Motivation

Random numbers play different roles in cryptographic systems. Mostly, they are used to generate keys or create uncertainty towards better security in different attack scenarios. Concerning the latter, it is often necessary to assure a certain minimum entropy of a random value, and to prevent coincidental equality of two random numbers chosen at different times or different places. While the former requirement is obvious, revealing the problem with the latter requires some more arguing: as a simple example, consider two independent persons A, B instantiating individual RSA (Rivest-Shamir-Adleman) encryption systems. Both choose large primes p_A, q_A and p_B, q_B, respectively, making up the key-parameters $n_A = p_A q_A$ and $n_B = p_B q_B$. If $\{p_A, q_A\} \cap \{p_B, q_B\} \neq \emptyset$ and $n_A \neq n_B$, then $\gcd(n_A, n_B) \in \{p_A, p_B, q_A, q_B\}$, which defeats security of both RSA instances. Adhering to recommended key-sizes, it is tempting to think that the chances of a match of two, say 512 bit long, primes is negligible. Even mathematically, the prime number theorem assures that there are at least 1.84×10^{151} primes within the range $\{2^{511}, \ldots, 2^{512} - 1\}$, so there appears to be no problem in choosing those parameters independently from each other. Unfortunately, reality differs from the theoretical expectations in a devastating manner: according to findings of [1], approximately 12,500 out of more than 4.7 million RSA-moduli could be factored by humble pairwise greatest common division computation!

At least for this reason, quantum randomness would – at first glance – be a good replacement for user-supplied randomness (such as mouse movements). However, a proper post-processing to authenticate a generator's output and to avoid random number generators coming up with identical outputs is nevertheless an advisable precaution.

Furthermore, while the statistical odds to accidentally hit the same integer over a search in the range of 512 bit or higher is sure negligible, reframing this possibility towards a potential attack scenario is worthwhile to look at. Especially so, as standard cryptosystems like RSA or ElGamal (and hence also the digital signature standard) can be attacked most easily, when the involved randomness source gets under the attacker's control or influence, regardless of whether or not the randomness is used to find primes or simply as a general input. We call this a *randomness substitution attack*. Scaling up this thought, distributed attacks on random number generators that make only a portion of those emit random numbers with low entropy may already suffice to establish a significant lot of RSA instances [2] that are vulnerable to simple gcd-based factorization, or instances of ElGamal signatures [3] [4] (such as the digital signature standard is based on), where the secret key sk can easily be recovered if the *same* signature exponent k in $r = g^k$ MOD $(p-1)$ is used twice, e.g., if the random number generator has been hacked.

The foremost danger of randomness substitution is not its sophistication, but its simplicity and apparent insignificance that may cause countermeasures to be hardly considered as necessary. Nevertheless, authentic random values with lower-bounded entropy and explicit avoidance of coincidental matches are easy to construct yet advisable to use.

The paper is organized as follows. In Section II, we will sketch the basic cryptographic building blocks used to embed certain additional information into a quantum-generated random bitstring. This additional information will not only assure distinctness of values generated by otherwise independent generators, but also assure uniqueness of values over an exponentially long range in the (infinite) sequence of random numbers emitted by the same generator. We call such numbers *nonces*. Section III shows the construction and how to verify the origin of a random number. Notice that in this context, we neither claim nor demand information-theoretic security (as would be common in a full-fledged quantum cryptographic setting), but our focus is on classical applications that use quantum randomness to replace user-supplied random values. However, replacing the generator itself is an issue that must as well be avoided, which is doable by classical techniques, as we will outline here.

II. Preliminaries

Let $x \in \{0,1\}^\ell$ denote bitstrings of length ℓ, and let $\{0,1\}^*$ be the set of all bitstrings (of arbitrary length). The notation $x\|y$ denotes any encoding of x and y into a new string, from which a unique recovery of x and y is possible (e.g., concatenation of x and y, possibly using a separator symbol). Sets are written in sans serif letters, such as M, and their cardinality is $|\mathsf{M}|$.

To establish a binding betweeen random numbers and their origin devices, and to assure uniqueness of random values over time and across different number generators, we will employ digital signatures with message recovery, and symmetric encryption. Recall the general framework of these, into which RSA-, Rabin or Nyberg-Rueppel signatures fit [5]: let $\mathsf{M} \subseteq \{0,1\}^*$ be the *message space*, and let M_S be the *signing space*, i.e., the set of all (transformed) messages on which we may compute a digital signature. Furthermore, let $R : \mathsf{M} \to \mathsf{M}_S$ be an invertible *redundancy function* that is publicly known, and for simplicity, equate $R(\mathsf{M}) = \text{Im}(R) = \mathsf{M}_S$. We define the mappings $Sign : \mathsf{M}_S \times \mathsf{K} \to \mathsf{S}$ and $Extract : \mathsf{S} \times \mathsf{K} \to \text{Im}(R)$ as the signing and verification functions, where S is the signature space and K is the keyspace, where the secret signature key and public verification key come from.

A digital signature is obtained by computing $s = Sign(R(m), sk)$. As we demand message recovery, the verification proceeds in four steps, assuming that we received the signature s^* to be validated:

1) Obtain the signer's public key pk from a valid certificate (also provided by the signer),
2) Compute $\widetilde{m} = Extract(s^*)$.
3) Verify that $\widetilde{m} \in \text{Im}(R) = \mathsf{M}_S$, otherwise reject the signature.
4) Recover the message $m = R^{-1}(\widetilde{m})$.

Our construction to follow in Section III will crucially rely on the recovery feature of the signature, so that resilience against existential forgery mostly hinges on a proper choice of the redundancy function R. In general, this choice should be made dependent on the signature scheme in charge, and to thwart existential forgery, the redundancy function should not exhibit any homomorphic properties. A possible choice would be $R(m) = m \| h(m)$, where h is a cryptographic (or universal) hash-function, where we emphasize that no rigorous security proof of this choice is provided here.

As a second ingredient, we will use a symmetric encryption E, writing $E_k(m)$ to mean the encryption of m under key k and transformation E. The respective decryption is denoted as $E_k^{-1}(m)$. Our recommended choice for practicality is the Advanced Encryption Standard (AES).

Finally, we assume that each random generator is equipped with a world-wide unique identification number, such as is common for network cards (Media-Access-Control (MAC) address) or smartcards (Integrated Circuit Card Serial Number (ICCSN) [6]). Hereafter, we will refer to this quantity as the ID of the generator.

III. CONSTRUCTION

Given a generator equipped with a unique identifier ID and an internal counter $c \in \mathbb{N}$ (initialized to zero), let $r \in \{0,1\}^*$ denote a raw random bitstring that the quantum random generator emits per invocation.

The final output of the random generator is now constructed over the following steps, (see Figure 1).

1) Increment $c \leftarrow c + 1$
2) Compute $x \leftarrow ID \| c \| r$
3) Apply a digital signature with message recovery, using the secret signature key sk, i.e., compute $s \leftarrow Sign(R(x), sk)$.

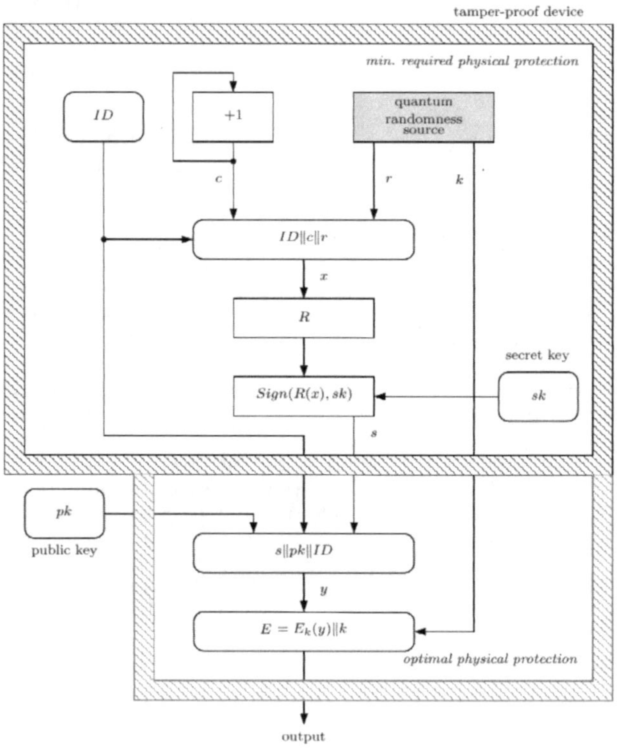

Figure 1. Schematic of post-processing for authentic nonces

4) Append the generator's public key pk and identity ID to get $y \leftarrow s \| pk \| ID$
5) Choose another (quantum) random number k and deliver the final output (the authentic nonce)

$$z := E_k(y) \| k.$$

It is easy to see that the so-constructed sequence of numbers enjoys all the properties that we are looking for. The last step ensures randomness, as parts of the random values (the public key and identity) remain constant over time. Note that all of the above transformations are invertible and hence injective. We examine each of the properties separately in the following.

a) Uniqueness: To this end, let $z_1 = E_{k_1}(y_1) \| k_1, z_2 = E_{k_2}(y_2) \| k_2$ be two outputs of a generator (possibly the same one or different devices). Uniqueness is trivial if $k_1 \neq k_2$, so assume a coincidental match between the two or the possibility that k_1, k_2 origin from an attacker. If z_1, z_2 match upon the least significant bits making up the keys $k_1 = k_2 = k$, then uniqueness requires $E_k(y_1) \neq E_k(y_2)$. Since E_k is injective, we hence look at $y_1 = s_1 \| pk_1 \| ID_1$ and $y_2 = s_2 \| pk_2 \| ID_2$. If z_1, z_2 come from the same generator so that $ID_1 = ID_2 = ID$ (e.g., if an attacker substituted the components), then the problem rests with the signature s_1 hopefully being different from s_2. Recovering $x_1 = ID_1 \| c_1 \| r_1$ from s_1 and $x_2 = ID_2 \| c_2 \| r_2$ from s_2, we ultimately have a difference, as in case the generator is the same, the counters are different by construction. In case the generators are different, the two IDs are different too. It follows that the entire output of the generator, regardless of adversarial influence at any postprocessing stage – excluding the signature generation – is unique. We refer the interested reader to [7] for a comprehensive discussion.

b) Authenticity: Having stripped all layers of signatures and encryptions as sketched above, we are left with two identity strings ID and ID' when we reach the innermost piece of data $x = ID\|c\|r$, being wrapped inside $s\|pk\|ID'$. One indicator of an attacker having made changes is a mismatch between ID and ID'. However, a stronger indication is provided by the digital signature verification, which is the primary measure to assure authenticity. At this point, it is important to stress the need for the manufacturer's certificate that links the public key of the generator to its ID (for otherwise, an attacker could create his own signature key pair and trick the user of the random number generator into using the wrong key to check authenticity). The certificate can be standard (say, X.509), such as used in most conventional public-key infrastructures.

c) Entropy and Min-Entropy: Notice that besides randomness that possibly went into the signature (e.g., if a Nyberg-Rueppel signature was in charge) or later stages of the postprocessing (i.e., the key k), the assured entropy coming out of the quantum random generator is limited by what has been authenticated. Hence, only the innermost value r can be used to lower-bound the entropy of the final output (assuming possible adversarial modifications), leading to the entropy bound $H(z) \geq H(r)$.

Besides Shannon-entropy H, min-entropy H_∞ of the generator's output may be of interest, as most applications demand high min-entropy for matters of randomness extraction. This is most easily done by extracting the authenticated quantum random bitstring r from the generator's output z. By our construction, it is possible to recover the true randomness from the generator's output, thus the above inequality holds in exactly the same fashion for H_∞ in place of H. This can be proven easily, as all processing functions are injective by construction and thus cannot lower the min entropy. These considerations lead to the min-entropy bound $H_\infty(z) \geq H_\infty(r)$.

We stress that the injectivity of the signature is vital for this bound to hold, and the inequality could be violated if the signature with message recovery were replaced by a conventional signature (for a hash-then-sign paradigm, the lack of injectivity in the hash function would invalidate the above argument).

IV. Security and Efficiency

Roughly, the postprocessing stage adds some redundancy to the randomness r, which depends on the specific implementations of the signature and encryption. In case of RSA and AES, we end up with (currently [8]) 4096 bits for $R(ID\|c\|r)$. Defining $R(m) = m\|h(m)$, where h is a 256-bit cryptographic hash function like the SHA-2 (Secure Hash Algorithm 2), and using a 128 bit counter as well as an 80 bit ID (e.g., an ICCSN in a smartcard taking 10 bytes), we are left with a remainder of $4096-256-128-80 = 3632$ bits of raw quantum randomness r. Attaching the ID and a short RSA public key pk (16 bits), we expand the input via AES-CBC (cipherblock chaining (CBC) with ciphertext stealing) to $4096 + 80 + 16 = 4192$ bits. Concatenating another 128 bits for the AES key k yields final output of $4192 + 128 = 4320$ bits, among which 3632 bits are pure quantum randomness. The relative overhead is thus $\approx 19\%$.

In addition, the application of digital signatures naturally puts the chosen signature scheme in jeopardy of a known-message attack. Assuming that the generator is tamper-proof, chosen- or adaptive chosen message attacks (cf. [9]) are not of primary danger in this setting. Yet, we strongly advice to take hardware security precautions to protect the secret key against physical leakage and backward inference. Nevertheless, to avoid an attacker replacing the randomness source by another one (with low entropy), the signature scheme must be chosen with care.

In the presented form, authenticity, i.e., protection of known-message attacks, is solely based on computational intractability properties. If one wishes employ information-theoretic security, the digital signature with message recovery may be replaced by a conventional Message Authentication Code (MAC), based on universal hashing and continuous authentication, as it is the case for quantum key distribution (QKD) [10]. There, an initial secret r_0 shared between the peers of a communication link, is used to authentically exchange another secret r_1, which is then used to authenticate the establishment of a further secret r_2, and so on. (in the application of [10], r_1 would be a quantum cryptographically established secret key).

We can play the same trick here by putting an initial secret r_0 in charge of authenticating the first random values emitted by our quantum random generator. Instead of signature with message recovery we will use a "MAC with appendix", i.e., we use a function $MAC : \{0,1\}^* \times \mathsf{K} \rightarrow \{0,1\}^\ell$ (e.g., a universal hash-family [11]) to authenticate the string $ID\|c\|r_1$ by concatenating a keyed checksum as $R(ID\|1\|r_1)\|MAC(R(ID\|0\|r_1), r_0)$, when r_1 is the first random number ever emitted by our generator. After that, the authentication is done using the respective last number r_i, i.e., we emit $R(ID\|c+1\|r_{i+1})\|MAC(R(ID\|c\|r_{i+1}]), r_i)$, whenever r_{i+1} follows r_i in the sequence (see Figure 2 for an illustration).

However, we might run into issues of synchronization here, thus opening another potential attack scenario, when the adversary succeeds in blocking some of the random values. In that case, we would either have to attach multiple MACs and maintain a list of past authenticators, or periodically re-synchronize the process (which requires a fresh authentic key exchange with the generator). Hence, this variant may not necessarily be preferable in practical applications.

V. Conclusions

Applications that require high-quality random sources like quantum physics based ones, most likely do so because the upper level cryptographic application crucially rests on the statistical properties of the involved random quantities. Binding a random number to its origin is thus perhaps an overlooked precaution to avoid working with low-entropy or potentially coincidental random values in a cryptographic application. Interactive proofs of knowledge, as well as recent empirical findings [1] on parameter selection for RSA and the digital signature standard, dramatically illustrate the need for such post-processing.

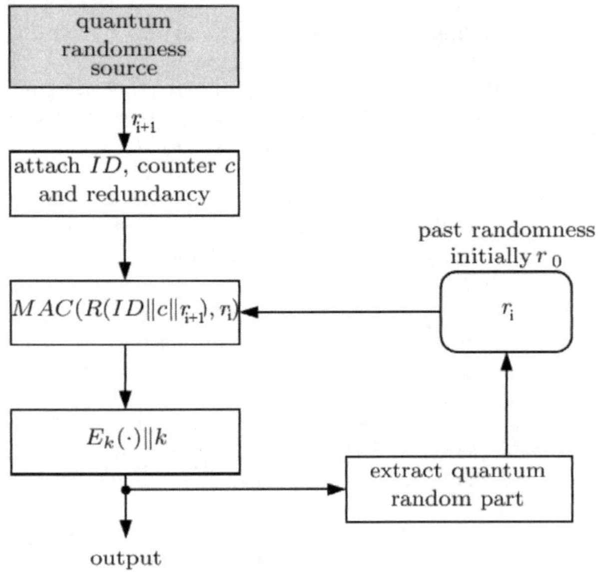

Figure 2. Variant with continuous authentication instead of digital signatures

REFERENCES

[1] A. K. Lenstra et al., "Ron was wrong, whit is right.", Cryptology ePrint Archive, Report 2012/064, http://eprint.iacr.org/ [retrieved: July 7th, 2018].

[2] R. L. Rivest, A. Shamir, and L. Adleman, "A method for obtaining digital signatures and public-key cryptosystems," Commun. ACM, vol. 21, no. 2, 1978, pp. 120–126.

[3] T. ElGamal, "A public key cryptosystem and a signature scheme based on discrete logarithms," in Proceedings of CRYPTO 84 on Advances in cryptology. New York, NY, USA: Springer New York, Inc., 1984, pp. 10–18.

[4] G. Locke and P. Gallagher, "Digital Signature Standard (DSS)," Federal Information Processing Standards (FIPS), Tech. Rep. FIPS PUB 186-3, 2009.

[5] A. Menezes, P. C. van Oorschot, and S. Vanstone, Handbook of applied Cryptography. CRC Press LLC, 1997.

[6] ISO/IEC, "ISO/IEC 7812-1:2006 Identification cards – Identification of issuers – Part 1: Numbering system," http://www.iso.org, ISO/IEC, 2006, [retrieved: July 7th, 2018].

[7] P. Schartner, "Random but system-wide unique unlinkable parameters," Journal of Information Security (JIS), vol. 3, no. 1, January 2012, pp. 1–10, ISSN Print: 2153-1234, ISSN Online: 2153-1242. [Online]. Available: https://www.scirp.org/Journal/PaperInformation.aspx?PaperID=16723

[8] D. Giry, "Bluecrypt – cryptographic key length recommendation," http://www.keylength.com/, October 2011, [retrieved July 7th, 2018].

[9] S. Goldwasser, S. Micali, and R. L. Rivest, "A digital signature scheme secure against adaptive chosen-message attacks," SIAM J. Comput., vol. 17, no. 2, Apr. 1988, pp. 281–308, [retrieved: July 7th, 2018]. [Online]. Available: http://dx.doi.org/10.1137/0217017

[10] G. Gilbert and M. Hamrick, "Practical quantum cryptography: A comprehensive analysis (part one)," 2000, uRL: http://arxiv.org/pdf/quant-ph/0009027 [retrieved: July 7th, 2018].

[11] M. Wegman and J. Carter, "New hash functions and their use in authentication and set equality," Journal of Computer and System Sciences, 1981.

Cyber-Security Aspects for Smart Grid Maritime Infrastructures

Monica Canepa
World Maritime University
Malmö, Sweden
e-mail: moc@wmu.se

Stefan Schauer
Austrian Institute of Technology
GmbH Vienna, Austria
e-mail: Stefan.Schauer@ait.ac.at

Giampaolo Frugone
University of Genova,
Genova, Italy
e-mail: frugone.xng@gmail.com

Riccardo Bozzo
DITEN, University of Genova
Genova, Italy
e-mail: riccardo.bozzo@unige.it

***Abstract*— Maritime ports are intensive energy areas with plenty of electrical systems that require an average power of many tens of megawatts (MW). Competiveness, profits, reduction of pollution, reliability of operations, and carbon emission trading are important considerations for any port authority. Current technology allows the use of a local micro-grid of the size of tens of megawatts, capable of isolated operation in case of emergency and moving toward a large energy independency. Ownership of its grid permits a large control on the prices of energy services and operation either on local electric market or generally on dangerous emission. Renewable energy generation has a large impact on costs since it features a low marginal cost, but it is random in nature. Since the smart grid is a critical asset within the port infrastructure, it is a high-level target for cyber-attacks. Such attacks are often based on malicious software (malware), which makes use of a controlling entity on the network to coordinate and propagate. In this paper, we examine the characteristics of a port smart grid and the typical characteristics of cyber-attacks. Furthermore, the potential ways to recognize these cyber-attacks and suggestion for effective countermeasures are also discussed.**

Keywords-Smart grid; maritime ports; energy efficiency; cyber attacks.

I. INTRODUCTION

The aim of this paper is to describe advantages of utilization of smart micro-grids in port areas and the requirements to protect them effectively from cyber-attacks. The paper stresses the advantages of this approach as a key factor of port competitiveness. Typical features of cyber-attacks against smart grid infrastructures are illustrated to suggest possible foundations for development of future research regarding mitigation and protection actions.

Efficient utilization of energy and sustainability of generation are critically important for port authorities and port operators due to obvious impacts on operational cost, business continuity, compliance to emission regulations, satisfaction for operators, attractiveness of the port and in last instance its competiveness [1].

In this paper, an operator is defined as an entity/organization active inside the port area that owns infrastructures, plants and buildings that is; an operator can perform simultaneously any of the following energy related operations: use of energy, generation of energy or storage of energy and change of generation /demand profile. Furthermore, the port authority can assume the role of market operator and consequently trade energy and services internally and externally.

Port electrical demand originates by:

- Civil and mechanical structures for shipbuilding activities and industrial installations, etc.
- Cruise ship terminals.
- Conveying systems, transfer towers, cranes, lighting and stockyards, refrigerated container, terminals to accommodate the movement of container
- Lighting systems for parking areas, roads, railway sidings, industrial shipbuilding yard
- Conditioning and heating system
- Electrical vehicles

From different points of view, port operators and port authorities look for competitiveness and also for profits, with a strong focus on energy efficiency and energy saving, which are related but different concepts (as efficiency implies savings but the vice versa is not necessarily true). Demand and generation have a flexible pattern in relation to the growth of port activities.

As per Theodoropoulos [2], energy efficiency and reduction of emissions is achieved by:

- Effective use of energy coming from traditional and renewables generations
- Enforce a general policy aimed to achieve the main energy objectives of the port
- Adjusting demand and supply of energy by flexible demand management, instantaneous load shedding or curtailment (both directions) and intelligent battery storage [3]
- Giving priority to renewable energy as primary resource
- Constantly moving generation and utilization of equipment to the their respective high efficient operating points

- Maximizing the use of electric transportation within a port
- Providing all operators with greater awareness on micro-grid status and current/forecasted prices in order to permit to anybody the correct planning of its own technical and economic operation

Protection of a smart micro-grid from cyber-attack is essential. A smart micro-grids is characterized by a set of distinctive aspects (extended geographical distribution, unmanned sub-systems, strong interaction between logical and physical level, strong requirements on service continuity, use of Internet communication services) that make traditional ICT defense techniques weaker or some time ineffective.

The sensitivity towards potential cyber-attacks increases in proportion to the growth of the complexity of micro grid control and intelligence, and is amplified by:

- Increasing interconnection also based on public networks between networks and micro grids, end users and power generation parks
- Increasing adoption of COTS (Commercial) Off-the-Shelf products in control (operating systems, DBMS, application software, etc.), and introduction of new technological paradigms of the ICT sector (virtualized systems)
- Extensive use of Internet based communication networks
- Data volume growth available and coming from non-homogeneous sources [4].

Technological evolutions introduce new vulnerabilities and criticalities of security and require accurate verification of compatibility with the requirements specified for the management of critical infrastructures.

The security context finds an additional dimension of interpretation in the analysis of the level of danger of potential attackers and their motivations, objectives and technical capabilities. The need to prevent events arising from well-organized attackers with strong financial capabilities, technical skills and the availability of state-of-the-art technological tools is widely shared. These attackers often have the ability to use "zero-day" vulnerabilities, bypassing signature-based attack detection systems and most current Prevention solutions / Detection of attacks.

Taking into account that the infrastructures of the electrical micro-grid generate a high dependence of almost all the other critical infrastructures and vital functions of the port, it is evident the possible impact that could have for a port a cyber-attack aimed at making these infrastructures not operational.

In this scenario, characterized by the combination of relevant factors, such as the logical-physical nature of the infrastructure, the need to guarantee a high level of continuity of service and the threat of technically competent and well-organized attackers, more needs arise, especially in field of attack prevention such as:

- the acquisition of feedback regarding the level of security of the physical infrastructure
- the correlation of information coming from the ICT security domain, physical security and Supervisory Control and Data Acquisition (SCADA).
- requirement of very low reaction times

In this scenario, an attacker could design malicious activities based on the contemporary perturbation of the SCADA and of physical equipment, but it could also operate a coordinated series of actions that could cause unexpected behavior of the micro-grid.

This situation greatly complicates the micro-grid security monitoring practices and the applicability of the technologies available today in ICT field.

II. WHY A SMART MICRO-GRID

A smart micro-grid is not a new concept since many large industrial areas and some ports are already operating an internal electrical grid powered by internal generation and connected to an external utility.

Irrespective of its smartness, a micro-grid consists of two major parts: on the one hand, the electrical infrastructure, i.e. the smart assets that generate, deliver, transform, protect and use energy and, on the other hand, communication and control systems, i.e., bidirectional communication and control system (SCADA) that operates the whole electrical smart micro-grid [5].

Most ports still use "dumb" micro-grids at certain marginal cost, rigidity of operations, level of reliability and resiliency. This implementation has a number of shortcomings, such as:

- Difficulty to fully exploit the potential of internal generation resources (often renewables such that large arrays of Photo Voltaic (PV) modules, biogas gas fired turbines, wind turbines, storage batteries, etc.)
- Difficulty to establish a customizable tariff policy that meets reward and economic and technical expectation of operators and remunerate them without tantalizing micro-grid performance and violating contractual requirements with the utility
- No easy way to support different control and regulations services required by external utility and by internal continuous activity related requirements, a fact that has an economic impact
- Difficulty to establish a customizable tariff policy that meets reward and economic expectation of operators without tantalizing grid performance and exceed contractual requirements
- Limited flexibility to server changing operators' needs
- Less reliability and resilience of dumb micro-grid
- Small possibility to trade services and actuate policies such as "Demand Response" (DR) and exploit "Time of Usage Tariff" (TOU).

A smart micro-grid generally overcomes these shortcomings, provides many other benefits [6] and therefore is a sensible solution to make a port an efficient and competitive infrastructure from the energy point of view.

Last but not least, a smart micro-grid provides a significant contribution to the process of generating revenues for port authority and operators. These revenues compensate some or all of the capital and operating costs incurred by operators during the micro-grid life cycle.

The U.S. Department of Energy (DOE) defines a micro grid as: "A group of interconnected loads and distributed energy resources with clearly defined electrical boundaries that acts as a single controllable entity with respect to the grid and can connect to and disconnect from the grid to enable it to operate in both grid-connected or island-mode" [7].

As stated in the "Micro-grid technology white paper" written by Muni-Fed – Antea Group Energy Partners, LLC in 2016, micro-grids are designed to allow delivering of excess energy into the incumbent utility grid as well as to import energy from the utility grid [11]. A micro-grid is a small-scale version of the traditional utility grid designed to optimize energy services through its intelligent pervasive controls, they can operate completely separated (that is islanded) from the utilities outside grid if properly sized internal generation and storage is provided.

Therefore, economic and technical objectives are enabling factors for a smart micro-grid deployment. Economic objectives aim to reach cost reductions and to stream revenues coming from operations of the smart micro-grid, specifically arbitrage/trading, minimization of cost associated to procurement of energy (including supply and bilateral contracts), correct definition of procurement contracts, avoiding penalties due to non-compliance with contractual terms (peaks, valleys, supply of services, emissions, etc.). Regarding the technical aspects, the fundamental objective is to deploy a stable, resilient, cyber-secure and reliable smart micro-grid capable of delivering high quality energy at the best prices to operators in relation to their past, present and forecasted behavior. These objectives are a function of availability of functionality, such as:

- Control at different levels capable to provide a cost effective, reliable durable, sustainable electric system able to serve efficiently its operators
- Enable independent (off the grid) operations in case of external adverse electrical conditions
- Reduce risk of general electrical collapse of micro-grid and permit faster detection, identification, isolation/clearing of fault and fast restoration to a normal state of operations
- Mitigate of the consequences of energy fluctuations through dispatching energy storage and switchable loads
- Improve energy-related operational efficiencies and coordinated use of energy storage systems
- Ensure continuous delivery of energy
- Face the stochastic nature of renewable generation
- Reduce peak load exposed to the utility
- Enable cranes with independent (often diesel) generation to inject excess of their generation, if economically viable and technically reasonable, into the micro-grid.
- Enable Vehicle to Grid (V2G) and Vehicle to Building (V2B) operations for port fleet of electrical vehicles
- Enable deployment and sound utilization of a Virtual Power Plant (VPP)
- Use energy normally wasted owing to braking operation through regenerative breaking.

III. MICRO-GRID DESIGN

Micro-grid design starts from specific port specifications like size of initial load and generation, its evolution as well mode of utilization of external energy supplies, operation schedules, and economic investment. Design Analysis is supported by some forecasting methods (e.g., it is possible to use spatial load forecasting, Support Vector Machine (SVM), time series analysis, Kernel Auto-Regressive Model with Exogenous Inputs (KARX), etc.

The preliminary design of electric micro-grid is done using network analysis packages such as loads and power flow, state estimation, stability and transient stability, voltage profiles, contingency analysis, etc.

Design Analysis is performed under various scenarios including the worst conditions, synchronization capability in connected and disconnected mode. Finally, risk analysis techniques like FMEA (Failure Mode and Effect Analysis) and FMECA (Failure Mode and Effect and Criticalities Analysis) are carried out as well to complete the preliminary project and permit an objective evaluation. These analyses are prerequisite for micro-grid risk management.

The smart micro-grid is also designed to support a "plug in type" approach to allow an easy horizontal and vertical upgrade as well as a seamless addition and integration of new equipment or replacement of existing one with a minimum of reconfiguration of existing configuration and reducing the risk of temporarily downgrading of the service. While the micro-grid planning criteria may come from a variety of sources, the most common is the need for high grid resilience to maintain active critical services during extended utility outages; other criteria include the increasing use of renewables, reducing emissions, managing energy costs and improving energy self-reliance, leading to state government regulations and incentives. (See figure 1).

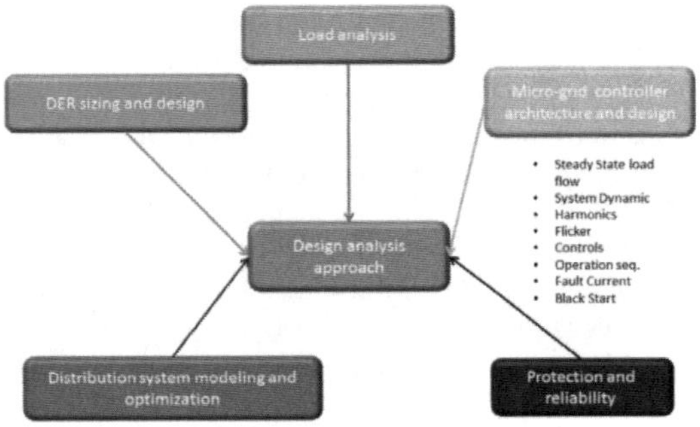

Figure 1. Micro-grid Design

Critical (that is must serve), no-critical loads and generating and storage farms are assigned to different feeders. Critical feeders are powered by dedicated generators and backed by their own storage so that required level of operability is always ensured.

For design purposes operators are categorized as active controllable or uncontrollable being the difference represented by the level of controllability, capability to respond to outside request to adjust load and/or generation profile and finally level of local intelligence. Design adheres to a general form of control that is hierarchical and decentralized, that means

- Each controllable operator can operate according to its own objective, preferences and policy
- Policy and objectives of the whole micro-grid are established by the controller at the highest level of the hierarchy
- A set of coordination principles takes into account the interaction of the processors (i.e. the fact they operate on their own according to a specific policy).

IV. CYBER-SECURITY ASPECTS OF SMART GRIDS

The cyber information security plays a fundamental role in management of smart micro-grids due to their strategic nature, since they represent the basis for the operation of several critical port infrastructures [11]. Because of this strategic role and considering the massive presence of intelligent components in the smart grid sector, the cyber-security of the smart micro grids (which includes attack prevention, detection, mitigation and resilience) represents a challenge for the future at the base of the research to be carried out. It is useful to reach the definition of models that are able to quantify potential consequences of a cyber-attack on the electricity grid, and this in terms of pressure drops, stability violations, and damage to equipment and / or economic losses.

According to a joint study by Iowa State University and the University of Illinois at Urbana-Champaign, after an appropriate risk assessment, the next step should be the development of an integrated set of security algorithms that can protect the network from multiple forms of cyber-attacks, such as denial of service attacks, malware-based attacks, etc. Such algorithms should take into consideration very sophisticated attacking modeled that could potentially cause a maximum level of damage. According to this study algorithms to mitigate the risk of an ICT attack should be developed through real-time correlation of the data streams and registers obtained from substations and control centers, algorithms that can prevent, detect and tolerate as well as mitigate cyber-attacks [8].

The protocols used in the SCADA, such as the inter-Control Center Communications Protocol ICCP also known as International Electro Technical Commission (IEC)/60870-6/Telecontrol Application Service Element 2 (TASE.2) [9], IEC 61850, Distributed Network Protocol 3 (DNP3) [10] (derived by GE-Harris from IEC 60870-5), if not properly protected, could potentially be used as carriers to launch cyber-attacks. This requires secure versions of these protocols.

A. *Kinds of Cyber- Attacks to Smart Grids*

A first type of attacks on the grid is represented by the "Intrusions": this type refers to exploiting the vulnerabilities of software and communication between the network infrastructures that then provides access to critical elements of the system. The "Malware" instead consists of malicious software that aims to exploit the existing vulnerabilities in the software system, programmable logical controllers, or protocols. Once the malware has gained access, it will try to cause damage in the system using the self-propagation mechanism.

The "Denial of service attacks aim to make services or resources managed by an organization unavailable for an indefinite period of time, denying the possibility to legitimate users of access them. This type of attack can aim to submerge the communication network (or a single server) with high volumes of traffic or loads of work to inhibit the operation of the attack lens.

Further, "Insider threats" are considered a great danger, by virtue of the privileged position that the potential attacker has, as it can operate from within the organization. Finally, "Routing attacks", in which cyber-attacks occur on internet routing infrastructures, should not be underestimated. Although this type of attack is not directly related to grid operations, it could have consequences on power system applications. Generally, it includes the following:

- Spear-phishing emails (from compromised legitimate accounts),
- Watering-hole domains,
- ICS infrastructure targeting and credential gathering
- Host-based exploitation,
- Industrial control
- Open-source reconnaissance

B. *Electrical Supply System: Vulnerability of Control Systems*

From a functional point of view, the micro-grids divided into: generation and storage, transmission and distribution.

Each functional division corresponds to systems whose task is the control of specific machines/devices. Each functional division has systems that control specific machines/devices and operate using dedicated communication signals and protocols. In this perspective, it is clear that each control system is subjected to specific vulnerabilities; in fact, they could constitute vectors of threats with a consequent potential impact on the operations of the whole supply system. Figure 2 shows a typical cyber-physical system.

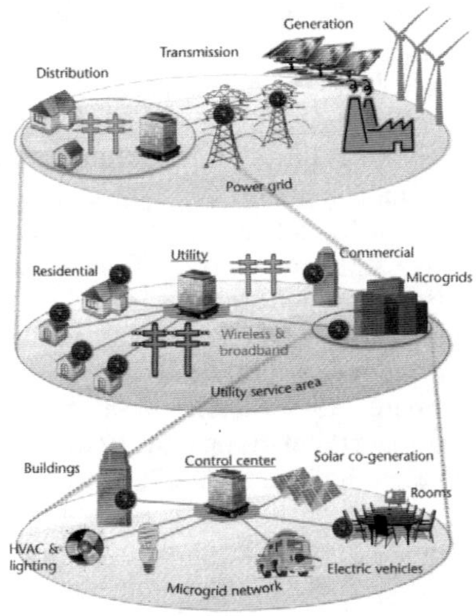

Figure 2. A typical cyber-physical system [12]

Resilience features of micro-grid control systems, includes

- Minimization of the occurrence of outages
- Mitigation of any unwanted incidents
- Minimization of the impact of outages
- Restoration of the normal working conditions of the grid in short time.

C. *Smart and Micro- Grid: Cyber- Security Aspects*

Cyber-security plays a very important role as observed in many ongoing projects, recommendations and standards, in particular in the United States NIST (National Institute of Standards and Technology) and within the EU by European Network and Information Security Agency (ENISA). However, there is currently no common approach and technology for applications in SCADA systems and this is even truer for the Smart Grids.

Therefore, in the specific case instead of investigating and proposing new technologies, we try to improve the process of defining the appropriate and measurable requirements of cyber-security for the micro-grid in order to define a realistic, efficient and scalable solution.

Computer security is an essential feature for the reliability of any control system today and is to be considered from the beginning of any project and not as an additional final component, as it sometimes happens. On the other hand, Cyber-Security for a smart micro-grid must be "smart" by itself, based on cost benefit and risk analysis, with negligible effect, if any, on performances. In this context, it is reasonable to recommend analysing from the beginning the specific needs of electrical equipment and the interconnections of data exchange [13].

Nowadays, the dedicated technology for ICS (Industrial control system) Cyber-Security consists mainly in analysis of network traffic at connection points relevant to the distributed control system. Current solutions range from easily configurable systems, which require traffic rules explicit and simple to self-learning machines that can separate autonomously normal and abnormal traffic, after a period of unsupervised training.

The "Defence in depth" is still at the initial stage and it's more expensive than filtering traffic, but it increases security of the single control nodes, independently of their interconnected topology. This approach is expected to become very valid, but in general it is justifiable only for new installations, while in other cases a mix between in-depth and filtering must be evaluated.

A good compromise for the choice has been proposed in the standard ANSI/ISA-99 [14], based on security zones and connection gateways. The term "Zone" means a grouping of logical or physical assets that share common safety requirements, based on factors such as criticality or others. The gateway connects different zones, is able to resist Denial of Service (DoS) or the injection of malware via back doors and protects the integrity and privacy of traffic on the network. The techniques of encapsulating areas guarantee the protection of much more areas from public networks; the deeper the encapsulation of an area is, the greater is its security.

There are several kinds of attacks to smart grids [15]:

Disruption attacks

Attacks whose purpose is the overpressure of a service for a certain period of time, creating an unavailability of the same usefulness for the purposes of decision-making processes:

- DDoS-attacks from outside targeting inside assets (Inbound attacks)
- DDoS-attacks from inside targeting inside assets (Internal attacks)
- DDoS-attacks from inside attacking targets outside (Outbound attacks)

- DDoS-attacks on certain user groups (selective harassment)

Destruction attacks

Unlike the interruption where the service can be restored after the attack, with destruction very often the infrastructure must be rebuilt:

- Disconnect households
- Destroy energy management
- Influence critical electrical nodes in the grid
- Alteration of sensor data
- Tamper with clock synchro

Theft

Stealing a commodity such as information to reveal to competitors:

- Espionage
- Ruin credibility of users:
- Sell long term data:
- Bill manipulation

Extortion schemes

Extortion attempts for demanding ransom achieving the releasing a captured:

- Commodity or service
- Threat of destruction
- Threat of DDoS
- Crypto-locker

Repurpose attacks

- Fake servers
- Proxies
- Distributed computing

D. Cyber-Security Objectives: Functional Improvements and Processes

The objectives of cyber-security are divided into functional improvements of process:

- Customized off-the-shelf solution, integrated into nodes (such as firewalls, hardening mechanism, strong authentication) and communication channels (such as Virtual Private Network (VPN) and encryption);
- An event correlator based on an active fault tree and supported by symptom detection technique tools analyses incidents, identifies abnormal ones and searches for hidden patterns among them. This event correlator is often associated with a security console which can be seen as a "mini security operation centre", such as decision support for the management of physical and logical security of the whole system.

Furthermore, non-functional objectives are associated with the procedures, e.g.:

- A new approach to the priority of the security requirements of logical components of Smart Grids, based on a specific analysis of risk weighted by appropriate critical parameters in order to identify reasonable, effective and timely countermeasures;
- A consequent logical partition of the smart or micro-grid in zones and communication channels that share security requirements homogeneous, allowing to customize cascade countermeasures.

A potential growing danger is the possibility that the supervision and control system (SCADA) of the micro-grid is deceived by false data coming from compromised peripheral units (RTUs, PLCs, Smart Inverters and other smart equipment) or through interconnections with other systems that are the object of successful attack. It is essential to distinguish between "genuine" data, incorrect data, whose error depends on malfunctioning of the peripheral instrumentation or the RTU "and data whose origin is dubious (potentially affected by malicious attacks). Methods for continuous monitoring of the security status of the infrastructure, through the acquisition, analysis and correlation of relevant data are key factors for security.

It is reasonable to use attack identification techniques based on the continuous analysis of safety events, states, alarms, measurements and commands coming / sent to the SCADA, from Metering and from ICT security systems. An appropriate use of these techniques allows to evaluate the overall behavior of the infrastructure, highlighting

- Presence of attacks (discriminating from really incorrect, but genuine, information)
- Changes in the level of risk.

A sophisticated attacker can attempt to modify the behavior of a SCADA and, in particular, directly or indirectly influence data (states, measurements, alarms) and commands (continuous and discrete) in such a way as to mislead the supervision and control system, protection and operators; what would trigger improper interventions, that in turns may be detrimental to the integrity of the equipment and interfere with the continuity of the service.

It is necessary to use techniques for the continuous monitoring of the safety of electrical infrastructures and to build identification of models to detect attacks.

It is useful to focus on the definition of methods for dynamically identifying the dependencies of the operational process of the micro-grid towards all the technologies served to it. In particular it necessary to study:

- the acquisition, standardization and correlation of security events coming from SCADA systems, from ICT systems with these correlated, from physical security systems

- determination of the stability status of the micro-grid by evaluating the data acquired in real time by the PV, systems
- the continuous monitoring of all the parameters describing the safety status of the logical, physical structures and the level of regularity and stability of the operational process, with a view to their correlation.

V. CONCLUSIONS AND FUTURE WORKS

The use of smart micro grid is to be promoted as a key element for port competitiveness and compliance with environmental regulations. Proper design of the micro-grid leads to benefits of port authority, port operators and external electrical utilities. It is important that the control and management structure reflects the organization and operation logics of port infrastructures, a fact that generally leads to a distributed hierarchical structure and a pervasive distribution of intelligence. Electrical and financial analysis supported by powerful forecasting tools is required to specify and deploy a micro grid that fit well with current and future requirements of the port. Modularity and upgradability is equally important as well as very friendly mode of operations.

Equally important is the cyber protection of the micro grids either in its smart equipment and control and information systems. This protection entails to points: defense of the information and control system as well as of communication infrastructure and recognition of electrical status that is not genuine and that would trigger dangerous control.

At the state of the art, in the face of a wide diffusion of solutions for the centralization and correlation of information security events it is possible to approach the problem using currently available technologies and planning developments aimed at extending the capacity of existing solutions.

Comprehensive control system with specialized optimizations tools needs to be developed together with sophisticated monitoring techniques. The role of forecasting and modeling cannot be neglected and its importance stems either or from management requirements or security model based constraints.

It should be noted that early recognition (in the order of a few minutes) may be sufficient to undertake protective actions and to initiate the resumption of operations. For instance, it is important to design and develop monitoring techniques capable of assessing whether and to what extent the monitored system is deviating from the normal state due to causes not due to actual failures or malfunctions. Equally important is development of optimization methods that decouple high and low level of control (that is port authority and port operators) and compensate individual behavior in line with high level policy and objectives.

Finally, a powerful but easily usable modeling and evaluation techniques is recommended to help port authority and operator to devise the best and long lasting solutions.

REFERENCES

[1] G. Parise et al., "Wise port & business energy management: Portfacilities, electrical power distribution", IEEE Transactions on Industry Applications, Vol. 52 , pp. 18-24, February 2016, doi: 10.1109/TIA.2015.2461176

[2] T . Theodoropoulos, "The port as an enabler of the smart grid", retrieved: September, pp. 1-37, Inte-Transit training workshop in Valencia, Nov 2014, http://www.fundacion.valenciaport.com/docs/inte-transit/T_InteTransit_5TTheodoropoulos.pdf

[3] Y. Yang, S. Bremnera, C. Menictas, and M. Kaya, "energy storage system size determination in renewable energy systems: A review', Renewable and Sustainable Energy Reviews" , vol. 91, August 2018, pp. 109 - 125, http://dx.doi.org/10.1016/j.rser.2018.03.047

[4] P. Bangalore, and L. B. Tjernberg, "Condition Monitoring and Asset Management in the Smart Grid" , Smart grids handbook 1, Wiely online library, August 2016, https://doi.org/10.1002/9781118755471.sgd061

[5] E. Lee, W. Shi, R. Gadh, and W. Kim, "Design and Implementation of a Microgrid Energy Management System", Sustainability, Vol. 8, 2016, https://doi.org/10.3390/su8111143

[6] G. Morris, C. Abbey, G. Joss, and C. Marnay, "A framework for the evaluation of the cost and benefits of microgrids", CIGRÉ International Symposium: The electric power system of the future, Lawrence Berkley National Laboratory, September 2011, https://building-microgrid.lbl.gov/publications/framework-evaluation-cost-and

[7] The US Department of Energy, Office of Electricity Delivery and Energy Reliability Summary Report , DOE Micro-grid Workshop Report, August 2011, California, https://www.energy.gov/sites/prod/files/Microgrid%20Workshop%20Report%20August%202011.pdf

[8] M. Govindarasu, A. Hann, and P. Sauer, "Cyber-Physical Systems Security for Smart Grid Future Grid Initiative", Iowa State University February 2012, https://pserc.wisc.edu/documents/publications/papers/fgwhitepapers/Govindarasu_Future_Grid_White_Paper_CPS_Feb2012.pdf

[9] International Electrotechnical Commission, "Telecontrol equipment and systems", IEC publication, April 2002, https://www.sis.se/api/document/preview/559181/

[10] International Electrotechnical Commission, "IEC Smart Grid Standardization Roadmap" , SMB Smart Grid Strategic Group (SG3) , June 2010, http://www.iec.ch/smartgrid/downloads/sg3_roadmap.pdf

[11] Muni-Fed – Antea GroupEnergy Partners, LLC and The Port of Long Beach, Micro-grid Technology White Paper, August 2016, http://www.polb.com/civica/filebank/blobdload.asp?BlobID=13595

[12] Yogesh Simmhan et al., " Cloud-based software platform for data-driven smart grid management", University of Southern California, 2013,http://citeseerx.ist.psu.edu/viewdoc/download?doi=10.1.1.458.1106&rep=rep1&type=pdf

[13] S. Sridhar, A. Hahn, and M. Govindarasu, Jan 2012, "Cyber Physical System Security for Electric Power Grid," Proceedings of the IEEE, Vol. 100, January 2012, http://powercybersec.ece.iastate.edu/powercyber/download/publications/11.pdf

[14] The International Society of Automation, "ISA99-Industrial Automation and Control Systems Security", retrieved: August, 2018, https://www.isa.org/isa99/

[15] P. Eder-Neuhauser, T. Zseby, J. Fabini, and G. Vormayr, " Cyber attack models for smart grid environments. Elsevier-Sustainable Energy, Grids and Networks, Volume 12, December 2017, Pages 10-29, http://dx.doi.org/10.1016/j.segan.2017.08.002

Practical Risk Analysis in Interdependent Critical Infrastructures - a How-To

Sandra König, Stefan Schauer
Austrian Institute of Technology GmbH
Digital Safety & Security Department
Vienna, Austria
{sandra.koenig,stefan.schauer}@ait.ac.at

Stefan Rass, Thomas Grafenauer
Universität Klagenfurt
Institute of Applied Informatics
Klagenfurt, Austria
{stefan.rass,thomas.grafenauer}@aau.at

Abstract—**Critical infrastructures (CIs) have become more and more interconnected in the recent past. Disturbances in one affect many others and consequences tend to become unpredictable due to manifold interdependencies and cascading effects. A decent amount of various stochastic models has been developed to capture this uncertainty and aid the management of security and risk. However, these models are not frequently used in practice, not to the least because many experts feel that there is a gap between theory and practice. In this article, we illustrate how to apply such a model by investigating the situation of a water provider that is part of an entire network of CIs step by step and describe the results of the analysis. While the data used is for illustration purpose only and describes the situation of a fictitious water provider, the assignments are based on several discussions with experts from the field. Besides pure damage prevention, simulations of incident propagation may be of independent interest for trust management and reputation.**

Keywords–critical infrastructure; dependencies; stochastic model; risk propagation; water supply.

I. Introduction

Critical infrastructures such as power or water providers, food systems, health care and transportation networks satisfy the basic needs of society. Each of them is crucial for the functionality of a society and significantly contributes to the economic welfare of people as well as their security. During the last years, mutual dependencies among CIs have become stronger; e.g., a hospital depends on electricity, water, food supply and working transportation lines. The increasing sensitivity of this network of connected CIs has been illustrated in the past by incidents such as the disruption of electric power in California in 2001 [1], the power outage in Italy in 2003 [2] or the hacking attack on the Ukrainian power grid in 2015 [3], only to name a few. The dependencies are getting more complex in nature, i.e., a water provider does not only need electricity for the pumps but also to keep the monitoring systems, e.g., Supervisory Control and Data Acquisition (SCADA) systems or Industrial Control Systems (ICSs), running. This increasing complexity makes it even harder to predict the consequences of a limited availability of one CI on other connected CIs. This is the main reason why we apply a stochastic model to investigate the consequences of interdependencies on the impact of a risk. Since electricity is a commonly fundamental provider for many CIs built on top, we pick the water supply as one example of these, to illustrate how incidents like the reported ones could affect a water provider *depending* on electricity (amongst others). More complex examples like hospitals are conceptually similar yet substantially more complex to describe, and are thus outside the scope of this current work.

Incidents of interest for simulation can be of various kind, including natural events, but also man-made unwanted interventions like cyber-attacks or human error. Especially cyber-attacks have recently (in 2016) been moved into the center of attention by the EU Directive 2016/1148 on cyber security [4]. The consequences of cyber incidents primarily relate to matters of privacy breaches and communication infrastructures, yet extend up to potential dangers of damaging infrastructures through cyber-attacks causing malicious configurations to vital parts of the system (such as the Stuxnet worm did). We stress that this kind of incident is its own kind of challenge to describe in the terms of the model that we study, yet no different in the simulation. To ease matters in the following, we thus confine ourselves to physical events and dependencies, leaving aspects of cyber-dependencies as straightforward adaptions.

Related Work

The increasing interest in interconnections and dependencies between CIs (and the effects on other utility providers) yields a growing number of publications investigating these dependencies. Various methods are used, including Hierarchical Holographic Modeling (HHM) [5], a multi-graph model for random failures [6] or input-output models [7]. Due to the unpredictability of consequences, stochastic models gained a lot of attention. A Interdependent Markov Chain (IDMC) model is used to describe cascading failures in interdependent infrastructures in power systems [8], where every infrastructure is described by one discrete-time Markov chain and the interdependencies between these chains are represented by dependencies between the corresponding transition probabilities.

A stochastic model that allows different degrees of failure while still being easy to implement is introduced in [9]. To some extent, simulation methods are available, e.g., [10], and allow comparing of different models for specific situations. Motivated by recent incidents, there is also a growing interest in the resilience of critical infrastructures [11]. An overview on models on interdependent CIs is presented in [12], while [13] gives an extensive overview on different models on cascading effects in power systems and presents a comparison of the various approaches.

When it comes to the domain of water supply and water providers as CIs, the amount of research seems to be more limited. In the context of the water sector, some research has been focusing on the security weaknesses of ICSs and SCADA systems and how to find good practices for water providers [14]. Further, effects of an Advanced Persistent Threat (APT) on a water utility provider have been investigated in [15] and [16] due to the increasing number of incidents based on such complex attack strategies. However, there is only little research specifically looking into the situation of a water provider depending on and influencing CIs in its vicinity.

Paper Outline

The remainder of this article is organized as follows: Section II describes the considered use case, Section III analyses the use case, which is further discussed in Section IV and Section V provides concluding remarks.

II. The Situation of a Water Provider

We describe the situation of a hypothetical water provider that we are going to analyze in the next section. Therefore, we are using information which is obtained from discussions with experts from a real-life water provider. The main goal is to illustrate how to analyze the consequences of a risk scenario affecting a CI that is part of a entire network of interdependent CIs. We investigate a utility organization that provides water to more than one hundred municipalities in its surrounding region. The main focus lies on availability of drinking water as well as on the water quality. In order to ensure a sustainable water quality, the provider supports water processing and sewage cleaning by an ICS. For our use case, we assume the existence of a well and a river head, each supported by a pump that conveys the water to the plant where it is further treated (e.g., undesired chemicals are removed or minerals added). A further source of water is a mountain spring nearby. Due to the geography of the landscape transportation paths are short and the number of necessary lines is low. A number of reservoirs are available to ensure supply with water needed to extinguish fire.

Further, the water provider depends on an transportation system, in particular on roads, e.g., to be able to check wells and springs. As any other CI, a water provider crucially depends on electricity (e.g., electric pumps). An internal power plant contributes approximately 30% of the required energy while the rest comes from external providers. Redundancy in the system and an existing emergency power supply help to mitigate this dependency on an electricity provider. In case of a (temporary) interruption of electricity, the utility provider is able to guarantee supply with drinking water up to three days due to available emergency power.

On the other hand, the water provider is important for a number of other infrastructures. In particular, it supplies drinking water to hospitals and grocery stores but also cooling water for hospitals and industrial companies. The actual importance of each of these connections can only be assessed by the CIs that depend on the water provider, which requires discussions with the corresponding experts and thus goes beyond the scope of our use case. A visualization of the use case is given in Figure 1.

Based on a desktop research and discussions with experts, the following risks have been identified as the most significant ones for a water provider:

- R_1: flooding
- R_2: extreme weather conditions
- R_3: leakage of hazardous material (water contamination)

In order to analyze the effects of a realization of one of these risks, we performed a qualitative risk assessment with experts from the water domain. The next section presents the results of this assessment together with a discussion on the consequences of such an incident.

III. Model-based Analysis of an Incident

The situation of the fictitious water provider described above will be analyzed in this section to illustrate how a practical risk analysis based on a theoretical model can be conducted. Based on the stochastic dependency model between CIs [9], consequences of an incident are simulated and the results are then visualized and discussed. All the assessments and estimates given in this paper are of illustrative use only, since it is not possible to disclose the water provider's original sensitive data. However, the data used is based on discussions with experts of the field to be as realistic as possible.

The model we apply is aligned with standard risk assessment methods like ISO31000, and considers a set of interdependent assets, being individual parts of a CI; a water-provider in our case. The water provider maintains a list of *assets*, each of which can be affected by a certain risk scenario. Each asset carries, among others, the following information:

- *Criticality*: How important is the asset for the overall function of the CI (a related question is that on the importance of the CI itself for other depending CIs or the society itself. Such assessments are outside the scope of this article, yet briefly sketched in Section IV to illustrate a possible post-processing of the simulation that we will describe later).
- *Dependencies*: How critical is the asset for the functionality of other related assets? E.g., how important is the mountain spring or well for the water plant (i.e., how much of the water supply is covered by the

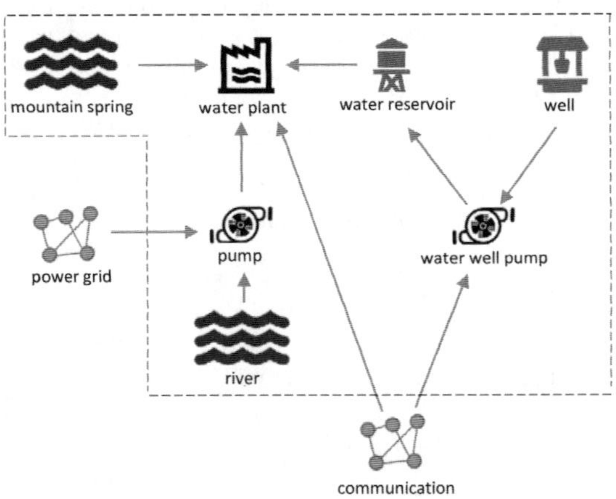

Figure 1. Visualization of Water Use Case

spring, how much is covered by the well, etc.)? How important (e.g., for control and signalling matters) would the company communication or office network be for the service as such, if an outage by a cyber incident or attack occurs?

- *Status indicator*: In normal operation, the assets would all be in working state, but can be in several other states, too (e.g., maintenance). For the risk assessment, the status can be related to the impact when the asset is affected. We shall use the scale $\{1, 2, 3\}$ to express increasing degrees of affection, ranging from status 1 ="working" up to the worst case status 3 ="outage", with the intermediate status level expressing anyhow limited functionality. More status levels are of course admissible, yet not used hereafter for the sake of simplicity.

Remark 1: It is important to stress that we use the general term "asset" as a link to standard risk management literature. As such, the term is appropriate for risk management *within* a CI. Adopting a more high-level perspective, such as national authorities may have, their view is on a whole network of CIs, such as power providers, hospitals and water suppliers, with those again depending on each other and so forth. From this high level perspective, a CI is itself an "asset" to the country/nation itself, and we can synonymously exchange the terms CI and asset. Since our focus in this work is on risk management from a single CI provider's perspective, we will hereafter use the term *assets*.

The simulation model will assume a certain incident to "just occur", which in the first place affects some assets by putting them from functional into affected or even outage state. The simulation then uses the dependency information to update the status of related (dependent) assets accordingly, where each asset may undergo individually different status changes, depending on the importance of the other asset (e.g., a mild affection may occur if the failed asset provides only a small part of the supply, or a severe affection may occur if an asset vitally depends on another yet failed asset). This reveals *cascading effects*, i.e., indirect impacts of a realization of a risk scenario.

The status transitions are generally probabilistic to cover cases of deterministic dependency (e.g., such as a pump continuously depending on electricity supply), and probabilistic dependencies (e.g., such as water supplies can temporarily be covered from backup water reservoirs). The main duty of the modeling then boils down into two major tasks:

1) Enumerate all assets and identify their interdependencies as detailed as possible. Hereafter, we let the arrow notation $A \to B$ denote a dependency of asset B on asset A (cf. Figure 1, e.g., where the pump B depends on the water A, and similar).
2) Use this information to specify probabilities for status changes in a dependent asset B, if the provider asset A has a status $\neq 1$ (i.e., any abnormal condition, not in normal working state).

The first of these two steps is typically a matter of compiling information that is already known and available to the CI provider. The actual difficulty is the specification of transition probabilities in step two of the above. We believe that this is a general issue in any probabilistic model (not only applying to [9] but also to many others of the references). Nonetheless, the remainder of this work will discuss both aspects in order of appearance.

A. *Identification of Dependencies*

In the beginning, it is necessary to identify all dependencies between the different components of the system. This is not limited to visible (physical) connections but also includes logical connections as in the case of a control system. During the upcoming analysis, it is necessary to assess every link between two components. If the network is large, it may be handy to classify dependencies according to their properties and assign values to every class of connection. In our small example, we refrain from categorizing the connections but rather assess every single connection.

B. *Expert Assessment of Risks*

Once the various components and the interdependencies have been identified, we focus on the assessment of the considered risks and its consequences of a realization in the network. The risk assessments are based on discussions with domain experts that rate each risk as "negligible", "low", "medium", "high" or "very high" while the recovery time is either rated as "short", "medium" or "long". The assessments are given in Table I.

TABLE I. OVERALL LIKELIHOOD ASSESSMENT FOR RISKS

Risk		Occurrence	Failure	Impairment
R_1:	flooding	medium	negligible	negligible
R_2:	extreme weather conditions	medium	negligible	medium
R_3:	leakage of hazardous material	low	negligible	medium

A flooding may affect single sites (e.g., a well), but is not critical for the overall functionality for the water supply as recent incidents like the flooding in central Europe in 2013 have shown. Still, single wells and springs may be used only partly as water may be contaminated by particles (germs, bacteria and others) induced by the flood. Depending on the degree of contamination, water can be boiled to make it drinkable. However, if this is not enough to ensure drinking water quality, the water needs to be purified technically which is a costly and time-consuming process. A realization of risk R_1 may thus yields a limited operation of wells and springs. The risk of an extreme weather situation needs to be considered in further detail based on the type of weather condition. Heavy rain is not a severe problem in our case, since the main source of the water provider is groundwater. It might cause smaller damage to the infrastructure, but will not interrupt water supply. As another extreme, droughts need to be considered, since they are likely to become more frequent in the future. Various sources may dry up, such as rivers or wells, so we may assume (here) that at least some sources like ground water remain available. The drought implies an increased water consumption and yields to peak consumptions that in turn challenge the infrastructure. The peaks will cause additional costs for the provider but are not considered here any further since this does not affect other parts of the system. As a realization of R_2, we assume an extraordinarily dry period, causing the well to produce only limited outcome while groundwater is still available; due to the drought, water consumption increases significantly at the same time. The realization of this risk may thus be similar as in the previous case which is why we combine the analysis with that of risk R_1.

The assessments related to leakage of hazardous material are challenging as the impact of such an event highly depends on the extent of the leakage. E.g., a bounded contamination is not a severe issue as long as the water network is close-meshed (i.e., there is enough redundancy in the network). Nevertheless, if groundwater or several wells are affected, water purification may take several months. Similarly as for the risk of flooding, the amount of hazardous material that has leaked matters a lot. For our use case, we assume that a limited amount affects some parts of the countryside used for water extraction so that a realization of risk R_3 affects the mountain spring. As contamination is a serious problem, we assume the spring switches into the worst state 3.

For our illustrative example, we here assume a scenario where communication is limited due to some internal problems. After some time, a realization of risk R_2 (an extremely dry period of time) or of risk R_3 (a contamination) yields to limited availability of the river source. In the remainder we model the consequences this event has on the other components of the water network. Note that the respective risks, say outages or resource shortages, may also be triggered by cyber-events, e.g., if a hacker switches off the pump or configures the systems towards reduced or zero supply volumes. As such, cyber events may constitute their own risks, but may also be reasons for risk scenarios to "kick in".

C. Discussions of Consequences of an Incident

While the simulation is able to describe the propagation of the consequences of an incident, the analysis of the overall impact on a specific CI requires knowledge about the effect of a failure of one single component. In particular, it is necessary to estimate how likely it is that a problem or a failure in one component affects the dependent components. These values can be estimated from two sources of information: data from past incidents and expert knowledge. The first source is of limited use when working with critical infrastructures since only few data is known (and even less is publicly available). As for the second source, experts may struggle or be reluctant to estimate precise values, despite their profound knowledge about the infrastructure. Systematic approaches like the Delphi method can help with this issue [17].

Aware of this problem, we avoid asking for exact estimates but rather look for an assessment on a qualitative scale, as is typically recommended in risk management (e.g., by the German Federal Office for Information Security (BSI) [18]). However, this yields to the problem of estimating a whole distribution (namely, all the likelihoods of changing to any of the possible states) from a few qualitative values. In this section, we show one way to approach this problem without pretending an accuracy that cannot be achieved in real life.

In order to determine the transmission probability t_{ij}, a CI needs to answer the following question:

> If your provider is in state i, how likely is it that this will put you into state j?

Since this is usually hard to answer, we replace it by two simpler questions, namely

1) "If your provider is in state i, what is the most likely state j that you will end up with upon this incident?"
2) "How certain are you about your assessment?"

The answers can be chosen from a set of predefined values, namely the number of states $\{1, \ldots, k\}$ for 1) and a set of possible confidence levels for 2). If the expert is unsure about the consequences, we still assume that he has an idea about the intensity of the consequences, i.e., if the expected consequences will be very bad or close to negligible. Because of this, we assume that in the case of uncertain assignments similar values as the predicted one are also possible.

This additional assignment of an assurance value is of twofold benefit. First, it takes pressure form the expert and allows him to choose the answer "I don't know" (represented by the statement that he is totally unsure about the prediction). Second, this information can be incorporated into the analysis by assigning some likelihood to neighboring values. We propose the following heuristic on an ordered scale of severity:

- If confidence is high ("totally sure"), assign all likelihood to the predicted value j from question 1 above.
- If confidence is medium ("somewhat unsure"), assign likelihood to direct neighbors $j-1$ and $j+1$ (as far as they exist on the scale) such that these are half as likely as the predicted value j.
- If confidence is low ("totally unsure"), assign the same likelihood to all possible values, i.e., choose a uniform distribution over all potential outcomes.

So, for the case of three possible states and the levels of assurance (i.e., the possible answers to question 2) form above) be "totally sure", "somewhat unsure" and "totally unsure" we take the uncertainty about the assessment into account as follows: if the expert chooses "totally sure", we assign the likelihood to the proposed status and all other states have a probability of zero. If he chooses "somewhat unsure", we assign some likelihood to the two neighboring states (i.e., the next smaller and the next larger integer). If we can assume a symmetric situation where a deviation to both sides is equally likely, one approach is to assign to both neighbors half the likelihood of the predicted value. Finally, if the expert chooses "totally unsure", we assume a uniform distribution over all possible states, representing the situation where we do not have any information at all. The described mapping from a predicted value and a level of uncertainty is explicitly given in Table II. In this table, a triple (p_1, p_2, p_3) represents the distribution over the three possible states, so state k is assumed with probability p_k $(k = 1, 2, 3)$. These estimated distributions then build up the rows of the transition matrices.

As it is quite difficult in practice to make predictions that are totally sure, we incorporate a small chance of an error even for these assessments. That is, we always assign a small probability ϵ to the states nearest to the predicted one, as exemplified in Table III. This makes the model more

TABLE II. DISTRIBUTION OVER THE CI'S POSSIBLE NEXT STATE BASED ON THE EXPERT'S ASSIGNMENT

prediction	totally sure	somewhat unsure	totally unsure
1	(1,0,0)	(2/3, 1/3, 0)	(1/3,1/3,1/3)
2	(0,1,0)	(1/4, 2/4, 1/4)	(1/3,1/3,1/3)
3	(0,0,1)	(0, 2/3, 1/3)	(1/3,1/3,1/3)

realistic and takes some pressure from the experts performing the assessment.

TABLE III. DISTRIBUTION OVER POSSIBLE NEXT STATE WITH POTENTIAL ERROR

prediction	totally sure	somewhat unsure	totally unsure
1	$(1-\epsilon, \epsilon, 0)$	(2/3, 1/3, 0)	(1/3,1/3,1/3)
2	$(\epsilon/2, 1-\epsilon, \epsilon/2)$	(1/4, 2/4, 1/4)	(1/3,1/3,1/3)
3	$(0, \epsilon, 1-\epsilon)$	(0, 2/3, 1/3)	(1/3,1/3,1/3)

In the upcoming analysis we will consider the cases $\epsilon = 1\%$. We discussed several scenarios with experts from the field to understand the dependencies between the different assets. The assessments are given in Tables IV, V and VI. We measure the impact on a three-tier scale "negligible" (state 1), "medium" (state 2) and "high" (state 3) while the experts' confidence in the provided prediction is described as "totally sure", "somewhat unsure" or "totally unsure". Note that these assessments are made for one specific connection and neither contain information about potential substitutes (e.g., if several pumps are available) nor the option of repair or recovery. It is only concerned about the nature of a specific dependence between two assets.

D. Simulation of Incidents

The input to the simulation is a network graph of connected critical infrastructures, where each component of the CI is in one specific state. This graph essentially resembles the picture in Figure 1, and augments each node with a matrix indicating the status change probabilities for each dependency and over time. The time aspect accounts for the fact that short-term outages of a provider may have different impact than long-term outages. E.g., if a power supply goes off, then emergency power supplies may cover for a limited time, thus causing no immediate service interruption. Consequently, the likelihood

TABLE IV. SHORT TERM IMPACT ASSESSMENT

Link	Problem	Prediction	Confidence
pump → water plant	limitation	negligible	totally sure
	failure	negligible	totally sure
mountain spring → water plant	limitation	negligible	totally sure
	failure	negligible	totally sure
communication → water plant	limitation	medium	somewhat unsure
	failure	negligible	totally sure
water reservoir → water plant	limitation	negligible	totally sure
	failure	negligible	totally sure
well → well pump	limitation	negligible	totally sure
	failure	negligible	somewhat unsure
communication → well pump	limitation	medium	somewhat unsure
	failure	negligible	totally sure
river → river pump	limitation	negligible	totally sure
	failure	negligible	somewhat unsure
power grid → river pump	limitation	negligible	totally sure
	failure	negligible	totally sure
river pump → water reservoir	limitation	negligible	totally sure
	failure	negligible	totally sure

TABLE V. MEDIUM TERM IMPACT ASSESSMENT

Link	Problem	Prediction	Confidence
pump → water plant	limitation	negligible	totally sure
	failure	negligible	somewhat unsure
mountain spring → water plant	limitation	negligible	totally sure
	failure	negligible	somewhat unsure
communication → water plant	limitation	negligible	totally sure
	failure	negligible	totally sure
water reservoir → water plant	limitation	negligible	totally sure
	failure	negligible	somewhat unsure
well → well pump	limitation	medium	somewhat unsure
	failure	high	somewhat unsure
communication → well pump	limitation	negligible	totally sure
	failure	negligible	totally sure
river → river pump	limitation	medium	somewhat unsure
	failure	high	somewhat unsure
power grid → river pump	limitation	negligible	totally sure
	failure	negligible	totally sure
river pump → water reservoir	limitation	negligible	totally sure
	failure	negligible	somewhat unsure

TABLE VI. LONG TERM IMPACT ASSESSMENT

Link	Problem	Prediction	Confidence
pump → water plant	limitation	negligible	totally sure
	failure	medium	somewhat unsure
mountain spring → water plant	limitation	negligible	totally sure
	failure	medium	somewhat unsure
communication → water plant	limitation	negligible	totally sure
	failure	negligible	totally sure
water reservoir → water plant	limitation	negligible	totally sure
	failure	medium	somewhat unsure
well → well pump	limitation	medium	somewhat unsure
	failure	high	totally sure
communication → well pump	limitation	negligible	totally sure
	failure	negligible	totally sure
river → river pump	limitation	medium	somewhat unsure
	failure	high	totally sure
power grid → river pump	limitation	negligible	totally sure
	failure	high	totally sure
river pump → water reservoir	limitation	negligible	totally sure
	failure	medium	somewhat unsure

for a pump, having an emergency supply, to go into outage state 3 if the electricity goes off is zero for the first couple of hours, and changes to 1 if the emergency generator runs out of fuel, unless the original power supply has been fixed. However, the same pump is vitally dependent on its water source, and if this runs dry, the pump will immediately go into outage state 3. Therefore, the simulation will need a state transition probability matrix *per dependency* $A \to B$ and *depending on the time scale*.

The simulation prototype we developed [19] embodies this by taking three such matrices, one for short-term, one for medium-term and one for long-term effects in which the probabilities $t_{ij} = \Pr(B \text{ is in state } j | A \text{ switches into state } i)$ describe the transition regime.

While the general model allows a recovery (i.e., switching back into a better status), this is not yet implemented in the current version of the prototype.

IV. RESULTS OF THE ANALYSIS

In a nutshell, the simulation delivers at least three output artifacts:

1) Textual sequence of events with time stamps, and showing the status of all assets at the given time (such lists are usually extensive and are thus not presented here

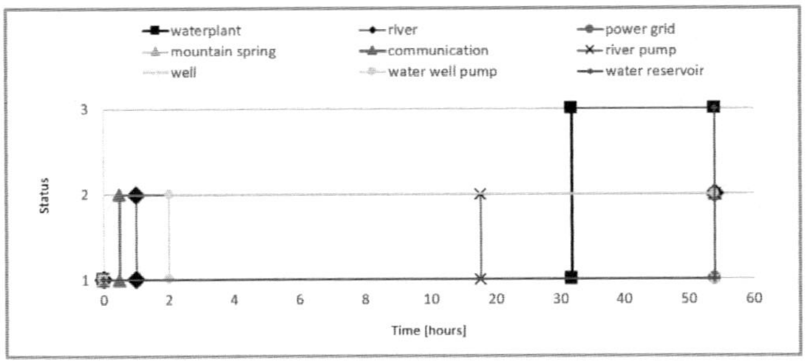

Figure 2. Example simulated time line for a water plant and its components

for space reasons). They are the basic data to compute further information for the risk management, such as the following:

2) Time-lines showing the evolution of the impact on different assets over time. Figure 2 shows an example for nine components in Figure 1.
3) Information about chances on when to expect status changes. Figures 3 and 4 show examples, with explanations to them and the preceding points following below.

Given a set of simulated scenarios, we can average the final states per asset to reflect the likelihood of this part of the CI (or CI network) to become affected (in a degree expressed by the state). For visualization, we apply color codes, ranging from green (symbolizing a working state) to red (symbolizing an outage), alerting about the criticality of the current condition. Numerically, the simulation results can be summarized as a table that lists the number of components which are on average in any of the possible states. We use `OMNeT++` as a tool to support the visualization and execution of our simulation.

Various additional outputs are possible, such as plots of time-lines relating to a single simulation run. This would display the times when a CI asset changes its state, and would show the temporal "evolution" of the cascading impacts. Figure 2 shows an example result for one simulation run.

If numerous simulations are conducted, we can compile the resulting state transition times into an empirical distribution, to learn the expected, median, mode or other characteristic feature of the time when an asset goes into malfunctioning state. E.g., we can measure the expected time until an outage of an asset. Figures 3 and 4 display examples of such a simulation output. Based on this data, we can easily compute the average, i.e., expected, time for a transition from working (1) $\rightarrow$ outage (3), for the asset "water plant" to be slightly less than five days (with and without the uncertainty of ϵ artificially added to the expert assessment; cf. Table III). In our example, introduction of a small uncertainty yielded to a different empirical distribution of the transition times. If this difference is significant needs to be checked in detail and is beyond the scope of this work but it indicates that potential errors need to be taken into account (just as the concept of trembling hand equilibrium does for game theory) and should not be ignored when analyzing cascading effects.

Usually, the state itself is not exactly a measure of real impact, and needs conversion into a measurable number for management matters. The simulation output will thus in most

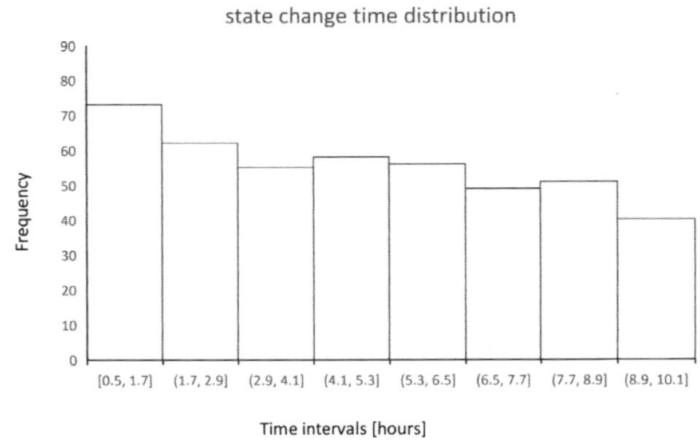

Figure 3. Simulated histogram of $1 \rightarrow 2$ state change times

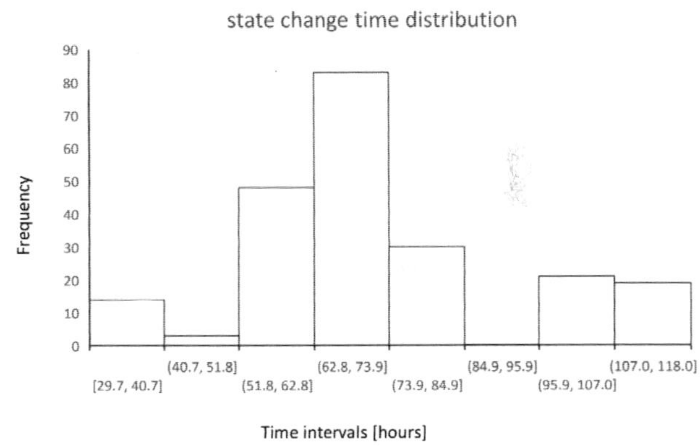

Figure 4. Simulated histogram of $1 \rightarrow 3$ state change times

cases undergo a post-processing that translates the status into a set of facts about what this status actually means, based on the criticality of the asset.

As for the case of a water utility provider, the degree of damage could depend on the number of affected customers, the time needed to fix the issue, the amount of resources needed to cover the outage, and so forth. Table VII displays an example of such a classification using artificial numbers (for obvious reasons of real data's sensitivity, as already pointed out above) to characterize criticality levels in numeric ranks. In general, criticality levels may also have different meaning for individual scenarios; e.g., if a pump or water tower fails for one day, the criticality may be higher than if water is contaminated, since in the latter case, households can be advised to boil the water before drinking it, whereas if the pump fails, the household would be cut off from water supply completely.

Knowing which parts of the CI network fail at which times and for how long it is a simple matter to apply conditions as exemplified in Table VII to determine the criticality level for this *single* round of simulation.

Repeating this procedure for many times and recording the relative frequencies of occurrence for all criticality levels, we end up with probabilities for each criticality level as $p_i :=$

TABLE VII. DETAILED DESCRIPTIONS OF CRITICALITY LEVELS

	Incident scenario			
Criticality level 1	#1	#2	#3	...
No. of affected households	< 1000	1001...5000	...	...
duration of problem	< 1 day	1...7 days	...	...
costs to fix it (per hour)	100	150	...	...
⋮	⋮	⋮		⋱
Criticality level 2	1	2	3	...
No. of affected households				
duration of problem				
costs to fix it (per hour)				
⋮				

Pr(criticality level i). These likelihoods quantify the odds for running into a certain amount of trouble in a given scenario. Partitioning the range $[0, 1]$ into a fixed set of levels, say in thirds, we can convert these probabilities into *warning levels*. That is, if criticality level 2 occurred in a fraction of 60% of the simulated runs, $p_2 \approx 0.6$ falls into $1/3 < p_2 < 2/3$, giving middle warning level (e.g., yellow alert). Likewise, if criticality level 1 occurred in 90% of the simulation runs, then criticality level 1 has warning level 3 (red alert) in the final output.

It must be kept in mind that the simulation cannot provide any detailed information about the likelihood for an incident as such to occur; the simulation starts straight away from the given scenario that is assumed to have happened.

V. CONCLUSION

A major challenge in the simulation of critical infrastructures is the expert assessment of probabilities for a stochastic simulation. In this context and for the example given in this article, it is important to specify dependencies on a local level only, meaning that the opinion must be formed with consideration on only directly dependent assets, and *not* the overall CI, since this is the purpose of the simulation. We stress that these dependencies are not constrained in nature and physical and cyber-aspects of a CI can be unified under the same modeling framework. Thus, simulation methods like the described one aid even a holistic cyber-physical view on incident propagation in a CI, if dependencies between physical assets (e.g., a hospital) and cyber assets (e.g., the telecommunication network on which the hospital relies for emergency communication and signalling) are included in one model.

An independent difficulty lies in assessing the temporal aspects like the meaning of short-term, medium term and long-term impacts. Certainly, these need to be distinguished, but good heuristics or models to support experts in these regards are rarely available. Polling multiple experts here creates the additional challenge of unifying opinions from different domains, say from experts on the physical matter (like water), vs. people specialized in cyber-security (none of which is necessarily skilled in the other's domain). Aggregating such different assessments into a single value for a simulation is a matter of opinion pooling and subject of supplementary research related to ours (e.g., [20]–[23]). As for future research, it is thus required to develop models that help parameterizing other models. Matters of describing system dynamics are well understood, but helping experts cast their domain knowledge into reasonable figures for a simulation is a challenge on its own. The main contribution of this work is the almost complete picture of the work flow, not least to display the difficulties besides the potential of simulation-based risk analysis in critical infrastructures. While many sophisticated methods of modeling exist, matters of *using* such models have received significantly less attention. Our discussion, though based on a concrete example and method, covers issues of wider applicability. Extending and studying possibilities to make stochastic models more useful is, in our view, an important and promising direction of future research.

ACKNOWLEDGMENT

This work was done in the context of the project "Cross Sectoral Risk Management for Object Protection of Critical Infrastructures (CERBERUS)", supported by the Austrian Research Promotion Agency under grant no. 854766. We thank the experts from Linz AG for fruitful discussions and valuable insights.

REFERENCES

[1] S. Fletcher, "Electric power interruptions curtail California oil and gas production," Oil Gas Journal, 2001.

[2] M. Schmidthaler and J. Reichl, "Economic Valuation of Electricity Supply Security: Ad-hoc Cost Assessment Tool for Power Outages," ELECTRA, no. 276, 2014, pp. 10–15.

[3] J. Condliffe, "Ukraine's Power Grid Gets Hacked Again, a Worrying Sign for Infrastructure Attacks," 2016. [Online]. Available: https://www.technologyreview.com/s/603262/ukraines-power-grid-gets-hacked-again-a-worrying-sign-for-infrastructure-attacks/

[4] European Parliament, "Directive (EU) 2016/1148 of the European Parliament and of the Council: concerning measures for a high common level of security of network and information systems across the Union," Official Journal of the European Union, 2016. [Online]. Available: https://eur-lex.europa.eu/legal-content/EN/TXT/HTML/?uri=CELEX:32016L1148&from=EN

[5] Y. Y. Haimes, "Hierarchical Holographic Modeling," IEEE Transactions on Systems, Man, and Cybernetics, vol. 11, no. 9, 1981, pp. 606–617.

[6] N. K. Svendsen and S. D. Wolthusen, "Analysis and statistical properties of critical infrastructure interdependency multiflow models," in 2007 IEEE SMC Information Assurance and Security Workshop, June 2007, pp. 247–254.

[7] R. Setola, S. D. Porcellinis, and M. Sforna, "Critical infrastructure dependency assessment using the input-output inoperability model," International Journal of Critical Infrastructure Protection (IJCIP), vol. 2, 2009, pp. 170–178.

[8] M. Rahnamay-Naeini and M. M. Hayat, "Cascading failures in interdependent infrastructures: An interdependent markov-chain approach," IEEE Transactions on Smart Grid, vol. 7, no. 4, jul 2016, pp. 1997–2006. [Online]. Available: https://doi.org/10.1109/tsg.2016.2539823

[9] S. König and S. Rass, "Stochastic dependencies between critical infrastructures," in SECURWARE 2017: The Eleventh International Conference on Emerging Security Information, Systems and Technologies. IARIA, 2017, pp. 106–110.

[10] S. Rinaldi, J. Peerenboom, and T. Kelly, "Identifying, understanding, and analyzing critical infrastructure interdependencies," IEEE Control Systems Magazine, 2001, pp. 11–25.

[11] A. Gouglidis, B. Green, J. Busby, M. Rouncefield, D. Hutchison, and S. Schauer, Threat awareness for critical infrastructures resilience. IEEE, 9 2016.

[12] S. M. Rinaldi, "Modeling and simulating critical infrastructures and their interdependencies," in 37th Annual Hawaii International Conference on System Sciences, 2004. Proceedings of the. IEEE, 2004, p. 8 pp.

[13] H. Guo, C. Zheng, H. H.-C. Iu, and T. Fernando, "A critical review of cascading failure analysis and modeling of power system," Renewable and Sustainable Energy Reviews, vol. 80, dec 2017, pp. 9–22.

[14] E. Luiijf, M. Ali, and A. Zielstra, "Assessing and improving SCADA security in the Dutch drinking water sector," International Journal of Critical Infrastructure Protection, vol. 4, no. 3-4, 2011, pp. 124–134.

[15] A. Alshawish, M. A. Abid, H. de Meer, S. Schauer, S. König, A. Gouglidis, and D. Hutchison, "Protecting water utility networks from advanced persistent threats: A case study," in HyRiM, S. Rass and S. Schauer, Eds. Springer International Publishing, 2018, ch. 6.

[16] A. Gouglidis, S. König, B. Green, S. Schauer, K. Rossegger, and D. Hutchison, "Advanced persistent threats in water utility networks: A case study," in HyRiM, S. Rass and S. Schauer, Eds. Springer International Publishing, 2018, ch. 13.

[17] J. Rohrbaugh, "Improving the quality of group judgment: Social judgment analysis and the delphi technique," Organizational Behavior and Human Performance, vol. 24, no. 1, 1979, pp. 73–92.

[18] I. Münch, "Wege zur Risikobewertung," in DACH Security 2012, P. Schartner and J. Taeger, Eds. syssec, 2012, pp. 326–337.

[19] T. Grafenauer, S. König, S. Rass, and S. Schauer, "A simulation tool for cascading effects in interdependent critical infrastructures," in Proceedings of the 13th International Conference on Availability, Reliability and Security, ARES 2018, Hamburg, Germany, August 27-30, 2018, 2018, pp. 30:1–30:8.

[20] S. Rass and S. Schauer, Eds., Game Theory for Security and Risk Management: From Theory to Practice, ser. Static & dynamic game theory : foundations & applications. Cham, Switzerland: Birkhäuser, 2018.

[21] S. Rass, J. Wachter, S. Schauer, and S. König, "Subjektive Risikobewertung – Über Da-tenerhebung und Opinion Pooling," in D-A-CH Security 2017, P. Schartner and A. Baumann, Eds. syssec, 2017, pp. 225–237.

[22] F. Dietrich and C. List, "Probabilistic opinion pooling generalized. Part one: General agendas," Social Choice and Welfare, vol. 48, no. 4, 2017, pp. 747–786.

[23] J. Wachter, T. Grafenauer, and S. Rass, "Visual Risk Specification and Aggregation," in SECURWARE 2017: The Eleventh International Conference on Emerging Security Information, Systems and Technologies, IARIA, Ed., 2017, pp. 93–98.

International Academy, Research,
and Industry Association (IARIA)
412 Derby Way
Wilmington, DE 19810

ISBN 978-1-5108-7215-8

CURRAN ASSOCIATES INC.
proceedings.com

Sixteenth International Conference on Networks (ICN 2017)

Held at NexComm 2017

Venice, Italy
23 - 27 April 2017

IARIA